THE CONGRESS OF THE
UNITED STATES 1789-1989

Editor

JOEL H. SILBEY

Advisory Editors

ALLAN G. BOGUE

JOSEPH COOPER

ROGER H. DAVIDSON

KERMIT L. HALL

A CARLSON PUBLISHING SERIES

See the end of the third volume of this title for a comprehensive guide to this twenty-three-volume series.

The United States Congress in a Partisan Political Nation, 1841-1896

Edited with a Preface by Joel Silbey

IN THREE VOLUMES

Volume One

CARLSON
Publishing Inc

BROOKLYN, NEW YORK 1991

See the end of Volume Three of this title for a comprehensive guide to all twenty-three volumes in this series.

Library of Congress Cataloging-in-Publication Data

The United States Congress in a partisan political nation, 1841-1896 /
    edited with a preface by Joel H. Silbey.
            p.   cm. — (The Congress of the United States, 1789-1989 : 6)
        Includes bibliographical references and index.
        ISBN 0-926019-33-3
        1. United States. Congress—History—19th century. 2. Political
parties—United States—History—19th century. 3. United States—
Politics and government—19th century. I. Silbey, Joel H.
II. Series.
JK1041.U65 1991
324.273'009'034—dc20   90-28962

Case design: Alison Lew

Index prepared by Scholars Editorial Services, Inc., Madison, Wisconsin, using NL Cindex, a scholarly indexing program from the Newberry Library.

Printed on acid-free, 250-year-life paper.

Manufactured in the United States of America.

Contents

Volume One

Volume Two

Volume Three

An Introduction
to the Series

Article I, Section 1, of the Constitution establishes "a Congress of the United States," consisting of a Senate and a House of Representatives, in which all national legislative power is vested. Section 8 of the same article empowers Congress "to make all Laws which shall be necessary and proper" to carry out its responsibilities. The first Congress under the new Constitution met in April 1789 and welcomed George Washington when he arrived in New York for his swearing-in ceremony as President. Since that beginning, Congress has met annually as one of the central actors on the national political stage.

Congress's role has been pivotal in guiding the course of American politics and governance and in reflecting, and helping to shape, the social, political and economic forces abroad in the nation at a given moment. For much of our history it has been a main arena for working out policy options, resolving interest group and regional differences, and developing public policies to meet the expressed needs of American society. At the same time, congressional actions have provided marking points that illuminate both the everyday routines of normal politics, from elections and policy making, to those moments of high importance when sharp divisions have burst out of their normal constraints to suggest that more was at stake, that the very nature and continuation of the polity was at issue. Understanding what goes on in the American Congress, therefore, has been an important entry into the nature and problems of American society at many different moments.

Recognizing Congress's significance, historians and political scientists have spent a great deal of effort studying the national legislature over its two-hundred-year history. Thousands of books and scholarly articles attest to their interest and efforts. The drama of Daniel Webster or John C. Calhoun debating the nature of the Union far into the night in the 1830s, or of a small group maneuvering to bring an issue of concern to the floor against intransigent opposition, or of the moment when a great moral dilemma is finally resolved—all are the stuff of many history books. At the same time, parts of the historical record are not easily recoverable. The articles, in particular, are widely scattered and have not been quickly accessible, certainly not in a form that allows the reader to follow the entire course of congressional history since the Constitution. The most important of these, those which provide a mosaic of that history, are brought together in these volumes.

The emphasis here is not primarily on the individual dramatic moment, great personality, or idiosyncratic episode, no matter how colorful. My concerns, rather, are primarily structural and developmental: to show how Congress has evolved and behaved over time and how it has particularly functioned within each of the distinct eras that make up Congress's history. The articles included provide insight into the entire dimension of the legislature's role over the whole course of American history as it has moved to meet its obligations, noting both the patterns of stability and moments of change that have characterized the institution. At the same time, while some differences between the House and the Senate have always existed and have often been important, the similarity of the congressional experience, regardless of the different chambers, has also been marked. The essays try to catch something of that, although all of the studies are focused on one house or the other. There is an imbalance as well; more work has been done on the House than on the Senate. Nevertheless, the two chambers, as well as Congress as a whole, have been opened up by the studies that are available.

Titles 1-4

Congress's history is both cumulative and episodic. The essays in the first title deal with the years comprising the legislature's origins and its first steps toward defining itself, establishing its purposes, and clarifying its boundaries. The articles provide some insight into the expectations and assumptions that America's first political leaders had about the legislative process. They also recount how external forces began to modify these as Congress got under way, ultimately shifting congressional behavior into channels other than were originally intended or expected at the Constitutional Convention.

The next three titles trace that which has been cumulative. Much about Congress over two hundred years has a timeless quality. The two houses look much the same physically as they always have done, and many of their rituals trace back many years; both suggest an unchanging institution. The Speaker and the President of the Senate, many of the activities, the location, not to mention the constitutional prescription as to duties and responsibilities, have not changed in form at all. But, substantially, much has shifted, much has been added. Congress is not the same today as it was at any particular point in the past. The articles emphasize that developmental quality. They are generally examinations of patterns, delineating and comparing chronological shifts in the various elements that comprise the congressional experience: the personnel, structure, agenda and behavior of the Senate and House.

The several thousand politicians and statesmen who have been elected to Congress since 1789 have reflected certain social realities of a rapidly changing country; their assumptions and expectations about their role and tenure have shifted. Similarly, Congress has organized itself in increasingly complex ways as the years have passed. Leadership positions and the committee structure have evolved to affect the role and power of any individual or bloc. Third, members of Congress have never come to Washington unadorned by commitments and previous knowledge. They have represented their states and districts to be sure, but they have also been members of political parties, of regional blocs, later of fairly well-defined economic, and other, interest groups. Whatever personal agendas existed, larger institutional forces, most particularly political parties, were always at play in the congressional experience to shape, modify, and subdue the idiosyncratic. But the relative role and power of these institutions have changed over time in dramatic ways.

Fourth, and most obviously, the policy agenda Congress has confronted has not been static, nor have been the country's assumptions about the scope and reach of congressional power. In the nineteenth century, an aggressive Congress pursued what has been labeled a developmental-distributive legislative agenda, parceling out the public lands, removing barriers to growth, and providing institutions which allowed freewheeling development to occur. Later, as its power has waned in comparison to the President's in the twentieth century, Congress's policy agenda has changed to become increasingly focussed on regulative and redistributive goals, emphasizing social welfare concerns and the fine-tuning of the economy. All of these changes have been recorded in the articles published here; they mark stages in the way Congress functions and allow us to understand why it has done what it has done in the way that it has.

Finally, in this category are a number of studies about what is referred to as Congress's electoral connection—the influence of popular elections in shaping the institution's central impulses and driving it into certain behavior patterns at different moments. Here, as elsewhere, Congress has been an institution constantly undergoing change as the balance between parties and individuals in the electoral equation has shifted, and the volatility of a member's security in his seat has varied considerably. As with all of the developmental and overview studies, each article provides a context within which to understand individual episodes, events, careers, pressures, and particular actions as something more than unique, and as aspects of a larger whole. Each allows us to grasp something of the reality of a moving, changing institution, never complete, always in process, always balancing change and stability.

Titles 5-8

In contrast, the next group of articles are organized by discrete chronological eras and focus on the range of matters central to each distinct period in Congress's past. The articles included in these chronological titles illuminate distinct problems and responses, as well as the specific ways in which Congress has moved each time to fulfill its constitutional obligations, meet the demands made on it, and react to pressures. After its organizing moments in 1789-1790, Congress faced an array of development, foreign policy, economic crisis, and nature of the Union matters, none for the last time. But in the period through 1841, the shaping of Congress's response to those problems lacked repetitive, predictable focus and direction; the policies developed were not always part of sustained, coherent agendas; rather, fragmentation and irregularity were the usual orders of the day. Large-scale organizing institutions or belief systems were only intermittently effective.

In contrast, after 1841 and through the 1890s, while the nature of the problems confronted changed little in substance or nature, the way that Congress moved to deal with them shifted markedly toward a certain kind of coherence. In the third era, after 1896, and through the post-World War II period, Congress had to try to deal with a new America, one in which industrialization, urbanization, and an energized demand for increased government regulation and vigor, along with our renewed role in world affairs, was played out in the institution. Members of Congress developed some new institutional forms to do so, while shucking some of their previous patterns of behavior. Finally, since the 1960s, a modern Congress has seen many rapid, extensive, and crisscrossing changes in every aspect of congressional life. The modern period was initially characterized, in the 1960s and 1970s, by fragmentation and dispersal of authority, reminiscent of the period before 1841, coupled with the heaviest legislative load in American history. Since then, however, the load remains about the same but some new coherence and institutionalization have begun to appear in the way Congress deals with its tasks. It adds up to a pattern unlike that of any other period.

Titles 9-10

Throughout its history, Congress has had to deal with a wide array of legislative topics, from tariffs and land policy in the early era, to the variety of social proposals, foreign policy issues, and economic matters that make up today's normal agenda. These topics are covered in the chronological titles. At the same time, scholarly interest in a number of the topics has produced an array of articles that, brought together, go into greater depth on these subjects. Two in particular, Congress's relations with the other two branches of the federal government and its handling of foreign policy issues in the twentieth century, have been particularly fruitfully and repeatedly examined. The rich literature available on them provide important insights into the subjects themselves and, more generally, into the way Congress has addressed recurring problems. To be sure, other subjects might have been chosen as well. But these are particularly rewarding examples of Congress's historical role and behavior within a complex, often contentious, federal system.

Even in a collection of articles as extensive as this, choices have had to be made about what to include and what must be left out. Almost all of the articles are from scholarly journals. With very few exceptions, I have not incorporated essays originally written for, or readily available in, collections of essays, for example, those in the various editions of the excellent *Congress Reconsidered* edited by Lawrence Dodd and Bruce Oppenheimer. Second, I have preferred to include more recent articles—from the last fifteen years or so—again with some exceptions. Among those, I have incorporated articles that have a clear historical bent. As we approach the present, my choices have been more and more selective. I have sometimes chosen one or two articles to represent a whole research tradition, secure in the knowledge that the references in the essays will lead those interested to the full corpus of work done. Finally, with those many, many essays that focus primarily on the contemporary Congress, I have been most selective, including only those that either resonate with recurring problems that reach back chronologically or that clearly sum up where Congress is at a particular moment.

The combination of external pressures shaping congressional personnel, agendas, and behavior and the way that Congress itself developed and organized to handle the demands of the external political world has been the major focus of scholarly research efforts. The focus of the articles chosen is always from inside Congress, looking out. The rest of the political world appears as it interacts with, and shapes, the history of Congress. There are many articles in which Congress and its members appear indirectly, as dependent factors as other political issues are probed: the development of political parties, elections, studies of various policy matters. These are included here only if the role of Congress is central or when they illuminate something important about the congressional experience: how the institution developed, how it behaves, what have been its major subject concerns, what have been the influences on it and what has been its response. In the section on the electoral connection, for example, I have not generally reproduced articles that focus on problems of the sources and nature of popular voting behavior as a general phenomenon. Rather, my choices lie in the area where such voting affects the way Congress goes about its business. Finally, there is more reliance on the most recently published materials as indicators of the direction current research is taking. In total, all represent much of the best work currently available on this most powerful and important institution.

Joel H. Silbey

Editor's Preface

When the twenty-seventh Congress of the United States met in early 1841, the American political system had just entered a new era, one different in form and substance from anything that had preceded it. The factional infighting that had dominated the political scene since 1815 had settled down, thanks to the activities of a number of skilled party leaders, into a bipolar confrontation superficially similar to that which had developed in the 1790s in the first days of the new government. This time, however, and unlike the earlier period, the commitment to parties had penetrated deep into the political soil, including strongly shaping the consciousness of the voters. National political parties of unparalleled strength, scope, and importance were now firmly settled on the scene and affected everything that went on. Elections at every level of politics were not only dominated by partisan labels, but also reflected the sharp ideological polarization represented by the Whig and Democratic parties. The voters responded by voting the party line for all of the offices contested on election day.

Congress, not unexpectedly, reflected the partisan forces that were at large in the political arena. Each party's national platform provided its legislative agenda. Members of Congress clearly identified themselves as partisans, promised to follow the party line, and constantly reported back to their constituents how well they were doing so. As a result, Congress, in its annual meetings, was a major arena of party activities. The House and Senate were all but completely partisan from 1841 onward, not briefly and incompletely, as had been the case earlier, but repeatedly and persistently. Members proved themselves to be partisans first, not independent statesmen (although some of the latter remained on the scene until the early 1850s). Most came up through their party's ranks. They believed in what the party stood for and felt themselves to be under the party's discipline in their behavior as well as in the shape of their careers. Their careers tended to be short under the party's aegis. There was a strong commitment to rotation in the office to allow others to have a turn, to reinvigorate the Congress with new, but still partisan, blood.

Such rapid turnover put a premium on some strong guidance for members as they came to Washington, often for the first time. It suggested, also, how much each was an all-but-interchangeable part of the partisan system, rather than an independent force in his own right.

When the members arrived on Capitol Hill, they entered party caucuses in each house to select each party's candidates for the various congressional offices elected at the opening of the session. Caucuses and all the rest of Congress's resources were dedicated to partisan purposes. Strong party leaders relentlessly pushed their policy agendas. The members were expected to follow the party line in debate, and most did. Committee chairs were partisans as well, and could be counted on to pursue their party's objectives in legislation. The result of this was clear-cut. The legislative process, from original definition to the roll-call voting on the range of issues that came before the House and Senate, was overwhelmingly determined by party membership. Even national emergencies and foreign crises saw little if any lessening of the partisan spirit. During the Mexican War and a number of similar crises, for example, the Whig-Democratic division remained sharp and dominant.

Other factors were also present, some of which remained influential within the domain of party. Group discipline based on partisan loyalties could be, and often was, challenged. Local and constituency pressures could still strongly affect outlook and behavior. Some members did dissent from a party line when they felt that they had to, based on these local pressures. Factionalism, rooted in other divisions, also remained an aspect of party and congressional affairs. But the force of these traditional determining elements was much less than ever before. Most issues and divisions, no matter how locally rooted they were in origin, were generally subsumed within the party apparatus and outlook. The parties built institutions, such as the conventions and caucuses, to work out whatever differences existed and to damp down challenges to the group perspective. And, for the first time, there was clear and repeated indication that the larger-scale perspectives fostered by parties could overcome these more narrowly rooted demands, tame factional infighting, and promote the larger focus of the two parties. The close national competition at the polls and to control Congress, between the Whigs and Democrats, also created pressures for party members to stay together, and act together, regardless of differences among them.

Only the sectionalism that divided North from South on the issue of slavery's expansion into the new territories (a division foreshadowed in an earlier period of Congress's history) resisted the omnivorous power of the party line and the pressure to conform to the dictates of the partisan steamroller. Sectional anger and confrontations repeatedly appeared in Congress. The parties proved able, at first, to control them. For almost a decade after 1841, whatever sectional anxieties existed were played down as contrary to the main lines that most members believed divided the political world. At the same time, Congress was able to forge compromises on these issues when they burst out of bounds, at least until a powerful electoral realignment in the mid-1850s severely (if temporarily) weakened the parties. The outbreak of violence in the territories under dispute foreclosed compromise and the playing down of sectional tensions as viable options in the second half of the 1850s. Congress continued to legislate but succumbed, as did the rest of the nation, to the force of sectionalism.

Of course, this sectionalism, while potent in its own right, also had a strong partisan cast affecting its shape and force. One indication of this was how quickly parties came roaring back on the American legislative scene (and elsewhere). The Civil War invigorated Congress. It had to spend much legislative energy by mobilizing resources to fight a war through the expansion of federal government authority. As Congress did so, the warfare between Democrats and Republicans dominated everything that went on. In putting down a rebellion and in supporting a strong president, Republicans in particular saw themselves as faced by not only a combative South but also a Northern Democratic bloc that was determined to frustrate the successful prosecution of the war. The latter defined matters in the same partisan way. The Democrats continued to be hesitant about the use of government power and resisted any vast social changes as a consequence of the war. These battles over the direction of the nation were unhesitatingly cast in partisan terms throughout the war years in the North. In the Confederate Congress as well, where political parties never formally took hold, similar partisan tensions, rooted in past memories and current problems, also appeared.

At the same time, America's wartime political experiences prompted a great deal of tension in both parties. The Democrats squabbled over the pressures imposed on them by the war, squabbles exacerbated by the frustration of their reduced power. Republicans in Congress, faced for part of the time with a much less potent Democratic opposition than usual, found themselves battling among themselves about policy and with the president over his powers and over patronage. At the same time, the president's power grew at Congress's expense and the latter kicked back. It effectively wielded its investigation power as both a Republican and a congressional weapon during the war, excoriating

Democrats and the president's appointees alike. All of these provoked sharp and bitter contentiousness, all of it colored by the partisan cast of the era. The parties remained largely united and in battle line against each other, regardless of their own internal difficulties.

Party lines continued to predominate in the congressional debates after the war as Congress debated the South's future and the social consequences of the war. Reconstruction politics dominated the congressional agenda for a decade after 1865, with a consequent expansion of legislative power to handle new responsibilities in the South, and in attempts to establish national standards over southern life in new and unparalleled ways. All of this was always partisan coated. The Republicans, although divided over means and extent, pushed for vigorous use of federal power in reconstructing the nation. The Democrats remained a party less willing to use the power of the national government to shape domestic life than either the Whigs or the latter's Republican successors. These battles were also shaped by the fact that, after a period of strong Republican dominance, the close electoral competition between the parties returned. The reinvigorated Democrats made sure that Congress would continue to be an arena of persistent partisan contentiousness. By the late 1870s and into the 1880s, the ways of partisanship had become the normal routine of Congress and characterized everything about it, and few of those participating, voters or members, would have understood any other way of operating.

Through all of this half century of powerful partisan warfare, Congress itself continued to change and grow more complex. Obviously its work load had increased a great deal during the war and its aftermath. Presidents and Congress continued to negotiate and fight over the enlarged agenda. The succession of single-term presidents after 1841 were fully involved in this partisan process and were considered the party's leaders. That, in some ways, promoted a working relationship between each of them and Congress when it was controlled by the president's own party. On the other hand, there was a quid pro quo involved. The presidents controlled patronage; members of Congress were not loath to ask them for a share. Partisan lubricants between executive and legislature were, therefore, always present. Their common partisanship often pulled them together; their extensive and competing powers often pulled them apart. After the wartime experience of presidential dominance in national affairs, the legislature came back strongly and tipped the balance the other way. It was again an equal partner—or something more. The postwar decades were labelled, in fact, an era of "congressional government," in Woodrow Wilson's famous phrase.

But it was no longer clear in the 1870s and afterward that Congress had the internal structural capabilities to meet its enlarged responsibilities. Members needed more and more knowledge to deal with a range of new problems and pressures, from what to do about the freedom in the South to their responsibility to the millions of veterans, with their demands for medical aid, rehabilitation services, and pensions. The recharging of American economic development and territorial expansion promoted new legislative demands in familiar policy areas: transportation, tariffs, immigration. Party platforms, and the perspectives behind them, provided general guides and promoted the establishment of legislative policy directions. At the same time, more and more specifics were needed. Specialized committees, and congressmen with special knowledge, were increasingly overburdened. It was a confusing, hectic, and, to some, overwhelming legislative situation.

The articles included in this volume set out the unique qualities that defined this partisan era of congressional history and explore the processes affecting that institution and the problems it had to confront. The focus of most of the essays remains on the partisan quality of political life over a fifty-year period—describing it, measuring its importance and impact, and considering the limitations on it from sectionalism and party factionalism. At the same time, as with the other volumes in this collection, a number of the articles illuminate the ongoing process of internal congressional development and change, and explore Congress's shifting relationship with the president and the remainder of the government.

Joel H. Silbey

The United States Congress in a Partisan Political Nation, 1841-1896

The Party, Going Strong:
Congress and Elections in the
Mid-19th Century

MICHAEL LES BENEDICT
The Ohio State University

It is a commonplace of American political science that party plays a smaller role in determining national legislative behavior in the United States than in most other parliamentary democracies. Moreover, studies over the past three decades into both legislative and mass political behavior suggest that the role of party in both areas has been diminishing. The respected journalist, David Broder, has summarized the situation for a popular audience by punning *The Party's Over* (1972).[1]

Studies of the electorate have indicated not only that party identification and loyalty have eroded over the past thirty years, but that voters' comprehension of issues and of the positions of candidates and parties is vague.[2] Suggested by studies of the electorate in presidential elections, the foregoing seems to be even truer for congressional elections (Stokes and Miller, 1962; Hinckley, Hoffstetter, Kessel, 1974; McKay, 1979).

Congressional behavior mirrors this political environment and perhaps reinforces it. In a political environment in which party labels have diminishing attraction for voters and in which party institutions have atrophied, most congressmen find the responsibility for getting elected and reelected falling primarily upon their own individual efforts. Most congressmen run their own independent election campaigns, with money they have raised themselves and staffed by people they have recruited; they strive primarily to establish among voters positive, personal images often irrelevant to that of their party; they take positions on issues that will be popular in their own districts, even if contrary to the general position of their party, and they eschew those that will be unpopular; they fulfill a service function for their constituents; and they take care to conciliate powerful local interests. In short, congressional politics turns upon what David R. Mayhew (1974) has called "the electoral connection" rather than party competition.[3] Party leaders recognize this reality by tolerating mavericks, eschewing sanctions in favor of persuasion when trying to secure support for party positions, and even encouraging colleagues to "duck" or desert the party position on votes that would jeopardize their chance of reelection. When exerting pressure for party loyalty, often party leaders go through influential constituents (Matthews, 1960: 118-146, *passim.*; Clapp, 1963: 150-158, 286-290, 313-320; Ripley, 1967: 73-77, 145-148; Rieselbach, 1973: 105-112; Mayhew, 1974: 99-105). Naturally, this blurs the policy differences between the parties, while

Reprinted by permission of the United States Capitol Historical Society and The American University.

the relationship between individual congressmen and party policy is even fuzzier.

However, recent political events must bring into question the permanence of this political environment. The election of 1980 witnessed an extraordinary degree of unity among Republican officeholders, candidates, and activists—a unity which has been transferred from the campaign into Congress, where party-line voting may be becoming more common than it has been in years.[4] Republican party strategists buy media-time and space for promotion of the party, actively recruit attractive candidates, run seminars in campaign methods, and seek diligently to identify all Democrats with party leaders perceived to be unpopular such as Speaker Thomas P. O'Neill and "liberal, big-spender" Edward M. Kennedy. Democrats are reacting by also urging a stronger party response to the Republican offensive (CQ 39 (1981): 137-40, 993-995, 1367; Kondracke, 1980; Malbin, 1980).[5]

All this suggests that Americans may be entering a new phase of political competition. Recent research into the history of the American political system indicates that the American electorate and American political institutions undergo periods of realignment, with intense party competition and increased political awareness and interest among voters. Such periods are followed by the slow deterioration of the new alignment, a time when party differences diminish, party lines in government slacken, control of various branches of national government is divided, there is general inertia in government policymaking, and partisan attachments among voters weaken (Key, 1955; Burnham, 1965, 1970; Sundquist, 1973; Clubb et al., 1980: esp. 132-152, 162-184, 228-239). It may well be that the patterns of behavior researchers have found in recent Congresses, and the lack of "saliency" of party and party issues in congressional election contests, reflect, at least in part, these circumstances. For example, Clubb, Flanigan, and Zingale (1980: 228-239) find a much higher degree of partisan cleavage on congressional roll calls in the aftermath of partisan realignments than during their deterioration. A major finding in Brady's (1973: 43-92) analysis of the House of Representatives from 1896 to 1900 was "the pervasiveness of party voting." By looking at Congress and the electorate during a period in the immediate aftermath of realignment, one may find patterns different from those to which modern researchers are accustomed.

PARTY IN THE 19TH CENTURY

The 1860s and the early 1870s were such a period, the early years of what political scientists and historians perceive to be the third party system. In these years, the great struggle over slavery that had led to the birth of the Republican party and to civil war was still fresh in the mind of the electorate; they worshipped at "the shrine of the party" (Polakoff, 1973:3-12).[6] This was reflected by the pervasiveness of party in the Reconstruction-era Congresses. This is not to say that every issue was a party issue, especially when defined by the strictest measure. The median Rice indices of party likeness on final votes on substantive legislation were 36 and 56 in the Thirty-ninth and Fortieth Congresses, respectively; they were 56 and 39 in the Senate.[7] And, as Tables 1 and 2 show, partisan differences were concentrated overwhelmingly in the area of Reconstruction legislation. But by far the largest number of votes in a single area that the two houses recorded involved that subject. In fact in the succeeding Congresses the proportion of Reconstruction to other legislation decreased, and as Clubb *et al.*'s (1980) figures show, so did the degree of partisan division, at least in the House, where their figures are more certainly reliable (Clubb and Traugott, 1977. See also Note 7, *supra*). When Republicans won the presidential election of 1868 on a promise that their victory would mark the end of the great conflict over slavery, pledging in the words of one orator "peace . . . upon the basis of a restored Union, of results already accomplished and of a state of things already existing," they were consciously interring the issue that had led to the partisan realignment upon which their coalition was based (Schurz, 1913: I, 419; see also Benedict, 1975: 323-334). Naturally, within a few months Republican congressmen were lamenting the collapse of party unity. "The Republicans are of one party only in name," complained one leader.[8] And Republican politicians and factions defeated in intra-party battles began to urge a fundamental restructuring of the party leadership.[9] This erosion of party unity continued until spring, 1871, when Ku Klux Klan outrages in the South rekindled the slavery issue and Republicans responded with the Force Act. A small number of Republican dissidents refused to go along with this resurrection of a "dead issue" and organized the ill-fated Liberal Republican movement. But for most Republicans the Force Act restored party elán. As Attorney General Amos T. Akerman wrote a political ally, "[A]ll that is necessary to hold the majority of the northern voters to the Republican cause, is to show them how active and cruel the Confederate temper still is in the South."[10] From that point until the realignment of the 1890s, Republicans regularly waved what battered opponents disgustedly called "the bloody shirt."[11]

3

TABLE 1

Median Indices of Republican-Democratic Likeness on Various Issues,
House of Representatives,
39th-40th, 43rd-44th Congresses

Issue	Number of Roll-Call Votes	Median Index of Likeness
Reconstruction		
39 Congress, 1 Session	(122)	10.5
39 Congress, 2 Session	(45)	6.1
40 Congress	(111)	6.0
43 Congress	(40)	22.6
44 Congress	(23)	21.8
Black Rights		
39 Congress, 1 Session	(Black Suffrage; votes = 11)	24.0
39 Congress, 2 Session	(Black Suffrage; votes = 5)	5.1
40 Congress	(Nonsouthern Black Rights; votes = 5)	0.1
43 Congress	(Civil Rights; votes = 17 not including filibuster)	9.9
44 Congress	(Civil Rights; votes = 1)	27.1

TABLE 1 (continued)

Southern Contested Elections

43 Congress	(10)	13.5
44 Congress	(6)	7.1

1876 Electoral Vote Count

44 Congress	(66)	11.4

Corruption in Government and Civil Service Reform

44 Congress	(Civil Service Reform; votes = 8)	42.4
44 Congress	(Corruption Investigation; votes = 7)	5.3

Tariff

39 Congress	(6)	41.0
43 Congress	(6)	21.8
44 Congress	(2)	23.8

Anti-Monopoly and Regulatory Legislation

39 Congress	(5)	24.3
40 Congress	(9)	74.9
43 Congress	(6)	31.3

Corporate Subsidies

39 Congress	(16)	31.1
40 Congress	(14)	86.8
43 Congress	(11)	64.2
44 Congress	(6)	89.3

Presidential Term

43 Congress	(3)	37.0
44 Congress	(7)	56.5

Fiscal Policy

39 Congress	(20)	67.8
40 Congress	(16)	71.0
43 Congress	(23)	88.4
44 Congress	(26)	46.5

Public Works

43 Congress	(16)	76.5
44 Congress	(6)	92.5

Bankruptcy

39 Congress	(5)	93.7
43 Congress	(1)	93.9
44 Congress	(1)	84.2

NOTE: Near-identical votes on dilatory motions and amendments were generally excluded. These figures are the result of tedious search, and slight variations due to human error or differences in judgment might occur if another investigator embarked on the same project.

TABLE 2

*Median Indices of Republican-Democratic Party Likeness on Various Issues, Senate,
39th-40th, 43rd-44th Congresses*

Issue	Number Votes	Median Index of Likeness
Reconstruction		
39 Congress, 1 Session	(293)	7.7
39 Congress, 2 Session	(67)	18.5
40 Congress, 1 Session	(60)	51.8
40 Congress, 2 Session	(57)	24.3
40 Congress, 3 Session	(59)	26.7
43 Congress	(25)	12.5
44 Congress	(General Reconstruction; votes = 52)	11.4
44 Congress	(Loyalty Oaths and Amnesty; votes = 4)	74.3
44 Congress	(Protection of Voting Rights; votes = 20)	0.0
Civil Rights		
43 Congress	(14)	10.4
Southern Contested Elections		
43 Congress	(8)	10.8
44 Congress	(15)	11.0
Army Appropriations		
43 Congress	(10)	33.4
44 Congress	(9)	21.1
Indian Policy		
43 Congress	(12)	29.8
44 Congress	(14)	44.9
Tariff		
39 Congress	(40)	56.5
43 Congress	(3)	19.5
Southern and Wartime Claims		
43 Congress	(7)	46.7
44 Congress	(2)	41.5
1876 Electoral Vote Count		
44 Congress	(31)	42.1
Corporate Subsidies		
39 Congress	(6)	54.4
40 Congress	(16)	60.1
43 Congress	(6)	61.5
44 Congress	(21)	73.7

5

TABLE 2 (continued)

Anti-monopoly and Regulatory Legislation

39 Congress	(3)	37.5
40 Congress	(5)	70.4
43 Congress	(10)	65.1

Civil Service Reform

43 Congress	(1)	61.0
44 Congress	(4)	91.3

Public Works

43 Congress	(24)	75.4
44 Congress	(23)	67.7

Fiscal Policy

40 Congress	(12)	77.8
43 Congress	(52)	88.8
44 Congress	(1)	74.9

Debt Funding

43 Congress	(4)	92.7
44 Congress	(3)	60.9

Bankruptcy

39 Congress	(1)	81.7
43 Congress	(6)	92.9

During these years (the 1860s to mid-1870s), the institutions of party leadership in Congress were stronger than they have been recently—particularly the party caucus, which met regularly to devise legislation that all elements of the party could support.[12] Thaddeus Stevens' legendary "dictatorship" over Republicans in the House emanated from the forcefulness with which he enforced party, especially caucus, decisions (Benedict, 1975: 34-35).

It was on the slavery and the related Reconstruction issues that congressional Republicans most differed from Democrats in the 1860s and 1870s,[13] and the electorate mirrored that division. Despite the insistence of many of the so-called "new political historians" that anti-Catholicism, nativism, prohibitionism, and Sabbatarianism were more important ingredients in Republicanism than antislavery, in their most recent work they have had to concede that Republicans' evangelical Protestant values were expressed primarily through what one of them has called "broad anti-southernism" (to escape the humanitarian connotations of "antislavery") (Kleppner, 1979: 70-71; see also Holt, 1978 and cf. Holt, 1969). In fact, from 1865 through 1876 the Republicans constantly stressed sectional issues—what Democrats, wishing they would go away, insisted were dead, "bloody shirt" issues, and what Progressive historians insisted were all-too-successful smokescreens to deflect the electorate's attention from the "real," economic issues of the time.[14]

Republican leaders suppressed nativist, anti-Catholic, prohibitionist, and Sabbatarian agitation throughout the era, and it did not begin to revive until the mid-

TABLE 3

Common Northern State Political Platform Planks
1866-1872

Reconstruction and Race	Number of Planks	
	Republicans	Democrats
	(N = 40)*	(N = 33)
Endorsing State Rights, Opposing "Centralization"	0	19
Endorsing Congressional Reconstruction Policy	16	0
Condemning Congressional Reconstruction Policy	0	9
Pro-Test Oath, Anti-Amnesty	3	0
Anti-Test Oath, Pro-Amnesty	4	6
Pro-Black Suffrage	9	0
Anti-Black Suffrage	0	8
Protection of Voting Rights (after 1868)	4	0
General Endorsement of Equality in Unspecified Rights, 1871-72	7	4
Acquiescence in the Results of Reconstruction, 1871-72	—	8
Thanks to Union Soldiers	6	4
Bounty Equalization	0	3
Economic Issues		
Pro-Protective Tariff	17	0
Anti-Protective Tariff	1	12
Anti-National Banking System	0	5
Pro-Government Aid for Economic Development	4	1
Anti-Government Aid for Economic Development	11	4
Pro-Currency Inflation, Anti-Currency Contraction	2	1
Anti-Currency Inflation, Pro-Currency Contraction	3	1
Pro-Reserving Public Lands for Settlers Only	10	4
Anti-Monopoly	2	1
Government Operation		
Pro-Civil Service Reform	7	3
Pro-Reduction of Expenditures	3	4
Pro-Reduction of Taxation	9	11
Social Issues		
Pro-National Government Promotion of Education	2	1
Pro-State Promotion of Education	6	0
Pro-Prohibition	3	0
Anti-Prohibition	1	2
Pro-Religious Tolerance	0	2
Anti-Sectarian Influence in Schools (implicitly anti-Catholic)	2	0
Pro-Immigration and Protection of Naturalized Citizens	3	3

*N = number of platforms. If more than one plank was devoted to one subject, the subject was nonetheless counted once.

7

TABLE 4

Coefficients of Determination Between Party Voting Patterns and Referenda

	Republicans		Democrats	
	Black Rights	Prohibition	Black Rights	Prohibition
Illinois, black exclusion,				
1848/1856 presidential vote	.42		.28	
1858 congressional vote	.16		.28	
Michigan, black suffrage,				
1850/1856 presidential vote	.37		.22	
1858 congressional vote	.31		.41	
Indiana, black exclusion,				
1851/1856 presidential vote	.35		.27	
1858 congressional vote	.23		.08	
Ohio, license,				
1851/1856 presidential vote		.03		.31
1858 congressional vote		.10		.32
Michigan, prohibition,				
1853/1856 presidential vote		.26		.30
1858 congressional vote		.48		.42
Rhode Island, license,				
1853/1856 presidential vote		.77		.29
1858 congressional vote		.56		.53
Wisconsin, prohibition				
1853/1856 presidential vote		.18		.23
1858 congressional vote		.07		.23
Pennsylvania, prohibition,				
1854/1856 presidential vote		.12		.18
1860 presidential vote		.23		.14
Illinois, prohibition,				
1855/1856 presidential vote		.58		.66
1858 congressional vote		.49		.55
Iowa, prohibition,				
1855/1854 congressional vote		.90		.71
1856 presidential vote		.13		.31
1858 congressional vote		.02		.18
Wisconsin, black suffrage,				
1857/1857 gubernatorial vote	.64		.96	
1858 congressional vote	.19		.14	
Iowa, black suffrage,				
1857/1857 gubernatorial vote	.06		.25	
1858 congressional vote	.11		.25	
1860 congressional vote	.26		.34	
Oregon, black exclusion,				
1857/1858 gubernatorial vote	.58		.56	
1860 presidential vote	.61		.07	
New York, black suffrage,				
1860/1860 presidential vote	.77		.81	
Connecticut, black suffrage,				
1865/1865 gubernatorial vote	.74		.96	

8

	Republicans		Democrats	
	Black Rights	Prohibition	Black Rights	Prohibition
Minnesota, black suffrage, 1865/1865 gubernatorial vote	.66		.79	
Wisconsin, black suffrage, 1865/1865 gubernatorial vote	.85		.90	
Kansas, black suffrage, 1867/1868 presidential vote	.58		.76	
Minnesota, black suffrage, 1867/1867 gubernatorial vote	.61		.74	
Ohio, black suffrage, 1867/1867 gubernatorial vote	.96		.98	
Iowa, black suffrage, 1868/1868 presidential vote	.88		.94	
Michigan, prohibition, 1868/1868 presidential vote		.62		.52
Minnesota, black suffrage, 1868/1868 presidential vote	.96		.96	
New York, black suffrage, 1869/1864-1868 mean party vote	.81		.67	
Michigan, black suffrage, 1870/1864-1868 mean party vote	.71		.26	
Ohio, license, 1874/1870-1873 mean party vote		.31		.16
Michigan, license, 1876/1872-1876 mean party vote		.37		.04
Kansas, prohibition, 1880/1880 presidential vote		.22		.38

9

NOTE: Voting patterns are based on the proportion of the total eligible electorate voting for each party. The coefficient of determination is the square of the simple Pearsonian correlation coefficient (r). It expresses the proportion of the variation in the voting patterns on referenda explained by the Republican and Democratic voting patterns in years noted. In every case voting patterns in favor of black rights and prohibition correlated positively with Republican voting patterns and negatively with Democratic voting patterns.

1870s.[15] A look at state party platforms from 1866 to 1872, gleaned from Edward McPherson's political manuals for those years, confirms this (1875: 123, 243-248; 478-488, 622-624, 1872: 132-181). (Party platforms do not predict very accurately what a party will *do* when in power, of course, but they do constitute the issues which leaders think will win them votes.) As Table 3 shows, planks on the national issues of Reconstruction, economics, and government operations far outnumbered the handful dealing with what may be called "social issues." Party differences were clearest in the areas of Reconstruction and black rights (especially before the Democratic "New Departure" of 1871-1872, in which Democrats tried to put the catastrophic war issues behind them), state rights, the protective tariff, and the national banking system.

Although nativism, prohibitionism, and antislavery seem to have been rooted in the same soil of evangelical Protestant values, Table 4 shows how strongly Republican voters identified with the party's antislavery mission by the 1860s. In the formative years of the third party system, until about 1856, voting patterns in prohibition referenda and in referenda on expanding the rights of black residents of the northern states (an issue closely related to antislavery) correlated at about the same level with Republican voting patterns. But by 1860 Republican voting patterns almost exactly paralleled the patterns of support for black rights, accounting for over 80% of the variation of those patterns.

10

Of course, the fact that the voting *patterns* were similar did not mean that every Republican voted to expand black rights in their states. Indeed until the war's end a large proportion of Republicans opposed so radical a step as enfranchising black men living among them. However, after the Confederate surrender support for black rights became virtually a party issue, dividing the electorate as completely as it did party leaders. Table 5 provides estimates of individual voting behavior derived from regression coefficients.[16] It indicates that only in Kansas was there major Republican opposition to the enfranchisement of black state citizens after 1865, and there was even less Democratic support. Where Republicans were unenthusiastic, they signified their dissatisfaction by abstaining; they could not bring themselves to vote for a position now completely identified with the Democratic party.

PARTY AND PERSONAL AMBITION

The powerful political partisanship of the mid-1860s and early 1870s alters many of the conclusions derived from Mayhew's postulate of "the electoral connection"— that each congressman's activities are best understood as a personal effort to win reelection. Naturally in such an environment party must have played a larger role in each congressman's calculation of just what conduct would reelect him. Moreover, even the premise may not have been true. With party and a single set of issues playing so crucial a role in politics, the ethic of the times seems to have been against such egocentric political calculations. In the 1860s and 1870s Americans believed that the man should not seek office; the office should seek the man, and he reluctantly agreed to a nomination for the sake of the principles that *his party* espoused. Thus George W. Julian recalled that he first stood for Congress "in compliance with the wishes of my anti-slavery friends, and by way of doing my part of the work" of organizing an antislavery party (1884: 116-117). Henry Watterson began his short stay in Congress although "holding office, especially going to Congress, had never entered any wish or scheme of mine. Office seemed to me ever a badge of bondage." What happened? "[T]he opportunity sought me out" (1919, II:22). Campaigning for a nomination, which suggested a desire for personal preferment, seems to have been regarded as unseemly. James A. Garfield wrote a friend shortly before his Republican district convention met to decide his renomination, "My policy . . . has been this: to secure the support of my constituents by doing my duty here (in Congress) in such a manner as to honor the District and myself . . . rather than by palaver and begging them to give me their votes. This is the only way for me to preserve my self-respect."[17]

TABLE 5

Republicans, Democrats, and Black Suffrage Referenda

VOTES ON BLACK SUFFRAGE REFERENDA

	REPUBLICANS		
	% For	% Against	% Not Voting
Connecticut, 1865[1]	60.2	0 (−3.2)	43.1
Minnesota, 1865[1]	72.4	22.7	4.9
Wisconsin, 1865[1]	84.5	8.5	6.9
Kansas, 1867[2].	47.7	' · 59.0	0 (−6.7)
Minnesota, 1867[1]	77.3	0	32.7
Ohio, 1867[1]	94.7	1.0	4.3
Iowa, 1868[2]	86.0	3.2	6.8
Minnesota, 1868[2]	92.2	5.1	2.7
New York, 1869[2]	61.7	4.0	34.5
	DEMOCRATS		
Connecticut, 1865[1]	0 (−2.1)	100.5	1.6
Minnesota, 1865[1]	0 (−7.6)	91.6	16.0
Wisconsin, 1865[1]	5.5	83.9	2.2
Kansas, 1867[2].	0 (−8.4)	94.5	14.9
Minnesota, 1867[1]	0 (−11.9)	59.0	18.3
Ohio, 1867[1]	0 (−3.5)	102.7	.9
Iowa, 1868[2]	1.9	93.1	1.0
Minnesota, 1868[2]	0 (−2.8)	98.3	4.5
New York, 1869[2]	6.3	84.2	9.1

[1]With gubernatorial vote of the same year.
[2]With 1868 presidential vote.

In his reminiscences the voluble Indiana Democratic politician, David Turpie, could not bring himself to say much about his political maneuvering. Naturally he claimed to have been drafted for his first state legislative race. Years later "in my absence, I was unanimously nominated by the Democratic convention of the ninth district as a candidate for Congress." Evidently without any action on his part, this occurred three consecutive times. A few years after that, "in the summer of 1874 . . . I was nominated by acclamation . . . as one of the candidates for the legislature. Having always been of the opinion that a member of our party should not decline a call thus made, I accepted the nomination." (1903: 109, 194, 232). That retiring butterfly Roscoe Conkling also had to be seduced into his first run for Congress. "At first Mr. Conkling refused to allow his name to be used," his brother remembered in his biography of him, "but his political friends would not take 'no' for a reply." (Conkling, 1889: 75). The researcher becomes so used to this pattern that he is shocked by the candor of Schuyler Colfax's 1868 campaign biographer, who wrote frankly, "it is certain that at a very early day, when most boys are thinking of their games and play, he made up his mind to enter upon the stormy and uncertain career of politics at the first practicable moment, and to rise as high and as quickly as his ability would permit." (Martin, 1868: 13). Rutherford B. Hayes' campaign biographer, William Dean Howells, was more traditional. Of Hayes' first congressional nomination, he wrote, "He had not, of course, sought the nomination, but at the urgence of friends, he had let the matter take its course. . . ." (1876: 89-99).

Now beneath this decorous exterior, the politicians of the 1860s and 1870s must have been as ambitious for personal benefits and honor as other men. Their behavior suggests it. Despite his protestations, Garfield fought like a lion to secure renomination the one time he was really threatened by local insurgents, after he was tainted by the Credit Mobilier scandal (Smith, 1925, I: 547-562; Peskin, 1978: 551) Charles Sumner resisted pressure by associates to seek the United States Senate nomination from the Democratic-Free Soil coalition that had won control of the Massachusetts legislature in 1850. "I have never been accustomed to think highly of political distinction," he wrote one of them. "I have not been able at any time in my inmost heart to bring myself to desire the post, or even to be willing to take it."[18] But he refused to withdraw his name even when the reluctance of some of the Democrats to support him deadlocked the legislature for three months. He would not bargain for the office; nor would he give it up.[19]

But this does not mean that these diffident politicians were not sincere. As he struggled for his 1874 renomination Garfield confided in his diary, "I can fight battles for others but to fight men for disliking me, for disapproving of my course, hurts my pride and self-love more than anything I have been called upon to meet." (Smith, 1925, I: 551).

The diary of Rutherford B. Hayes also indicates a deep ambivalence about his pursuit of political advancement. The researcher can look in vain for an avowal of ambition, for an apparently selfish thought. Every act is justified in terms of moral duty. And yet the acts themselves are not much different from those that a calculating self-seeker would undertake.[20] Perhaps the best example of the inability of mid-nineteenth century politicians to admit their own ambition, and their compulsion to justify it in terms of other commitments, is a letter Salmon P. Chase wrote to an old friend in April, 1868. "I really think that I am not half so ambitious of place as I am represented to be," he wrote. "Certainly I never used any of the ordinary means to get place. I worked for ideals and principles and measures embodying them; and was always quite willing to take place, or be left out of place, as the cause, in the judgment of its friends, required."[21] As he wrote, the old antislavery radical was coquetting for the *Democratic* nomination to the presidency, since it had become clear he could not win that of the Republicans. Even his friend and sympathetic biographer had to concede, "Never was a heart more self-deceived than was the heart of our hero when he wrote that letter and others of like import." (Warden, 1874: 683).

The consequence of this aversion to public personal promotion, or perhaps to the public expectation that one should not engage in it, was the tendency to promote one's party rather than oneself when campaigning. A candidate to the House of Representatives was expected to stump his district thoroughly every two years.

Slogging by carriage from one small town to another, at each of which he would be expected to speak for hours before a few hundred of the voters in what was both an entertainment and a civic duty to them, the candidates developed a largely set piece that served with minor changes for the duration. One can find them in local weekly newspapers and in the daily press of the large cities. Almost invariably, these speeches were arraignments of the opposing party and encomiums for one's own.[22] Rarely did a candidate ask for a vote for himself. Garfield recognized congressional elections as "the time . . . when the people . . . inspect the work of their servants to see if it has been done honestly and wisely." But he did not perceive it to be individual politicians who were judged. To Garfield, it was axiomatic that "the political party whose doctrines and aspirations accomplish most in this direction will enjoy the confidence of support of our people."[23]

13

Candidates even articulated party positions where none really existed, so as to get their own views before the public. Julian, for example, drew a distinction between the Democratic and Republican positions on his pet scheme to reserve all government-owned western lands for actual settlers, ending the railroad landgrant system.[24] One would be hard-pressed to sustain the distinction based on congressional action. Garfield likewise insisted that only Democrats favored "repudiating" the national debt by paying off wartime bonds in greenbacks.[25] He must have known better, but if the position were popular, he wanted his party to have credit for it. Nothing would have been more alien to him than Ohio Democratic Representative Thomas L. Ashley's remarks in 1980 about his role in passing major housing legislation while in Congress: "My proudest feeling about that is that it was done with absolutely bipartisan support." (Columbus (O.) *Daily Dispatch*, Dec. 14, 1980: E, 11). With their congressman taking such a nonpartisan view, perhaps it is not surprising that the constituents of Ashley's overwhelmingly Democratic district showed similar tolerance by electing his Republican opponent.

So complete was the identification in Garfield's mind between party and candidate that after he arraigned the Democratic party for favoring repudiation of the national debt during the elections of 1868, he concluded, ". . . [T]he people of the Nineteenth District . . . will not now, I believe, . . . become repudiators of the national obligations. But if they do, I should consider myself dishonored by accepting or continuing to hold office on any such terms." (1883, I: 407). One can hardly imagine a modern congressional candidate threatening to refuse his office if the rest of his party's ticket is defeated, even as a rhetorical device—an explicit rejection of ticket-splitting, even in one's favor.[26]

Perhaps nothing displayed better this aversion to personal politics than the reaction in the North to Andrew Johnson's unusual campaign tour of 1866, designed to win support for his conservative Reconstruction policy. This policy had divided him from the Republican party, and yet he refused to affirm himself a Democrat. Without a party with which to identify, he continually had to refer to "my policy" rather than to his party's policy. The number of references to "my policy" and uses of the first person in his speeches became a political joke. Satirist David Ross Locke dedicated a poem to the President, in honor of his campaign: "I, Me, I, Me, I, Me, I, Me, I, Me, I, Me, I, Me," were its last two stanzas (Toledo *Daily Blade*, September 6, 1866). Needless to say, the tour was a political disaster.

Given the degree of the mid-nineteenth century partisanship, however, there was little danger in making such threats as Garfield's to refuse election if the rest of the ticket were defeated. The simple fact was that the congressman's success was intimately bound to that of his party. In the case of those aspiring to the United States Senate, the mode of election itself required such a symbiosis. Since senators were elected by state legislatures, their fortunes depended on party success in their states. Any politician who hoped to get the party legislative caucus to select him was expected to campaign strenuously for his party throughout the state. But even House candidates could not expect to succeed if the rest of their party's ticket failed. Party lines were too rigid for that. Whether in a presidential year or in an off-year, there was far less variation between the congressional vote and that for candidates

14

TABLE 6

Roll-off Between Congressional Vote Percentages and Presidential or Gubernatorial Vote Percentages for Six States

	Ill.	Iowa	Mass.	N.J.	Ohio	Penn.
1848	12	2	31	2	13	2
1850			20	0		
1852	4	1	16	0	1	1
1854			3*			7
1856	7	1	3	1**	1	1**
1858			0			
1860	1	1	7	1	0	4
1862			7	2		
1864	1	0	0	1	0	1
1866			0			0
1868	0	0	3	1	2	2
1870			0			
1872	1	4	0	1	3	8
1874			2	1		
1876	2	1	0	5	0	1
1878			3***			
1880	0	4	0	0	1	4

Mean roll-off in presidential years, 1856-1880 = 1.7

Mean roll-off in non-presidential years, 1858-1878 = 1.7

Mean roll-off, 1856-1880 = 1.7

NOTE 1: Unless otherwise noted, the parties are Whigs and Democrats through 1854 and Republicans and Democrats from 1856.

NOTE 2: Non-presidential year roll-off percentages are between congressional and gubernatorial votes.

*Democratic and American parties.

**Democratic and combined American and Republican parties.

***Combined Democratic and Greenback parties and Republican party

TABLE 7

Correlations Between Whig-Republican Congressional and Presidential or
Gubernatorial Votes for Six States

	Ill.	Iowa	Mass.	N.J.		Ohio	Pa.	
1848	.50	.88	.49	.75		.66	.81	
1850			.72		.96			
1852	.56	.83	.72	.99		.67	.79	
1854			.97					.73
1856	.86	.90	.86	−.06*		.95	.54	
1858			.98					
1860	.99	.99	.97	.98		.92	.91	
1862			.84		.96			
1864	.86	.99	.98	.99		.92	.96	
1866			1.00					.98
1868	.93	1.00	.97	.98		.99	.98	
1870			.81					
1872	.97	.96	.99	.96		.97	.96	
1874			.74		.98			
1876	.84	.85	.92	.53		.98	.97	
1878			.86					.65
1880	.97	.99	.95	.99		.99	.90	

15

*Republican congressional vote compared to Peoples Party presidential and gubernatorial votes.

Median Pearson r for presidential years, 1856-1880 = .96

Median Pearson r for non-presidential years, 1856-1880 = .91

NOTE: Non-presidential year correlations are between congressional and gubernatorial vote patterns.

for other offices than what we expect today. Looking at the difference between election percentages among candidates running for different offices in the same year, Paul T. David has found that the average difference for Republicans was 5.3% from 1872 to 1894, as compared to 8% from 1932 to 1970. For Democrats the figures are 6% and 8%, respectively, (David, 1972: 16).

But closer analysis of returns for 1856 through 1880 indicates that the differences were even slighter. Table 6 shows the roll-off between the congressional vote and the presidential and gubernatorial vote from 1848 to 1880 in six typical states. From 1856 to 1880 the mean roll-off of the two-party vote for both presidential year and off-year elections in the average county was merely 1.7%. Moreover, Tables 7 and 8 suggest how futile it was between 1856 and 1880 for a congressional candidate to hope that the basic voting patterns would be any different for him than for the rest of his ticket. The median Pearson product-moment correlation between the congressional and presidential or gubernatorial vote over the counties in the six states was .96—fully 92% of the variation in the congressional vote could be explained by the presidential vote in presidential years or the gubernatorial vote in nonpresidential years. Therefore, even if a candidate were selfishly concerned with his own personal election, the best way to secure it was to promote the success of the whole party.

16

TABLE 8

Correlations Between Democratic Congressional and Presidential or Gubernatorial Votes for Six States

	Ill.	Iowa	Mass.	N.J.	Ohio	Pa.	
1848	.62	.90	.02	.99	.74	.79	
1850			.30	.99			
1852	.69	.64	.79	.99	.76	.85	
1854			.92				.70
1856	.99	.86	.55	.99	.96	.97	
1858			.95				
1860	.93	.98	.59	.95	.85	.86	
1862			.66	.98			
1864	.87	.98	.99	1.00	.97	.96	
1866			1.00				.99
1868	.99	.98	.93	.96	.99	.98	
1870			.94				
1872	.99	.93	.99	.97	.94	.84	
1874			.74	.98			
1876	.93	.92	.95	.98	.96	.98	
1878			.77				.24
1880	.93	.69	.99	.99	.99	.68	

Median Pearson r for presidential years, 1856-1880 = .96

Median Pearson r for non-presidential years, 1856-1880 = .93

NOTE: Non-presidential year correlations are between congressional and gubernatorial vote patterns.

Yet another reason that congressional candidates may have stressed party rather than individual virtues while campaigning was the relative lack of commitment to a congressional career that characterized most of them. Scholars have long recognized that the nineteen-century Congress, especially the House, was marked by high turnover, few members with long terms of consecutive service, and slight regard for seniority (Polsby, 1968; Price, 1971; Fiorina et al., 1975; Nelson, 1975). Many of those congressmen who served only short stints in Congress looked forward to holding other elective or appointive office and their prospects, especially for patronage positions, depended on general party success.

Finally, the whole party organizational system demanded that candidates work for party rather than individual success. The party organization was sustained primarily through the custom of providing activists with positions in the national, state, and local civil service. The large number of political appointees were expected to devote time and a portion of their incomes from government service to the party; reciprocally, party activists expected such rewards for their efforts. However, these rewards could be secured only if the party won control of the major appointing offices: the presidency, the state governorship, and local executive offices, (see Dobson, 1972: 25-34; White, 1954: 332-343). Party activists, who controlled party nominations, were hardly likely to feel kindly toward a congressional candidate who won political office for himself but ignored the rest of the ticket, to their own detriment.

Conclusion

All of this may have reinforced partisan behavior in Congress. An elected congressman must have felt that he *owed* more to his party than present-day congressmen do. As already noted, nowadays (or at least until the last election), electioneering involves almost entirely the efforts of individual congressmen in their own districts with little help from their party as a whole. That simply was not true of the elections of one hundred and twenty years ago. Not only did the patronage system assure a supply of party workers and money, but because of the nature of the system everyone owed his election to everyone else. They had all stressed the importance of a party vote on party issues, and the electorate had responded. Part of the congressional party's job was to keep those issues salient by proposing legislation involving them. Therefore, for the mid-nineteenth century, and perhaps for other periods following partisan realignments, Anthony Down's (1957) economic model of political action, which makes parties the units of analysis, may be more relevant than that of Mayhew (1974) and others who stress individual desire for reelection as the prime determinant of congressional legislative behavior.[27]

Given American political history, it seems unlikely that the process of decay in party loyalty among voters and officeholders can continue much longer. Past experience suggests that when Americans feel that their parties no longer provide vehicles for dealing with salient questions, party lines are either reorganized or revitalized. This process may have already begun, and if so, the congressional elections of the future may begin to look more like the party-oriented contests of the 1860s and 1870s.

17

Notes

[1]See also Shafer, 1981; Scott and Hrebener 1979; and Burnham, 1970: 19-134.

[2]For scholarly statements, see Pomper, 1975: 18-41. Of course there has been a strenuous debate over just how tenuous the link between issues, voters' positions on them, and their electoral decisions is. But no one really disagrees with the observation that voters generally do not have a very thorough or sophisticated knowledge of public policy issues. The argument seems to be more over the degree to which even vague generalizations about parties, candidates, and issues determine voter behavior, and just how sophisticated about issues voters must be in order to be characterized as "responsible." See Lazarsfeld *et al.*, 1954; Campbell *et al.*, 1954, 1960, 1966; Converse, 1964, 1975: 206-61; V. O. Key. Jr., 1966; Nie, 1974; Stimson, 1975. Even Jack Walker's (1966) powerful challenge to the notion that such political ignorance is a permanent characteristic of the electorate still seemed to concede the accuracy of the description for the electorate as then constituted. The major challenge to the notion that during the 1960s and 1970s voters had only superficial knowledge of party and candidate positions on issues is Pomper, 1975, esp. 166-85.

[3]See also Jones, 1966; Leuthold, 1968; Agranoff, 1972; Jackson, 1974; Tacheron and Udall, 1966; Clapp, 1963: esp. 501-101, 158-60, 313, 333-84; Matthews, 1960: 119, 224-28; Miller and Stokes, 1963; Huitt, 1961; Ripley, 1967; Abramowitz, 1981; and Parker, 1981.

This should not be taken to mean that congressmen are insensitive to party ties. Evidence is abundant that they prefer to support their parties, if possible, and party cleavages still outnumber voting cleavages along other lines. Matthews, 1960: 121-23; Froman and Ripley, 1967: 141-45; Clapp, 1963: 314-16; Shannon, 1968; Truman, 1959; Clausen, 1973.

[4]*Congressional Quarterly* reported that the average Senate Republican supported his party on party votes 80% of the time from January to August, 1981, compared to a range of 68-72% from 1973 through 1980 (*CQ* 39 (Jan. 10, 1981): 80; (Sept. 12, 1981): 5.) Moreover the median Republican backed his party 86% of the time. The average Republican House member supported his party 79% of the

time—the highest figure in 25 years (*CQ* 39 (Aug. 22, 1981): 1583).

[5]For a scholarly analysis of the growing power and activity of the party national committees, especially the Republicans, see Cotter and Bibby, 1980.

[6]See also Marcus, 1971: 3-21. Recent analysts of mass political behavior in the mid-nineteenth century have challenged the belief that the slavery issue precipitated the partisan realignment of the 1850s. I do not find their interpretations of the evidence convincing, for reasons I will sketch below and discuss in more detail in my forthcoming book *Let Us Have Peace: Republicans and Reconstruction, 1869-1880*. For the new view, see Kleppner, 1970, 1979; Formisano, 1971; Holt, 1969. However, even these analysts agree that for one reason or another the parties that emerged from the realignment finally divided most completely on the slavery question in the national arena. For a view closer to my own, but not coinciding exactly, see Holt, 1978.

[7]The Rice index of party likeness is found by subtracting the percentage of one party's members voting for a measure from the percentage of the other party's members voting for it, always subtracting the smaller number from the larger. The difference is subtracted from 100 and then multiplied by 100. Thus a roll call on which the parties split 75-25 percent and 25-75 percent respectively would have an index of likeness equal to that on a roll call on which they split 90-10 and 40-60 respectively (that is, 50.00). An index equalling less than 50.00 marks a rather large disagreement. (See L. F. Anderson *et al.*, 1966; Benedict, 1975: 46-48). These figures differ somewhat from those offered by Clubb *et al.*, 1980: 231, 236. There are two reasons. First, Clubb *et al.* based their figures on all votes on substantive legislation. While Clubb *et al.*'s method is satisfactory for the purpose they have in mind—a comparison of party division in Congress over time—it is less accurate as a measure of party division in individual Congresses, because it does not account for the large series of identical and similar votes on amendments to legislation, or even filibuster votes, which can run into the dozens. So long as these are randomly distributed among Congresses, it will not skew their comparison of Congresses over time.

However, a second potential problem is more serious. The ICPR data, which is based on the *Congressional Directory*, generally identifies congressmen by their party affiliation when first elected. In the large House, with its high nineteenth century turnover, this is not very serious. But in the smaller Senate, with its longer terms, it may affect the findings significantly, as by 1862 several Senators elected as Democrats attended the Republican caucus and Whig Senators had divided between the parties. If Clubb *et al.* did not correct for this, it would explain why their Rice indices of "unlikeness" are so much lower than mine (and also explain why changes in party division in the House correlated with distance from the year of partisan realignment while changes in the Senate did not).

[8]Senator Daniel D. Pratt, quoted in the *Cincinnati Daily Commercial*, June 9, 1870.

[9]I will discuss this more fully in Benedict, forthcoming.

[10]Akerman to Foster Blodgett, November 8, 1871. (Akerman Letterbooks, Alderman Library, University of Virginia, Charlottesville, Virginia).

[11]The foregoing suggests that there may be two different ways in which increased partisan division may occur in Congress. There may be increased polarization across all issues, which is what is usually presumed to occur in times of strong partisanship; but increased polarization may also be due to increased attention to selected issues—even a single issue—of great party saliency. That is certainly true of the Thirty-ninth through Forty-fourth Congresses, as Tables 1 and 2 indicate. It is interesting to note that Clubb, Flanigan, and Zingale (1980) found an extremely high index of party "unlikeness" in the Fifty-first House, an extreme deviation from the pattern of declining partisan division they found from the 1860s through the 1890s. That strong division is also reflected in their Senate figures, although it does not deviate from so clear a pattern. This was the Congress (1889-1891) that considered the Force bill of 1890, the last Republican attempt to protect black voting rights in the South. Likewise the declining partisan division Clubb *et al.* found was reversed in the late 1870s, when a great partisan confrontation took place over repeal of laws permitting the national government to protect voting rights in the South.

[12]Republican caucuses framed the first Reconstruction resolutions, the Fourteenth Amendment, and the Reconstruction Act of 1867, the key pieces of Republican Reconstruction legislation. The Senate Republican caucus limited and directed business in the critical first session of the Fortieth Congress; the House caucus determined the process by which members considered impeachment (see Benedict, 1975: 25-26, 140-42, 185-86, 235-36, 238, 245, 253; 1973: 23-24, 52, 55.) The Republican

18

caucus arranged the process by which Republicans reached a compromise on the bitterly contested currency issue, the Resumption Act of 1875, one of the most important fiscal laws of the nineteenth century and one of the few laws of the 1860s and 1870s equal in importance to those concerning Reconstruction (Unger, 1964: 253-256, and 234-253 for background.)

[13]Besides Tables 1 and 2 above, see Linden, 1966, 1967 and Seip, 1974.

[14]See Beale, 1930, an assessment of the congressional elections of 1866; Benedict, 1975: 188-209, 257-78, for the elections of 1866 and 1867; Coleman, 1933, for the election of 1868; Ross, 1919: 152-77, for the election of 1872; for the election of 1876, Gillette, 1979: 300-311.

[15]Although temperance reform played a large role in the organization of the anti-Democratic coalition in Wisconsin, for example, by 1856 "the party's gravediggers buried its connection with the issue," after discovering "that the Maine law issue could loose a flood of opposition" in the heavily German state (Byrne, 1958-1959: 119-117). The same was true in Iowa, where Germans also made up a large proportion of the population (Clark, 1908). (Note how this parallels the declining correlation between the prohibition referendum of 1855 and the Republican vote from 1854 to 1857 in Table 4). Although Democrats tried to keep the issue alive—a clear indication of whom they thought it benefitted—there was little temperance agitation during the Civil War and Reconstruction years (Martin, 1925; Clark, 1908; Krout, 1936). Even in Maine, home of the "Maine law," Republican regulars worked to keep temperance crusader Neal Dow from committing the party to his cause (Byrne, 1961).

Appeals to nativisim played a similar role. Important in the realignment of 1854-1856, anti-foreign, anti-Catholic issues were quickly relegated to obscurity once the Republicans had established their basic constituency and had begun to look beyond it for the votes needed to gain power. In Ohio, Republicans in the late 1850s began "systematically weeding out" old Know-Nothings from leadership ranks to conciliate Germans (Dannenbaum, 1978. See also Herriott, 1913; Emery, 1971; Bergquist, 1971; Holt, 1969: 286-92; Brand, 1927; Baum, 1978.)

Republican efforts to divorce their party from prohibition and nativist agitation as much as possible seem to have borne fruit. Although they never could gain the support of a majority of Wisconsin, Iowa, or Michigan Germans, the proportion of them voting the Republican ticket rose dramatically in each state from 1856 to 1860. Formisano's figures indicate a median 16% Democratic loss in German Lutheran areas of Michigan and about a 10% loss in Detroit's German wards (1966: 301-302). See also Shafer, 1927: 140-158 and 1981; and Emery, 1971: 170-174. Swierenga (1971), taking a close look at an Iowa Dutch community, records that the Republican vote rose from 25% in 1856 (and a mere 17% in 1857) to 34% in 1860. Germans voted heavily Republican in St. Louis (Kamphoefner, 1975), and Illinois Republicans won about half the German vote (Bergquist, 1971: 196-226). Holt's (1969) figures show a drop in the correlation between Catholic and Democratic voting patterns from +.93 to +.56 between 1856 and 1859 in Pittsburgh, and a drop in the negative correlation between German voting patterns and Republicanism from −.54 to −.29.

[16]For the method for deriving individual behavior from aggregate statistics, and the assumptions that must be made to justify its use, see Shively, 1969; Kousser, 1973; Goodman, 1953, 1959. These figures are estimates, accurate to the degree that voting groups behaved the same way over all counties. Therefore some estimates are less than 0% and more than 100%. These are given in parentheses in Table 4.

[17]Garfield to Harmond Austin, June 21, 1868, quoted in Smith, 1925, I: 433.

[18]Sumner to Charles Francis Adams, December 15, 1850, quoted in Pierce, 1893, III: 233.

[19]*Ibid.*, 231-44; also Donald, 1961: 189-202.

[20]See, for example, Hayes' flirtation with the idea of permitting dissident Republicans to join with Democrats to elect him to the United States Senate over the nominee of the Republican caucus, (Hayes, 1922-26, III: 210-11). Ostensibly Hayes decided he could not in conscience encourage Republicans to bolt their regular nomination. In fact, he risked defeat and ostracism from a party with which he was dissatisfied on moral grounds. See also Hayes' professed indifference to the result of his 1875 gubernatorial and 1876 presidential contests, and contrast it to the obvious evidence of his passionate interest (Hayes, 1922-26, III: 268-85, 289-422 *passim*). See also the more detailed presidential diary edited by T. Harry Williams, 1964.

[21]Chase to Gerritt Smith, April 2, 1868, quoted in Warden, 1874:683.

[22]Some of these are in collections and are thus easily available. See, for example, Blaine, 1887: 48-54, 61-71, 95-103, 119-24; Boutwell, 1867: 347-55; Garfield, 1883, I: 216-42, 390-407, 610-31; Julian,

19

1872: 399-414.

[23]"Political Issues of 1870," in Garfield, 1883, I: 610-11.

[24]"The Seymour Democracy and the Public Lands," in Julian, 1872: 399-414.

[25]"Political Issues of 1868," in Garfield, 1883, I: 390-407.

[26]See also Blaine, "Presidential Election of 1864—Lincoln Against McClellan," in Blaine, 1887: 54.

[27]Mayhew specifically rejected the Downs formulation.

References

Abramowitz, A. I. 1981. "Party and Individual Accountability in the 1978 Congressional Elections," in Maisel, L. S. and J. Cooper, eds., *Congressional Elections*. Beverly Hills: Sage.

Agranoff, R. 1972. *The New Style in Election Campaigns*. Boston: Holbrook Research Institute.

Anderson, L. F., M. W. Watts, Jr., and A. R. Wilcox. 1966. *Legislative Roll Call Analysis*. Evanston: Northwestern University Press.

Baum, D. 1978. "Know-Nothingism and The Republican Majority in Massachusetts: The Political Realignment of the 1850s," *Journal of American History* LXIV: 959-86.

Beale, H. K. 1930. *The Critical Year: A Study of Andrew Johnson and Reconstruction*. New York: Frederick Ungar.

Benedict, M. L. 1973. *The Impeachment and Trial of Andrew Johnson*. New York: W. W. Norton.

——.1975. *A Compromise of Principle: Congressional Republicans and Reconstruction, 1863-1869*. New York: W. W. Norton.

——.Forthcoming. *Let Us Have Peace: Republicans and Reconstruction, 1869-1880*. New York: W. W. Norton.

Berelson, B. R., P. Lazarsfeld, and W. H. McPhee. 1954. *Voting*. Chicago: University of Chicago Press.

Bergquist, J. M. 1971. "People and Politics in Transition: The Illinois Germans, 1850-1860," in F. C. Luebke, ed., *Ethnic Voters and The Election of 1860*. Lincoln, Neb.: University of Nebraska Press.

Blaine, J. G. 1887. *Political Discussions, Legislative, Diplomatic, and Peculiar, 1856-1886*. Norwich, Conn.: Henry Bill Publishing Co.

Boutwell, G. S. 1867. *Speeches and Papers Relating to the Overthrow of Slavery.* Boston: Little, Brown.

Brady, D. W. 1973. *Congressional Voting in a Partisan Era: A Study of the McKinley Houses and a Comparison to the Modern House*. Lawrence, Kansas: University Press of Kansas.

Brand, C. F. 1922. "History of the Know-Nothing Party in Indiana," *Indiana Magazine of History* XVIII: 281-98.

Broder, D. S. 1972. *The Party's Over: The Failure of Politics in America*. New York: Harper and Row.

Burnham, W. D. 1970. *Critical Elections and the Mainsprings of American Politics*. New York: W. W. Norton.

——.1965. "The Changing Shape of the American Political Universe," *American Political Science Review* LIX 7-28.

Byrne, F. L. 1958-1959. "Maine Law Versus Lager Beer: A Dilemma of Wisconsin's Young Republican Party," *Wisconsin Magazine of History* XLII: 115-20.

——.1961. *Prophet of Prohibition: Neal Dow and His Crusade*. Madison: State Historical Society of Wisconsin.

Campbell, A., G. Gurin, and W. M. Miller. 1954. *The Voter Decides*. Evanston, Ill.: Row, Peterson.

Campbell, A., P. E. Converse, W. E. Miller, and D. E. Stokes. 1960. *The American Voter.* New York: John Wiley.

———.1966. *Elections and Political Order.* New York: John Wiley.

Clapp, C. L. 1963. *The Congressman: His Work as He Sees It.* Washington: The Brookings Institution.

Clark, D. E. 1908. "The History of Liquor Legislation in Iowa, 1846-1861," *Iowa Journal of History and Politics* VI: 55-87.

Clausen, A. R. 1973. *How Congressmen Decide: A Policy Focus.* New York: St. Martin's Press.

Clubb, J. M., W. H. Flanigan, and N. Zingale. 1980. *Partisan Realignment: Votes, Parties, and Government in American History.* Beverly Hills: Sage.

Clubb, J. M. and S. A. Traugott. 1977. "Partisan Cleavage and Cohesion in the House of Representatives, 1861-1974," *Journal of Interdisciplinary History* VII: 382-83.

Coleman, C. H. 1933. *The Election of 1868: The Democratic Effort to Regain Control.* New York: Columbia University Press.

Conkling, A. 1889. *Life and Letters of Roscoe Conkling, Orator, Statesman, Advocate.* New York: C. C. Webster.

Converse, P. E. 1964. "The Nature of Belief Systems in Mass Publics," in D. E. Apter, ed., *Ideology and Discontent.* New York: The Free Press.

———.1975. "Public Opinion and Voting Behavior," in F. I. Greenstein and N. W. Polsby, eds., *The Handbook of Political Science* 4 vols. Reading, Mass.: Addison Wesley.

Cotter, C. P. and J. F. Bibby. 1980. "Institutional Development of Parties and the Thesis of Party Decline," *Political Science Quarterly* XCV: 1-27.

Dannenbaum, J. 1978. "Immigrants and Temperance: Ethnocultural Conflict in Cincinnati, 1845-1860," *Ohio History* LXXXVII: 125-39.

David, P. T. 1972. *Party Strength in the United States, 1872-1970.* Charlottesville: University Press of Virginia.

Dobson, J. M. 1972. *Politics in the Gilded Age: A New Perspective on Reform.* New York: Praeger.

Donald, D. 1961. *Charles Sumner and The Coming of the Civil War.* New York: Alfred A. Knopf.

Downs, A. 1957. *An Economic Theory of Democracy.* New York: Harper and Row.

Emery, C. W. 1971. "The Iowa Germans in the Election of 1860," in F. C. Leubke, ed., *Ethnic Voters and the Election of Lincoln.* Lincoln, Neb.: University of Nebraska Press.

Fiorina, M. P., D. W. Rohde, and P. Wissel. 1975. "Historical Change in House Turnover," in N. J. Ornstein, ed., *Congress in Change: Evolution and Reform.* New York: Praeger.

Formisano, R. P. 1966. *The Birth of Mass Political Parties: Michigan, 1827-1861.* Princeton: Princeton University Press.

Froman, L. A., Jr. and R. B. Ripley. 1965. "Conditions for Party Leadership: The Case of The House Democrats," *American Political Science Review* LIX: 52-63.

Garfield, J. A. 1883. *The Works of James Abram Garfield,* ed. by B. A. Hinsdale. 2 vols. Boston: James R. Osgood and Co.

Gillette, W. 1979. *Retreat from Reconstruction, 1869-1879.* Baton Rouge: Louisiana State University Press.

Goodman, L. A. 1953. "Ecological Regressions and the Behavior of Individuals," *American Sociological Review* XVIII: 663-64.

———.1959. "Some Alternatives to Ecological Correlation," *American Journal of Sociology* LXIV: 610-25.

Hayes, R. B. 1922-1926. *Diary of Letters of Rutherford B. Hayes, Nineteenth President of the United States,* ed. by C. R. Williams. 5 vols. Columbus: Ohio State Archaeological and Historical Society.

21

——.1964. *Hayes: Diary of a President, 1875-1881*, ed. by T. H. Williams. New York: David McKay Co.

Herriott, F. I. 1913. "The Germans of Iowa and the 'Two Year' Amendment of Massachusetts," *Deutsch-Amerikanische Geschichtungsblatter* XIII: 202-308.

Hinckley, B., C. F. Hofstetter, and J. H. Kessel. 1974. "Information and the Vote: A Comparative Election Study," *American Politics Quarterly* II: 131-58.

Holt, M. F. 1969. *Forging a Majority: The Formation of the Republican Party in Pittsburgh, 1848-1860*. New Haven: Yale University Press.

——.1978. *The Political Crisis of the 1850s*. New York: John Wiley.

Howells, W. D. *Sketch of the Life and Character of Rutherford B. Hayes*. New York: Hurd and Houghton.

Huitt, R. K. 1961. "Democratic Party Leadership in the Senate," *American Political Science Review* LV: 331-44.

Jackson, J. E. 1974. *"Constituencies and Leaders in Congress: Their Effects on Senate Voting Behavior.* Cambridge, Mass.: Harvard University Press.

Jones, C. O. 1966. "The Role of the Campaign in Party Politics," in M. K. Jennings and L. H. Ziegler, eds., *The Electoral Process*. Englewood Cliffs, N.J.: Prentice-Hall.

Julian, G. W. 1872. *Speeches on Political Questions (1850-1868)*. New York: Hurd and Houghton.

——.1884. *Political Recollections, 1840-1872*. Chicago: Jansen, McClung and Co.

Kamphoefner, W. D. 1975. "St. Louis Germans and the Republican Party, 1848-1860," *Mid-America* LVII: 69-88.

Key, V. O. Jr. 1955. "A Theory of Critical Elections," *Journal of Politics* XVII: 3-18.

——.1966. *The Responsible Electorate: Rationality in Presidential Voting*. Cambridge, Mass.: Harvard University Press.

Kleppner, P. 1979. *The Third Electoral System, 1853-1892: Parties, Voters, and Political Cultures*. Chapel Hill: University of North Carolina Press.

——.1970. *The Cross of Culture: A Social Analysis of Midwestern Politics*. New York: The Free Press.

Kondracke, M. 1980. "The G.O.P. Gets Its Act Together," *New York Times Magazine* (July 13): 18-24, 42-47.

Kousser, J. M. 1973. "Ecological Correlation and the Analysis of Past Politics," *Journal of Interdisciplinary History* IV: 237-92.

Krout, J. A. 1936. "The Maine Law in New York Politics," *New York History* XVII: 260-72.

Leuthold, D. A. 1968. *Electioneering in a Democracy: Campaigns for Congress*. New York: John Wiley.

Linden, G. M. 1966. "Radicals and Economic Policies: The Senate 1861-1873," *Journal of Southern History* XXXII: 189-99.

——.1967. "Radicals and Economic Policies: The House of Representatives, 1861-1873," *Civil War History* XIII: 51-65.

Malbin, M. J. 1980. "The Republican Revival," *Fortune* CII (Aug. 25): 85-88.

Marcus, R. D. 1971. *Grand Old Party: Political Structure in the Gilded Age, 1880-1896*. New York: Oxford University Press.

Martin, A. E. 1908. "The Temperance Movement in Pennsylvania Prior to the Civil War," *Pennsylvania Magazine of History and Biography* XLV: 226-30.

Martin, E. W. 1868. *The Life and Public Services of Schuyler Colfax*. New York: United States Publishing Co.

Matthews, D. R. 1960. *U.S. Senators and Their World*. Chapel Hill: University of North Carolina Press.

Mayhew, D. R. 1974. *Congress: The Electoral Connection*. New Haven: Yale University Press.

McKay, D. H. 1979. "The United States in Crisis: A Review of the American Political

22

Literature," *Government and Opposition* XIV: 373-85.

McPherson, E. 1872. *Handbook of Politics for 1872.* 5th Ed. Washington, D.C.: Philip & Solomons.

———.1875. *Political History of the United States of America During the Period of Reconstruction.* 2nd ed. New York: Solomons & Chapman.

Miller, W. E. and D. E. Stokes. 1963. "Constituency Influence in Congress," *American Political Science Review* LVII: 45-56.

Nelson, G. 1975. "Change and Continuity in the Recruitment of U.S. House Leaders, 1789-1975," in N. G. Ornstein, ed., *Congress in Change: Evolution and Reform.* New York: Praeger.

Nie, N. H. 1974. "Mass Belief Systems Revisited: Political Change and Attitude Structure," *Journal of Politics* XXXVI. 540-87.

Ornstein, N. J. ed. 1975. *Congress in Change.* New York: Praeger.

Parker, G. R. 1981. "Incumbent Popularity and Electoral Success," in L. S. Maisel and J. Cooper, eds., *Congressional Elections.* Beverly Hills: Sage.

Peskin, A. 1978. *Garfield: A Biography.* Kent, Ohio: Kent State University Press.

Pierce, E. L. 1893. *Memoir of Letters of Charles Sumner.* 4 vols. Boston: Roberts Brothers.

Polakoff, K. I. 1973. *The Politics of Inertia: The Election of 1876 and the End of Reconstruction.* Baton Rouge: Louisiana State University Press.

Polsby, N. W. 1968. "The Institutionalization of the U.S. House of Representatives," *American Political Science Review* LXII: 1448-68.

Pomper, G. M. 1975. *Voter's Choice: Varieties of American Electoral Behavior.* New York: Dodd, Mead.

Price, H. D. 1971. "The Congressional Career—Then and Now," in N. R. Polsby, ed., *Congressional Behavior.* New York: Random House.

Rieselbach, L. N. 1973. *Congressional Politics.* New York: McGraw-Hill.

Ripley, R. B. 1967. *Party Leaders in the House of Representatives.* Washington: The Brookings Institution.

Ross, E. D. 1919. *The Liberal Republican Movement.* New York: Rumford Press.

Schurz, C. 1913. *Speeches, Correspondence, and Political Papers of Carl Schurz,* ed. by F. Bancroft. 6 vols. New York: G. P. Putnam's Sons.

Scott, R. K. and R. J. Hrebenar. 1979. *Parties in Crisis.* New York: John Wiley.

Seip, T. L. 1974. "Southern Representatives and Economic Measures During Reconstruction: A Quantitative and Analytical Study." Unpubl. Ph.D. dissertation, Louisiana State University.

Schafer, J. 1927. *Four Wisconsin Counties: Prairie and Forest.* Madison: State Historical Society of Wisconsin.

———.1941. "Who Elected Lincoln?" *American Historical Review* XLVII: 51-63.

Shafer, B. E. 1981. "Anti Party Politics," *The Public Interest* No. 63: 95-111.

Shannon, W. W. 1968. *Party, Constituency, and Congressional Voting: A Study of Legislative Behavior in the United States House of Representatives.* Baton Rouge: Louisiana State University Press.

Shively, W. P. 1969. "Ecological Inference: The Use of Aggregate Data to Study Individuals," *American Political Science Review* LXII: 1183-96.

Smith, T. C. 1925. *The Life and Letters of James Abram Garfield.* 2 vols. New Haven: Yale University Press.

Stimson, J. A. 1975. "Belief Systems: Constraint, Complexity, and the 1972 Election," *American Journal of Political Science* XIX: 393-417.

Stokes, D. E. and W. E. Miller. 1962. "Party Government and the Saliency of Congress," *Public Opinion Quarterly* XXVI: 531-46.

Sundquist, J. L. 1973. *Dynamics of the Party System: Alignment and Realignment of Political*

Parties in the United States. Washington: The Brookings Institution.

Swierenga, R. P. 1971. "The Ethnic Voter and the First Lincoln Election," in F. C. Leubke, ed., *Ethnic Votes and the Election of 1860.* Lincoln, Neb.: University of Nebraska Press.

Tacheron, D. G. and M. K. Udall. 1966. *The Job of the Congressman: An Introduction to Service in the U.S. House of Representatives.* Indianapolis: Bobbs-Merrill.

Truman, D. B. 1959. *The Congressional Party: A Case Study.* New York: John Wiley.

Turpie, D. 1903. *Sketches of My Own Times.* Indianapolis: Bobbs-Merrill.

Unger, I. 1964. *The Greenback Era: A Social and Political History of American Finance, 1865-1879.* Princeton: Princeton University Press.

Walker, J. 1966. "A Critique of the Elitist Theory of Democracy," *American Political Science Review* LX: 285-95.

Warden, R. B. 1874. *An Account of the Private Life and Public Services of Salmon P. Chase.* Cincinnati: Wilstach, Baldwin, and Co.

Watterson, H. 1919. *"Marse Henry": An Autobiography.* 2 vols. New York: George H. Doran Co.

White, L. D. 1954. *The Jacksonians: A Study in Adminstrative History 1829-1861.* New York: Macmillan.

24

WHIGS REFORM THE "BEAR GARDEN": REPRESENTATION AND THE APPORTIONMENT ACT OF 1842

Johanna Nicol Shields

No issue more deeply affects the character of democratic government than the substantive meaning a people impart to the term representation. Colonial Americans had questioned what representation meant before the birth of the republic, but the issue became central as patriots framed an ideology to justify their resistance to British taxation. Pointing out that they were not actually represented in Parliament, Americans rejected the British assertion that they were virtually represented, as were other Englishmen. But, as J. R. Pole has noted, "no linear process of transition" marked the transfer of ideas from Europe to America.[1] When Americans debated constitution-making, they demonstrated the continuing vitality of both actual and virtual concepts of representation. They wanted legislators to be delegates who directly reflected the opinions of their constituents, but they also hoped statesmen would be wise and virtuous trustees of the common good.[2] Students of the Federalist and Jeffersonian eras

---

Ms. Shields is a member of the Department of History and Philosophy at the University of Alabama in Huntsville.

[1]J. R. Pole, *The Gift of Government: Political Responsibility from the English Restoration to American Independence* (Athens, Ga. 1983), 142. Pole's major contribution to this subject remains *Political Representation in England and the Origins of the American Republic* (New York 1966).

[2]The fullest discussion of these continuing influences is found in Gordon S. Wood, *The Creation of the American Republic, 1776-1787* (New York 1972), but see also J. G. A. Pocock, *The Machiavellian Moment: Florentine Political Thought*

JOURNAL OF THE EARLY REPUBLIC, 5 (Fall 1985). © Society for Historians of the Early American Republic.

---

have connected the rise of parties with declining popularity of the trustee theory, and by the 1830s partisan enthusiasts proclaimed that the new democracy made legislators true delegates.[3] Nonetheless, political scientists studying twentieth century legislatures still find conflicting definitions of representation in which eighteenth century tensions reverberate.[4] This fundamental issue in the American polity remains surrounded by ambiguity.

Part of that ambiguity stems from the intervention of parties in the relationship between legislators and their constituents, a pattern that became fixed during the Jacksonian period. Parties were much more than passive filters in the representative process when they selected candidates, controlled information through

26

and the Atlantic Republican Tradition (Princeton 1975), esp. ch. 15, "The Americanization of Virtue."

[3]Especially relevant for the period before 1828 are David Hackett Fischer, The Revolution of American Conservatism: The Federalist Party in the Era of Jeffersonian Democracy (New York 1965); James S. Young, The Washington Community, 1800-1828 (New York 1966); Noble E. Cunningham, Jr., The Jeffersonian Republicans in Power: Party Operations, 1801-1809 (Chapel Hill 1963) and The Process of Government under Jefferson (Princeton 1978); William N. Chambers, Political Parties in a New Nation: The American Experience, 1776-1809 (New York 1963); and Richard Hofstadter, The Idea of a Party System: The Rise of Legitimate Opposition in the United States, 1780-1840 (Berkeley 1969). Useful for general attitudes on the newer parties of the 1830s and 1840s are Richard P. McCormick, The Second American Party System: Party Formation in the Jacksonian Era (Chapel Hill 1966); Rush Welter, The Mind of America, 1820-1860 (New York 1975); and Marvin Meyers, The Jacksonian Persuasion: Politics and Belief (Stanford 1957).

[4]The best overview of the historical evolution of the concept of representation is Alfred de Grazia, Public and Republic: Political Representation in America (New York 1974 [1951]). There are useful essays on representation from political scientists in Samuel C. Patterson, ed., American Legislative Behavior: A Reader (Princeton 1968); see esp. the reprint there of a modern "classic" by Heinz Eulau, John C. Wahlke, William Buchanan, and LeRoy C. Ferguson, "The Role of the Representative: Some Empirical Observations on the Theory of Edmund Burke," American Political Science Review, 53 (Sept. 1959), 742-756. Building upon this influential article, Roger H. Davidson explored attitudes toward representation in the Eighty-eighth Congress (1963-1964) in The Role of the Congressman (New York 1969). More recent analyses based on the perceptions of state legislators are Donald J. McCrone and James H. Kuklinski, "The Delegate Theory of Representation," American Journal of Political Science, 23 (May 1979), 278-300, and Donald A. Gross, "Representative Styles and Legislative Behavior," Western Political Quarterly, 31 (Sept. 1978), 359-371. It would, of course, be a mistake to assume that modern trustee concepts are based solely on persisting notions of republican wisdom and virtue, since the highly specialized nature of contemporary lawmaking offers a newer source of legislative elitism.

newspapers, and shaped decisions of legislatures.[5] Skeptics as different as Edward Pessen and Ronald P. Formisano have questioned whether these innovations made politics more democratic, but it has proved difficult to uncover mechanisms through which critical decisions were made, much less to ascertain what interests prevailed.[6] That problem has impeded our understanding of lawmaking in the House of Representatives, where partisan committees framed important legislation in closed sessions. The indirect evidence that parties dominated congressional decisions is overwhelming; yet no scholar has asked how this development affected meanings of representation.[7]

Theories of representation were not commonly addressed in congressional debates, which rarely centered upon abstract political theory. Theories did become relevant, however, when in 1842 Congress linked major reform of the legislative process to the decennial apportionment of the House. The Whig party barely controlled the Twenty-seventh Congress and Whig leaders steered the apportionment bill through both houses, but their discussions highlighted internal stresses in Whig ideology. For years Whigs had defended legislative prerogatives against executive usurpation and had assailed the military discipline of the Democracy. Now in a position to act upon their campaign rhetoric, Whig leaders found their history a handicap. No viable plan for legislative reform could neglect the real power of parties.

27

---

[5]Among recent works, broad studies that emphasize the active role of parties in the electoral process include Jean H. Baker, *Affairs of Party: The Political Culture of Northern Democrats in the Mid-Nineteenth Century* (Ithaca 1983); William J. Cooper, Jr., *The South and the Politics of Slavery, 1828-1856* (Baton Rouge 1978); and Michael F. Holt, *The Political Crisis of the 1850s* (New York 1978). The results of partisan power in Congress are demonstrated in Joel H. Silbey, *The Shrine of Party: Congressional Voting Behavior, 1841-1852* (Pittsburgh 1967), and Thomas B. Alexander, *Sectional Stress and Party Strength: A Study of Roll-Call Voting Patterns in the United States House of Representatives, 1836-1860* (Nashville 1967).

[6]Pessen's skepticism is sharply expressed in Edward Pessen, *Jacksonian America: Society, Personality, and Politics* (rev. ed., Homewood, Ill. 1978). Formisano is more cautious in tone but perhaps as skeptical in fact; see Ronald P. Formisano, *The Transformation of Political Culture: Massachusetts Parties, 1790s-1840s* (New York 1983).

[7]I have elsewhere discussed in broader terms the changing conceptions of congressional roles in the antebellum period; see Johanna Nicol Shields, *The Line of Duty: Maverick Congressmen and the Development of American Political Culture, 1836-1860* (Westport, Conn. 1985).

Ideological differences rooted in sectionalism also prevented a coherent justification for the Whigs' reform. Throughout the nation they, like their opponents, blended new ideas with the republican heritage, a secure anchor in the fluctuating currents of popular opinion. But party ideologies changed slowly and unevenly as a consequence of pluralism, a point thoroughly demonstrated by recent studies of state politics like Formisano's for Massachusetts and Marc W. Kruman's for North Carolina.[8] John Tyler's refusal to accept the economic measures of the congressional Whigs—especially Henry Clay's revived national bank—was purging the party of its most extreme state-rights ideologues, but sectional differences persisted. Many historians have claimed that the social conservatism of the southern region fostered a backward-looking ideology. Most recently, Daniel Walker Howe has described southern Whiggery as captured by tensions "between the bourgeois values represented by the national party and the premodern values encouraged by southern society itself."[9] Southern Whigs supported the progressive economic legislation of the Twenty-seventh Congress, but their

28

[8]Formisano, *Transformation of Political Culture*, and Marc W. Kruman, *Parties and Politics in North Carolina, 1836-1865* (Baton Rouge 1983). See also J. Mills Thornton, *Politics and Power in a Slave Society: Alabama, 1800-1860* (Baton Rouge 1978).

[9]Daniel Walker Howe, *The Political Culture of the American Whigs* (Chicago 1979), 239. Howe finds the diverse strands of Whig ideology resting upon a broader base of common political culture. His view of southern Whiggery is influenced by that of Eugene Genovese, but the differences between southern and northern Whigs have been analyzed from various viewpoints. The oldest line of investigation, still current, focused on the class basis of the party in the South; see, for example, Arthur C. Cole, *The Whig Party in the South* (Washington 1914), and Charles Grier Sellers, Jr., "Who Were the Southern Whigs?" *American Historical Review*, 59 (Jan. 1954), 335-346. Many recent studies have attempted, with varying degrees of success, to integrate ideology, political behavior, and class influences on party affiliation. Cooper, *South and Politics*, while asserting the centrality of slavery interests in southern politics, clearly exposes the "democratic" nature of Whig and Democratic practices. Of the recent state studies for the South, Michael P. Johnson, *Toward a Patriarchal Republic: The Secession of Georgia* (Baton Rouge 1977), argues most forcefully for the conservatism of southern Whigs. Thornton describes Whigs and Democrats as equally democratic and egalitarian in their rhetoric, but questions the congruence between rhetoric and practice at various levels of party organization in Alabama. *Politics and Power*, esp. 160-162. Relevant also is Thomas Brown, "Southern Whigs and the Politics of Statesmanship, 1833-1841," *Journal of Southern History*, 46 (Aug. 1980), 361-380.

views on representation were clearly conservative.[10] Indeed, while northern Whigs did not embrace political change with an encompassing new theory, many southern Whigs flatly resisted "progress" in the legislature, grounding their objections in a pronounced commitment to eighteenth century values.

There were two important reforms attached to the apportionment act of 1842. The first—the primary focus of this essay—called for a reduction in the size of the House of Representatives. Revolutionary arguments about the nature of representation echoed through the debate over the House's size as politicians spoke seriously about their own responsibilities. The second reform mandated the division of states into contiguous and uniform congressional districts. Although this requirement, like the reduction reform, was original with the 1842 act, most states already used districts, and the debate was largely diverted into an arid discussion about the meaning of constitutional language.[11] Ironically, partisan influence in the election process was openly (if sometimes critically) acknowledged, but congressmen and senators did not admit that the organizations behind their elections should influence their voices in Washington. Thus the debate over reforming the House by reducing its size proceeded from beginning to end with an element of unreality at an essential point.

The apportionment act in many respects was an unsuitable vehicle for reform. When James Madison observed in No. 55

29

---

[10]Cooper terms southern Whig economic nationalism in the early 1840s "the great aberration" in *South and Politics,* ch. 5, title. Nationalism among southern Whigs appears more persistent in the voting behavior studies of Alexander and Silbey.

[11]By supporting the districting requirement, Whigs implicitly affirmed one aspect of a delegate concept of representation, and that tacit position affected the content of the debate over the size of the House. It seems to me, however, that it is analytically useful to separate the two reforms. Districting focuses on one aspect of the representative's role: his interface with his constituents. Decisions favoring districts had already been made in the states, and whether Congress acted or not, most states would certainly continue to use districts. The decision to reduce the size of the House hinged upon two aspects of a representative's role: the constituent relationship and the responsibilities of a member in the House. Moreover, the internal consideration was completely under congressional control, or the control of individual congressmen. If congressmen had real concerns about the meaning of representation—that is to say, if they thought seriously and spoke candidly about their responsibilities—a broader view should emerge from the reduction debate, which considered both aspects of the theory.

of the *Federalist Papers* that "no political problem is less suscep-
tible of a precise solution than that which relates to the number
most convenient for a representative legislature," he anticipated
the controversies that have persistently surrounded
apportionment.[12] Conflicts between large and small states, slave
and free states, eastern and western states, urban and rural areas,
and the personal interests of House members complicated every
apportionment. Because these problems were so thorny, Congress
had generally adopted a hands-off position, tampering with the
process as little as possible. It is not clear what motivated Whigs
to attach reform measures to the 1842 act, but partisan interests
were much more obvious in the districting measure than in the
reduction reform.

Party allegiance dominated voting about districting and acceptance of the whole bill, but Whigs were divided about reduction. Their lack of unity is indicated by a brief analysis of cohesion levels in votes for the bill and its parts (see Tables 1 and
2).[13] On eighty percent of the votes for districting and the entire

30

---

[12]Madison, in Alexander Hamilton, James Madison, and John Jay, *The
Federalist Papers,* ed. Clinton Rossiter (New York 1961), 341. The standard history
of apportionment is Laurence F. Schmeckebier, *Congressional Apportionment*
(Washington 1941). Very useful in assessing the impact of apportionment on
individual states are two atlases: Stanley B. Parsons, William W. Beach, and
Dan Hermann, *United States Congressional Districts, 1788-1841* (Westport, Conn.
1978); and Kenneth C. Martis, *The Historical Atlas of United States Congressional
Districts, 1789-1983* (New York 1982), which contains a helpful introduction
and summary of the subject. There is a growing body of literature on the develop-
ment of the House, much of it stimulated by the seminal article of Nelson W.
Polsby, "The Institutionalization of the U. S. House of Representatives,"
American Political Science Review, 62 (Mar. 1968), 144-168. See, for example,
Allan G. Bogue, Jerome M. Clubb, Carroll R. McKibbin, and Santa A.
Traugott, "Members of the House of Representatives and the Processes of
Modernization, 1789-1960," *Journal of American History,* 63 (Sept. 1976), 275-302.
Indispensible for research in that body of literature is Robert U. Goehlert and
John R. Sayre, *The United States Congress: A Bibliography* (New York 1982). Cur-
rent trends in the study of the legislature are summarized in Joel H. Silbey,
" 'Delegates Fresh from the People': American Congressional and Legislative
Behavior," *Journal of Interdisciplinary History,* 13 (Spring 1983), 603-627; other
useful suggestions for continuing study are in Robert Zemsky, "American
Legislative Behavior," in Allan Bogue, ed., *Emerging Theoretical Models in Social
and Political History* (Beverly Hills 1973).

[13]Levels of cohesion were calculated using a computer program that
organizes legislators by party and region. This program was furnished by Pro-

bill in both houses of Congress, at least seventy percent of Democrats and Whigs from North and South voted with their regional and party colleagues. In contrast, votes on the size of the House produced far lower levels of cohesion across the board, suggesting that neither partisan nor sectional interests were of overriding significance.

Partisan arguments about districting were straightforward in regard to both constitutional theory and practice. Districting was historically familiar, and the system had been manipulated since early in the colonial period. Although districting was not required

TABLE 1

COMPARISON OF COHESION LEVELS IN THE HOUSE FOR ROLL CALLS ON
THE SIZE OF THE HOUSE AND THE DISTRICTING REQUIREMENT
OR WHOLE BILL

PERCENTAGE OF ROLL CALLS IN EACH LEVEL OF COHESION

Cohesion Level	Northern Democrats		Southern Democrats		Northern Whigs		Southern Whigs	
	House Size	District-ing	House Size	District-ing	House Size	District-ing	House Size	District-ing
90-100%	27%	80%	0	40%	18%	60%	9%	20%
80-90%	45%	0	0	20%	0	20%	0	40%
70-80%	9%	0	27%	40%	9%	0	9%	20%
60-70%	18%	20%	36%	0	18%	20%	73%	20%
50-60%	0	0	36%	0	55%	0	9%	0

fessor Thomas B. Alexander of the University of Missouri, Columbia, to whom I am grateful. Cohesion levels describe how frequently particular groups of legislators voted together on specific roll calls. In Table 1, for example, the first entry in the column headed Northern Democrats means that 90% of all northern Democrats in the House voted together on 27% of the roll calls evaluated. Southern delegations include legislators from all slave states but Delaware.

The same roll-call votes were used in calculating cohesion levels and cluster blocs (see below), and some features of these warrant comment. In all analyses represented in the tables here except that for House votes on districting or the whole bill, there were sufficient numbers of roll calls in the House and Senate *Journals* to exclude duplicate votes or those with unclear implications. In the case of the five House votes on districting and the whole bill, only one roll call was taken on districting *per se,* while the other four votes are on the entire bill (two for the bill with the House ratio included and two for the bill with the Senate ratio included). For the Senate, the opposite is true, as most votes of the ten included were on districting rather than the whole bill. For the House size issue, eleven roll-call votes in the House fixed only on three ratios (50,169,

TABLE 2

COMPARISON OF COHESION LEVELS IN THE SENATE FOR ROLL CALLS ON
THE SIZE OF THE HOUSE AND THE DISTRICTING REQUIREMENT
OR WHOLE BILL

PERCENTAGE OF ROLL CALLS IN EACH LEVEL OF COHESION

Cohesion Level	Northern Democrats		Southern Democrats		Northern Whigs		Southern Whigs	
	House Size	District-ing	House Size	District-ing	House Size	District-ing	House Size	District-ing
90-100%	0	50%	0	50%	0	60%	0	30%
80-90%	29%	30%	21%	30%	14%	10%	21%	20%
70-80%	14%	10%	50%	10%	7%	10%	29%	30%
60-70%	29%	10%	7%	10%	64%	10%	0	20%
50-60%	29%	0	21%	0	14%	10%	50%	0

in the Constitution, debates about the basic frame of government showed a clear preference for district representation. By 1842 only a few states used alternative systems.[14] Some states, most notably New York and Pennsylvania, allocated plural membership to urban districts rather than dividing cities. Other states elected delegations on a general ticket (sometimes called at large), a practice through which partisan slates could capture a whole state's delegation. Whigs were outraged that in 1840 Alabama's Democratic legislature had converted the state from a district to a general ticket system, eliminating the Whig representation, and party leaders may have hoped that they could exploit their fragile national majority to regain seats in some states.[15] In any case, while each party's members insisted that the others would corrupt any system, most legislators agreed that equality of representation was a desirable goal and that uniform districting might increase the fairness of elections. The constitutional issue was finally the sticking

---

68,000, and 70,680) while in the Senate much higher ratios (up to 92,000) were considered in the fourteen roll calls analyzed.

For readers not familiar with the analysis of legislative voting, a non-technical explanation with examples of various techniques is in Richard E. Beringer, *Historical Analysis: Contemporary Approaches to Clio's Craft* (New York 1978), ch. 18. For a more comprehensive explanation, see Lee F. Anderson, Meredith W. Watts, Jr., and Allen R. Wilcox, *Legislative Roll-Call Analysis* (Evanston 1966).

[14]Martis, *Historical Atlas,* 2-5, presents a convenient overview of the systems used in selecting representatives.

[15]Thornton, *Politics and Power,* 94, suggests that an underlying reason for

point, as Whigs found ample power to coerce the states into districting while Democrats argued that coercion was acceptable only in exceptional circumstances.

Since the Constitution plainly required Congress to fix the size of the House, customary partisan arguments about strict or loose construction did not enter into the reduction debate, nor was it clear how partisan interests would be served by a smaller body. Historically, Congress had taken the path of least resistance to apportionment, allowing the size of the House to drift upward with the population and thereby avoiding much of the unpleasantness associated with cuts in House membership for many states. The size of the basis upon which membership was allocated had been enlarged from 30,000 in 1789 to 47,700 in 1842, with the size of the House growing from 65 to 244 members.[16] Given enormous variation in the rate of population growth, Whigs could not safely predict that a decrease would serve their interests everywhere. Booming western states or states with rapidly expanding urban populations would make relative gains with any ratio for apportionment, while slow-growth states would face a relative decline. With partisan and regional interests clouded by local circumstances, and with no major constitutional issue involved, Whigs were free to speak their personal concerns.

Many Whigs believed that the conduct of the House of Representatives in the Twenty-seventh Congress was the best evidence of the need for reform. Disorder in the House had become so notorious that newspapers called it the "bear garden," a phrase often repeated on the floor of the House and Senate.[17]

33

---

the Democrats' action was the promotion of their own party's unity in the Alabama legislature.

[16]See the useful tables in Schmeckebier, *Congressional Apportionment,* Appendix C, 226-233.

[17]Accounts of Whig difficulties include Clement L. Eaton, *Henry Clay and the Art of American Politics* (Boston 1957); George Rawlings Poage, *Henry Clay and the Whig Party* (Gloucester, Mass. 1965); Robert J. Morgan, *A Whig Embattled: The Presidency under John Tyler* (Lincoln 1954). William R. Brock has recently interpreted Whig problems in the Twenty-seventh Congress in *Parties and Political Conscience: American Dilemmas, 1840-1850* (Millwood, N.Y. 1979); see ch. 3, "Party Government—Experiment and Failure."

A correspondent of Levi Woodbury, Democratic senator from New Hampshire, wrote in the summer of 1842, "I have never in my whole life known the people so savage towards Congress"; Gilbert Davis to Levi Woodbury, July 5, 1842, Levi Woodbury Papers (Library of Congress). Democrats were

Democrats were understandably amused that the sources of the disruption were within the Whig party. The *Congressional Globe* recorded the taunting remark of one Democrat: " 'Quem Deus vult perdere, prius dementat.' Whom the gods would destroy, they first made mad. [Laughter.]' "[18] The first source of disarray was the conflict between regular Whigs and Tyler's "corporal's guard," a legacy of the special session called by William Henry Harrison before his untimely death.[19] Tyler Whigs were led in the House by the new president's good friend Henry Wise, an intemperate Virginian who was a skilled debater and ardent defender of state rights. Wise was also in the middle of the second intraparty fray—the gag-rule controversy—in which his prime antagonist was the aging ex-President John Quincy Adams. As a result of their battle, conservative Indiana Whig Richard Thompson noted privately in January 1842 that the House had

34

pleased to blame the Whigs but privately recognized that the problems were more general. As Silas Wright wrote, "I have never seen such a state of things before as exists here now, and has existed ever since we have been here. There is neither form nor organization any where. Our friends seem well disposed and kind towards each other, but wholly apathetic, and there is nothing in the position, or acts, of the majority to rouse them out of it. On the other side all is distraction, disorganization, and bitterness, and bad as we have seen the late representative Houses, we have never seen one so utterly without form, as abject, as this." Wright to Martin Van Buren, Jan. 12, 1842, Martin Van Buren Papers (Library of Congress).

Robert McClellan, Democratic congressman from New York, wrote Van Buren in a similar vein about the "bear garden"; McClellan to Van Buren, Feb. 6, 1842, *ibid.* There is a running commentary on the disorder of the House in Richard W. Thompson, Diary for 1842, Richard W. Thompson Papers (Library of Congress). Whigs were defended in John Pendleton Kennedy, *Defence of the Whigs. By a member of the Twenty-seventh Congress* (New York 1844).

[18]*Congressional Globe,* 27th Cong., 2d sess., July 8, 1842, 736. House Whigs elected as speaker a follower of Senator Henry Clay, John White of Kentucky, and White proceeded to appoint committee chairmen and committee majorities who would enact the Whig program. In the Senate, where organization was less consistent, Whig Samuel Southard of New Jersey presided over most of the special session, to be replaced upon his death in 1842 by Willie P. Mangum, a North Carolina Whig.

[19]Conflict between Tyler and Congress is described in Morgan, *A Whig Embattled;* Poage, *Clay and the Whig Party,* 67-100, *passim;* and in Oliver P. Chitwood, *John Tyler: Champion of the Old South* (New York 1964 [1939]), 217-251. The gag-rule controversy is thoroughly discussed in Henry H. Simms, *Emotion at High Tide: Aboliton as a Controversial Factor, 1830-1845* (Richmond 1960).

become "the subject of almost universal reproach and censure."[20] The sectional tenor of the gag-rule debate was more intense than that of the Tyler-Whig struggle, but with Wise and Adams visibly entangled in both, the latter issue assumed a sectional air not wholly mitigated by the fact that Tyler's Whig opponents were both southern and northern.

Although most Whigs were more interested in economic issues than in apportionment, when the census was completed by January 1842, the constitutional obligation could not be shirked. Beginning early in the year there were calls for consideration of an apportionment bill. In the House a special committee was created to manage the bill, a committee chaired by Whig Horace Everett of Vermont. Although the committee made its first report in late January, the measure did not receive consideration by the full House until April. With some state legislatures near the end of sessions in which they would have to reapportion for elections to the Twenty-eighth Congress, there was considerable pressure for speedy action.[21]

Whig divisions about reform were evident from the earliest House action, for there was no consensus about the exact size of the new apportionment basis to be written into law. Under the circumstances the House agreed on April 21 to consider motions for a basis beginning with the highest number proposed and working down until some figure could be approved by a majority. Voice votes began on a proposal by Whig Joseph Underwood of Kentucky for 141,000 people per representative, a ratio that would halve the size of the House, but tellers were called for only when the number reached 100,000. Rancor characterized the debate from its opening, when Wise attacked the "deterioration" of the House, "all owing, as he believed, to its overgrown size." This assault prompted a Kentucky Whig to insist, in an "animated" and "indignant" fashion, that the House would behave better if Wise left it, since "God knew there was no one man in it whose absence would so highly improve it." Wise himself proposed a basis of 70,680, the figure finally to be enacted, but there was no consensus for any number on that day, and the

35

---

[20]Thompson, Diary, Jan. 26, 1842.

[21]Everett's first report is noted in *Congressional Globe*, 27th Cong., 2d sess., Jan. 22, 1842, 160-161.

discussion was postponed.[22] In the next two weeks the debate ranged over numbers from 50,000 to 70,680 until in early May the measure was sent to the Senate with a basis of 50,179, a figure which entailed no reduction. The House bill did mandate districting, however, thus embodying one significant reform element.

The Senate extended the reformist nature of the bill. There it was managed by the Judiciary Committee headed by Senator John M. Berrien of Georgia. Berrien, a Clay supporter who had served as Andrew Jackson's attorney general from 1829 to 1831, preferred a larger ratio than that of the House bill, and he believed that he had to oppose the district requirement because Georgia was one of the few states using the general ticket system. After extensive but relatively calm debate the Senate agreed to the 70,680 ratio preferred by Berrien, but it did not retreat from the district measure despite repeated efforts of Democrats to eliminate it.[23]

When the amended apportionment bill returned to the House in June, the immediate reaction of the congressmen seems to have been anger that the Senate dared to tamper with the figures closer to the interests of House members than of senators. Senators might consider with some objectivity a basis which could reform the House; as Thomas Hart Benton had put it: "A high or a low number was the question—a numerous or a small body was the point . . . ." For a representative, even one who was concerned about the quality of the House, the "high or low number" could

36

[22]For voice votes on the size of the basis and the remarks of Wise, see *ibid.,* Apr. 21, 1842, 437.

[23]For Berrien's career, see *Dictionary of American Biography,* II, 225-226. There are autobiographical and biographical sketches in the John M. Berrien Papers (Southern Historical Collection, University of North Carolina Library, Chapel Hill); his role in the Whig party in the early 1840s is briefly discussed in Cole, *The Whig Party in the South,* 81, 94-102; and Berrien described his position on the House bill shortly after the Senate opened debate, *Congressional Globe,* 27th Cong., 2d sess., May 24, 1842, 526. The Senate version of the bill also added a provision for the representation of fractions greater than one-half of the remainder over the basis, a measure that had been advocated from the earliest apportionments, but most notably by Daniel Webster in the previous apportionment; see Schmeckebier, *Congressional Apportionment,* 113. The fractional amendment was agreed to by the House without significant discussion, and succeeding congresses did allow for fractional representation, though not through the Webster method.

be critical to his congressional seat. As Senator James Buchanan had noted in debate, the most visible advantage of the 50,179 ratio passed by the House was that it would result in the loss of not a single seat.[24]

For whatever reasons, the House initially refused to accept the Senate figure, with John Quincy Adams adamantly announcing that "he should vote for the number in the bill as it went from the House, and adhere to it . . . even if this, and twenty other apportionment bills, should be lost." Nonetheless, after the Senate also refused to move, the Whig leadership was able to gain assent to the higher ratio, and late in June 1842 the apportionment bill was sent to Tyler. Although a veto was anticipated by some Whigs, Tyler found himself willing, in this instance, to abide by the "solemnly pronounced opinion of the representatives of the people and the States," and he signed the bill.[25]

37

Given the history of the apportionment bill's enactment, managed by Whig committee chairmen through a Whig-dominated House and Senate, many Whigs were willing to let it stand *in toto* as a Whig reform. Robert Toombs of Georgia, then serving as a prominent member of the state legislature, wrote Berrien recommending that he stand by the act despite its impact on Georgia's general ticket system:

I think nothing could be more unfortunate than for Congress to recede from the measure in the slightest degree. The die is cast, we must stand by it. . . . If the system of repealing and abandoning measures by the Whigs in Congress is persued [*sic*], the Whigs out of Congress have will no influence on the public mind. If Congress will only not injure us we can manage the Democrats in the South, we ought to stand by every thing we have done

---

[24]Benton, *Congressional Globe*, 27th Cong., 2d sess., May 27, 1842, Appendix, 402; Buchanan, "Remarks, May 26, 1842, on the Apportionment Bill," *The Works of James Buchanan*, ed. John Bassett Moore (12 vols., Philadelphia 1908-1911), V, 256.

[25]Adams, *Congressional Globe*, 27th Cong., 2d sess., June 13, 1842, 620. Tyler signed the bill with a message detailing his objections to the districting measure, producing a strong objection from House Whigs to his procedure; see Morgan, *A Whig Embattled*, 55n. The protest was led by John Quincy Adams, who called the combination of signature and message an "amphibious production" which violated the separation of powers. *Congressional Globe*, 27th Cong., 2d sess., Aug. 16, 1842, 895.

in Congress firmly, decidedly. It is better, infinitely better for our prospects in 1844, to be *beaten* on our measures than to repeal or modify a *single* one of them.[26]

But a few leading Whigs opposed the reduction of the House, the most important of whom was Henry Clay. Clay had departed for "Ashland" in March and was busily planning, like Toombs, for the election of 1844. He counseled his Senate friends by letter, probably repeating ideas he had expressed before he left Washington. Clay wrote to Kentucky colleague John J. Crittenden less than a week after the Senate's ratio was established, approving Crittenden's opposition to the 70,680 figure. Shortly afterwards, Clay commented to President *pro tem* Willie P. Mangum that he would "have been in the minority on the question of the ratio," though he knew that Mangum had voted with the majority.[27]

The opposing positions of these southern Whig leaders parallel divisions among the rank and file. Using cluster bloc analysis, a statistically simple descriptive technique made possible for large groups by use of the computer, the groups of congressmen and senators who most consistently supported and opposed the larger ratio-smaller House proposals can be identified. (See Tables 3 and 4.)[28] Although partisan divisions were sharp on most issues

[26]Toombs to Berrien, July 6, 1842, John M. Berrien Papers.

[27]Clay to Crittenden, June 3, 1842, John J. Crittenden Papers (Library of Congress); Clay to Mangum, June 7, 1842, in *The Papers of Willie Person Mangum*, ed. Henry Thomas Shanks (5 vols., Raleigh, N.C. 1950-1956), III, 356. The relationship between Crittenden and Clay is fully explored in Albert D. Kirwan's excellent biography, *John J. Crittenden: The Struggle for the Union* (Lexington 1962). There is a brief biographical sketch of Mangum in his *Papers;* see also the laudatory treatment by Stephen B. Weeks in Thomas Meritt Pittman, *Sketches from the Biographical History of North Carolina* (n.p., n.d.).

[28]Majorities shifted in both houses as legislators responded to pressures from constituents and party leaders, and as negotiations between the two chambers took place. Because the numerical ratio most suitable to a state is not an absolute matter, particularly when the inclusion of fractional ratios is considered, it cannot be assumed that a congressman or senator who favored one very low ratio would favor all other low ratios over all high ones. For these reasons, cluster bloc analysis, which only describes similarities in voting, is most useful. The cluster bloc computer program was also provided by Professor Alexander. In cluster bloc analysis, for a selected group of roll calls the votes of each member of a legislature are compared with the votes of every other member. In the process used here, the analysis produces a square matrix containing every possible pair of legislators and, within the cell defined by each pair, the percentage of votes on which they agreed (when both responded). Percentages were

TABLE 3

REGION AND PARTY COMPOSITION OF HOUSE BLOCS

House Bloc Favoring Reduction			House Bloc Opposing Reduction		
Region/Party	% of Bloc	(N)	Region/Party	% of Bloc	(N)
Northern Democrats	5%	(3)	Northern Democrats	53%	(23)
Northern Whigs	55%	(30)	Northern Whigs	28%	(12)
Southern Democrats	11%	(6)	Southern Democrats	14%	(6)
Southern Whigs	29%	(16)	Southern Whigs	5%	(2)

TABLE 4

MEMBERSHIP OF SENATE BLOCS

Senate Bloc Favoring Reduction			Senate Bloc Opposing Reduction		
Name	State	Party	Name	State	Party
Bayard	Delaware	W	Bates	Massachusetts	W
Evans	Maine	W	Benton	Missouri	D
Sevier	Arkansas	D	Choate	Massachusetts	W
White	Indiana	W	Crittenden	Kentucky	W
Calhoun	South Carolina	D	Huntingdon	Connecticut	W
Fulton	Arkansas	D	Kerr	Maryland	W
Mangum	North Carolina	W	Morehead	Kentucky	W
Clayton	Delaware	W	Simmons	Rhode Island	W
			Smith	Connecticut	D
			Sprague	Rhode Island	W
			Tappan	Ohio	D
			Wilcox	New Hampshire	D
			Wright	New York	D

not calculated for men with less than 5 shared responses. For a percentage threshold in assigning bloc membership, 80% was selected, meaning that men who voted together less than 80% of the time were not included in the same bloc. Fringe members—those who voted with most, but not all, members of a bloc at the 80% level—were also not included.

Tables 3 and 4 describe only the largest blocs found in the analysis of the House and Senate votes. Blocs were identified in order to discover whether Whig explanations about legislative reform approximate the patterns suggested by Whig voting, not to determine precisely what interests shaped the voting. In a political system ostensibly responsive to the popular will, it is often important to know what interests affected a particular policy, but it is equally significant to ascertain how well public discourse describes decision-making. The composition of the major blocs suggests that an interplay of partisan, sectional, local, ideological, and personal interests were involved in voting, but debates poorly reflect those complexities.

in the Twenty-seventh Congress, the voting blocs on the reduction reform are not exclusively partisan. In the House Whigs from
both North and South consistently supported the reform, about
thirty percent of all House Whigs being members of the bloc.
In the predominantly Democratic House bloc opposing reduction, there were, nonetheless, twelve northern Whigs (thirteen
percent of all northern Whigs). The composition of the smaller
Senate blocs is less revealing, but parties were also divided in
the Senate, and again northern Whigs voted both for and against
the reduction proposal.[29] Although cluster bloc analysis merely
describes bloc membership, such a statistical description can provide an objective account of voting patterns against which to place
explanations offered by the participants themselves.

Two prominent members of the opposition blocs in the House
and Senate, John Quincy Adams and Thomas Hart Benton,
privately recorded their own analyses of the voting. Curiously,
neither identified the large amount of Whig support for the reduction measure, but both stressed sectional motivations. Adams
observed bitterly in his diary after the final House vote:

> An out-of-door negotiation with Southern slave-holders and North-
> ern Five-Points Democrats has accomplished this revolution in
> the voting of the House, all linked together by a common hatred,
> envy, jealousy, and fear of one man. It is an exact counterpart
> of the restoration of the gag-rule, effected in the same manner
> and by the same tactics.[30]

---

[29]By way of reminder, the range of bases considered in the Senate was
far broader than that considered in the House; there were also more numbers
considered. The result was a fragmentation of preferences, so that the largest
bloc was composed of those who would accept 92,000 and all other numbers
down to the 70,680 figure finally placed in the bill. The small size of the Senate
blocs does make it easy to identify the specific interests of some states. A quick
glance at the apportionment populations for Rhode Island and Delaware (108,828
and 77,043) suggests reasons for the respective positions of their four Whig
senators. With or without fractions, a basis of 50,179 would give Rhode Island
two representatives and a small remainder; with or without fractions, a basis
of 70,680 would give her one representative and a large remainder. Any number
near to or above Delaware's tiny population would give that state maximum
advantage. It is worth noting that Delaware was the smallest and Rhode Island
the third smallest state in the Union, demonstrating that a simple large/small
state formula for explaining the voting is inadequate.

[30]Charles Francis Adams, ed., *Memoirs of John Quincy Adams* (12 vols.,
Philadelphia 1874-1877), XI, 179.

41

The United States Capitol, ca. 1846

This daguerreotype, attributed to John Plumbe, Jr., has been furnished through the courtesy of the Senate Historical Office, United States Senate, Washington, D.C.

Adams' egocentric interpretation fixed on the "revolution in the voting" that caused the House to accept the Senate ratio. While other opponents of the measure had publicly blamed a Whig caucus, Adams targeted southerners and Democrats.

Benton focused blame on southerners, not Democrats, in a letter to Martin Van Buren. His analysis, however, was directed at debates rather than the final voting:

> The debates in the two Houses at present have some interest in them. Two movements which have made such discussion, are from the South; that is to say, districting the States for election to the H. R. and reducing the numbers of the H. R. These are aimed against the populous States which are the nonslaveholding. Most of your friends go against both . . . .[31]

Benton correctly described Democratic opposition to the House

---

[31]Benton to Martin Van Buren, June 3, 1842, Martin Van Buren Papers.

bill, but he, too, failed to mention northern Whigs who were voting for reduction.

The deficiencies in the analyses of Adams and Benton, both extremely acute if biased observers, are partly explained by the character of the debate that accompanied the votes on decreasing the House. Strangely, although northern Whigs, especially in the House, voted to support the reduction reform, they were silent when it came to defending their position. Party regulars like Horace Everett and Ways and Means Committee Chairman Millard Fillmore spoke briefly for reduction but most of the argument for reform was carried by southern and border state representatives or senators. At the same time Whigs failed to participate in the arguments *against* the reduction reform, with the notable exceptions of John Quincy Adams in the House and John J. Crittenden in the Senate. Participation in the debates, then, had a skewed sectional character.

There were also sectional undercurrents in the content of the debate, but in that regard the context of discussion should be taken into account. Congressional debates in the 1840s had two primary audiences. Legislators spoke to persuade each other, but they also spoke through the debates to their constituents. Many of the issues involved in an apportionment decision were never discussed because they were too parochial. As each legislator voted he not only had to calculate the impact of different bases on his state and district but also to assess the probable weight of local political circumstances on districting at various sizes. How could minutely examined particulars be rhetorically effective when the conduct of twenty-six state delegations was involved? Yet once the rhetorical conflict was opened, many legislators felt compelled to explain the merits of their positions, whether from a sense of public responsibility or from more pragmatic considerations. In explaining what they thought important about the reduction measure, speakers emphasized two issues: what size House would most effectively exercise its legislative responsibilities, and what size district would best promote a proper relationship between a representative and his constituents. Each issue had fundamental import for both legislators and voters, and each was basic to the quality of the representative process.

Within these perspectives perhaps the most striking feature of the debate was the backward-looking tone and structure of

42

the argument made by the predominantly southern reformers.[32]
For the proponents of the smaller House, the terms of the debate
were very nearly defined by Madison's contributions to the
Federalist Papers, although they quoted not only Madison but
debates in the constitutional and state ratifying conventions as
well. Whig public discourse generally relied upon the resonance
of republicanism, but in this debate the rhetoric of an earlier
era served southerners especially well, providing them with
theoretical premises and a familiar vocabulary to explain their
position.

Often citing the disorders of the Twenty-seventh Congress
as *prima facie* proof, the reformers argued that large legislative
bodies produced mob government and destroyed the rationality
and virtue that Whigs typically ascribed to statesmanlike conduct. However much some Whigs may have admired the
parliamentary system, anti-British sentiments were often incorporated into their critique of the oversized House. Joseph Underwood of Kentucky, usually an enthusiastic Clay supporter but
probably the most talented of the House reformers, insisted that
large numbers tended toward "mob government, by confusion,
crowing like cocks, braying like asses, shuffling with feet, coughing,
and other similar expedients now pursued in the House of
Commons . . . ."[33] Citing the founders, and presenting a
familiarly Whiggish theory of human nature, another Kentucky
Whig agreed with Underwood's assessment of mob government:

43

---

[32]The fullest discussion of early American ideas about the character of
republican legislatures is found in Wood, *Creation of the American Republic,* esp.
363-372, 446-453. Madison's ideas have been reinterpreted in Garry Wills,
Explaining America: The Federalist (New York 1981), 156-161, and Part Four,
"Representation," *passim.* The current scholarly controversy about the meaning and significance of early republican thought is summarized in Jean Yar-
brough, "Republicanism Reconsidered: Some Thoughts on the Foundation and
Preservation of the American Republic," *The Review of Politics,* 41 (Jan. 1979),
61-95. Richard P. McCormick has found the lawmakers who adjusted the processes of the electoral college dominated by a similarly backward-looking attitude; see his *The Presidential Game: The Origins of American Presidential Politics*
(New York 1982), esp. 162-163, 205-206.

[33]*Congressional Globe,* 27th Cong., 2d sess., Apr. 21, 1842, 436; manuscript
autobiographical and biographical sketches of Joseph Underwood can be found
in the Oscar W. Underwood Papers (State of Alabama Department of Archives
and History, Montgomery).

Large assemblies are always tumultuary; and the spirit of a mob seems to pervade the numbers of a mob, the world over. . . . From the frailty of our nature, our physical and moral organization, we follow the impulses of those around us. The responsibility of doing wrong is not only not felt, but we are allured to error by example; and the present apparent popularity of a measure, and not deliberation, decides our action: if the thought, in the tumult, occurs, that we are erring, it is overwhelmed by blind sympathy, and the reflection that it is a divided responsibility. Diffuse responsibility; destroy, by numbers, the calmness, and quietude, and facility of intercommunication requisite for deliberation,—and your House of hundreds will be inert and emasculated as to all unity and concentration of purpose: like any other mob, it will concentrate and act as led by passion and leaders, and not from reason and deliberation.[34]

The critics of mob government painted a dismal picture of a weakened House, irrational and dominated by passion, failing to uphold its part in the constitutional system, and breaking down the checks and balances upon which republican liberty rested.[35]

Southern Whigs commonly suspected executive tyranny lurking behind opposition to the smaller House. William Archer of Virginia warned that "the *degradation* of the branch of the Legislature which was the direct representative of the people, must be fatal to liberty." The danger of executive tyranny "was demonstrated in the warning pages of our recent history":

We stand now . . . on the narrow isthmus which intercepts the union, ever fatal, of executive power and popular encroachments. This body [the Senate] constitutes the dividing barrier between that tide of executive power which is ever working to undermine,

[34]John B. Thompson, *Congressional Globe,* 27th Cong., 2d sess., June 21, 1842, Appendix, 884.
[35]Some feared that the smaller and more elevated Senate might thus come to dominate the House. Francis W. Pickens, a South Carolina Democrat, predicted that eventuality and even described its likely occurence because of a plot by oligarchical House members. He asserted that John Quincy Adams and other supporters of a large House were actually seeking to make the House "unfit for discussion and practical legislation" so that the "aristocratic" Senate might prevail. Adams, on the other hand, insisted that the reduction plan was designed to weaken the House and favor the "aristocratic Senate." *Congressional Globe,* 27th Cong., 2d sess., June 13, 1842.

and that wave of popular excitement which is ever rolling to dash over the safeguards of a guarded and regulated liberty.[36]

Archer's fear of "popular excitement," like the warnings against "mob government," derives in language and substance from the antidemocratic tendencies present in the republican ideas of the constitution-makers. Reformers also borrowed their antiparty sentiments from the same sources.

In one sense smaller-House advocates backed into the antiparty argument as a result of defending themselves against the accusation that they were antidemocratic. Attacking a large House as "mob government" was not undemocratic because a large House was democratic in appearance only. Repeatedly the reformers quoted Madison's warning:

> [With] every addition to their representatives . . . the countenance of the government may become more democratic, but the soul that animates it will be more oligarchic. The machine will be enlarged, but the fewer, and often the more secret, will be the springs by which its motions are directed.[37]

The secret springs could only be party leaders, managing legislation through committees whose discussions were not recorded, shutting off debate to hasten action, and substituting machine-like regularity for rational deliberation. All knew that these were "the signs of the times," Senator Archer insisted, and the signs were portentous. "Large bodies," he warned, "could not act, unless by guidance. They fell inevitably under dictation. And what guidance? Whose dictation? Of the modest—the most meritorious? No: of the interested—the violent—the designing."[38] James Buchanan, one of the few Democrats who spoke for the reduction reform, tied the arguments together. Making again the damaging comparison with the House of Commons, and quoting Madison's "beautiful language" directly, Buchanan insisted that continued growth would "finally concentrate all power and all influence in the hands of a few party leaders," thus true democracy would be lost. "If," he argued, "from the very number of the

---

[36]Archer made perhaps the most complete presentation of the case for a smaller House. *Ibid.,* May 27, 1842, Appendix, 436-437.

[37]Madison, No. 58, *Federalist Papers,* 360-361.

[38]Archer, *Congressional Globe,* 27th Cong., 2d sess., May 27, 1842, Appendix, 437.

House, it follows, as a necessary consequence, that a few prominent members and party leaders must transact the whole of the
important business, then, in order to influence a majority of the
House, it will only be necessary to influence or corrupt these
leaders.''[39]

In depicting the House as a place where statesmen of wisdom
and virtue protected the national welfare without partisan interference, Whig reformers returned to the ambivalent concept
of representation prevalent in the late eighteenth century. Their
opponents were quick to fasten upon the deferential implications
of this view, and they pushed the point that attaining a smaller
House must incur the disadvantage of diminishing the close relationship between a congressman and his constituents. But some
reformers eliminated the logical inconsistency inherent in historical
meanings of representation in America and openly repudiated
the notion that a congressman should mirror his constituents'
will. Close relationships were unnecessary, they argued, because
representatives were trustees, not delegates. Arthur Bagby, one
of Alabama's Democratic senators, recommended the reduction
plan because it would "place the rights of the people in the hands
of such trustees as would best secure the trust, and at the same
time exercise the trust itself most efficiently.''[40] An extended constituency, Congressman Underwood argued, would reduce "mere
shake-hands and grog-shop influence, and would require more
weight of character to secure a man's election." A trustee, he
asserted, would make decisions based on his independent assessment, not upon the power of "mere numbers.''[41]

46

---

[39]Moore, ed., *Works of Buchanan,* V, 258-259, 267.

[40]*Congressional Globe,* 27th Cong., 2d sess., May 30, 1842, 549.

[41]*Ibid.,* Apr. 21, 1842, 437. A few self-styled reformers, almost all of them
southern Democrats, stated outright that it simply did not matter whether a
congressman knew his constituents with a "fireside acquaintance" or not. According to Henry Wise, "neigborhood representation" was unnecessary.
Domestic issues, which required close knowledge, were the domain of the
"General Assemblies of the States," Senator William Preston of South Carolina
asserted. James McKay, a North Carolina congressman, pointed out that if
representation were considered in this light, there were already over 4,500
legislators in the country, or one representative for "every 350 men able to
bear arms." *Ibid.,* Apr. 21, 1842, 437; May 30, 1842, 549-550; June 13, 1482,
622. This argument from state-rights principles was not a major theme in the
debate, but even its infrequent mention probably fed the suspicion of those
already concerned by the southern cast of speakers. Because of the three-fifths

Predictably, then, a frontal assault on the trustee theory of representation was the central theme of the Democratic argument against a smaller House. New Hampshire Democrat Charles Atherton stated the matter bluntly, declaring that the trustee idea was "based on an assumption which is altogether fallacious, and contrary to the spirit of our institutions; which assumption is, that it is the wisdom of the Representatives, *'per se'* . . . which is to govern the country, and not the popular opinion . . . ." Representatives were to be "the agents of the people," not their guardians. Less theoretically, Democrat Charles Brown of Pennsylvania observed:

> [I]f they could squeeze this Government down to that of *one man,* they would have a more practicable, more efficient, and more quiet one than that they now had; and though that one man might be the Representative of the American people, he would not be the kind of Government the American people desired or would approve.[42]

47

While the relative merits of the trustee and agent theories of representation might be open to academic discussion, in the "era of the common man" popular opinion was undoubtedly with Atherton and Brown. Awareness of that opinion influenced the tone of debate, if not the voting patterns.

Those who argued for a smaller House could make a persuasive appeal for its qualitative advantages, but they had difficulty dealing with the subject of enlarged constituencies. On the other hand, those who wanted a larger House found the maintenance of a small constituency to be a powerful argument in their favor, while they had real problems justifying how the quality of government could be improved by an increase in the size of the legislature.

Some large-House advocates used romantic rhetoric to defend their position. William Allen, prominent Democratic senator from Ohio and an outspoken advocate of a large body, repeated

---

clause a representative from a state with a large slave population practically had a much smaller constituency than a free state representative. It should be noted, however, that in the Senate bloc favoring a smaller House, the only southerner from a lower South state was Calhoun, and in the House bloc, only 7 of the 22 southerners favoring a smaller House were from the heavily slave-populated lower South.

[42]*Ibid.,* Apr. 25, 1842, Appendix, 350; *ibid.,* Apr. 21, 1842, 436.

several times his basic belief that "there was something awfully sublime in the spectacle of a congregated mass of representatives." Conservative Whig Senator Crittenden spoke of a large House ensuring the "full operation of that congregated mass of intellect which pervades the people at large."[43] Romantic flights like these, common though they were, unfortunately could not be developed without substituting fancy for political thought, and they were more often than not simply stated and abandoned, having served their purposes by placing the speaker on the side of democracy. John Quincy Adams was more cautious in advocating the democratic merits of a large House, insisting that he "did not profess to be an advocate of pure Democracy, in the party and general sense of that term; but he was a Democrat so far as the representation in the House of Representatives was concerned." Even that much concession to the popular argument led Francis Pickens to comment sarcastically that it was "a strange spectacle to see the gentleman from Massachusetts assuming to be the guardian of democratic principles."[44]

Large-House supporters also used more restrained republican ideology. A large House, Benton told the Senate, would be less corruptible and purer, thus rendering "liberty safest." Acknowledging that a large House might be rowdy, he asserted that "decorum was a good thing, but liberty was better."[45] Although the notion that "in multitudes of counsellors there is safety" was commonly enough associated with early republican ideas, on the whole large-House advocates appear to have recognized that their position was weak when it relied on either the sublimity or purity of large bodies. For the most part, therefore, they stressed democratic arguments about representation, like the reformers ignoring partisan influences, but unlike them defending the sovereign will of the people.

Perhaps it is unreasonable to look for intellectual consistency in working politicians, even in regard to their own roles and responsibilities, but the reduction debate reveals a distressing inattention to the chasm between representative theory and the practice of representation in America. Democrats, who advocated limited government and executive democracy, might cheerfully

[43]*Ibid.*, May 27, 1842, 546, May 26, 1842, 538-539.
[44]*Ibid.*, June 13, 1842, 620, 621.
[45]*Ibid.*, May 27, 1842, Appendix, 402-403.

see the turbulent House as a fine mirror of an unbounded society, even a proper protection against excessive lawmaking. Whigs, conversely, called for an effective government to guide social progress and abhorred chaotic upheaval anywhere, so a rational legislative process seemed essential. For Whigs, internal paradoxes and sectional divisions in their ideology were serious impediments to reform.

The most conservative spot on the Whig party's ideological spectrum belonged to the reforming southern Whigs. They advocated progress through retrogression, describing an improved House in language that denigrated the majoritarian and partisan tendencies in contemporary politics. When they depicted the ideal House as a body of responsible individuals reaching decisions through calm and rational deliberation, they reflected a persisting trustee concept of representation. These southerners made no overt appeals to regional interests and their language was not sectional, but their motives were certainly suspect in the eyes of men like Adams, whose gag-rule struggle had heightened fears of a pervasive slave power. Furthermore, their position appeared sectional because their northern Whig colleagues did not support the southerners' arguments for reform.

The silence of those northern Whigs who consistently voted for the reduction measure is perplexing. Some may have worried about their constituents' reactions to the antidemocratic implications of the southern position. The possibility remains open, moreover, that northern Whigs wanted a smaller House for reasons they were unwilling or unable to articulate. As the debate opened, Richard Thompson suggested a rationale that required little theoretical justification when he insisted that it would be "better to have a Legislature consisting of a comparatively small number of well-informed business men, than a much larger number of those destitute of business habits and fond of debating."[46] His image of a quietly businesslike body may reflect a desire for a more respectable legislature than the disorderly Twenty-seventh Congress he lambasted in his diary. Whether

49

---

[46]*Ibid.,* Apr. 21, 1842, 436. Chairman Everett's statement that "the opinion of no member would be changed by debate," as he moved the previous question on accepting the Senate bill, suggests a similarly businesslike perspective on his responsibilities. *Ibid.,* June 13, 1842, 620.

it also suggests a departure from a trustee concept of representation depends upon the undefined sources of his businessmen's information. Was a congressman to be well informed by his own wisdom and virtue, by his constituents' opinions, by his party, or by some inexplicable combination of the three? Neither Thompson nor any other northern Whig clarified this ambiguity in debate.

Only Henry Clay, who opposed the reduction measure, provided insight into a significant modification of the concept of representation by the presence of parties, and his comments were made, in a letter to Willie P. Mangum, in the form of a frank analysis from one party leader to another:

> The argument in favor of a small house assumes that the house is a bad thing and that the less you have of it the better. I think that the experience of the Extra Session demonstrated that, with suitable rules, a large House can get along as well as a small one. Indeed the House proceeded at the Session with more despatch than the Senate. It is a mistake therefore to suppose that the proper transaction of business depends upon the size of the body; it depends on its rules.[47]

Clay's remarks were couched exclusively in the context of the legislative experience he shared with Mangum, not in republican sentiments, but the nature of their experiences made the meaning clear. Through the committee system, where partisan majorities could covertly shape legislation, a cumbersome body of ill-informed and inexperienced congressmen could be shaped to the will of party leaders, "secret springs" of decision-making, indeed, but altogether appropriate ones.

Clay's observation implies a significant shift in the meaning of representation, a revised view in which responsibility to party was incorporated into the role of a representative. To the extent that his party clarified and focused popular will through the election process, a legislator could continue to be a delegate from the people; but within the House he could act as a new kind of trustee. His personal wisdom and virtue might guide his decisions, but they would also be influenced by knowledgeable party leaders, expediting the lawmaking process to accomplish national party purposes rather than the goals of fragmented local interests.

---

[47]Clay to Mangum, June 7, 1842, in Shanks, ed., *Papers of Mangum*, III, 356.

Tensions arising from these joint influences of private judgment, popular opinion, and party leaders could be reconciled in the security of closed meetings, making it possible for party members to develop a common justification for their decision well in advance of the need for disclosure in floor debate. The full development of this modified conception of representation would require major innovations in Whig ideology, most importantly a complete commitment to the need for parties in the American system.[48] It is no wonder, then, that no Whig stepped forward to proclaim its relevance to the issues of 1842.

The Whig reforms embodied in the apportionment act of 1842 did not have a permanent impact on the legislative process. Districting continued to be the prevalent practice in most states, but it was not effectively guaranteed until well into the twentieth century.[49] The act, moreover, only reduced the size of the House

51

---

[48]Whig antiparty ideas and the handicap they presented to Whig success have been treated in Lynn L. Marshall, "The Strange Stillbirth of the Whig Party," *American Historical Review*, 72 (Jan. 1967), 445-468. Howe sees many Whig leaders accepting parties as legitimate (Adams more slowly than others) and stresses Clay's creativity: "By putting the new idea of a party system into the service of the old antiexecutive objectives of the 'country' tradition, Clay showed himself an imaginative political ideologist." *Political Culture of the American Whigs,* 143. For an explication of some of the complexities involved in any analysis of the relationship between ideology and political change, see Quentin Skinner, "Some Problems in the Analysis of Political Thought and Action," *Political Theory,* 2 (Aug. 1974), 277-303. The tension created by the juxtaposition of antiparty ideas and incessant manipulation of the party system is a major theme in McCormick, *Presidential Game,* summarized for the period of the second party system at 205-206. Brock suggests in *Parties and Political Conscience,* ch. 3, that Whigs in the Twenty-seventh Congress moved tentatively toward a system of party responsibility in government, but the apportionment debate does not reveal any substantial rationale to support such a move.

I would hasten to add, lest the shortcomings of Whig ideology be overstated, that congressmen still differ about the relative importance of party in decision-making; see Davidson, *Role of the Congressman,* 146-162. In the words of a political scientist who has written thoughtfully about conceptual problems in representation, " 'representation,' despite its important role in democratic philosophies and practices, is unlikely ever to meet with common understanding as a concept." Charles E. Gilbert, "Operative Doctrines of Representation," in Patterson, ed., *American Legislative Behavior,* 23.

[49]The Democratic majority in the House of the Twenty-eighth Congress ignored the districting provision, seating the representatives from four states which held general-ticket elections. Although the use of the general ticket system declined in the second half of the nineteenth century, states continued to elect some representatives at large, perhaps most frequently when a state's popula-

from 244 to 233 members, and that at the cost of substantially enlarging each member's constituency. The principle of limiting growth affected two succeeding apportionments, but after the Civil War Congress returned to the practice of increasing the size of the House as the population grew. Only after World War I was the ceiling permanently fixed at 435, the present number of the House.[50] More fundamentally, most reforms of the House have rested upon alterations in the processes by which the majority party dominates legislation, as Clay anticipated. Increasingly, the modern "bear garden" has become the domain of legislative specialists, and legislative reform has become so arcane a subject that informed public discussion about it is rare. In an odd way, then, the conduct of northern Whigs in 1842 foreshadowed a future pattern.

The consistently pragmatic character of American politics was already clear by the 1840s, when rapid changes in the practice of party politics were quite imperfectly reflected in slowly changing ideologies. In the reduction debate, congressional rhetoric served as much to obscure the realities of lawmaking as to bridge the information gap between legislators and the public.[51] In general, Whig ideology integrated assumptions about human nature, the social order, and political institutions; but such was not the case for ideas about representation, except for those of the nostalgic southern Whig reformers. The apportionment act of 1842 illustrates again the basic problems that burdened the Whig party as it confronted the legislative responsibilities of a pluralistic and progressive nation with an ideology founded upon an increasingly irrelevant republican tradition.

52

---

tion had grown and the legislature could not agree upon a new plan for districting. Not until after the landmark Supreme Court decisions in *Baker* v. *Carr* (1962) and *Wesberry* v. *Sanders* (1964) did the national government begin to impose uniform districting upon the states. Schmeckebier, *Congressional Apportionment*, 113-117; Martis, *Historical Atlas*, 2-5.

[50]*Ibid.*

[51]Pole portrays the "two-way traffic over this bridge" as "traffic in knowledge." *The Gift of Government*, 140.

CENSURING OLD MAN ELOQUENT: FOREIGN POLICY AND DISUNION, 1842

by

Lynn Hudson Parsons

The attempted censure of John Quincy Adams in 1842 is one of the most dramatic chapters in the life of that statesman, as well as in the history of Congress. For two weeks, from January 25 to February 7, the House of Representatives was ensnarled in bitter invective, parliamentary maneuvering, and political intrigue. Before it was over, Adams accused a major antagonist—Henry A. Wise of Virginia—of once having entered the House with his face and hands stained with the blood of a slain colleague, and mercilessly taunted Thomas F. Marshall, of Kentucky, with the latter's drinking problem. Wise called Adams a traitor and accused him of making faces at him. Representative Thomas J. Campbell, Democrat of Tennessee, punched Representative William W. Boardman, Whig of Connecticut, in front of Gadsby's Hotel as a result of remarks made on the House floor.[1] There was, wrote a Washington newspaper correspondent, "a general determination of the friends of peace to adjourn every day at 4 o'clock, firmly believing that a candle-light sitting would bring in riot, fighting, the use of knives and pistols, and murder. . . ."[2] "The papers will inform you of the afflicting scenes passing in the House of Representatives," wrote Henry Clay to a friend. "They will fill every patriot bosom with distress."[3] Many

[1]U.S. Congress, House, *Congressional Globe*, 27th Cong., 2d sess., vol. XI, 168–215. (All future references to the *Congressional Globe* will be from this volume.) This account is incomplete and should be supplemented by the *National Intelligencer's* reports of Adams's speeches, 11–15 Feb. 1842.

[2]*American* (New York), quoted in *Daily Democrat* (Rochester, N.Y.), 2 Feb. 1842.

[3]Henry Clay to Francis Brooke, 27 Jan. 1842, *The Private Correspondence of Henry Clay*, ed. by C. Colton (New York, 1856), 456.

Originally published in *Capitol Studies*, 3 (Fall, 1975). Reprinted by permission of the United States Capitol Historical Society.

54

John Quincy Adams: A rare daguerreotype, dated 1843. (credit National Portrait Gallery, Smithsonian Institution, Washington, D.C.)

newspapers reported a decline in the prestige of the House, and of Congress generally.[4]

John Quincy Adams's "offense" was the introduction of a petition, signed by forty-six residents of Haverhill, Massachusetts, asking that Congress "immediately adopt measures peaceably to dissolve the Union of these States." The reasons given were: no union was possible without reciprocal benefits; the resources of one portion of the union were being drained into another; the history of other such inequitable unions indicated violence and civil strife as the inevitable result.[5] Adams introduced the petition with the recommendation that a committee be appointed to report an answer "showing the reasons why the prayer of it should not be granted," explaining ambiguously that it was "not yet time" for such measures. Despite this, Representative Thomas Walker Gilmer, of Virginia, promptly moved a short resolution that Adams had "justly incurred the censure of this House." The next day Representative Marshall, nephew of the late Chief Justice, also moved that Adams be censured for having "disgraced his country, through its representatives, in the eyes of the whole world."[6] The elements of political drama followed quickly: overflow crowds in the galleries, profound and petty debates, alliances, charges, strategies. And always central was the stubborn, defiant personality of "Old Man Eloquent." It was a graphic demonstration of the metamorphosis of Adams, from the stuffy young Federalist who attacked the radicalism of Jefferson and Paine in the 1790's, to the elderly scourge whom the Richmond *Enquirer* attacked, inconsistently, as "a bore and a nuisance and a firebrand."[7]

55

Bennett Champ Clark, Gilbert Hobbs Barnes, and Samuel Flagg Bemis, each wrote accounts of this bizarre event.[8] Clark drew upon his experiences in congressional politics to produce a vivid picture, while Barnes benefitted from the newly-discovered papers of Theodore Dwight Weld, the abolitionist who lent valuable assistance to Adams during the incident. Neither Clark nor Barnes had access to Adams's unpublished papers; Bemis was among the first to gain permission from the Adams family to use them. Yet none of these historians probed the complex background of the event. None sought to place it within the partisan political framework of the day, and none paid close attention to the debates, nor investigated their coverage by the nation's press. The purpose of this essay is to examine more closely the partisan and

[4]*Daily Democrat*, 10 Feb. 1842; *U.S. Gazette* (Philadelphia), quoted in *Tribune*, (New York), 1 Feb. 1842; *Evening Post* (New York), 28 Jan. 1842; *Globe* (Washington), 3, 4 Feb. 1842.

[5]*Congressional Globe*, 168. The petition may have been drafted by the abolitionist poet John Greenleaf Whittier, a Haverhill native. See A. T. Pickard, *Life and Letters of John Greenleaf Whittier*, (2 vols., Boston, 1907), I, 179–80; Whitman Bennett, *Whittier, Bard of Freedom* (Chapel Hill, 1941), 179–80.

[6]*Congressional Globe*, 168–70.

[7]*Enquirer* (Richmond), 1 Feb. 1842.

[8]Bennett Champ Clark, *John Quincy Adams* (Boston, 1932), 394–407; Gilbert Hobbs Barnes, *The Anti-Slavery Impulse 1830–1844* (New York, 1932), 177–87; Samuel Flagg Bemis, *John Quincy Adams and the Union* (New York, 1956), 416–39.

sectional aspects of the incident. Not merely a dramatic episode in the long, tumultuous career of John Quincy Adams, it concealed an attempt to remove him as Chairman of the House Foreign Affairs Committee, was an important test of the cohesiveness of the Whig party, and was a demonstration of the sharp increase in disunionist sentiment in the North.

The accounts of Clark, Barnes, and Bemis depicted the attempt to censure Adams as either a simple sectional battle or the result of the Whig leadership's decision to "get" Adams in retaliation for his insurgency on the matter of receiving anti-slavery petitions. Clark said "the whole controversy was a sectional rather than a partisan one."[9] According to Barnes, Whig leaders were furious with Adams for his disruptive effect on the party's legislative program: "A caucus of Southern members decided that on the first pretext that offered, Adams should be censured; and Northern leaders concurred in their decision."[10] Bemis followed Barnes fairly closely on this point.[11]

The identity of the northern Whig leaders cited by Barnes and Bemis was never given. In fact, an examination of the vote in the House which finally tabled the censure motion shows only two northern Whigs in opposition, neither of whom could be classified as a leader. Indeed, not only did northern Whigs overwhelmingly oppose the censure attempt, but so did a significant number of southern Whigs. Contrary to Clark, Barnes, and Bemis, the pattern of voting was partisan, not sectional, and became more so with each roll call. (See Table.)[12] In the end, a majority of Whigs *of both sections* favored the tabling of the censure motion, while a similar majority of Democrats favored a continuation of the debate. Close examination reveals that the key factor in the defeat of the censure attempt was a gradual but massive shift of southern Whigs, from their initial opposition to tabling the motion, to a vote in favor. Equally significant, the proportion of northern Democrats favoring censure, or at least opposing a tabling of the motion, increased slightly but perceptibly over the two-week period. The final vote to table saw the Whigs favoring it, 95–18, while the Democrats opposed it, 75–10.[13]

An analysis of the roll calls in the Adams censure affair supports the contention, so persuasively argued in Joel Silbey's *The Shrine of Party*, that partisan ties were generally more binding than sectional ones among con-

56

[9]Clark, *John Quincy Adams*, 400.

[10]Barnes, *Anti-Slavery Impulse*, 185.

[11]Bemis, *Adams and the Union*, 427. The caucus referred to actually occurred after, not before, the original censure motion against Adams. See *Congressional Globe*, 169–70, 211.

[12]The roll call results may be found in the *Congressional Globe*, 169, 177, 191, 200–201, 214–15. Party affiliations were gleaned from the *Biographical Directory of the American Congress, 1774-1927* (Washington, 1928) and Joel Silbey, *The Shrine of Party* (Pittsburgh, 1967).

[13]On February 2, Adams and thirteen anti-slavery Whigs voted against tabling the censure motion, fearing a pro-slavery attempt to cut off Adams's defense. With this and one or two other exceptions, it is argued that the position taken on the vote against tabling the censure motion is a good indication of the pro- and anti-Adams sentiment, especially among southern Whigs and northern Democrats.

TABLE
Analysis of Five Roll Calls on Tabling The Censure of John Quincy Adams

Date		January 25		January 26		January 29		February 2		February 7	
		Number	Percent	Number	Percent	Number	Percent	Number	Percent	Number	Percent
Northern Whigs	For	72	34.95	66	34.74	68	33.01	58	28.86	72	36.18
	Against	4	1.94	3	1.58	5	2.43	14	6.97	2	1.01
Southern Whigs	For	9	4.37	16	8.42	19	9.22	22	10.95	23	11.56
	Against	29	14.08	24	12.63	23	11.17	18	8.96	16	8.04
Northern Democrats	For	12	5.83	7	3.68	9	4.37	9	4.48	9	4.52
	Against	36	17.48	34	12.63	40	19.42	40	19.90	40	20.10
Southern Democrats	For	0	0	0	0	0	0	0	0	1	0.50
	Against	41	19.90	38	20.00	40	19.42	38	18.91	35	17.59
Totals	For	94*	45.63	90*	47.37	97*	47.09	89*	44.28	106*	53.27
	Against	112§	54.37	100¶	52.63	109¶	52.91	112§	55.72	93	46.73

*Includes one southern independent (Williams, N.C.)
§Includes one northern independent (Adams, Mass.) and one southern independent (Sprigg, Ky.)
¶Includes one southern independent (Sprigg, Ky.)

57

gressmen in the 1840's. Resisting the sectionalist interpretation of American history typified by Frederick Jackson Turner, Frank L. Owsley, and Avery Craven, Silbey and others have pointed out the danger in assuming that, since armed conflict broke out between the sections in 1861, most ante-bellum history must be understood in terms of sectionalism.[14] The ultimate failure of the attempt to censure John Quincy Adams, and the reasons behind that failure, seem to substantiate the newer view.

A glance at the table will show that, for at least the first three roll calls, the anti-Adams forces had the possibility of success, since the overwhelming majority of Democrats were allied with a large minority of Whigs. Ultimately, party lines tightened, and even the remaining handful of southern Whig defectors was not enough to prevent the Whig-dominated House from tabling the matter.

The censure attempt cannot be fully explained in terms of Adams's insurgency over the gag rule against anti-slavery petitions which, after all, had been going on for five years.[15] Nor can it be explained solely in terms of the Haverhill petition, for similar sentiments had already been expressed, publicly and privately, by some of Adams's severest critics. What was new in 1842, was Adams's chairmanship of the House Committee on Foreign Affairs at a critical point in United States foreign relations. He had become chairman only a few weeks before, as a result of the continuing power struggle between the "national" Whigs led by Henry Clay, and the small group of extreme state-rights, pro-slavery Whigs loyal to President John Tyler. The chairmanship had first been held by Caleb Cushing of Massachusetts, but Cushing made a number of anti-Clay, pro-Tyler statements in the autumn of 1841.[16] As a result, when Congress reconvened in December, Cushing was ousted by the Speaker of the House, a Clay Whig, and replaced by John Quincy Adams, whose credentials for the post in normal circumstances would have been unchallengeable. But the divisions within the Whig party that followed the death of President William Henry Harrison created an abnormal situation. A series of issues in foreign policy made that area one of particular concern to pro-slavery and state-rights elements in both parties.

At the beginning of 1842, many observers, including Adams, believed a third war with Great Britain to be a distinct possibility.[17] A variety of questions, including the international slave trade and the right of search upon

[14]Silbey, *Shrine of Party*, 5–6, 143–46; Silbey, "The Civil War Synthesis in American Political History," *Civil War History*, X (June 1964), 130–40. Thomas B. Alexander, *Sectional Stress and Party Strength* (Nashville, 1967). [The vote on the Adams censure motion was dealt with in Silbey's book, but it is unclear to what degree. See 242–43.]

[15]The battle against the gag rule is described in Russel Nye, *Fettered Freedom* (East Lansing, 1964) 41–66; and Robert P. Ludlum, "The Anti-slavery 'Gag Rule': History and Argument," *Journal of Negro History*, XXVI (April 1941) 203.

[16]Claude M. Feuss, *Caleb Cushing*, (2 vols., New York, 1923), I, 303, 326–33.

[17]Bemis, *Adams and the Union*, 456.

the high seas, Texas annexation, the *Creole* incident, and the northeastern boundary dispute, threatened to break the more than quarter-century of peace between the two nations, which Adams had helped to negotiate in 1814. At that time, his appointment to the chairmanship of any committee dealing with foreign policy would have been hailed by knowledgeable Anglophobes. Since then, however, Adams's views had changed. His opposition to the annexation of Texas angered expansionists, his defense of the kidnapped Africans from the illegal slave ship *Amistad* dismayed pro-slavery forces, and the modification of his once-adamant position in defense of neutral rights on the high seas (to allow for the right of "inspection" by the British of suspected slave ships flying the American flag) upset those who were anti-British.[18] In November, Adams supplied his critics with new ammunition by defending Britain's questionable role in the Opium War with China.[19] Finally, when Congress reconvened, he told the Anglophobic Cushing, who was moving steadily into the Tylerite camp, that the United States was wrong on all outstanding issues with Britain except the Maine boundary dispute.[20] The catapulting of a man with such opinions into the Chairmanship of the House Foreign Affairs Committee could only be viewed by pro-slavery forces and Tyler Whigs as an outright challenge.

59

Adams's new-found sympathy for the British was a reflection of his growing militancy on the slave question. He had come to regard the international slave trade as a form of piracy, not subject to the usual protections of international law, and welcomed Britain's attempts to suppress it.[21] The Washington *Globe*, a Democratic organ, stressed the connection between Adams's defense of Britain in the Opium War and his alleged abolitionism.[22] The Richmond *Enquirer* (which, along with the *Globe* and the Albany, N.Y. *Argus* constituted the Big Three of the Democratic party's newspapers) was more explicit, complaining that "this reckless vindicator of the British attack upon China" had been put in charge of the very committee "before whom the case of the Creole, and perhaps other questions deeply interesting to the South are to be brought."[23] The Tylerite Washington *Madisonian* claimed, soon after Congress reconvened, that the crucial Ways and Means Committee, along with that on Foreign Affairs, had been stacked

[18]*Ibid.*, chaps. XVIII, XIX; R. R. Stenberg, "John Quincy Adams, Imperialist and Apostate," *Southwestern Social Science Quarterly,* XVI (March 1936), 37–50; George T. Tade, "The Anti-Texas Address," *Southern Speech Journal*, XXX (July 1965), 185–98; Samuel Flagg Bemis, *John Quincy Adams and the Foundation of American Foreign Policy* (New York, 1949), 423–29; George Dangerfield, *The Era of Good Feelings* (London, 1953), 7; Hugh G. Soulsby, *The Right of Search and the Slave Trade in Anglo-American Relations* (Baltimore, 1935), 9–47.
[19]John Quincy Adams, *Memoirs*, ed. by Charles Francis Adams (12 vols., Philadelphia, 1874–77), XI, 1877, 30–31.
[20]Adams, *Memoirs*, XI, 35–57 (9, 11 Dec. 1841).
[21]Bemis, *Adams and Foreign Policy*, 428–29.
[22]*Globe* (Washington), 9, 11, 21, 27 Dec. 1841, 10 Feb. 1842.
[23]*Enquirer*, 25 Jan. 1842.

with enemies of the administration, even though the administration's party was nominally in control of Congress.[24] As the year began, there was major concern among both Jacksonian Democrats and Tylerite Whigs with this return to prominence and power of John Quincy Adams, once thought safely confined to the back benches. While sectional considerations no doubt played a role in this concern, evidence suggests that partisanship was, at this stage, more important.

On January 9, Adams received a petition allegedly from Clarksville, Georgia, dated December 30, 1841, requesting his dismissal as chairman of the Foreign Affairs Committee on grounds of "monomania" on all matters dealing with the darker peoples of the world. The genuineness of this petition may be doubted, for it appears to have been written on congressional stationery, and the Democratic congressman from the Clarksville district denied its authenticity. A similar, later petition is additional evidence of the determination on the part of the pro-slavery element to get rid of Adams as chairman.[25] Mrs. John Quincy Adams, in letters to her son Charles Francis Adams, was convinced that a conspiracy existed to replace her husband with Cushing. She implicated Daniel Webster, Tyler's Secretary of State and a close friend of Cushing, who had fallen out with Adams many years before.[26]

The pro-slavery assault upon the Foreign Affairs Committee, led by Jacksonian Democrats and Tylerite Whigs, forms an essential part of the background of the attempt to censure John Quincy Adams. The Clarksville petition, Adams told the House, involved deeper questions, such "as whether we shall go to war with England to prevent the suppression of the slave trade, or whether we shall go to war with England on the question whether infamous slave traders shall be indemnified for their abominable traffic." The day after the speech, Adams received an anonymous note warning him that Henry A. Wise intended to move his expulsion.[27] If a censure or expulsion motion passed, Adams would be forced to go back to his district and seek re-election. In the meantime, he could be replaced with someone more acceptable to the pro-slavery and anti-British forces in the House.

In seizing upon the Haverhill petition, which unquestionably antagonized a majority in both parties, the Tylerites—Gilmer, Wise, and a few other southern representatives who were referred to derisively by their opponents as the "corporal's guard"—hoped to separate southern Whigs from their party

60

---

[24]*Madisonian,* (Washington), 15 Dec. 1841.

[25]James Playfair to Adams, 30 Dec. 1841, and James Linch to Adams, 8 Jan. 1842, Adams Manuscript Trust, Microfilm Reel 520, Massachusetts Historical Society. For doubts as to the authenticity of the Clarksville petition, see *Congressional Globe,* 207, and Adams, *Memoirs,* XI, 98–99.

[26]Louisa Catherine Adams to Charles Francis Adams, 11, 25 Jan., 3, 5 Feb. 1842. Adams Manuscript Trust, Microfilm Reels 520–21.

[27]*Congressional Globe,* 163; Theodore Dwight Weld to Angelina Grimke Weld, 23 Jan. 1842, quoted in Bemis, *Adams and the Union,* 426; *Globe* (Washington), 24 Jan. 1842. Anonymous to Adams, 22 Jan. 1842, Adams Manuscript Trust, Microfilm Reel 520.

in a burst of indignation over Adams's conduct. They then hoped to unite them with Jacksonian Democrats and create a new coalition dedicated to state-rights and pro-slavery expansion. Such a coalition had been discussed since the day Tyler took office.[28] Had the "corporal's guard" been successful in the censure motion, it would have been not only a bitter personal blow to Adams, it also would have crippled the entire Whig party. For, although Adams, up to this point, had refused to associate himself with either party (and there were many occasions when neither party chose to associate with him), his political ideology—an expanded view of federal power, hostility to pro-slavery expansion, and opposition to the "gag" rule—was clearly the direction in which the majority of Whigs, even in the South, were headed. As the censure debate proceeded, its importance to the future of the Whig party, particularly in the South, and to Whig chances for success in 1844, became obvious. For this reason, the most prominent speakers in favor of tabling the censure motion came from the South: Thomas D. Arnold of Tennessee, Joseph R. Underwood of Kentucky, and John M. Botts of Virginia.[29] The speeches of Wise, who painted a picture of a pro-English-abolition-dissolution party headed by Adams, and who pointedly called upon the Democrats to rescue the South and the nation, also were marked by personal attacks upon Henry Clay, who stood in the chamber along with a number of other senators as part of the immense audience to the debates.[30] It is not surprising, therefore, that Clay Whigs from Kentucky, Virginia, and Tennessee provided most of the southern votes against censure. Even Marshall, who was not a Tylerite, but who had broken with Clay over expansion, disassociated himself from Wise.[31]

61

Marshall introduced his own censure resolution, as a substitute for Gilmer's.[32] Marshall's resolution became the focal point of the debate, and served to confuse the strategy of the "corporal's guard," inadvertently aiding Adams. Whereas Gilmer's original motion concluded merely that Adams had "justly incurred the censure of this House" without going into the whys and wherefores, Marshall's substitute consisted of three lengthy paragraphs of a strongly nationalist flavor, accusing Adams of complicity in "perjury" and "high treason."[33] By using those fateful words, the Kentuckian gave the Yankee the opportunity to array himself as the defendant in a court and claim all the rights of the Sixth Amendment. This led to prolonged wrangling over the nature of the Marshall resolution and the proceedings themselves. In vain did Marshall protest that it was the Haverhill petition, and not Adams, that

[28]Abel P. Upshur to N. Beverly Tucker, 11 Oct. 1841, Williamsburg, College of William and Mary Library, Tucker Collection, brings this point out.
[29]*Congressional Globe*, 180–84, 201.
[30]*Ibid.*, 171–77, 194.
[31]*Ibid.*, 187.
[32]*Ibid.*, 211.
[33]Both resolutions are conveniently printed by C. F. Adams in his father's *Memoirs*, XI, 72–73.

had advocated perjury and treason: The damage was done. From that time on, Adams referred to the affair as his "trial," and he demanded, and for the most part received, not only the right to defend himself but the right to subpoena documents to aid in that defense.[34] Thus, in sidetracking the crisply-worded Gilmer resolution, Marshall unwittingly helped to bring about the failure of the censure attempt.

A close reading of the debates reveals not only the intrigue surrounding the Foreign Affairs Committee, the purposes of the Tylerites, and the confusion following the introduction of Marshall's substitute resolution, but also reveals a certain ambiguity of thought and purpose in the mind of Adams with regard to the Haverhill petition. His cryptic remark that it was "not yet time" to consider the prayer of the petition was leaped upon by his opponents as proof of his ultimate disunionism.[35] The qualification was subject to one of two interpretations: either that the alleged abuses to which the North had been subjected had not reached the point at which dissolution was justified, or that, from a tactical standpoint, the time had not yet come to move effectively in that direction. Adams generally put the former interpretation upon his words. "If they have mistaken the remedy," he said of the Haverhill petitioners, "the House should . . . tell these men that their grievances are not to be remedied by a dissolution of the Union; that there are other remedies in their power. . . ."[36] Repeatedly, he emphasized his opposition to disunion by citing his long career and quoting from past orations.[37] The Democratic press consistently omitted his initial statement of opposition to the petition. But his adversaries maintained that the "not yet time" proviso made his opposition irrelevant. To them, he was following a calculated course in which he would publicly deny sympathy with disunion, yet knowingly encourage it by his actions. The same interpretation explained his opposition to immediate abolition of slavery, even in the District of Columbia. The Washington *Globe* described what it thought was the method of John Quincy Adams:

His long experience in diplomacy had taught him that in politics, the safest and sometimes the surest way to accomplish an object, is to disclaim it. Whilst doing, profess not to do it. Lament, deprecate the end, heap suspicions and epithets on others, whilst steadily pushing on, by acts stronger than words, and by words, hot and galling, when any pretext affords the opportunity, to the end proposed. He hastens others on, but is in no haste himself. He does not take positions himself until he has made them by others, and then points to them as things which *will* be. Surely and diligently he digs at the foundations of the Union, and prepares the dark mine for its overthrow.[38]

---

[34]*Congressional Globe,* 191–202.
[35]*Argus* (Albany), 4 Feb. 1842; *Globe* (Washington), 12 Feb. 1842; *Madisonian,* 28 Jan. 1842.
[36]*Congressional Globe,* 170; *National Intelligencer,* 15 Feb. 1842.
[37]*National Intelligencer,* 11–15 Feb. 1842.
[38]*Globe* (Washington), 12 Feb. 1842.

Henry A. Wise was also convinced of Adams's ultimate purpose:

The gentleman's doctrine was, "Not yet, not yet; wait a little longer; keep up the excitement; agitate—agitate; keep the slaves in this District, like mice in a receiver, to make experiments with; make a further experiment with religious zeal; try how foreign influence will work; hold on to the bone of contention; agitate." This was the gentleman's policy. His cry was "not now," and that was the worst feature in the proceeding.[39]

Adams believed that discussing the possibility of a peaceful dissolution of the Union could serve a constructive purpose. "There were questions pending before different portions of the country that ought to be agitated and discussed fully," he told the House near the close of the debate.[40] Had his accusers read his diary, they would have found more ammunition, dating as early as 1820 when, after a conversation with John C. Calhoun, Adams wrote:

A dissolution of the Union for the cause of slavery would be followed by a servile war in the slave-holding states, combined with a war between the two severed portions of the Union. It seems to me that its result must be the extirpation of slavery from this whole continent; and, calamitous and desolating as this course of events in its progress must be, so glorious would be its final issue, that, as God shall judge me, I dare not say that it is not to be desired.[41]

He kept these sentiments to himself until, in 1836, he shocked the South by suggesting, on the floor of the House, that the door to emancipation could be opened under the war powers of the federal government should civil war break out between the sections.[42] And, in his oration given on the fiftieth anniversary of the Constitution, he told the members of the New-York Historical Society that:

If the day should ever come (may Heaven avert it!) when the affections of the people of these states shall be alienated from each other . . . the bands of political association will not long hold together parties no longer attracted by the magnetism of conciliated interests and kindly sympathies; and far better will it be for the people of the disunited states to part in friendship from each other, than to be held together by restraint.[43]

What helped to blunt the attack of the anti-Adams coalition was the argument of Adams and the southern Whigs that, if indeed his support of the Union was qualified, it was no different from that of many of those who urged his censure. Adams pointed out that Representative Robert Barnwell Rhett of South Carolina was known to have kept in his desk drawer a resolution calling for the appointment of a select committee to investigate the

---

[39]*Congressional Globe*, 175.
[40]*National Intelligencer*, 12 Feb. 1842.
[41]Adams, *Memoirs*, V, (29 Nov. 1820) 205–11.
[42]U.S. Congress, House, *Register of Debates*, XII, pt. 4, 4036–49 (25 May 1836).
[43]*National Intelligencer*, 12 Feb. 1842.

63

possibilities of peaceful dissolution.[44] Even more devastating was the public exchange of letters among John M. Botts, Henry A. Wise, and President Tyler's Secretary of the Navy, Abel P. Upshur (a close friend of Gilmer and Wise), in which Botts sought to prove, with some success, that Upshur's support of the Union was conditioned upon the continued repression of the abolitionist movement in the North. The Botts-Upshur-Wise correspondence was reported in newspapers all over the nation. The revelation and underscoring of an apparent double standard of fidelity to the Union did the anti-Adams coalition no good. In summary, the censure motion had the paradoxical effect of strengthening the national Whig party against Tylerite attempts to disrupt it and, at the same time, provoking the frankest discussion of dissolution yet heard in Congress.

64

Bemis, and to a certain extent John Quincy Adams himself, claimed that a rising tide of northern journalistic opinion caused Congress to retreat from censure.[45] This is unlikely for two reasons: first, the time lag in this pre-telegraph era prevented public opinion from crystallizing until after the affair was terminated, and second, as has already been shown, the major shift of opinion in the House occurred among Southern Whigs who were unlikely to be influenced by the northern press. Whatever shift occured among northern congressmen occurred among Democrats, and that, as the table shows, was slightly *away* from Adams, and in favor of continuing the debate. A sampling of reaction, as seen through the press, confirms the dual nature of the event described above: a division along party, not sectional lines, coupled with a heightened frankness concerning dissolution of the Union, especially in the North.

Adams's own city of Boston offers the best case for the partisan interpretation of the attempted censure, where the *Morning Post* and the *Bay State Democrat*, both Jacksonian papers, favored it. The *Post* referred to his "disappointed ambition" and "traitorous revenge," while the *Democrat* repeated, in editorial form, the arguments used by Wise and Gilmer in their attacks upon Adams, the national Whigs, and the unlimited right of petition.[46] In Ohio, the Jacksonian-dominated state legislature condemned Adams by a strictly partisan vote.[47] In New York, the powerful Albany *Argus,* the voice of William L. Marcy and Martin Van Buren (whose son John, as a New York representative, repeatedly voted to continue the censure debates), denounced Adams's "reckless criminality" and blamed him for a decline in the prestige of the House of Representatives.[48] The New York *Post*, edited by the anti-slavery Democrat, William Cullen Bryant, was

---

[44]*Congressional Globe*, 182, 193.

[45]Bemis, *Adams and the Union*, 436; *Congressional Globe*, 208.

[46]*Bay State Democrat* (Boston), 1,2, 4 Feb. 1842; *Morning Post* (Boston) 28 Jan., 2 Feb. 1842.

[47]*Daily Advertiser* (Rochester, N.Y.), 15 Feb. 1842; *Enquirer*, 8 Feb. 1842. The censure was later expunged.

[48]*Argus*, 2 Feb. 1842.

predictably more restrained, deploring the whole affair, and contenting itself with the somewhat inaccurate claim that the business was the fault of the Whigs, and that the Democrats had nothing to do with it.[49] But it was the Washington *Globe*, edited by the redoubtable Francis Preston Blair, that set the tone for most of the Democratic press, North and South. It had laid the groundwork through its attack upon Adams during the previous two months, primarily in relation to his chairmanship of the Foreign Affairs Committee. In reporting the presentation of the Haverhill petition, the *Globe* omitted reporting Adams's opposition to it, however qualified.[50] Since most Democratic papers copied the *Globe's* account of all congressional proceedings, the overwhelming majority of Democratic readers in the country probably believed that John Quincy Adams had advocated the immediate peaceful dissolution of the Union. The *Globe* stopped short of supporting Adams's censure, and concentrated on Adams's alleged relationship with the abolitionists, the anti-slavery petition campaign, and the British. The *Globe* was careful to deny Democratic responsibility for the incident, pointing out that the debates had consistently been between Whigs.[51]

65

The Whig press reflected the division in the party between the Tylerites and the national Whigs. The leading paper, the *National Intelligencer*, aspired to do for the Whigs what the *Globe* did for the Democrats, but without success. When Adams presented the Haverhill petition, the *Intelligencer* recorded the fact in its daily report of Congressional proceedings (including Adams's opposition to the substance of the petition), but a week went by before it made editorial comment. Even then, the *Intelligencer* merely announced that it would make no comment.[52] Shortly thereafter, a quarrel broke out between Adams and the editors of the *Intelligencer* over their coverage of the debates, particularly of Adams's speeches. On the morning of the final vote to table the censure motion, the *Intelligencer* loftily announced that it would no longer report any of Adams's speeches unless he furnished a copy. Finally taking a stand, it upheld the right of petition, opposed the censure, and criticized Adams's judgement.[53]

With no "party line" emanating from Washington, Whig papers around the nation were on their own, and tended to reflect factional interests within the party. The conservative *Journal of Commerce*, published in New York, described Adams's conduct as "opposed to the public good, anti-patriotic, and in every point of view reprehensible."[54] The Alexandria, Virginia *Gazette*,

[49]*Evening Post*, 29 Jan., 7, 9 Feb. 1842.
[50]Quoted in *Globe* (Washington), 2, 10 Feb. 1842. Compare with *Congressional Globe*, 168.
[51]*Ibid.*, 27 Jan., 2 Feb. 1842. The Washington *Globe* also avoided printing the final roll call on tabling, since that would have shown all but 10 Democrats in favor of continuing the affair. Instead, it printed the roll call on the acceptance of the Haverhill petition itself, which showed all but two Democrats rejecting it. *Ibid.*, 7 Dec. 1842.
[52]*National Intelligencer*, 25, 27, 31 Jan. 1842.
[53]*Ibid.*, 7 Feb. 1842.
[54]Quoted in *Globe* (Washington), 2, 10 Feb. 1842.

a Tylerite journal, wrote of Adams: "He adds the passion of a fanatic to the obstinancy of a mule."[55] But further South, the congressional correspondent of the Richmond *Whig* praised Adams's "thrilling narrative and touching eloquence" in defending himself. The *Whig,* while careful to disassociate itself from the Haverhill petitioners, attacked Adams's antagonists and supported "the right of American citizens to petition for a dissolution of the Union—when in their judgement it has become intolerable—when the evil exceeds the benefit; nor from our abhorrence of Abolition would we be driven to surrender a right which may at least prove an available mode of making known to Rulers, the sentiments of the people."[56] Still further South, the New Orleans *Daily Picayune* took a tolerant view of the affair, concentrating on the Botts-Upshur-Wise dispute, and asserting that Botts had prevailed over Upshur and Wise.[57]

66

Most northern Whig newspapers at first did their best to isolate the abstract issue of the right of petition from that of disunion, and from Adams's tactics in raising it. Horace Greeley's fledgling New York *Tribune* called the petition "ill-timed," and referred to anonymous men "who are in the daily practice of dishonoring the national character by their political Gladiatorship on the floors of Congress."[58] "Mr. Adams is right in the abstract . . ." said the Rochester *Daily Democrat* midway through the debate. "The *expediency or propriety*, however, of presenting such a petition at the present time may well be doubted, and we think no prudent man would have done so."[59] The Boston *Atlas* was also critical of Adams's "eccentricities."[60] With the passage of time, and as the motivations behind the attack upon Adams became more manifest, most northern Whig papers tended to make him a hero. The New York *American* led in attacking the designs of the Tylerites. Southern Whigs, said its correspondent, "have found themselves involved in a scheme artfully designed by their worst enemies to alienate them from their only friends, which could have as its result the re-established dominion of Locofocoism. . . ." Later, the same correspondent reported that southern Whigs were "delighted with [Adams's] recent movements, and are quite willing to let him go on to the extermination of the new united forces of Tylerism and Loco-Focoism. All are agreed that this is rapidly becoming a party question."[61]

Such being the case, the survival of John Quincy Adams became synonymous with the survival of the Whig party. Accordingly, most of the reservations expressed earlier were forgotten. The New York *Tribune* rejoiced in Adams's victory, describing him as a "pure and upright though not always

[55]Quoted in *ibid.*
[56]*Whig*, 28 Jan., 1, 8, 15 Feb. 1842.
[57]*Daily Picayune* (New Orleans), 17 Feb. 1842.
[58]*Tribune*, 31 Jan. 1842.
[59]*Daily Democrat*, 3 Feb. 1842.
[60]*Atlas*, 29 Jan. 1842.
[61]Quoted in *Daily Democrat*, 11 Feb. 1842.

discreet and politic Statesman."[62] The Rochester *Democrat* forgot its earlier qualms about Adams's "prudence," and quoted with approval the judgement of the *Albany Advertiser*: "Every day that he occupies the floor is a Sabbath day to liberty. Even the brow of hostility begins to relax its frown as he goes on triumphantly from day to day . . . Noble Patriot! Venerable Man!"[63] In Boston, the *Atlas* omitted further mention of Adams's "eccentricities" and concluded that "Mr. Adams is right in his course in regard to the reception of petitions. The whole North will eventually and thoroughly sustain him." And a correspondent added: "He will at last triumph. Civilization—Christianity—eternal truth—the constitution and Heaven are on his side."[64] With such formidable allies, some northern Whigs must have wondered why the final vote was so close.

Whether he had intended it or not, Adams forced his uneasy allies in the Whig party into a stronger defense of the right of petition than ever before. His victory on February 7, over the pro-censure alliance of Tylerites and Democrats, laid the groundwork for the ultimate rescinding of the gag rule some two years later.[65] He also brought about—perhaps unintentionally—a serious discussion in the North of disunion. Discussion of this subject, though heard frequently in New England during the era of the War of 1812, had come to be regarded as a virtual southern monopoly by 1842. The phrase "to calculate the value of the Union," first used by the English-born South Carolinian, Thomas Cooper, in the 1820's, had come to be associated exclusively with the proslavery cause.[66] Suddenly the monopoly was broken with the introduction of the Haverhill petition. "Mr. Adams' movement has caused much excitement," reported the ever-watchful John C. Calhoun. "It is the first open development of abolition towards disunion."[67] It was a remarkable coincidence that Adams's introduction of the Haverhill petition in Washington was followed almost immediately by the adoption of a disunionist resolution by William Lloyd Garrison's New England Anti-Slavery Society, meeting in Boston. There is no evidence whatsoever to suggest collusion. In reporting to Adams the resolutions of the convention, Edmund Quincy, a Garrisonian and the son of Adams's lifelong friend Josiah Quincy, added a few comments:

I am happy to say that these are but a portion of the signs of the times which show a deep change in the public mind in regard to our relation to Slavery . . . You hear men far enough from being technical Abolitionists seriously looking to India for our future supplies of cotton and curbing the

[62]*Tribune*, 10 Feb. 1842.
[63]Quoted in *Daily Democrat*, 11 Feb. 1842.
[64]*Atlas*, 31 Jan., 7 Feb. 1842.
[65]Clark, *John Quincy Adams*, 407; Bemis, *Adams and the Union*, 446–48.
[66]William W. Freehling, *Prelude to Civil War* (New York, 1966) 130; Charles S. Sydnor, *The Development of Southern Sectionalism* (Baton Rouge, 1948), 178, 189.
[67]Calhoun to James H. Hammond, 4 Feb. 1842, "Correspondence of John C. Calhoun" ed. by J. F. Jameson, *Annual Report of the American Historical Association, 1899* (2 vols., Washington, 1900), II, 504.

insolence of the Southern braggarts who would claim the monopoly of threatening the dissolution of the Union, but who tremble when the proposition is seriously made by men who can stand alone by themselves. Well did a witty friend of mine say that the Town's poor might as well talk of dissolving their Union with the Selectmen.[68]

At about the same time a Rochester, New York, correspondent asked Adams:

When a Union fails of the ends for which it was formed, why should not freemen be allowed to "right the wrong"? I agree with you in hoping that it is not too late to save our country, but if the present state of things continues much longer, the north to a man will spurn a union cemented by fetters and chains.[69]

68   Pro-censure southerners reacted vigorously against the notion of disunion, peaceful or otherwise, in spite of the insistence of Adams and the southern Whigs that it was they who had first "calculated the value of the Union."[70] Wise repeatedly asserted his loyalty to the Union, maintaining doggedly that there was not a disunionist in his district.[71] Marshall pronounced peaceful dissolution to be an impossibility, and lamented the apparent turnabout of the sections since the days of his uncle and Adams's father. "It is the detestation of the South to [sic] abolition that makes her a Unionist. And it is the love of the North for abolition that has brought her in favor of dissolution."[72]

As the debate unfolded, most of the northern Whig press became more militant, not only in their defense of Adams, but in their defense of the North's right to discuss seriously the whole matter of disunion. The New York *American* claimed that the South had raised the issue so many times that many in the North had concluded that the free states "would gain power, wealth, and importance by cutting loose from the weaker and dependent South. . . ." Resistance to disunion was therefore ebbing. "We now say to the South," it concluded, "Beware—you have taught us to calculate the value of the Union, *and we have calculated it*—push us not to the conclusion."[73] The more conservative New York *Courier and Enquirer* professed to see the Haverhill petition as a "cloud no bigger than a man's hand." Southern talk of disunion had always been bluster, it asserted confidently, but northern discussion was something else. "The North could live without the South. The South could not exist without the North."[74] The Boston *Courier* printed Abel P. Upshur's letter explaining his qualified support of the Union, and agreed with its reasoning:

[68]Edmund Quincy to Adams, 31 Jan. 1842, Adams Manuscript Trust, Microfilm Reel 520.
[69]Samuel D. Porter to Adams, 1 Feb. 1842, *ibid.*, Reel 521.
[70]*Congressional Globe*, 168.
[71]*Ibid.*, 174.
[72]*Ibid.*, 190.
[73]Quoted in *Daily Democrat*, 3 Feb. 1842.
[74]Quoted in *ibid.*, 4 Feb. 1842.

We would much sooner see the Union dissolved than submit it to the indignities that are almost daily cast upon the people of the northern states, and their representatives in Congress, by southern slave-holders and duellists. We should much prefer a dissolution of the Union to a continuance of the present degraded subjection and embarrassment endured by the free white laborers of the North, in order that the lazy, prodigal, domineering aristocracy of the South may grow rich by the labor of their negroes.[75]

At least one Democratic newspaper, which admitted it had not given much coverage to the Adams affair in hopes that it would blow over, conceded that "if the Northern people have got tired of the bond—if they wish no longer to rally around the flag of a common country—let them secede from the Union by a convocation of the people in the would-be seceding States. . . ."[76]

Evidence indicates that when the Tylerites chose to move against John Quincy Adams, they uncovered a seething sense of frustration, which had been building in the North since John Tyler's accession to the presidency, and of which both the Haverhill petition and the Garrison resolutions were symptoms. A gap had opened, at least temporarily, between the voting behavior of southern Whig congressmen, who overcame sectional considerations in order to unite with their northern brothers and suppress the censure, and the new militancy of most northern Whig newspapers. The historian is thus faced with the dilemma: Which is the more significant development? The Turner school would emphasize the heightened expressions of northern discontent with the Union, while more recent scholarship would concentrate on the assertion of Whig unity and the ultimate failure of the would-be censurers. No account of the event is complete without reference to both.

Although Adams complained privately of a lack of support among his Whig colleagues, most usually voted for him.[77] At the end, his standing with them rose, as did theirs with him. Friendly relations were also maintained with those southerners who had provided the crucial votes needed to table the censure motion.[78] Henry Clay, in temporary retirement that summer, even professed to see Adams, aged seventy-four, as a potential presidential candidate.[79] When he returned in triumph to face re-election in Massa-

69

---

[75]*Courier*, 4 Feb. 1842.

[76]*Daily Advertiser*, 12 Feb. 1842.

[77]Adams, *Memoirs*, XI, 73–79, 86.

[78]*Ibid.*, 99. The following month the House formally condemned anti-slavery Whig Joshua Giddings, of Ohio, for introducing resolutions pertaining to the case of the domestic slave transport ship *Creole*, whose cargo had mutinied and sailed to the British Bahamas. Significantly, the Tylerite-Jacksonian alliance was not in evidence, the censure motion being introduced by Botts of Virginia, who had vociferously opposed the censure of Adams. Giddings lacked Adams's prestige, the right of petition was not involved, and he was not permitted any real defense. Whig party unity was for the most part unimpaired, though a number of northern Whigs, including Adams, resisted the attempt. Giddings resigned his seat, went back to his district and was re-elected with an increased majority.

[79]Bemis, *Adams and the Union*, 442–43.

chusetts, for the first time in his life Adams ran openly as a Whig. His heart was with the party, he said, and the welfare of the country depended upon Whig unity.[80] He might have added that upon it had also rested the welfare of John Quincy Adams. Thus, not only did the censure attempt provide a successful test of the cohesiveness of the Whig party and the occasion for a marked rise in northern calculation of the value of the Union, it also led to a rare occurrence in American political history: an Adams openly embracing a political party. He remained identified with the Whigs until the end of his days.

70

[80]*Ibid.*, 445.

The "War of Words":
The Cass-Webster Debate of 1842–43

On 24 August 1842, John Quincy Adams called upon Secretary of State Daniel Webster to offer congratulations on the successful treaty negotiation with Lord Ashburton. During the course of their conversation Webster denounced the conduct of Lewis Cass, the U.S. minister to France. Cass, Webster said, had tried to make "political headway upon a popular gale" with his unauthorized protest of 13 February against the Quintuple Treaty.[1] The gale soon picked up momentum and turned into a storm. On 17 September, Cass requested permission to retire from his post, and on 3 October he composed a second protest. This time Cass's ire was directed against his own government.

The letter of 3 October was the opening round fired in what Cass later characterized as the "war of words" between himself and Webster over the joint-cruising convention established by Article VIII of the Treaty of Washington.[2] Webster responded to Cass on 14 November, Cass penned a counterresponse on 11 December, Webster made a further reply on 20 December, and the debate concluded with a fifty-two-page missive by Cass on 7 March 1843. The Cass-Webster controversy is contained in these five documents.

Historians have paid little attention to the Cass-Webster dispute and have totally overlooked its importance as a debate over basic American foreign policy. While this neglect may be due to the vagaries of scholarship, it also may be related to Cass's miserable handwriting. He began a letter to Webster dated 20 February 1842 with the comment that he would "not inflict upon" the secretary of state a communication in his own hand, perceiving "it would be too great a tax upon your forbearance."[3] Aware of

---

[1] Charles Francis Adams, ed., *Memoirs of John Quincy Adams,* 12 vols. (Philadelphia, 1874–77), 11:21.
[2] Lewis Cass to Daniel Webster, 7 March 1843, Dispatches from U.S. Ministers to France, RG 59, National Archives, Washington (hereafter cited as Dispatches from France).
[3] Cass to Webster, 20 February 1842, Dispatches from France.

Originally published in *Diplomatic History*, 5 (Spring, 1981). Reprinted by permission of Scholarly Resources, Inc.

the problems his nearly indecipherable scrawl created for others, Cass usually employed the services of an amanuensis while serving as minister to France from 1836 to 1842. On 11 December 1842, Cass apparently had little desire not to tax Webster's forbearance, for the letter of that date could be entered into a contest for the worst handwriting of the nineteenth century. The clerks at the Department of State who prepared the copy of that letter for publication in *Senate Documents* began by misdating it to 1843. Their text of the letter itself contains frequent and serious errors. For example, one sentence in *Senate Document* No. 223 has Cass stating: "I remark that England never urged the United States to enter into a conventional arrangement by which joint action of the two Countries in the suppression of the slave trade might be secured."[4] By misreading *then* for *never,* those who prepared the document for publication implied the opposite of what Cass had in fact written. Whether or not Cass's appalling handwriting explains the neglect, the Cass-Webster controversy has not been given the attention it merits. The purpose of this article is to fill a gap in historical scholarship by providing a concise account of the "war of words" and to assess its importance to the history of American foreign policy.

When the Whig party came to power for the first time in 1841, Cass, unlike most Democratic holdovers, was not removed from his post. By what turned out to be an irony of history, Cass seems to have retained his position because Secretary Webster used his influence with William Henry Harrison and John Tyler to keep him in Paris.[5] Both Cass and Webster were born and raised in New Hampshire, and they had been schoolmates at Phillips Exeter Academy in the 1790s. In an autobiographical fragment that Webster wrote in 1829, he mentioned that he had formed an enduring friendship with Cass in 1796–97. Cass had been friendly toward the younger Webster, and though their careers diverged after graduation from Exeter, they retained cordial feelings toward one another.[6]

While Webster opposed the War of 1812, cultivated friendships with Englishmen, and became a leading Whig politician in the postwar era, Cass moved in the opposite direction. During the War of 1812 he acquired a strong prejudice against the British. He fought against them in that conflict, rising from the rank of colonel to that of brigadier general. In 1813, shortly after the Battle of the Thames in which he participated with distinction, Cass was appointed governor of the Michigan Territory. He

---

[4]U.S., Congress, Senate, *Senate Documents,* 27th Cong., 3d sess., 1843, ser. 416, no. 223, p. 40.

[5]Cass to Webster, 5, 15 March 1841, Papers of Daniel Webster, Dartmouth College, Hanover, NH.

[6]Charles M. Wiltse and Harold D. Moser, eds., *The Papers of Daniel Webster, Correspondence, Volume 1, 1798–1894* (Hanover, NH, 1974), p. 9; and Frank B. Woodford, *Lewis Cass: The Last Jeffersonian* (New Brunswick, NJ, 1950), p. 16.

retained the governorship until 1831 when he entered Andrew Jackson's cabinet as secretary of war. In 1836 he left the cabinet to become U.S. minister to France. Lewis Cass, then, was a partisan Democrat and an Anglophobe. While in Paris, Cass also became something of a Francophile. He insisted on writing his notes to the Foreign Office in French until ordered to use English by Secretary of State John Forsyth.[7] Had it not been for the old school ties with Daniel Webster, it is likely that Lewis Cass would have been removed from his post in Paris in 1841.

The correspondence between Washington and Paris was uneventful until February 1842, when Cass sent Webster a copy of his unusual protest to French Foreign Minister François Guizot against the Quintuple Treaty. That agreement of 20 December 1841 between Austria, Britain, France, Prussia, and Russia allowed the cruisers of the signatories to visit and search the merchant vessels of one another that were suspected of being engaged in the slave trade. In addition to establishing a limited mutual right of search, the accord declared the commerce in slaves to be piracy.[8] Although delivered to Guizot, Cass's protest was aimed at Lord Aberdeen and England, for the British government had been the moving force behind the Quintuple Treaty. Aberdeen called it a "Holy Alliance . . . of mercy and peace."[9] Had the Quintuple Treaty been ratified and implemented, it would have gone a long way toward making the right of search to suppress the slave trade an accepted practice of international law. It would have established a kind of international naval police force armed with a right of search, with the United States isolated as the only important maritime nation outside the treaty system.

Ever suspicious of British intentions, Cass immediately adopted a jaundiced view of the Quintuple Treaty. In February 1842 he anonymously published *An Examination of the Question, Now in Discussion, Between the American and British Governments, Concerning the Right of Search, By an American*. The theme of Cass's pamphlet was that the true British motive in trying to establish a right of search to suppress the slave trade was anything but humanitarian. He began his analysis with an alleged quotation from the *Times* (London): "When we doubted, we took the trick," and he concluded that the real British objective in promoting the Quintuple Treaty was to establish maritime supremacy by driving legitimate American commerce from the seas.[10] After reading Cass's pamphlet,

73

---

[7]John Forsyth to Cass, 21 January 1840, Diplomatic Instructions of the Department of State, RG 59, no. 42, National Archives (hereafter cited as Diplomatic Instructions).

[8]For the Quintuple Treaty see Clive Parry, ed., *The Consolidated Treaty Series,* 165 vols. (New York, 1969–), 92:438–69.

[9]Aberdeen to Edward Everett, 20 December 1841. Enclosure in no. 4, Everett to Webster, 28 December 1841, Dispatches from Britain, RG 59, National Archives.

[10]Cass's pamphlet as reprinted in William T. Young, *Life of General Lewis Cass* (Detroit, 1852), pp. 136, 139.

Webster assessed it as ardent with "American feeling," but "as a piece of law logic, quite inconclusive."[11]

Cass moved beyond anonymity on 13 February. Acting on his own authority, he lodged a formal protest against the Quintuple Treaty with the French government. Cass depicted the agreement as a diabolical scheme of the British to make visit and search during peacetime part of the fabric of international law. He emphasized that the right to board merchant vessels belonged only to belligerents during time of war, and he asked Guizot to reconsider the implications of French adherence to the pact. The Quintuple Treaty, Cass stated, could lead to collisions between the two countries.[12]

Cass's note of 13 February was both vigorous and presumptuous. Without instructions he had embroiled himself and the United States in a European treaty negotiation. Cass even later proudly took credit for France's failure to ratify the Quintuple Treaty.[13] Speaking in Parliament, Lord Brougham lambasted Cass for intruding into matters "which in nowise concerned him." In addition to personifying hostility toward Britain, he continued, Cass had no more conception of the rudiments of international law "than of the languages that were spoken in the moon."[14] In a similar vein, U.S. Minister to Britain Edward Everett wrote that Cass had improperly interfered in European affairs.[15] Finally, Adams characterized Cass's impertinent protest as "a compound of Yankee cunning, of Italian perfidy, and of French légèrté, cemented by shameless profligacy, unparalleled in American diplomacy."[16]

On 15 February, Cass informed the secretary of state of what he had done. In justification Cass argued that there was no way to reconcile the American and British positions on the question of search. The "great principle" of American independence could not be compromised, and the United States should undertake "instant and extensive arrangements for offensive and defensive war." He also suggested that the Tyler administration should require Lord Ashburton to disavow any pretended right to search American vessels before entering into negotiations with him. "Your course," Cass melodramatically concluded, "is perfectly free to avow or to disavow my conduct."[17]

In fact, Tyler and Webster had little choice. Although Cass had acted in an unorthodox manner, the president shared his views about the danger

74

---

[11]Webster to Everett, 26 April 1842, as cited in George Ticknor Curtis, *Life of Daniel Webster,* 2 vols. (New York, 1870), 2:118.

[12]Cass to Guizot, 13 February 1842. Enclosure in no. 141, Cass to Webster, 15 February 1842, Dispatches from France.

[13]Woodford, *Lewis Cass,* p. 212.

[14]*Hansard's Parliamentary Debates,* 3d ser. (London, 1843), 68:605–6.

[15]Everett to Webster, 3 March 1842, Papers of Edward Everett, Massachusetts Historical Society, Boston (hereafter cited as Everett Papers).

[16]Adams, *Memoirs of John Quincy Adams,* 11:338.

[17]Cass to Webster, 15 February 1842, no. 141, Dispatches from France.

that the Quintuple Treaty posed to the traditional American doctrine of freedom of the seas. In his first annual message to Congress of 7 December 1841, Tyler had specifically denied that the mutual search treaties of other nations could in any way be construed so as to allow the detention of American vessels in African waters.[18] Moreover, one of the items on the agenda of the forthcoming Webster-Ashburton negotiations was the African slave trade, and Tyler felt that Cass's remonstrance gave the United States "more sea-room with Lord Ashburton."[19] On 5 April, the same day that Lord Ashburton arrived in Washington, Webster informed Cass that the president approved his letter of 13 February and warmly commended "the motives which animated you in presenting it."[20]

In May, Cass reported that the Quintuple Treaty would not be ratified by France, and he transmitted a note from Guizot stating that the French government had never contemplated the establishment of a new principle of international law that permitted the vessels of nonsignatories to be searched.[21] From the spring to the fall of 1842, however, most of the correspondence between Paris and Washington dealt with such matters as the establishment of lighthouses on the coast of France and the French system for administering justice.[22] On 9 August, Ashburton and Webster signed the Treaty of Washington, and eleven days later the U.S. Senate voted its approval by a vote of 39 to 9. Then on 29 August, Webster sent Cass a carefully worded letter explaining Article VIII of the Treaty of Washington.[23] Aware of Cass's strong feelings on the subject of visit and search because of previous correspondence,[24] Webster emphasized that the joint-cruising convention did not "place the police of the seas in the hands of a single Power." Although the United States had obligated itself to act concurrently with Britain to suppress the African slave trade, it had not entered into a mutual search agreement. Rather, each nation would maintain a separate and independent naval force on the coast of Africa, and the two distinct squadrons would cooperate with one another. Thus, the United States would contribute to ending "that great reproach of our times," while retaining its freedom to act as an independent maritime state.[25]

75

---

[18]James D. Richardson, ed., *A Compilation of the Messages and Papers of the Presidents, 1789–1897*, 10 vols. (Washington, 1896–99), 4:77–78.

[19]Tyler to Webster [n.d.], as cited in Curtis, *Life of Daniel Webster*, 2:183.

[20]Webster to Cass, 5 April 1842, no. 62, Diplomatic Instructions.

[21]Cass to Webster, 26 May 1842, no. 151; and Guizot to Cass, 26 May 1842. Enclosure in no. 153, Cass to Webster, 31 May 1842, Dispatches from France.

[22]For example see Cass to Webster, 29 May 1842, no. 152; and Cass to Webster, 5 September 1842, no. 159, Dispatches from France.

[23]Webster to Cass, 29 August 1842, no. 68, Diplomatic Instructions.

[24]Cass to Webster, 15 February 1842, no. 141, Dispatches from France; Cass to Webster, 12 March 1842, Aberdeen Papers, British Museum; and Webster to Cass, 25 April 1842, Papers of Lewis Cass, University of Michigan, Ann Arbor.

[25]Webster to Cass, 29 August 1842, no. 68, Diplomatic Instructions. For Article VIII of the Treaty of Washington see Hunter Miller, ed., *Treaties and Other International Acts of the United States of America*, 8 vols. (Washington, 1931–48), 4:369.

Cass's initial response to news of the Treaty of Washington came on 17 September. He stated that since that accord ended any prospect of immediate difficulties with Britain, the public interest no longer required his presence in Europe. Accordingly, he requested permission to "retire" as U.S. minister to France and said that he intended to leave Paris in early November.[26] Then on 3 October, before the requested permission had been granted, Cass sent off a letter of resignation. He could no longer remain at his post with honor or represent the United States advantageously, he wrote, because the Treaty of Washington had placed him "in a false position," the only escape from which was to return home without delay.[27] The Cass-Webster controversy had begun.

Before plunging into the "war of words," it needs to be pointed out that the debate was sometimes confusing. In March 1843, after reading what he called "the strange correspondence" between Cass and Webster, John Quincy Adams found his brain filled with "teeming fancies" as he tried to find a "way out of the thicket."[28] Cass was the primary source of Adams's perplexity.[29] Webster's letters were generally written in a cold, logical methodical, and precise manner, while those of Cass were heated, occasionally contradictory, unsystematic, and often ambiguously worded. They were very different men with different qualities of mind. This does not mean that Webster necessarily had more valid arguments than Cass, but it does mean that great care must be exercised in trying to interpret Cass's hazy prose.

In the letter of 5 October, Cass explained his resignation as a necessary response to the Treaty of Washington. His "reputation" and "official conduct" as embodied in the protest to Guizot were closely related to the search issue, he said, and the treaty had failed to deal adequately with that question.[30] Had Cass confined his comments to an explanation of his reasons for resigning, there might not have been a prolonged correspondence with Webster, but he went on to interpret the joint-cruising convention as a departure from George Washington's maxim of "avoiding combinations upon subjects not American." This violation of Washington's "Great Rule of Conduct" might have been justifiable, Cass continued, had the United States as a condition prior to the negotiations extracted from the British a renunciation of their offensive pretension to a right of visit and search. Obviously, the Tyler administration had not done so.[31]

[26]Cass to Webster, 17 September 1842, no. 160, Dispatches from France.
[27]Cass to Webster, 3 October 1842, no. 161, Dispatches from France. The letter granting Cass permission to terminate his mission was sent on 11 October. See Fletcher Webster to Cass, 11 October 1842, no. 70, Diplomatic Instructions.
[28]Adams, Memoirs of John Quincy Adams, 11:341–43.
[29]Ibid., 11:338.
[30]Cass to Webster, 3 October 1842, no. 161, Dispatches from France.
[31]Ibid.

In his response of 14 November, Webster reminded Cass that he was U.S. minister to France, not Britain.[32] Since the Treaty of Washington was literally none of Cass's business, it could not possibly have placed him in a "false position." More important, by misconstruing Article VIII in "the imposing form of a public dispatch" Cass had damaged the "public interests." Cass's protest to his own government might allow the British to put forth the very construction of the joint-cruising convention to which Cass objected. Webster then denied that Article VIII constituted a departure from the principles of George Washington. He reminded Cass that the U.S. Congress had taken the lead in declaring the slave trade unlawful in statutes enacted in 1794 and 1820.[33] The initiative for the joint-cruising arrangement, moreover, had come from President Tyler, not Lord Ashburton. Thus, "the abolition of the African Slave Trade is an American subject, as emphatically as it is a European subject," and even more so. Webster dismissed Cass's objection that the United States should have obtained a prior renunciation of the British claim of a right of search as counterproductive. Such a disclaimer only would have weakened the American position, which rested on the solid bedrock of international law. In a phrase that stung Cass, Webster characterized the overall contents of his letter of 8 October as "a tissue of mistakes."[34]

77

Cass landed at Boston on 6 December, and on 11 December he fired another round in the escalating controversy with Webster. He began his second contribution to the debate by denying that his letter of 8 October was a "protest or remonstrance." Rather, it was simply a reply to Webster's instruction of 29 August explaining the Treaty of Washington, which, Cass added, "left us in a worse position than it found us." In any event, diplomats had a responsibility to express their honest differences to their superiors. Cass could think of "no government, certainly none this side of Constantinople, which would not encourage rather than rebuke the free expression of the views of their representatives in Foreign countries." Since he had not written his dispatch for publication, he did not see how it could promote the interests of Britain or injure those of the United States. As far as Cass was concerned, his comments could be "buried in the Archives of the Department and thus forgotten and rendered harmless."[35] Cass then asserted that the Treaty of Washington was his business and denied that he had behaved improperly.

Cass also reasserted his belief that the Tyler administration had been ill advised in not making the abandonment of the British pretension of a

---

[32]Webster to Cass, 14 November 1842, no. 73, Diplomatic Instructions.
[33]The law of 1794 made the slave trade illegal and that of 1820 declared it to be piracy punishable by death. See U.S., *Statutes at Large,* 1:347–49; and U.S., *Statutes at Large,* 3:600–601.
[34]Webster to Cass, 14 November 1842, no. 73, Diplomatic Instructions.
[35]Cass to Webster, 11 December 1842, Dispatches from France.

right of search "a previous condition to any conventional arrangement" on the African slave trade. The silence of the treaty on the question of search allowed the British to subject American merchant vessels to "naval inquisition" all over the globe. Cass disagreed fundamentally with Webster about the importance of international law, which provided "but a feeble barrier" when it stood in the "way of power & ambition." Had he been in the Senate, Cass wrote, he would have voted for the Webster-Ashburton accord, but only after amending it to include a declaration denouncing the British claim to search American ships. By omitting that vital stipulation, the treaty had been "unfortunate for the Country."[36]

Cass then focused his attention on the "serious charge" that his letter of 8 October was a "tissue of mistakes." If he were incorrect in believing that Britain had taken the initiative in fashioning the joint-cruising convention, then the situation was even worse than he had imagined. Although he did not contest Webster's assertion that the United States had been the first nation to move against the international slave trade, Cass continued to argue that Article VIII constituted a violation of the precepts of the Founding Fathers. Specifically, the slave-trade provision was one of those " 'entangling alliances' " against which Thomas Jefferson had warned. The joint-cruising agreement, moreover, established a dangerous precedent. It would lead to similar "alliances with every maritime nation." Most ominously, it was based upon an elastic principle that allowed the United States to enter into binding commitments with other countries if the issues were humanitarian in nature. Such an approach to foreign policy would bring America to "ruinous consequences."[37] While ostensibly maintaining the position that he had set forth on 8 October, Cass had in fact shifted ground. Unable to counter Webster's factual statements, he had defined the isolationist tradition differently by using Jefferson instead of Washington as his frame of reference.

Webster made his second reply to Cass in a letter bearing the date 20 December. Cass, however, did not receive this document until sometime after 24 February 1843 when President Tyler submitted the entire correspondence to the U.S. Senate.[38] Although Cass had conferred with Secretary Webster in Washington in January, nothing had been said at that time about the document that ostensibly had been written on 20 December. When Cass eventually did receive a copy, he noticed that it had been posted at Washington on 23 February.[39] This sequence of events, and the contents of the letter of 20 December itself, suggest that the secretary of state was trying to get in the final word.

---

[36]Ibid.

[37]Ibid.

[38]In an undated note, probably written in February 1843, Tyler directed Webster to send his correspondence with Cass for publication to the Senate. "Let the whole blast be at once over," the president wrote. See Tyler to Webster [n.d.], Papers of Daniel Webster, New Hampshire Historical Society, Concord.

[39]Cass to Webster, 7 March 1843, Dispatches from France.

In the document dated 20 December, Webster informed Cass that he was closing their correspondence "with a few remarks." He went on to write a sixteen-page, point-by-point refutation of the arguments contained in Cass's fourteen-page letter of 11 December. Invoking the president's name, Webster stated that Tyler had considered Cass's unsolicited notes "quite irregular from the beginning." The president not only interpreted the letter of 3 October as a protest, but also as an "attack upon his administration." Like any American, Cass was free to express his views, and had he done so in the capacity of a private citizen, there would have been no problem. Instead, sitting in a hotel room in Paris, Cass had written in a "public dispatch" a history of a "very delicate part of a negotiation" conducted in Washington with which he had had "nothing to do" and about which he possessed "no authentic information." The manner of Cass's remonstrance, according to Webster, was inappropriate and unprecedented.[40]

After criticizing form Webster moved on to substance. He dwelt upon what he called Cass's acknowledged error in assuming that the British had initiated the joint-cruising proposal. Such mistakes underscored the speculative nature of Cass's analysis, which converted inferences into facts. Above all, Webster focused his rebuttal on the precondition argument, which he interpreted as Cass's major objection to the Treaty of Washington. Rather than seeking a British disclaimer of a right of search, the administration had preferred to act boldly and independently in asserting the American position as the president had done in his message to Congress of 7 December 1841. The United States, Webster continued, depended upon the correctness of its principles as confirmed by international law and upon "its own power" in upholding its maritime rights. The vague declaration proposed by Cass as an amendment to the treaty would have been no more "effectual than the Chinese method of defending towns by painting grotesque and hideous figures on their walls, to fright away assailing foes." Finally, had Cass's advice been adopted the British probably would have countered with a statement of their views, thus leaving the question of search where it had been before the negotiations with Ashburton had commenced.[41] In this final letter to Cass, Webster did not discuss his opponent's Jeffersonian interpretation of isolationism. He seemed more concerned with scoring debaters' points against the weakest parts of Cass's letters and with emphasizing the superior realism of the Tyler administration's approach to foreign policy.

Despite Webster's express desire to "close the correspondence,"[42] Cass got in the final words. He did so in a fifty-two-page, pamphlet-size letter dated 7 March, which, along with the previous correspondence, was

79

---

[40]Webster to Cass, 20 December 1842, Diplomatic Instructions.
[41]Ibid.
[42]Ibid.

published during March 1843 in the Washington *Globe* and the *National Intelligencer.* Cass began his extraordinary document by stating that he too had hoped that the "war of words" was over. Because of Webster's discourteous and undignified letter of 20 December, however, Cass had to write again in order to avoid "serious injury" to his reputation. He also informed the secretary of state that he did not want this final defense of his honor to be "buried in the Archives of the Department of State." His comments were directed to "that great tribunal of public opinion, which is to judge between us," and would be released to the newspapers.[43]

Much of what Cass wrote on 7 March was repetitious, but he also elaborated upon some of his previous objections and broadened the scope of his critique of the Treaty of Washington. He took Webster to task for what he had and had not done. On the one hand, since Webster's letter to Ashburton of 8 August 1842 on impressment had led "to nothing," it was useless and should not have been published along with the treaty. On the other hand, Cass faulted the secretary of state for secret diplomacy, for not publishing any notes, protocols, or records, thereby leaving the negotiations with Ashburton remarkably undocumented. Cass also ridiculed Webster's Chinese wall-painting analogy as "a reductio ad absurdum," and he repeatedly criticized the "tissue of mistakes" phrase as "undignified language" and as reflecting a false assumption of superiority on Webster's part.[44] As in his previous letters, however, Cass emphasized the right of search issue and the shortcomings of the joint-cruising convention.

The "fatal error" of the Treaty of Washington was the absence of a stipulation by which the British renounced the right of search. This "sin of omission" was Cass's "principal charge" against the treaty and explained his resignation. "I was not," he lamented, "sufficiently supported." Although the Tyler administration had given "paper approval" to his protest of 13 February to Guizot, it had in fact abandoned his ideas and undercut his diplomatic career by failing in the treaty to resist the British on the search issue. The error lay in negotiating an agreement on the slave trade, while at the same time permitting the British to maintain their claim of a right of search. This mistake, Cass predicted, would produce serious consequences, for the British in their unrelenting "march towards universal domination" could be counted on to persist in such self-serving pretensions. Wherever the English had "planted a foot, whether on Marsh, Moor or Mountain, under the polar circles, as under the tropics," they had almost never withdrawn it. Visit and search led directly to impressment and the subjection of American commerce to British control. Cass articulated a nineteenth-century version of the domino theory: "It is

[43]Cass to Webster, 7 March 1843, Dispatches from France.
[44]Ibid. For Webster's letter on impressment see James W. McIntyre, ed., *The Writings and Speeches of Daniel Webster,* 18 vols. (Boston and New York, 1903), 11:318–26.

the slave trade today, but it may be the sugar trade tomorrow and the cotton trade the day after." The remedy was not that weak barrier called international law, it was military power. As for himself, Cass would "meet the first exercise" of visitation upon an American vessel "by war."[45]

Finally, the joint-cruising convention was "an improvident arrangement" that departed from "the wholesome maxim of non-combination." The humanitarian obligation of the United States to suppress the slave trade could have been performed fully without a European entanglement. Instead of adhering to the wisdom of the Founding Fathers, however, the Tyler administration imprudently had abandoned in Article VIII an old principle "of our political faith."[46]

Webster did not respond to Cass's massive letter of 7 March, and the debate ended inconclusively with neither man convincing the other. In assessing the Cass-Webster controversy it should be recognized at the outset that it was in part political in nature. In 1841, as his biographer puts it, Cass became infected with "a virus commonly known as the presidential bug." He returned to the United States in late 1842 in order to promote his candidacy for the Democratic nomination for the presidency.[47] Webster had been infected with the same virus long before 1841, but his political prospects were virtually nonexistent in 1842–43. Tainted by his association with an unpopular president who had been disowned by the Whig party, Webster knew by the fall of 1842 that he had no chance for any elective office, even in his home state of Massachusetts. Webster's responses to Cass were more a matter of pride than of politics. Considering the Treaty of Washington to be his greatest achievement as secretary of state, Webster could not allow one of the strongest contemporary critiques of that agreement to go unanswered.[48]

More than pride and politics, however, was involved in the Cass-Webster dispute. As Cass stated, his differences with Webster were "quite as much" matters of feeling "as of reasoning."[49] On the emotional level Cass's views were colored by his virulent anti-British prejudice. On 7 March he wrote that one of the "offences" he was least likely to commit was to favor the "pretensions of England,"[50] and all of his letters were sprinkled with invidious comments about the British. Cass was a true Anglophobe. It would be an overstatement to call Webster an Anglophile, but he was less suspicious of British motives than Cass and thought that

81

---

[45]Cass to Webster, 7 March 1843, Dispatches from France.
[46]Ibid.
[47]Woodford, *Lewis Cass,* p. 215.
[48]Webster to Everett, 27 April 1843, Everett Papers. In 1846, with considerable pride, Webster favorably compared his negotiation with Ashburton to the labors of Castlereagh, Nesselrode, Metternich, and Talleyrand. See "Defence of the Treaty of Washington" in McIntyre, *Writings and Speeches,* 9:94.
[49]Cass to Webster, 7 March 1843, Dispatches from France.
[50]Ibid.

English and American statesmen could amicably compromise the out-standing issues between the two countries. By contrast Cass felt that Webster had conceded too much and had not been demanding enough in the negotiations with Ashburton. A basic underlying issue in the "war of words" was just how far the United States should go in trusting the British.

On a more rational level Cass and Webster articulated sharply divergent views about international law. While both were realists in the sense that they saw power as the ultimate arbiter in international relations, Webster held the law of nations in much higher regard than did Cass. The veteran of the War of 1812 expressed a very low opinion of the efficacy of international legal norms, while the opponent of that conflict looked upon them as solid barriers against incursions upon American maritime rights.

82   Cass and Webster also clashed over the question of whether the Treaty of Washington violated the traditional policy of isolationism. In terms of historical significance this was the most important aspect of the Cass-Webster debate. By the 1820s isolationism, which called for avoiding permanent alliances and keeping to a minimum involvement in the political affairs of Europe, had become a basic dogma of American foreign policy. The only subject open to serious discussion was the appli-cation of the principles of isolationism to particular situations. Such dis-cussions had occurred in 1825–26 over the proposal of President John Quincy Adams to send delegates to the Congress of American States in Panama and in 1849–52 over whether the United States should support the liberal revolutions that had broken out in Europe in 1848.[51] The Cass-Webster correspondence contains the only important debate over isola-tionism carried on between 1825 and mid-century.

Neither Cass nor Webster questioned the wisdom of the policy of isolationism, but they disagreed substantially over the question of whether the slave-trade provision of the Treaty of Washington violated that commonly accepted American heritage. Webster countered Cass's asser-tion that Article VIII constituted an entanglement in a European matter by stressing the limited nature of the commitments undertaken in the joint-cruising convention and by using historical evidence to demonstrate that the slave trade was a long-standing humanitarian concern of the United States. Unfortunately, he did not choose to respond to Cass's subsequent categorical assertions that the joint-squadron provision was an "entangling alliance" that would lead to further involvements and ultimately to disas-trous consequences. Still, Webster had written enough to provide some insights into the intellectual dynamics of antebellum American foreign policy.

While Webster's views seem to have been derived from George Washington's Farewell Address of 17 September 1796, Cass's seem to

---

[51]For an analysis of the debates of 1825–26 and 1849–52 see Richard W. Leopold, *The Growth of American Foreign Policy: A History* (New York, 1962), pp. 22–26.

have relied more on Thomas Jefferson's "entangling alliances with none" inaugural message of 4 March 1801. Washington's "Great Rule of Conduct" had allowed for "temporary alliances" for extraordinary situations, while Jefferson had been more categorical in advising against political connections with European states.[52] To put it another way, while Webster looked more toward the past, Cass looked more toward the future when American policymakers like William Henry Seward tended to accept a doctrinaire definition of isolationism and to ignore Washington's qualifying phrases.

The bitterness of the correspondence of 1842–43 led to a seven-year estrangement between Cass and Webster. Not until 1850, when they found themselves on the same side in the struggle to preserve the Union, did they resume their friendship. That common cause healed the breach between them, and in 1851 Webster directed Everett, who was in the process of editing *The Works of Daniel Webster*, to "by all means, spare Genl Cass" because "I do not wish that he should be held up to ridicule."[53] Webster died in 1852, but Cass lived until 1866 and served as secretary of state during the Buchanan administration. When British cruisers began seizing slavers flying the American flag in 1857, Cass proved that he had not changed his views. He threatened to abrogate the joint-cruising convention negotiated by Webster, and the British backed down. In 1858 they formally abandoned their pretension of a right to search American vessels during peacetime in order to suppress the slave trade.[54] Ironically, Cass found both the Treaty of Washington and that "feeble barrier" international law to be instrumental in persuading the British to discard their pretension of a right of search.

83

[52]Richardson, *Messages and Papers of the Presidents,* 1:213–24, 321–24.

[53]Webster to Everett, 22 September 1851, Everett Papers. See also Woodford, *Lewis Cass,* pp. 283–86. Everett's edition of Webster's *Works* was published in six volumes in Boston in 1851.

[54]See Hugh G. Soulsby, *The Right of Search and the Slave Trade in Anglo-American Relations, 1814–1862* (Baltimore, 1933), pp. 143–57.

Southern Senators and the Right of Instruction, 1789-1860

By CLEMENT EATON

IN THE DEVELOPMENT OF REPRESENTATIVE GOVERNMENT in the United States an important question arose whether federal senators were bound to obey instructions of state legislatures. This question was debated at length in the first Congress when Thomas Tudor Tucker of South Carolina proposed to incorporate the right of instruction in the first amendments of the Constitution. Four states, North Carolina, Pennsylvania, Massachusetts, and Vermont, had included in their original constitutions the right of the people to instruct their representatives.[1] Since federal senators were chosen by the legislatures they were regarded as peculiarly responsible to instruction from the legislatures. Indeed, in the nineteenth century the doctrine of mandatory instruction came to apply only to senators. Almost invariably the instructing resolutions read that senators were "instructed" and the representatives merely "requested" to vote in accordance with the will of the majority of the legislature.

During the debate on Tucker's proposal the Federalist senators clearly presented the evils that would flow from the practice of this doctrine. Thomas Hartley of Pennsylvania observed that the exercise of the right of instruction had been attended with bad consequences both in England and America. "When the passions of the people are excited," he warned, "instructions have been resorted to and obtained to answer party purposes; and although public opinion is generally respectable, yet at such moments it has been known to be often wrong; and happy is the

---

[1] F. N. Thorpe (ed.), *The Federal and State Constitutions* . . . (7 vols., Washington, 1909), III, 1892, V, 2802, 3084, VI, 3764.

Originally published in *The Journal of Southern History*, 18 (August, 1952). Copyright 1952 by the Southern Historical Association. Reprinted by permission of the Managing Editor.

Government composed of men of firmness and wisdom to discover and resist popular error."[2] Instructions, he maintained,
would embarrass representatives in consultation and in the compromise of differences and would substitute the rule of the partial
or local view for the broad view in considering proper legislation
for the country. James Madison, who had once violated instructions as a delegate of Virginia in the Continental Congress, also
opposed binding the representative by a constitutional amendment to vote according to instructions. Consequently, Tucker's
amendment was defeated by a vote of 41 to 10.

Nevertheless, the doctrine of the right of instruction was frequently used in states controlled by the early Republican party.
For six years, from 1789 to 1795, the Senate, in contrast to the
House of Representatives, sat behind closed doors, and not until
1802 did it permit a record of its debates to be published. Finally,
it was compelled to abandon this aristocratic policy as a result of
the protests of southern states. The instrument that opened the
doors of the Senate to the American public was the exercise of the
doctrine of instruction, for in 1789-1791 the southern states forced
the issue by instructing their senators to use "their utmost en-
deavors" to obtain free admission of the American people to the
Senate.[3] Perhaps the staunchest upholder of the right of instruction in the Senate was William Maclay of Pennsylvania, who expressed the Republican doctrine that senators, being servants of
the people, were responsible to the will of their states and therefore in voting should follow the instructions of their legislatures.[4]

The doctrine of instruction was elaborated by the legislature of
Virginia in 1812 during the course of a controversy with the
state's senators over instructions for them to vote against the re-
charter of the Bank of the United States. One of the Virginia senators, Richard Brent, refused to obey this order; the other, William Branch Giles, acquiesced although he denied the right of
mandatory legislative instruction. Thereupon, the legislature
adopted a set of resolutions written by Benjamin Watkins Leigh,

[2] *Annals of Congress*, 1 Cong., 1 Sess., 761 (August 15, 1789).

[3] Elizabeth G. McPherson, "The Southern States and the Reporting of the Senate
Debates, 1789-1802," in *Journal of Southern History* (Baton Rouge, 1935-   ), XII
(1946), 228-33.

[4] E. S. Maclay (ed.), *Journal of William Maclay, United States Senator from
Pennsylvania, 1789-1791* (New York, 1890), 193, 220, 399-400.

a young representative from Petersburg, which censured the conduct of both senators. This able document, after reviewing the history of the practice of instruction in England, asserted that it was the indubitable right of the legislature to instruct the state's senators in Congress on all points, either constitutional or political, and that the senators were bound to obey or resign.[5] Likewise, John Taylor of Caroline vigorously affirmed the right of instruction in the sixth section of his *An Inquiry into the Principles and Policy of the Government of the United States* (1814). In approving this work Jefferson wrote to Taylor that "it settles unanswerably the right of instructing representatives, and their duty to obey."[6]

87

During the decade of the 1830's a violent struggle arose between Whigs and the Jackson party over the question of the legislative instruction of senators. The exultantly victorious Jacksonians were disposed to use their power ruthlessly, without a sense of responsibility, and they found the doctrine of instruction a ready instrument at hand for their purposes. The conservative Whigs, on the other hand, were cast in the role of defender of minority rights and upholders of the federal Constitution, which they thought were threatened by the practice of instruction. The dramatic struggle which occurred over this issue provided the backdrop for a remarkable display of moral courage and independence of thought by certain southern senators, notably Willie P. Mangum, John Tyler, and Benjamin Watkins Leigh. It illustrated the fact that strong conservatives do at times advance the cause of liberalism.

The immediate occasion for the great debate over the right of senatorial instruction in the decade of the 1830's was the bitter controversy between the Jacksonians and the Whigs over the removal of the deposits from the Second Bank of the United States and over the expunging of the censure of the President by the Senate for this action. On February 10, 1834, the Whig majority in the Virginia legislature instructed the senators and requested

[5] "The Right of Instruction. Preamble and Resolutions," February 20, 1812, in Virginia General Assembly, *House Journal*, 1834-1835, Doc. No. 9, p. 6.
[6] P. L. Ford (ed.), *The Works of Thomas Jefferson* (12 vols., New York, 1904-1905), XI, 528. John Taylor argued in favor of instruction of representatives by districts. See John Taylor, *An Inquiry into the Principles and Policy of the Government of the United States,* ed. by Roy F. Nichols (New Haven, 1950), 364-70.

the representatives from the state to use their best exertions to obtain the restoration of the deposits.[7] John Tyler favored this policy and obeyed orders, but William Cabell Rives, an ardent administration supporter, resigned rather than violate his convictions.[8] Promptly his place was filled by the election of Benjamin Watkins Leigh, a strong opponent of Jackson.[9]

On March 28 the Senate by a vote of 26 to 20 passed Henry Clay's resolution of censure of Jackson for ordering the removal of the deposits. Shortly after the passage of this rebuke of the President, Senator Thomas Hart Benton announced that he would introduce a resolution to expunge the censure from the Senate journal. Furthermore, a bitter Jacksonian protagonist, Senator Isaac Hill of New Hampshire, on June 23 presented resolutions from his state legislature approving Jackson's course in the bank controversy, instructing the senators to vote for an expunging resolution, and requesting Senator Samuel Bell to resign since he misrepresented the opinions of a majority of his constituents.[10] It was a day when partisanship knew no bounds. Jackson's personality, his program, and his methods were as effective in polarizing men into Jackson haters and Jackson enthusiasts as were Franklin Roosevelt and the New Deal a hundred years later.

This violence of faction was demonstrated in North Carolina during the struggle to instruct the senators to vote for expunging. The chief Jackson foe in North Carolina was Senator Willie P.

[7] *Congressional Debates*, 23 Cong., 2 Sess., 2840 (February 27, 1834). The Virginia instructions were presented to the United States House of Representatives by William Fitzhugh Gordon.

[8] Draft of letter of resignation to the General Assembly, February 22, 1834, in William Cabell Rives Papers (Division of Manuscripts, Library of Congress). In a letter to John T. Brown, December 5, 1834, Rives wrote that he did not resign to make up an issue before the people and the legislature but because the resolutions had instructed him to vote, not for a specific law, but for "*abstract declarations of principles or opinions*" which were contrary to his convictions. *Ibid.*

[9] John W. Murdaugh, a member of the Virginia legislature, described Leigh's hostility to Jackson as follows: "I met Mr. Leigh & Jno. Robertson yesterday, they are unceremonious in the use of their terms when speaking of his Majesty." Murdaugh also reveals the practice in this period of the instruction of state legislators by their constituents. He wrote to John N. Tazewell to oppose all attempts "to instruct me & my colleague to vote approval of the Proclamation or condemnation of nullification — I'll be D———d if I'll do either." Murdaugh to Tazewell, January 16, 1833, in Littleton W. Tazewell Papers (Southern Collection, University of North Carolina Library).

[10] *Cong. Debates*, 23 Cong., 1 Sess., 1813 (March 28, 1834), 2061-62 (June 23, 1834).

Mangum, who until the emergence of the nullification and bank controversies had been a supporter of the President. On December 22, 1833, he wrote to Governor David L. Swain: "The only check to an absolute power as that in Russia is found in the Senate. The policy of the man in power is to destroy that body in public opinion. Every other branch of the Gov.t is unquestionably and almost unqualifiedly subservient to the will and passions of one man—or to speak more truly to the will and passions of a cabal that gives a decided direction to the Executive."[11] This "man worship" of Jackson infuriated the Whigs. James Whitaker of Franklin County, North Carolina, wrote to Mangum that there were many people in his county "who seem to think that Andrew Jackson can do no rong [sic]."[12] Much of Jackson's power, Mangum observed, was due to the belief that he was invincible. Judge William Gaston, one of the greatest of the North Carolina Whigs, wrote gloomily to Mangum deploring "our thralldom to corrupt and factious misrule," which he attributed to a combination of popular infatuation, the discipline of party, and the bribes of office.[13]

89

On November 28, 1834, Dr. John Potts threw a firebrand into the legislature by introducing resolutions asserting the right of instruction and instructing the senators to vote for expunging. In the rough and tumble of debate which followed, some Whigs maintained that the legislature did not possess the right of instruction but that this power belonged only to the people in their sovereign capacity, acting through a specially elected convention. Hugh McQueen of Chatham County introduced a resolution that the people "possess the right of instructing our Senators on questions of national policy connected with their own immediate interest and not upon questions of constitutional law."[14] Senators,

[11] Willie P. Mangum to David L. Swain, December 22, 1833, in Willie P. Mangum Papers (Division of Manuscripts, Library of Congress).

[12] James Whitaker to Mangum, June 13, 1834, ibid.

[13] William Gaston to Mangum, December 3, 1834, ibid. At this same period the Virginia Whigs were expressing similar sentiments. Hugh Mercer of Fredericksburg condemned "the glaring usurpations of the Federal Executive over laws & Constitutions" and declared that "this baneful spirit of party will soon or later dissolve the union unless put down." Hugh Mercer to Littleton W. Tazewell, January 20, 1834, in Tazewell Papers.

[14] North Carolina General Assembly, Senate and House Journals, 1834-1835, p. 83.

he held, should be allowed discretion in deciding on the constitutionality of bills before Congress.

The strongest speech made against the resolutions for instructing the senators to expunge was delivered on December 17 by William A. Graham. Graham was an outstanding leader of the North Carolina Whigs, later to be United States senator, Secretary of the Navy, and vice-presidential candidate of the Whig party. At no point in the speech did he challenge the right of instruction, but he argued against its expediency and justice. His main contentions were that the alarming exercise of executive power by Jackson threatened the independence of the Senate, that Congress had a constitutional right to censure the President, and that it would be futile to mutilate the journal of the Senate. He opposed the instruction of Senator Mangum, for it would make him violate his conscience in revoking his honest opinion as to the preservation of the Constitution.[15]

Notwithstanding, the resolutions to instruct Mangum (the other senator, Bedford Brown, was a Jacksonian and needed no instruction) passed the House of Commons December 11 and the Senate December 27. The vote in the House of Commons asserting the right of instruction was 99 to 28, but the resolution instructing Mangum was carried by the narrow margin of 69 to 57 votes.[16] Graham declared that the Jacksonian majority were first inspired to begin the move for instruction by their success in re-electing Bedford Brown over the Whig candidate, Governor David L. Swain, which gave them full confidence.[17] The Whig newspapers, the Raleigh *Register* and the Raleigh *Star*, printed speeches of Graham, John Branch, and Mr. Fleming of Burke County against the resolutions of instruction and protested against the man-worship of Jackson by the party representing King Numbers.[18] After the Whigs were defeated on the instruction issue they tried to discredit the instructions by maintaining that the state senators who voted for the resolutions came from

[15] Raleigh *Register and North Carolina Gazette,* January 27, 1835.

[16] North Carolina General Assembly, *Senate and House Journals,* 1834-1835, pp. 188, 189.

[17] William A. Graham to Mangum, December 8, 1834, in William A. Graham Papers (North Carolina Department of Archives and History).

[18] Raleigh *Register and North Carolina Gazette,* December 2, 16, 23, 1834, January 27, 1835.

counties containing a minority of the population of the state by the federal ratio. The Jacksonian *North-Carolina Standard,* on the other hand, maintained that this Whig calculation was insulting to the people of the state, for it placed white freemen in the same scale with Negroes.[19] It strongly supported the right of instruction and accused Mangum and the Whigs of being aristocrats.

Mangum now had to make a decision whether to obey, resign, or refuse to heed the instructions. In the Mangum correspondence in the Library of Congress there are numerous manuscript resolutions from various meetings in the state urging him to disregard the instructions. Michael Holt, the pioneer textile manufacturer, wrote, "I hope you will not be drove so easily."[20] Only one prominent man, Burton Craige of Rowan County, advised him to resign, on the ground that public opinion sanctioned the right of instruction and that it would be politically expedient to take such a course and seek to change the composition of the legislature in the summer election, which he predicted would result in his re-election.[21] Among his correspondents was John Chavis, a free Negro, who had taught Mangum in a white private school. Chavis bitterly opposed both expunging and the abolitionists.[22]

In two letters to William A. Graham, December 16 and 17, Mangum revealed the inner conflict of his mind over the dilemma presented by the instructions. He declared that were he to consult his pride or his desire to recover his wrecked popularity he would resign instantly. However, regarding the Senate as the only barrier to the virtually absolute power of the Executive, he believed that if he resigned he would give countenance to the perversion of the spirit of the Constitution. The doctrine of instruction, he pointed out, was being used to reduce office in the Senate to a mere tenancy at will and by mining and sapping to convert the Senate to a less stable branch of the legislature than the House of Representatives. If he yielded to the popular infatuation, he would be lacking in moral courage. Therefore, he announced that he had no intention to resign to the present legislature.[23]

---

[19] Raleigh *North-Carolina Standard,* January 9, 1835.
[20] Michael Holt to Mangum, December 13, 1834, in Mangum Papers.
[21] Burton Craige to Mangum, January 21, 1835, *ibid.*
[22] John Chavis to Mangum, April 4, 1836, February 1, 1837, *ibid.*
[23] Mangum to Graham, December 16, 17, 1834, in Graham Papers.

In addition to this high moral ground he gave a political reason for refusing to resign: "If I resign Jackson will be able to command the Senate in the *next* Congress—if I stand firmly the opposition will continue in the ascendancy in the *next* Congress."[24] He observed that Senators Gabriel Moore of Alabama and John Black of Mississippi would probably be placed in the same predicament in which he was and that his course would be decisive of their action. They had declared to him that it would be impossible for them to withstand the storm if he yielded. On March 3, 1835, in presenting the instructions of the North Carolina legislature to the Senate, he announced that he would disregard them. He maintained that the legislature had no right to require him to become the instrument of his own degradation.[25]

The Alabama resolutions instructing the senators to vote for expunging, presented by Senator William R. King on January 28, 1835, touched off an acrimonious debate in the Senate on the subject. A month previously Mangum had written: "Gov. [Senator] Moore of Ala. has this morning recd intelligence of the resolutions having passed the Ala. legislature by so large a majority that the firmness of his friends at home is much shaken; & he in turn is so deeply shaken in his purpose that I think his resignation at the close of this session exceedingly probable."[26] Mangum expressed the gloomy thought that if there should be a general yielding by the Whig senators, "the power of resistance in the Senate would be lost and it will settle practically the Constitution in the South." When Senator King, a Jacksonian, introduced the resolutions of his state in the Senate, and announced that he felt bound to obey them, his colleague, Gabriel Moore, refused to obey. Although Moore acknowledged the right of instruction by the legislature on all questions of policy and the obligation of the senator to obey, he declared that on subjects involving constitutional questions he felt himself not bound by instructions but "by higher and paramount obligations due to his conscience."[27] King yielded to Benton the honor of introducing the expunging resolution, which the latter did on February 18.[28] Calhoun, Clay,

[24] *Id.* to *id.*, December 17, 1834, *ibid.*
[25] *Cong. Debates*, 23 Cong., 2 Sess., 722 (March 3, 1835).
[26] Mangum to Graham, December 28, 1834, in Graham Papers.
[27] *Cong. Debates*, 23 Cong., 2 Sess., 256 (January 28, 1835).
[28] Thomas Hart Benton, *Thirty Years' View . . . from 1820 to 1850* (2 vols., New York, 1854), I, 524-50.

George Poindexter of Mississippi, Leigh, and Alexander Porter of Louisiana made bitter atacks on these resolutions which they regarded as stultifying the Senate.

In Virginia the storm center in the fight over instruction and expunging was Benjamin Watkins Leigh. The Virginia legislature was scheduled to choose a senator for the regular term of six years early in 1835, and Leigh was the candidate of the Whigs. The Democrats, under the lead of the veteran editor, Thomas Ritchie of the Richmond *Enquirer*, engaged in a feverish campaign to defeat Leigh and restore Rives by starting a movement in the counties to instruct their representatives in the legislature to defeat the aristocrat, Leigh.[29] Leigh won by the narrow margin of 85 to 81 votes in a joint ballot of both houses of the legislature. The administration Democrats claimed that Rives had been defeated by the flagrant violation of instructions. Some representatives, they charged, ignored the mandate of a majority of signatures of voters in the county by "swelling" the number of voters and then claiming that the list of signatures did not represent a majority.[30]

It is surprising that a man of Leigh's haughty personality could win high office in Virginia, for he was never popular, particularly in western Virginia.[31] Small in stature, "of striking manly beauty, with hair of silky, soft, chestnut brown, floating in curls," and gray eyes, he was distinctly a patrician in appearance. His voice was "soft, clear, flute-like . . . a murmuring music," and his mannerisms, according to Henry A. Wise, always excited sympathy for his infirmity, a short leg, for which he compensated by wearing a cork on the sole of his shoe.[32] Leigh was a man of commanding intellect, a very able lawyer, cultivated, and master of a style "equal to that of the Elizabethan age of English litera-

93

[29] State Senator Thomas P. Atkinson resigned December 26, 1834, because he could not conscientiously obey instructions of the people of Mecklenburg and Halifax counties to aid in the elevation to the United States Senate of Rives, "an avowed advocate of the Proclamation and Protest." Virginia General Assembly, *Senate Journal*, 1834-1835, p. 39. See also H. H. Simms, *The Rise of the Whigs in Virginia, 1824-1840* (Richmond, 1929), 94.

[30] Alex. Brown to Rives, January 9, 1835; Jno. L. Anderson to Rives, January 30, 1835; A. B. Davies to Rives, February 6, 1835, in Rives Papers.

[31] For a brief biographical account of Leigh, published two years after his death, see *Southern Literary Messenger* (Richmond, 1838-1864), XVII (1851), 123-27, 148-49.

[32] Henry A. Wise, *Seven Decades of the Union* (Philadelphia, 1876), 139-42.

ture."[33] In the Virginia constitutional convention of 1829-1830 he had been one of the leaders of the conservatives. Working for the selfish economic interests of the eastern slaveholders, he had opposed granting fair representation in the legislature to the West and the expansion of the suffrage. During the convention he had made a statement which caused him to be burned in effigy in the West and which plagued him in his later political career. He compared the farmers beyond the Blue Ridge to peasantry who occupied the same position in Virginia's economy as the slaves of the East, and he boldly asserted that those who depended on their daily labor for subsistence could never enter into political affairs.[34] Indeed, he looked with disdain upon the Jackson rabble, its electioneering methods, its elevation of mediocre men into office, and its disregard of constitutions.

The Democrats ardently wished to retire this exponent of aristocratic doctrines from his office as senator. Their victory in the spring elections of 1835 gave them control of the legislature. In the following February they used their recently acquired majority to force through the legislature resolutions instructing the senators, Tyler and Leigh, to vote for Benton's expunging measure. Declaring that it was the solemn duty of the legislature "to re-assert" the right of instruction, they passed the resolution declaratory of the principle of instruction by a vote of 114 to 14 in the House of Delegates.[35] Governor Littleton W. Tazewell, however, refused to forward the instructions to Virginia's senators on the ground that they were "a palpable violation of the Constitution."[36]

Both Tyler and Leigh were uncompromisingly opposed to carrying out the instructions of the legislature, which were really designed to vacate their offices and make way for the election of Jackson men. Most Whigs desired that the two senators should act in unity, but Tyler and Leigh chose different courses in responding to the legislative mandate. According to Leigh, Senator

[33] Quoted by Claude G. Bowers, *The Party Battles of the Jackson Period* (Boston, 1922), 321.

[34] Charles H. Ambler, *Sectionalism in Virginia from 1776 to 1861* (Chicago, 1910), Chap. V; Simms, *Rise of the Whigs in Virginia*, 38-39.

[35] Virginia General Assembly, *House Journal*, 1835-1836, p. 111.

[36] Rebecca S. Luttrell, "The Campaign to Expunge the Resolution of Censure, 1834-1842" (M.A. thesis, University of North Carolina). See also Charles H. Ambler, *Thomas Ritchie: A Study in Virginia Politics* (Richmond, 1913), 178.

William C. Preston of South Carolina, a native Virginian, jealous because of "a notion he has that there is some rivalry between us as to reputation for oratory," began an intrigue to persuade Tyler to resign and thus discredit Leigh, who had no intention of resigning.[37] In this crisis the Whig leaders gave him conflicting advice. John Hampden Pleasants, powerful editor of the Richmond *Whig*, urged him to resign for political expediency.[38] The Washington *Globe*, spokesman for Jackson, insinuated that a motive for Tyler's resignation was to offer "a small oblation in order to be candidate for Vice President."[39]

Tyler was so devoted to consistency of political conduct that at times he turned a virtue into a vice.[40] The fact that he had in 1811 introduced a motion to censure the Virginia senators for their cavalier attitude to legislative instructions had great weight with him on this occasion. On February 19, 1836, he sent his resignation to the legislature. His letter reaffirmed his belief in the right of legislative instruction. Since he could not obey the instruction to vote for expunging without in his opinion violating the Constitution, he felt obliged to offer his resignation. He declared that he would not resign for every difference of opinion between himself and the legislature but that he would not hold office for an hour against the settled wishes of his constituents. He observed, however, that the right of instruction might degenerate into an engine of faction, an instrument of the outs to get in office.[41] Tyler's resignation gave the Jackson men in the legislature the opportunity to return Rives to the Senate on March 3, 1836.

Seven months before the legislature had passed the resolutions of instruction, Leigh had anticipated the event and had determined neither to obey nor resign. "I will not be instructed out of my seat," he wrote Tyler. "I will not obey instructions which

95

[37] Leigh to Littleton W. Tazewell, February 18, 1836, in Tazewell Papers. Henry A. Wise offered another explanation for the refusal of Leigh to resign, namely that Leigh had earlier advised Mangum not to resign. Wise, *Seven Decades*, 140.

[38] Lyon G. Tyler, *The Letters and Times of the Tylers* (2 vols., Richmond, 1884-1885), I, 525-27.

[39] Washington *Globe*, March 1, 1836.

[40] Oliver P. Chitwood, *John Tyler, Champion of the Old South* (New York, 1939), Chap. X.

[41] Virginia General Assembly, *House Journal*, 1835-1836, pp. 171-75; and Doc. No. 49.

shall require me to vote for a gross violation of the Constitution."[42] After the instructions arrived, he wrote to Tazewell: "I have refrained from all correspondence with the members of our Assembly; because I was resolved that no man should be committed, in any way, to share my fate and sacrifice their [*sic*] political hopes by sustaining me."[43] The Richmond *Enquirer* taunted the political-minded Whigs for changing their opinions in regard to obeying instructions. The editor of the Richmond *Whig*, it observed, belonged to the Resigning School now; with an eye on the polls in April, he was eager for Leigh to resign.[44]

96

On March 2 Leigh wrote a letter to the legislature explaining his recalcitrant position on obeying instructions. He announced that although he adhered to the right of instruction as stated by the Virginia resolutions of 1812 of which he himself had been the author, he had stipulated in those resolutions that a senator was not bound to obey instructions which required him to violate the Constitution or commit an act of moral turpitude. He could not vote for the expunging resolution, for he regarded it as a clear violation of the Constitution. At the same time he believed that his duty forbade him to resign. The real motive, he observed, behind the instructions was to instruct him out of his seat in the Senate. If he yielded, he would aid in the establishment of a pernicious practice by which the tenure of the senatorial term of office would be changed from six years to tenure at the pleasure of the legislature. The doctrine which the Jacksonian party wished to impose, he declared, was that the senator "has no right to exercise his own judgment at all, or consult his own conscience; he is not in this case a moral agent."[45] The abuse of the right of instruction, he also pointed out, would give a President who was checked by senatorial opposition an incentive to intervene in state politics and by using the patronage to secure the removal of his opponents in the Senate.

Leigh realized that it would be expedient for him to resign since most Virginians believed in the right of instruction. Nevertheless, he felt that he must "signalize his resistance to uncon-

[42] Tyler, *Letters and Times of the Tylers*, I, 523.
[43] Leigh to Littleton W. Tazewell, February 18, 1836, in Tazewell Papers.
[44] Richmond *Enquirer*, March 3, 1836.
[45] Virginia General Assembly, *House Journal*, 1835-1836, pp. 186-94; and Doc. No. 50.

stitutional instructions" by remaining at his post in the Senate.[46] Thus he deliberately sacrificed his political career to maintain his principles inviolate. On April 4 he made a powerful speech in the Senate against the adoption of the expunging resolution and the surrender to party spirit. Three months later he resigned for personal reasons but reaffirmed his views on instruction. On December 31 the legislature condemned Leigh's letter of March 2 as "sophistical and unsatisfactory" and reasserted that it was the duty of a senator to obey instruction or resign.[47] After Leigh's defiance of popular opinion on this occasion, he never afterwards held political office except from 1839 to 1841 when he served as reporter of the Supreme Court of Appeals in Virginia.

The fate of the Whig senators in the South who opposed Jackson in the expunging controversy was far from happy. Senator Willie P. Mangum resigned his seat in November, 1836, after North Carolina had elected another Democratic legislature.[48] Alexander Porter, Whig senator from Louisiana, who had delivered a long speech against expunging, followed a somewhat similar course by resigning voluntarily in 1836 after a Democratic legislature had been elected.[49] The bitter, vituperative George Poindexter of Mississippi was defeated for re-election by Robert J. Walker. The legislature of Alabama tried to recall Gabriel Moore by passing resolutions requesting him to resign because of his opposition to Jackson policies, but he refused to do so, filling out his term until 1837.[50] The fight of the anti-Jackson senators against legislative instruction to expunge the censure of the President was a powerful force in the growth of the Whig party in the South.[51]

The use of the doctrine of legislative instruction was not con-

[46] Ibid., Doc. No. 50, pp. 8-9.

[47] Ibid., 256-57.

[48] For Mangum's career as a Whig leader, see Joseph G. deR. Hamilton, *Party Politics in North Carolina, 1835-1860* (Durham, 1916), 32-33, 41-42.

[49] Wendell H. Stephenson, *Alexander Porter, Whig Planter of Old Louisiana* (Baton Rouge, 1934), 97-100.

[50] *Niles' Weekly Register* (Baltimore, 1811-1849), XLVII (January 10, 1835), 317.

[51] Professor A. C. Cole in his study of *The Whig Party in the South* (Washington, 1913) devotes little attention to the significance of the expunging controversy in developing the Whig party in the South; for recent studies, see Paul Murray, *The Whig Party in Georgia, 1825-1853* (Chapel Hill, 1948), and Clement Eaton, *A History of the Old South* (New York, 1949), Chap. XIII.

fined to the southern states. Both New Jersey and Ohio instructed their senators to support Jacksonian policies, but Senators Samuel L. Southard and Thomas Ewing from those states proved "recreant" to the doctrine of obedience to instruction. The legislature of New York on January 26, 1835, ordered the senators from that state to vote for expunging the censure of Jackson in the manner indicated by the Virginia legislature, namely, "by causing black lines to be drawn around the resolution in the original manuscript journal, and these words plainly written across the face of the said resolution and entry: 'Expunged by order of the senate of the United States.' "[52] The Vermont legislature two years later instructed the senators and requested the representatives from the state to present antislavery resolutions to Congress and to work toward their fulfillment.[53]

The practice of instructions in the 1830's constituted a standing invitation to the President to intervene in state politics and purge his opponents, as was illustrated in the history of instruction in Tennessee. Senator Hugh Lawson White was conscientiously opposed to expunging although he was willing to vote to repeal or rescind the Senate vote of censure without mutilating the Senate journal. Accordingly, when a Jackson supporter, Joseph C. Guild, introduced a resolution to instruct the senators to vote to expunge, the friends of Judge White, regarding this resolution as an effort to expunge Judge White from his seat in the Senate, bitterly opposed it.[54] President Jackson urged his lieutenants in the state to promote meetings in the counties for the purpose of instructing the representatives to the legislature to vote for instructions to the senators to expunge. The "Old Hero" did not scruple to draft resolutions instructing the Tennessee senators to vote for expunging and to send them to Governor William Carroll to present to the legislature.[55] Thus he hoped to prevent the re-election

98

---

[52] J. M. Mathews and C. A. Berdahl, *Documents and Readings in American Government* (New York, 1930), 324.

[53] United States Congress, *Senate Journal*, 25 Cong., 2 Sess., 144.

[54] The Nashville *Republican*, February 25, 1836, declared that Jackson used his frank freely to influence the adoption of expunging resolutions. The Nashville *Union*, September 18, 30, and November 24, 1835, on the other hand, urged the legislature to pass the instructing resolutions. See also J. C. Guild, *Old Times in Tennessee* (Nashville, 1878), 145-54.

[55] Andrew Jackson to James K. Polk, August 13, 1835, in John Spencer Bassett (ed.), *Correspondence of Andrew Jackson* (6 vols., Washington, 1926-1935), V, 18.

of Senator White, who had become independent of executive dictation. But the legislature tabled the instructing resolutions and later re-elected White.[56]

The practice of instructions proved to be a double-edged sword. In January, 1838, the Whig majority in the Tennessee legislature, for example, tried to drive the old Jackson warhorse, Felix Grundy, from his seat in the Senate by instructing him to vote against the Sub-Treasury scheme of Van Buren.[57] Grundy turned the tables on his opponents, however, by obeying instructions and throwing the responsibility of his act upon the legislature.[58] In a delightful letter of irony, written February 6, 1838, he observed: "You, by your instructions, have taken upon yourselves the responsibility of the vote I am required to give, and I am relieved from it. The people will look to you as the principal and to me merely as the agent, in performing an act expressly required by those in whom I recognize the right to instruct."[59] During the next year the Democrats won control of the legislature and instructed the Whig senators, Hugh Lawson White and Ephraim H. Foster (Grundy had in the meantime resigned to become Attorney General of the United States), to vote for Van Buren's Sub-Treasury bill, in effect forcing them to resign. Foster resigned almost immediately after the passage of the instructing resolutions, and Grundy was re-elected to fill the vacancy. White, however, postponed his resignation until January 14, 1840, when the Sub-Treasury bill was introduced in the Senate. Thus, the doctrine of legislative instruction developed virtually into a form of recall of senators, anticipating the Progressive Movement for the recall in the early twentieth century.

The driving of such a venerable and eminent senator as Hugh Lawson White from his office by the instrument of instructions undoubtedly contributed toward discrediting its use in Tennessee. White was a republican of the old school, noted for his independence of mind and his incorruptible virtue. Although he sincerely believed in the right of the legislature to instruct and

99

[56] Joseph H. Parks, *John Bell of Tennessee* (Baton Rouge, 1950), 109-11.
[57] Tennessee General Assembly, *House Journal*, 1837-1838, pp. 402-403, 515-18; the resolution passed January 23 by a vote of 39 to 19.
[58] Joseph H. Parks, *Felix Grundy, Champion of Democracy* (University. La.. 1940), 309-17.
[59] *Niles' Register*, LIV (March 10, 1838), 20-21.

the obligation of a senator to obey or resign, he felt keenly that by the abuse of instructions he had been sacrificed on the altar of his principles. In the Senate he gave his "swan song" reaffirming his principles, and at a farewell dinner he bitterly condemned "that monster, party spirit," which had banished him from the service of his country because he would not recant his principles.[60] For thirty-eight years White had been in public service, and now his abrupt dismissal by the partisan use of instruction was shocking to many people in Tennessee who loved and respected him.

In the same year of White's instruction the Whig majority in
100 the North Carolina legislature passed some resolutions hostile to Van Buren's administration and condemning the expunging resolution of 1837. The Democratic senators of the state, Bedford Brown and Robert Strange, refused either to carry out the will of the legislature or to resign. They declared that they regarded resolutions of the legislature which did not explicitly instruct them as advisory only.[61] Senator Henry Clay, on the other hand, maintained that the North Carolina senators should carry out the intent of the legislature without quibbling over technical terms. As for his own position, he stated that he supported the doctrine of instruction "as it stood in 1798," namely that the representative should vote in matters of expediency but not on questions of constitutionality in accordance with the will of his constituents.[62]

The doctrine of the right of instruction was subjected to a devastating criticism by John Bell of Tennessee in a speech before the Senate, February 23, 1858. Bell had just received instructions from the Tennessee legislature disapproving of his vote against the Kansas-Nebraska bill four years before, virtually inviting him to resign, and instructing the Tennessee senators to vote for the admission of Kansas under the Lecompton Constitution. Bell re-

[60] The instructing resolutions were not presented by White until January 13, 1840; the resolutions and a brief summary of his farewell remarks are found in *Cong. Globe,* 26 Cong., 1 Sess., 116-17 (January 16, 1840); N. N. Scott (ed.), *A Memoir of Hugh Lawson White* (Philadelphia, 1856), 397; and L. P. Gresham, *The Public Career of Hugh Lawson White* (Nashville, 1945). See also Powell Moore, "James K. Polk: Tennessee Politician," in *Journal of Southern History,* XVII (1951), 502-503.

[61] *Cong. Globe,* 25 Cong., 3 Sess., 109-12 (January 14, 1839).

[62] Calvin Colton, *The Life, Correspondence, and Speeches of Henry Clay* (6 vols., New York, 1864), VI, 134-38.

fused to obey instructions and maintained that such a practice had long ago been discarded by the Whig party. He traced the origin of the practice of instruction to the period of the Confederation, when delegates to Congress were regarded as ambassadors. He declared that legislative instruction had no warrant in the Constitution and that it was resorted to chiefly as "an engine of party and to promote party ends." Senators, he argued, did not represent the legislatures but the people, and therefore they were no more responsible to the fluctuating opinions of factions in control of legislatures than was the President to the electoral college.[63]

The doctrine of the right of legislative instruction became obsolete after 1860. It had matured in a period of great political partisanship during which the two-party system was emerging. Although in theory the doctrine of instruction seemed to be a noble expression of representative government, in actual practice it was subject to dangerous abuses which thoroughly discredited it. Hezekiah Niles in 1834 pointed out that the frequent use of instruction would render the legislation of the country uncertain and would unsettle business and commerce.[64] Indeed, the partisan use of instruction in the 1830's caused thoughtful men to reflect upon the dangers of an unrestrained and irresponsible majority in a democracy. Later, Calhoun was to incorporate this distrust of a partisan majority in his theory of government. Moreover, the record of those Southerners who opposed tyrannical instructions forms a sober annotation to the history of freedom of thought in the Old South, a rubric written, not by liberals, but by conservatives who withstood the storm of unpopularity rather than sacrifice their political principles. The adoption of the Seventeenth Amendment in 1913 gave a final blow to the venerable doctrine of instructions which had been transplanted from England. Nevertheless, long before that date the development of the Solid South rendered the practice of instructions below the Potomac an act of supererogation. Like the duel and virtually at the same time, the practice of legislative instruction disappeared from the mores of the American people.

[63] *Cong. Globe*, 35 Cong., 1 Sess., 804-806 (February 23, 1858).
[64] *Niles' Register*, XLVII (November 15, 1834), 61.

101

MISSISSIPPI'S ANTEBELLUM CONGRESSMEN: A COLLECTIVE BIOGRAPHY

103

By Daniel P. Jordan*

From 1817 to 1861, fifty-two individuals represented Mississippi in the United States Congress. Thirty-two of these persons served only in the House, fifteen only in the Senate, and five in both. These men formed the crest of the state's public leadership in the antebellum period and included virtually every major politician from David Holmes to Jefferson Davis. The preeminence of the group invites systematic study, perhaps best conducted in the form of a collective biography. This technique identifies significant personal characteristics — such as education, religion, economic interests, and the like — and constructs a profile by categories. The resulting composite portrait provides a basis for assessing the process and personalities of Mississippi politics

*Dr. Jordan, a native Mississippian, is associate professor of history and acting chairman of the Department of History of Virginia Commonwealth University, Richmond, Virginia.

[1] For a complete list of Mississippi's antebellum congressmen and their respective terms, see Daniel P. Jordan, Jr., "A Statistical Analysis of Mississippi's Antebellum Congressmen" (Unpublished M.A. thesis, University of Mississippi, 1962), 35-37.

Originally published in *Journal of Mississippi History*, 38 (May, 1976). Reprinted by permission of the *Journal of Mississippi History*.

before the Civil War.[2]

Mississippi's antebellum congressmen were not of native stock.[3] Only three of the fifty-two individuals were born within the state or its old territorial limits.[4] In geographic origin, twenty-one came from the South Atlantic sector (Virginia to Georgia) and fourteen from Kentucky and Tennessee. The Middle Atlantic region (Maryland to New York) produced nine, and New England furnished three. One representative, William Henry Hammett, was reputed to have been from Ireland, thus being the only foreigner in the group. By states, Virginia and Tennessee each claimed nine, with the former having eight senators and the latter the same number of representatives.[5] North Carolina with seven and Kentucky with five were the only other states with over three sons in Mississippi's congressional ranks.

The vast majority of these men came as part of a human flood which poured into the Old Southwest in the early decades of the nineteenth century. They became associated with the state's boom period, during which

104

[2] For a discussion of the importance of the congressmen and of their various vital roles in antebellum Mississippi, see Jordan, "Statistical Analysis," iii-vi, 1-2, which also covers the methodology of collective biography. On the latter technique, one might also consult Robert P. Swierenga, ed., *Quantification in American History: Theory and Research* (New York, 1970), 345-347, with its extensive footnotes, and Lawrence Stone, "Prosopography," *Daedalus*, 100 (Winter, 1971), 46-79 — also available in Felix Gilbert and Stephen R. Graubard, eds., *Historical Studies Today* (New York, 1972), 107-140. Useful for methodology and for providing a basis for comparing the congressional profile with that of other southern political elites are Thomas B. Alexander and Richard E. Beringer, *The Anatomy of the Confederate Congress: A Study of the Influences of Member Characteristics on Legislative Voting Behavior, 1861-1865* (Nashville, 1972); Richard E. Beringer, "A Profile of the Members of the Confederate Congress," *Journal of Southern History*, XXXIII (November, 1967), 518-541; and Ralph A. Wooster, *The People in Power: Courthouse and Statehouse in the Lower South, 1850-1860* (Knoxville, 1969).

[3] Pertinent tabulations are given in Jordan, "Statistical Analysis," 38-41.

[4] Mississippi's native congressmen were William T. S. Barry, J. F. H. Claiborne, and Wiley P. Harris, all of whom served in the House of Representatives.

[5] The Old Dominion's striking contribution to the leadership of other states in this period is detailed in Richard Beale Davis, "The Jeffersonian Virginia Expatriate in the Building of the Nation," *Virginia Magazine of History and Biography*, LXX (January, 1962), 49-61.

her total population increased from 75,448 in 1820 to 606,526 just thirty years later.[6] Of the fifty-two men under consideration, three were natives and four came as children with their parents. Thus, forty-five journeyed to Mississippi by design, and of this group, the average age on arrival was twenty-seven. Of these individuals, twenty-four established permanent residence, five left temporarily then returned, and the other sixteen eventually moved to new locations. Seventeen of the forty-five who came as adults had lived in two or more states prior to their appearance in Mississippi, and those who departed were to average 1.52 other state residences after leaving.[7]

105

Mississippi's antebellum congressmen were drawn to the Old Southwest by the desire for a rapidly improved position in life. During her early decades of statehood, Mississippi epitomized such an opportunity. Society was in constant flux, and the prospects for quick riches were particularly inviting. Like California, Alaska, and other boom frontiers to follow, Mississippi enjoyed a period of "flush times." With a distinctive blend, millions of acres changed hands, speculation ran amuck, plantations and towns alike appeared overnight, and fortunes were acquired and lost with equal speed. To the enterprising youth of older sections, the state appeared to be "a new El Dorado," as one contemporary citizen aptly labeled it.[8] And, because Mississippi was a

---

[6] U. S., Bureau of the Census, *Historical Statistics of the United States, Colonial Times to 1957* (Washington, 1960), 13. See also Thomas Perkins Abernethy, "The Great Migration," chapter XVI in his *The South in the New Nation, 1789-1819* (Baton Rouge, 1961), and Charles D. Lowery, "The Great Migration to the Mississippi Territory, 1798-1819," *Journal of Mississippi History*, XXX (August, 1968), 173-192.

[7] Jordan, "Statistical Analysis," 43-45.

[8] Quoted in Edwin A. Miles, *Jacksonian Democracy in Mississippi* (Chapel Hill, 1960), 119. A relevent, colorful, contemporary account is Joseph Glover Baldwin's *The Flush Times of Alabama and Mississippi* (New York, 1853).

democratic pace-setter in the Old South, her opportunities were political as well as economic.[9]

The recorded comments of her future senators and representatives explain Mississippi's appeal to many young Americans. John Anthony Quitman, a dynamic force in the state for almost half a century, questioned the value of living in his native New York when he said, "It is folly to remain in these parts when there are such wide fields open South and West, where much can be done with little money."[10] Quitman's search for "fame and fortune" soon ended in the deep South where he discovered that "money is there more plenty; trade is brisk . . . . The bar is not overcrowded with well-read lawyers and fees are high." [11] Shortly after his arrival in Natchez, Seargent S. Prentiss assured his parents in Maine ". . . should I settle in this State, I have no doubt I could make a fortune with the greatest of ease."[12] Forsaking eight years as a congressman from North Carolina, Jesse Speight joined the westward movement ". . . prompted by a desire to provide for his own household, and invited by the prolific soil, the general climate, and rich productions of Mississippi."[13]

Three future occupants of presidential cabinet positions — L. Q. C. Lamar, Jacob Thompson, and Robert J. Walker — were lured by family connections and glowing accounts of the opportunities for youthful

106

[9] Charles S. Sydnor, *The Development of Southern Sectionalism, 1819-1848* (Baton Rouge, 1948), 283-284; and Wooster, *People in Power*, 20-23, 107.

[10] John A. Quitman to his brother, March 21, 1819, in J. F. H. Claiborne, *Life and Correspondence of John A. Quitman* (2 vols., New York, 1860), I, 32. See also Troy B. Watkins, "John A. Quitman: Governor of Mississippi" (Unpublished M.A. thesis, University of Mississippi, 1948), 5.

[11] John A. Quitman to F. R. Backus, February 28, 1821, in Claiborne, *Quitman*, 59.

[12] Seargent S. Prentiss to his mother, November 18, 1828, in George Lewis Prentiss, ed., *A Memoir of S. S. Prentiss* (2 vols., New York, 1856), II, 92.

[13] *Congressional Globe*, Thirtieth Congress, First Session, 40.

members of the legal profession.[14] Powhatan Ellis came
with letters of introduction from General Andrew Jackson; federal appointments from President Thomas
Jefferson were responsible for the Mississippi territorial residences of David Holmes, the state's first governor, and Walter Leake and Thomas Hill Williams, who
subsequently became the state's first two senators.[15]
Franklin Plummer came to evade the hard times which
followed the Panic of 1819 in Massachusetts;[16] mercurial
Henry Stuart Foote arrived to escape the consequences
of an anti-dueling violation which had disbarred him
in Alabama;[17] and George Poindexter was reputedly
motivated to travel by a desire to avoid creditors in
his native Virginia.[18] Mississippi thus offered, if not a
guaranteed remedy for a person's ills, at least a more
salubrious atmosphere in which he might recover.

Many of the individuals who represented Mississippi in Congress started life within the state in an
humble fashion. The road to political success often began

107

[14] Wirt A. Cate, *Lucius Q. C. Lamar* (Chapel Hill, 1935), 32; Dorothy Z. Oldham,
"Life of Jacob Thompson" (Unpublished M. A. thesis, University of Mississippi,
1930), 15-21; Susie V. Powell, comp., *Source Material for Mississippi History:
Pontotoc County*, Works Progress Administration Historical Research Project,
Vol. 58, Part 3 (1936-1938), 197; and James P. Shenton, *Robert John Walker: A
Politician from Jackson to Lincoln* (New York, 1961), 10.

[15] Edwin L. Cobb, "Powhatan Ellis of Mississippi: A Reappraisal," *Journal of
Mississippi History*, XXX (May, 1968), 94; Frances Elizabeth Melton, "The Public
Career of David Holmes" (Unpublished M.A. thesis, Emory University, 1966), 13,
which notes that the appointment came from Jefferson, not Madison, as often
thought; Howard P. Hildreth, "David Holmes," *Virginia Cavalcade*, XVI (Spring,
1967), 38-39; Claude E. Fike, "The Administration of Walter Leake (1822-1825),"
Journal of Mississippi History, XXXII (May, 1970), 103; and Sidney H. Aronson,
Status and Kinship in the Higher Civil Service (Cambridge, Mass., 1964), 209-210.

[16] Edwin A. Miles, "Franklin E. Plummer: Piney Woods Spokesman of the
Jackson Era," *Journal of Mississippi History*, XIV (January, 1952), 2.

[17] John Edmond Gonzales, "The Public Career of Henry Stuart Foote, 1804-
1880" (Unpublished Ph.D. dissertation, University of North Carolina, 1957), 4-5.

[18] J. F. H. Claiborne, *Mississippi, as a Province, Territory, and State with
Biographical Notices of Eminent Citizens* (Jackson, 1880), 363n. For a contention
that this theory is unsubstantiated, see Mack Swearingen, *The Early Life of George
Poindexter: A Story of the First Southwest* (New Orleans, 1934), 23.

with a struggle against indigence. Quitman's plight was revealed in his first letter from Natchez: "I arrived here last night. I have $15 in my pocket, and the cheapest respectable board and lodging is $45 per month."[19] Displaying a supreme confidence characteristic of Mississippi's "flush times," Seargent S. Prentiss reached Natchez with only five dollars, which he quickly exchanged for a bottle of wine and a box of cigars.[20] According to tradition, Thomas Buck Reed arrived by river boat, and due to his penurious status, had difficulty getting his baggage transported from the landing.[21] The initial advantage enjoyed by Franklin Plummer was no more than a small parcel of clothing and five dollars cash.[22]

To avert poverty in the years before financial success was assured, the future congressmen often followed a temporary vocation. College-trained Walker Brooke, Christopher Rankin, and Seargent Prentiss found a convenient source of income in teaching, as did the Massachusetts pair, John Black and Franklin Plummer. L. Q. C. Lamar applied for a tutor's position at the University of Mississippi "to provide myself with ready money until I get a [lawyer's] practice."[23] A mechanic's skill aided Robert Huntington Adams, who was "without one advantage save his talents,"[24] while Foote and John Jones McRae were newspapermen prior to attaining repute as attorneys.

Difficult economic circumstances in the early years

[19] John A. Quitman to his brother, December 4, 1821, in Claiborne, *Quitman*, I, 70.

[20] Dallas C. Dickey, *Seargent S. Prentiss, Whig Orator of the Old South* (Baton Rouge, 1945), 29.

[21] Thomas Buck Reed Folder, Subject File, Mississippi Department of Archives and History, Jackson.

[22] Franklin E. Plummer Folder, Subject File, Mississippi Department of Archives and History, Jackson.

[23] Quoted in Cate, *Lamar*, 32.

[24] William H. Sparks, *The Memories of Fifty Years* (Philadelphia, 1872), 344.

were often only a prelude to wealth. Rags-to-riches stories are legion. Reuben Davis recalled how he had left Alabama "with three dollars in my pocket and no immediate prospect of adding to my store,"[25] and how that "at the end of four years, I had put by a surplus of twenty thousand dollars."[26] Adams and Reed rose quickly to positions of distinction in the Mississippi bar. Robert John Walker, who came to Natchez in 1826 with "no fixed income," [27] and Henry S. Foote, who arrived similarly twelve months later, both converted vast land speculations into immense wealth within five years. Jacob Thompson saw his limited property and four slaves in 1842 develop into 2,400 acres and eighty-three Negroes within a decade.[28]

109

Fulfilling his earlier economic prophecy in ten years, Seargent Prentiss acquired real estate valued up to $400,000,[29] and George Poindexter, who was "without resources other than ambition and intelligence" when he settled in Natchez, owned 400 acres within three years and thirty-two slaves after five.[30] William M. Gwin promptly became a land speculator on a grand scale, and John A. Quitman accumulated vast property holdings.[31] Again reflecting the vigorous currents of upheaval which pervaded antebellum Mississippi, fortunes were

[25] Reuben Davis, *Recollections of Mississippi and Mississippians* (Boston, 1889), 47.

[26] *Ibid.*, 57.

[27] Shenton, *Walker*, 14.

[28] Percy Lee Rainwater, ed., "Letters to and from Jacob Thompson," *Journal of Southern History*, VI (February, 1940), 96; Seventh and Eighth Censuses of the United States: Slave Schedules, Mississippi, Lafayette County, Mississippi Department of Archives and History, Jackson.

[29] Joseph Dunbar Shields, *The Life and Times of Seargent Smith Prentiss* (Philadelphia, 1884), 123, 368; Dickey, *Prentiss*, 95.

[30] Swearingen, *Poindexter*, 61, 83.

[31] Shenton, *Walker*, 13-14; D. Clayton James, *Antebellum Natchez* (Baton Rouge, 1968), 119-121, 138, 149, 158, 185.

as easily lost as gained — with most of the above-men-
tioned individuals being undercut by the Panic of 1837,
state repudiation, erratic judgment, or personal ex-
travagance.

In occupational terms, Mississippi's pre-war congressmen were almost without exception members of
the legal profession.[32] Of fifteen senators, nine were
practicing attorneys and four others combined law with
agricultural pursuits. For the thirty-two representatives, the equivalent figures are ten and nineteen respectively. The five men who served in both branches
of Congress included two lawyers and two lawyer-planters. Of the total fifty-two individuals, forty-six were
either lawyers or lawyer-planters. An examination of
delegations in ten-year increments from 1817 to 1861
reveals a consistent predominance of this class, with the
lowest ratio being fourteen of eighteen in the period
1842-1851. The professional training of these forty-six
varied from the *bona fide* law-school preparation of the
kind received by Powhatan Ellis, Wiley P. Harris, and
Otho Robards Singleton to — at the other extreme —
self-education as exemplified by Franklin Plummer, who
passed a bar examination after only six weeks' study.[33]
The usual route to legal knowledge was that of "reading
law" under an experienced attorney. Among those following this familiar path were Albert Gallatin Brown,
J. F. H. Claiborne, Walter Leake, and a clear majority
of their colleagues. The practice of law was so attractive
as to induce several persons to forsake earlier careers.
William M. Gwin and Reuben Davis originally prepared
in medicine, and Benjamin Duke Nabers shifted from a
commission merchant to the bar.[34] Non-lawyer congress-

[32] Jordan, "Statistical Analysis," 46-51.
[33] Miles, "Plummer," 4.
[34] William Barksdale, on the other hand, left a solid law practice for newspaper

men included two planter-soldiers, one medical doctor, one planter, plus William Henry Hammett, a combination Methodist minister-medical doctor-prosperous planter, and Jesse Speight, who seems to have made a career of holding public office.

If the legal training of Mississippi's congressmen was erratic, their formal education rested on more substantial grounds.[35] Almost fifty per cent of the group had college training; no less than nineteen persons held degrees. In lower educational categories, eleven congressmen received common or public school training, five had been enrolled in academies or preparatory institutions, nine had gained formal knowledge in some other fashion, and the records of four are unknown. From 1817 to 1861 the educational level of Mississippi delegations increased decidedly. During the first two decades only seven of twenty-two congressmen had the benefits of higher learning. But, from 1839 to 1861, the figure rose to twenty-two of thirty-seven.[36] The maximum level was registered from 1851 to 1861 with thirteen college products (eleven graduates) of a total nineteen congressmen.[37] Also significant is the caliber of institutions attended. Among the prominent schools with

111

ties, while maintaining planter interests as well. See James W. McKee, Jr., "William Barksdale: The Intrepid Mississippian" (Unpublished Ph.D. dissertation, Mississippi State University, 1966), 11-14. Gwin's career pattern was erratic. He was trained in law, switched to medicine, and then back to law, and — in the process — was a land speculator of grand proportions and a recipient of some federal patronage plums. See James, *Antebellum Natchez*, 119-121, 185; Shenton, *Walker*, 13-14, 32-33; and Joe Warlick Whitwell, "The Public Life of William M. Gwin in Mississippi" (Unpublished M.A thesis, University of Texas, 1930), 2, 6-7, 60.

[35] Jordan, "Statistical Analysis," 46-51.

[36] Robert J. Walker, whose senate years (1835-1845) spanned the two periods, was included in both tabulations; thus the total reads fifty-three instead of the actual number fifty-two.

[37] In the 1850s twenty-one positions were filled by nineteen men due to the fact that Jefferson Davis and Albert Gallatin Brown had terms in both houses during the decade.

alumni in Mississippi's congressional ranks were Bowdoin, Miami of Ohio, Princeton (two), the United States Military Academy, Washington College (later Washington and Lee), William and Mary, Yale, and the Universities of North Carolina (two), Pennyslvania, and Virginia (three). Academic excellence was attained by Jacob Thompson and Robert J. Walker, each of whom finished first in his class at the Universities of North Carolina and Pennsylvania, respectively.[38]

112   Religious orthodoxy was no prerequisite for political success in antebellum Mississippi if the activities of the congressmen are a measure for judgment. The paucity of church records — perhaps itself evidence of this fact — precludes any attempt to generalize about denominational preferences. But, based on the private comment and public conduct of several eminent members of the group, it seems safe to conclude that formal membership or even a pronouncement of faith was little related to vote-getting potential.[39] Robert J. Walker's "marked antipathy for sectarian belief" did not keep him from being a senator for ten years and President James K. Polk's Secretary of War.[40] The public image of Seargent S. Prentiss, who enjoyed immense popularity even past regional boundaries, was apparently untarnished by his questioning "the distinction of sects, and the necessity of belonging to any one of them."[41] An organization man *par excellence*, John A. Quitman was president, director, commander, or grand master of at least

[38] *Biographical and Historical Memoirs of Mississippi* (2 vols., Chicago, 1891) II, 898; Allan Johnson and Dumas Malone, eds., *Dictionary of American Biograph* (23 vols., New York, 1928-1958), XIX, 354.
[39] Tabulations of religious preference are found in Jordan, "Statistical Analysis," 77-79.
[40] Shenton, *Walker*, 5.
[41] Seargent S. Prentiss to his mother, August 27, 1833, in Prentiss, *Memoir* I, 127.

ten societies and institutions in Adams County;[42] however, according to his daughter, he was "not a confirmed member of the church."[43] William T. S. Barry described himself "as to religion, by education a Presbyterian, by taste an Episcopalian; in practice, nothing."[44] Although a Baptist in his youth, George Poindexter and the church parted company when certain pious brethren were too critical of his wearing a queue.[45] Raised in a Baptist home and educated by Catholic priests, Jefferson Davis did not join a sectarian group until he was past fifty and was serving as president of the Confederacy.[46] The only congressman to have been a minister, William Henry Hammett, was characterized by a contemporary as having "little of the ecclesiastic in his appearance, manners, or habits."[47] Ironically, he was reputed to have died outside the faith.[48]

113

Perhaps of more advantage than organized religion to the vote-conscious individual was a solid if not spectacular military record.[49] Whatever the political asset,

[42] In addition to his well-known political and military exploits, Quitman's fantastic leadership record included being president of local anti-gambling, anti-dueling, and anti-abortion societies, of regional railroad and state-wide cotton companies, and of the Mississippi States Rights Association; of being a director of the Mississippi Planters Bank, organizer and leader of the Natchez Fencibles, a trustee for Jefferson College and Natchez Academy, and Grandmaster of the Mississippi Masonic Lodge. See James, *Antebellum Natchez*, 117, 133, 191-192, 225-226, 249, 256, 259, 274-275, 281; and Dunbar Rowland, ed., *Encyclopedia of Mississippi History* (2 vols., Madison, Wis., 1907), II, 486.

[43] Rosalie Quitman Duncan, "Life of General John A. Quitman," *Publications of the Mississippi Historical Society*, IV (1901), 418. But James, *Antebellum Natchez*, 249, lists him as an Episcopal vestryman.

[44] Quoted in James D. Lynch, *The Bench and Bar of Mississippi* (New York, 1881), 298.

[45] Claiborne, *Mississippi, as a Province, Territory and State*, 360; Swearingen, *Poindexter*, 20-21.

[46] Hudson Strode, *Jefferson Davis: American Patriot, 1808-1861* (New York, 1955), 110-115.

[47] Claiborne, *Mississippi, as a Province, Territory and State*, 451.

[48] Charlotte Capers and William D. McCain, eds., *The Papers of the Washington County Historical Society, 1910-1915* (Jackson, 1954), 133.

[49] Jordan, "Statistical Analysis," 77-79.

most antebellum congressmen at one time or another marched with musket in hand. At least thirty-four of the fifty-two were participants in a variety of martial organizations ranging from Revolutionary War muster companies to the famed Natchez Fencibles. No less than eight held the rank of general in the state or territorial militia. Almost without exception, Mississippi's war heroes became successful officeholders. General Thomas Hinds, the preeminent military figure of the early statehood period, capitalized on his prestige and popularity as did Jefferson Davis and John A. Quitman a generation later. The lack of such a record, however, was not tantamount to political oblivion as signal vote-getters Foote, McRae, Prentiss, Plummer, and Walker often proved.

Mississippi's pre-war congressmen were almost unanimously family men.[50] The only possible exceptions are four individuals about whom information is deficient and one pioneer statesman, David Holmes, who, having suffered the fate of unrequited love in his early youth, resolved never again to participate in *les affaires de coeur*, and died faithful to the oath.[51] The propagation of children in abundance seems to have been standard practice, but a lack of records prevents accurate comment. Of those with complete statistics, the prodigious John A. Quitman exerted leadership in still another area and was the pace-setter with eleven offspring. A single divorce was noted — a particularly bitter one involving the controversial George Poindexter, who apparently suffered no political penalty from the matter.[52] Perhaps the most significant wedding in antebel-

---

[50] *Ibid.*
[51] William Boyd Horton, "The Life of David Holmes" (Unpublished M.A. thesis, University of Colorado, 1935), 83-84.
[52] Swearingen, *Poindexter*, 133-135.

lum Mississippi was that of a young Georgian at Emory College who fell in love with and married the daughter of the school's president. Afterwards, the father-in-law answered a call to become head of the infant University of Mississippi, and on arrival in his new location, beckoned for his daughter and her husband to follow. They came, and with the exception of a brief return trip to Georgia, the L. Q. C. Lamars were associated with the destiny of their adopted state from that point forward.[53]

115

Of the various means of analyzing Mississippi's congressmen, one of the most potentially rewarding remains blurred. Compilation of a general economic index would add much to an understanding of the fifty-two men. But, regrettably, such a construction encounters some overwhelming obstacles. One is the intermittent character of source materials. Personal tax rolls offer solid statistics, but missing years and illegible entries make success sporadic. In addition, the list of taxable items changed drastically at the midpoint between 1817 and 1861. Early figures relate primarily to acreage and its value as contrasted to the luxury items assessed in the two decades prior to the Civil War. To equate two watches, a piano, and three livery horses against one hundred acres and a town lot is to measure yards against ounces.

An imperfect but comprehensive base for economic analysis is slave ownership. Tax rolls, census reports, and the 1850 and 1860 slave schedules provide enough figures throughout the period from statehood to secession to construct valid generalizations. By determining the number of Blacks owned by each congressman in the

[53] Cate, *Lamar*, 30-32; and Frank E. Shanahan, Jr., "L. Q. C. Lamar: An Evaluation," *Journal of Mississippi History*, XXVI (May, 1964), 93.

116

year of his arrival in Washington, several contrasts of significance can be established.[54] With statistics available for fifty of fifty-two individuals, the average was 32.1 slaves per man, with the typical lower-chamber member having 1.5 times the number of a senator. Congressmen who served *after* 1839 possessed almost twice as many chattels as did their predecessors, and those in Washington during the 1850s held title to more slaves than belonged to any previous ten-year delegation. From 1817 to 1861, only two non-slave holders were elected,[55] but over a third of those owning Negroes had ten or less. Fifty or more slaves were owned by nine congressmen, four of whom had in excess of one hundred. While on Capitol Hill several Mississippians witnessed substantial if not phenomenal increases in their property. As previously mentioned, Jacob Thompson enlarged his slaveholdings from four when he was first elected to eighty-three at his retirement.[56] The self-styled non-slaveowners' champion, Albert Gallatin Brown, advanced from one bondsman during his initial term to sixty-one for his last,[57] and George Poindexter went from forty-one to ninety-five.[58] If the slave base is valid as an economic index, one must conclude that Mississippi's congressmen were elected from a financially flourishing element — one that became increasingly prosperous during the antebellum period.

Other grounds for analysis are age and years of

[54] For these tabulations and a compilation of other economic data, see Jordan, "Statistical Analysis," 52-57.

[55] The two non-slaveholders were Samuel J. Gholson and Wiley P. Harris. Robert J. Walker's personal claim to this distinction is belied by the 1835 Madison County Personal Tax Roll (Mississippi Department of Archives and History, Jackson) which credits him with owning seventeen.

[56] See footnote twenty-eight.

[57] Mississippi, Personal Tax Rolls: Copiah County, 1839, and Hinds County, 1860, Mississippi Department of Archives and History, Jackson.

[58] Mississippi, Personal Tax Rolls: Wilkinson County, 1818 and 1830, Mississippi Department of Archives and History, Jackson.

state residence.[59] In these categories, the prototype senator was older and not so long a Mississippian as his associate in the House. To be exact, on arrival in Washington, he was 3.8 years the senior of a representative and had lived in the state an average of eight months less. For the 1839-1861 era, Mississippi's senators and representatives alike were decidedly older with more tenure than their predecessors from 1817 to 1839. For the entire antebellum period, age and state residence averaged 39.1 and 17.2 years, respectively.

117

In terms of political experience, Mississippi's antebellum congressmen were far from being in the novice category.[60] In fact, only five of fifty-two were without earlier public positions. Thirty-three individuals had spent a staggering total of 114 years in a most practical training arena, the state legislature, while nineteen had 106 years in judicial capacities. Seven were former governors, and nine had served prior terms in a different branch of Congress. Mississippi politics rested on a democratic foundation, and successful, veteran politicians, like most of the congressmen, were skilled in the cultivation of grass-roots ties and electioneering techniques.

Congressional activity was frequently a stepping-stone to additional service. Subsequent appointments to presidential cabinets went to Jefferson Davis (between terms), Jacob Thompson, Robert J. Walker, and, in the post-war era, to L. Q. C. Lamar, who also became a justice of the United States Supreme Court. Either after or between congressional tours, seven individuals served as governor, and eight returned to Washington in a new branch of Congress. Of those who lived under

---

[59] Jordan, "Statistical Analysis," 58-62.
[60] *Ibid.*, 63-70.

the Confederacy, nine were members of its legislature, and Jefferson Davis labored as its lone chief executive. For twenty-two of Mississippi's fifty-two representatives and senators, however, political life terminated with their years in Congress; six died in office. The total political careers of the fifty-two pervade the executive, legislative, and judicial divisions of the state's pre-war government. Although Mississippi's suffrage laws were liberal, her political leadership was more oligarchical than democratic.

118

In Congress, Mississippians were appointed to standing committees which often reflected their state's frontier character.[61] Totals for both branches from 1817 to 1861 show 106 separate assignments, a third of them coming in the 1850s. Indian affairs, internal improvements, and land policy — all important concerns in western sections of the country — were frequent appointments. More specifically, the highest number of selections were to the following committees: Public Lands (twelve with three chairmanships), Indian Affairs (ten with one), District of Columbia (nine with two), Post Office and Post Roads (eight with one), Public Land Claims (eight with two), Military Affairs and Militia (eight with two), and Roads and Canals (seven). Of the seventeen chairmanships which went to Mississippians, eleven were in the Senate and only three were awarded prior to 1839.

Mississippi's most important congressional delegation was the one which went north in 1859. The responsibilities and subsequent actions of that group are well-known. However, mention should be made of several less-noted, aggregate characteristics which might open

[61] Committee assignments are listed in *ibid.*, 71-75.

new avenues of interpretation.[62] Collectively, this seven-
man bloc outdistanced all its predecessors in the categories of age, education, congressional experience, and
years of Mississippi residence. Paced by senators Jefferson Davis and Albert Gallatin Brown, it featured a composite age and a Mississippi residence of 43.4 and 29.5
years respectively. The total years in Congress came to
41.7, or 5.9 per individual, and six were college trained.
All had served in the immediately preceding session,
and except for Reuben Davis and John Jones McRae,
all had been in Washington more years than not during
the 1850s.

119

As far as the "peculiar institution" was concerned,
these men had a personal interest to match their political obligations. Of the seven, only McRae owned less
than fifteen slaves; the average was 43.5 per man. In
terms of occupations, six farmed extensive land holdings,
and five were also practicing attorneys. Representative
in a genuine sense, this group included spokesmen from
every geographic area in the state. Additional reinforcements were present in the form of ex-Mississippi
congressman William M. Gwin (a California senator)
and Jacob Thompson (Secretary of the Interior). Of all
pre-Civil War delegations, this was the best qualified
to interpret and express the state's wishes to the nation,
and vice versa. The group's judgment and leadership —
if considered faulty or "blundering" — cannot be explained by a lack of education, maturity, congressional
experience, economic interest, or empathetic relationship with their constituents.

When the fires of secession flamed in 1860-1861,
Mississippi's congressmen, in office and of earlier vin-

---

[62] *Ibid.*, 80. Capsule biographies are found in "The Mississippi Delegation in
Congress," *Harper's Weekly*, V (February 2, 1861), 66.

tage, added fuel to the growing conflagration within the state.[63] Seeds of disunion had been firmly implanted by the Quitman-Davis element in the early fifties[64] and were cultivated during the decade by orators like Albert Gallatin Brown. "It is futile," he warned, "if, indeed, it is not puerile to attempt a compromise of the slavery question. The difference between the North and the South is radical and irreconcilable."[65]

Prior to the fateful presidential campaign of 1860, William Barksdale, Reuben Davis, Otho Robards Singleton, and McRae had delivered defiant House addresses warning that the election of a black Republican would justify as well as cause a national schism.[66] Jefferson Davis maintained the right of secession to be "unquestionable," but realized that the exercise of that privilege would mean a war for which the South was not prepared.[67] Reuben Davis concurred by labeling "peaceful secession an idle dream."[68] In the event of such an ominous outcome, Barksdale, a Gettysburg fatality three years later, predicted with tragic inaccuracy that "the army that invades the South . . . will never return; their bodies will enrich southern soil."[69]

After Lincoln's victory in November 1860, Mississippi Governor John J. Pettus called a meeting of the

[63] For a general treatment of the disunion movement in Mississippi which emphasizes the roles of various congressmen, see Percy Lee Rainwater, *Mississippi: Storm Center of Secession, 1856-1861* (Baton Rouge, 1938). Numerous quotations about secession are given in "The Mississippi Delegation in Congress," 66.

[64] A discussion of the Quitman heritage in the secession current is found in John K. Bettersworth, *Confederate Mississippi: The People and Policies of a Cotton State in Wartime* (Baton Rouge, 1943), 1-8.

[65] Cited in M. W. Cluskey, ed., *Speeches, Messages, and Other Writings of the Hon. Albert G. Brown* (Philadelphia, 1859), 597; for similar, threatening language by another congressman, see McKee, "Barksdale," 104-105.

[66] *Congressional Globe*, Thirty-sixth Congress, First Session, Part I, 157; Part IV, App., 34-36, 53, 171.

[67] Strode, *Davis*, 363.

[68] Davis, *Recollections of Mississippi*, 403.

[69] McKee, "Barksdale," 105.

state's congressional delegation to discuss the secession question.[70] In the conclave, Jefferson Davis was
opposed to disunion except when all other peaceful
recourses had been exhausted. But after his colleagues
voted in favor of separate state action, he "reluctantly
and regretfully consented to it as a political necessity
for the protection of popular and state rights."[71] When
the Mississippi Secession Convention assembled in
January 1861, seven former congressmen were among
its hundred delegates. Five of the seven served on the
special committee of fifteen — headed by Lamar — which
drafted the ordinance of secession.[72] William T. S. Barry
was elected convention president, Wiley P. Harris was
"pre-eminently influential," and Walker Brooke led the
conservative "co-operationist" element which favored
a united South for purposes of "obtaining further
guarantees from the North, or failing in that, the formation of a Southern Confederacy."[73]

Soon after Mississippi's formal secession, Jefferson
Davis and his colleagues in Washington resigned their
positions in the United States Congress and journeyed
home. They immediately became involved in the formation of the Confederate States of America and in the
subsequent clash of arms which would terminate its
existence. From the ranks of Mississippi's ex-congress-
men came political leadership for the new government
and military commanders for its armies. Barry, Brooke,

[70] See James B. Ranck, *Albert Gallatin Brown, Radical Southern Nationalist*
(New York, 1937), 202; Rainwater, *Mississippi: Storm Center of Secession*, 168-
169; and McKee, "Barksdale," 106.

[71] Strode, *Davis*, 363; see also McKee, "Barksdale," 106.

[72] Thomas H. Woods, "A Sketch of the Mississippi Secession Convention of
1861 — Its Membership and Work," *Publication of the Mississippi Historical
Society*, VI (1902), 97; Rainwater, *Mississippi: Storm Center of Secession*, 202-
217; and Ralph A. Wooster, *The Secession Conventions of the South* (Princeton,
1962), ch. 3. Wooster erroneously omits William T. S. Barry and Walker Brooke
from his list of former congressmen serving as convention delegates (p. 29).

[73] Woods, "A Sketch of the Mississippi Secession Convention of 1861," 76.

and Harris were among the state's delegates at the Provisional Congress which established the new nation and elected Davis as its president. Brown, Reuben Davis, McRae, and Singleton were members of the regular Confederate Congress, which also included their former associates, the nomadic Henry S. Foote (Tennessee) and John A. Wilcox (Texas). Henry T. Ellett declined the position of Postmaster General in Davis's cabinet, but Walker Brooke and Jacob Thompson accepted judicial and diplomatic assignments, respectively. On the battle-field, ten former Mississippi congressmen fought as commissioned officers in the Confederate Army; eight held the rank of colonel or above. Barksdale was the lone fatality.[74]

If most of the state's ex-representatives in Washington were ardent supporters of the Confederate cause, at least two assumed a different position. In the northern camp was Robert J. Walker who became a devastating, "self-appointed . . . propagandist for the Union," at first as a journalist and subsequently as a financial agent for the United States in England.[75] Deep within Confederate territory, J. F. H. Claiborne, who had opposed secession and avoided official connection with the Confederacy, was active in the Gulf Coast contra-band trade as early as October 1862 and maintained contact with Federal authorities throughout the conflict.[76]

The public career of a composite antebellum Missis-

---

[74] Jordan, "Statistical Analysis," 64-70, 77-79. For further information — biographical data and voting patterns — on the Confederate congressmen, see Alexander and Beringer, *Anatomy of the Confederate Congress*, especially Appendixes I-III.

[75] Shenton, *Walker*, 186.

[76] Franklin L. Riley, "Life of J. F. H. Claiborne," *Publications of the Mississippi Historical Society*, VII (1903), 235; Bettersworth, *Confederate Mississippi*, 183; and Herbert H. Lang, "J. F. H. Claiborne at 'Laurel Wood' Plantation, 1853-1870," *Journal of Mississippi History*, XVIII (January, 1956), 1-17.

sippi congressman can be traced with little difficulty. Born in an older section of the country to parents financially able to provide a substantial degree of formal education, the prototype congressman came to Mississippi as an ambitious young adult seeking the opportunities of a booming frontier society. He found an atmosphere in which past performance was subordinate to present action, and where the measure of success related not to an initial economic and social advantage, but rather to an individual's diligence and ingenuity. On arrival his means were limited, and often the early years extracted sweat and sacrifice. When his financial foundation assumed a firmness, he entered the political arena at the local or state level. Meanwhile, he had married, become an officer in the resident militia unit, perhaps had speculated in land sales or at any rate had acquired property in the form of acres and slaves. Having thus attained a measure of economic stability and public standing, he sought or was selected to campaign for a congressional seat. After a tour in Washington, he continued to be active in Mississippi politics and to prosper financially. If pastures appeared greener elsewhere, however, he was not hesitant about relocation, frequently to another state. In short, he was an aspiring, aggressive, resourceful, and highly flexible creature in an environment which favored his species.

123

For the period 1817-1861, Mississippi's senators and representatives have different profiles.[77] In collective terms, the senators were predominantly natives of the South Atlantic states and arrived in Mississippi as older men than the representatives, whose origins favored Tennessee and Kentucky, as well as the South

---

[77] See the tables in Jordan, "Statistical Analysis," 38, 42, 46, 52, 58, 63.

Atlantic seaboard. The prototype senator was likely to have been better educated and in the legal profession exclusively; in terms of election-day statistics, he was slightly older, although not as long a state inhabitant as his colleague in the House. Mississippians in the two branches were about even in political experience, but the average representative owned much more slave property than a senator.

The study of Mississippi's pre-war congressmen generally confirms the traditional view about the location of political power in the state.[78] After providing ten of the first eleven Mississippi senators and representatives, the "Old Natchez District" or southwest area yielded her supremacy to newer, rapidly populating counties to the east and north. Although "Mother Adams" and her neighbors of the lower-river sector did surrender the state's political throne, they nevertheless remained contenders for its control. In fact, from 1831 to 1861, among Mississippi's six geographic divisions, the number of senators and representatives from the "Old Natchez District" was exceeded only by the "New Purchase" or Second Choctaw Cession (1820) area. The continued presence of a substantial bloc from this locale is even more unusual when the process of selecting congressmen is considered. Senators were chosen by the state legislature, which was dominated by no single geographic region. Members of the House of Representatives were selected on an at-large basis until 1846 when four districts were established. The state was then

124

[78] See Jordan, "Statistical Analysis," 59, for the geographic distribution of political power represented by the antebellum congressmen. The familiar story of a loss of power represented by the Southwest is told in Charles S. Sydnor, *A Gentleman of the Old Natchez Region: Benjamin L. C. Wailes* (Durham, 1938), 71-77; Sydnor, *Slavery in Mississippi* (New York, 1933), 247-248; and Miles, *Jacksonian Democracy in Mississippi*, 19-32. See also James, *Antebellum Natchez*, 97-98, 112-128.

divided into parallel east and west districts, of which North Mississippi had two.[79] The "Old Natchez District" thus maintained a political influence even while falling behind in population totals.

An attempt to determine the site of party strength by analyzing congressional elections is difficult. After the pre-Jacksonian or Republican era, campaigns were waged between the Democrats and Whigs (subsequently Union Democrats), with an occasional intra-party squabble. The Whigs won only twelve of forty-five seats and were triumphant but once after 1851. But, contrary to the actual location of conservative power, the dozen Whig victors came from every section in the state. Another confusing element is the presence of individuals with vacillating political ties. For example, party chameleon Henry S. Foote "— 'General Weathercock,' according to his detrators — was a Democrat in 1834, a Whig in 1835, a Democrat in 1836, a Whig in 1837, and a Democrat in 1840!"[80] Four senators elected as Democrats (and listed in the party totals) became Whigs during their terms in Washington.

An additional impediment to defining geopolitical power is the frequent relocation of individuals within the state. Foote and John D. Freeman both became congressmen while living in Jackson, but each was more closely associated with a former residence. Although products of the Natchez region, J. F. H. Claiborne and Robert J. Walker were very recent citizens of Madison County when elected to Congress. A native and lifelong inhabitant of Columbus (Lowndes County), William T. S. Barry moved across the state to Greenwood (Sun-

125

[79] James E. Baxter, "Congressional Redistricting in Mississippi from 1817 to 1938" (Unpublished M.A. thesis, Duke University, 1939), 18-40.
[80] Miles, *Jacksonian Democracy in Mississippi*, 164.

flower County) in 1852, and was therein chosen for the House, but three years later returned to his original location. Albert Gallatin Brown listed a different residence for each campaign success. In short, investigation of the antebellum congressmen suggests the caution which must be used in describing the political strength and party ties of Mississippi's geographic sections.[81]

126

Within the limits of this study, the parochial attitude assumed by Mississippi political leaders in the 1850s is paradoxical. Rigid, defiant sectionalism seems incongruous in a group whose congenital and educational heritage was beyond the Deep South. Active national ties through party lines, military tours, and Washington residence should have been additional deterrents to staunch regionalism. Reflecting a distinctly nomadic pattern which ordinarily would vitiate extreme emotional attachment to any particular locale, the congressmen were also immersed in a state whose populace was ever-changing and whose currents of social and economic upheaval gave fixed positions an ephemeral foundation. But, these factors to the contrary, a narrow, doctrinaire posture developed rapidly in the two decades prior to Fort Sumter.

The theory that southern leadership declined sharply in the antebellum era[82] is not substantiated in several vital categories by a profile analysis of Mississippi congressmen. A revealing basis for interpretation is the division of congressmen chronologically between groups before and after 1839. Contrasted with his predecessor, the average member of Congress from 1839 to 1861 enjoyed a signally higher degree of education and had much more legislative experience. In addition, he was an

[81] Residential patterns are covered in Jordan, "Statistical Analysis," 60-62.
[82] For examples, see Syndor, *Development of Southern Sectionalism*, 289-293; and Clement Eaton, *Freedom of Thought in the Old South* (Durham, 1939), 62-63.

older man when he took office and could claim a considerably longer association with the people whose interests he represented. The argument that the wealthy planter class withdrew from politics after it became "tainted" with democracy is questionable; of the four Mississippi congressmen elected while owning in excess of a hundred slaves, all four served after 1843, and two were in Washington during the late fifties. The average number of slaves held by individual senators and representatives *prior to 1839* was *21.95*, while the equivalent post-1839 figure was *38.5*, an estate which in 1860 would have placed the prototype congressman in the upper fraction of Mississippi slaveholders.[83] An analysis of congressional delegations does not mirror the complete picture of the state's political hierachy, and leadership ability is determined by many more factors than those mentioned herein. However, within the scope of this study, certain characteristics usually considered desirable in public officials were on the *increase* during the antebellum period.

In a sense, the collection and tabulation of silent numerals is an ignoble reference to the men who represented Mississippi in the halls of Congress from 1817 to 1861. Statistics conceal the flare and vitality of colorful, complex, and important personalities. Some of the fifty-two congressmen attained national prominence and registered lasting fame. Others faded quickly from center-stage and were destined to die in obscurity. But, regardless of the historical favor each received, all were significant as part of a leadership panorama which transcended state boundaries. Insight into their lives provides a deeper understanding not only of antebellum Missis-

127

---

[83] See Jordan, "Statistical Analysis," 58; and Sydnor, *Slavery in Mississippi*, 193.

sippi, or of that distinctive time and place — the Old
South — but also of a critical era in American history.

128A

ARRANGING THE PRELIMINARIES OF A TREATY BETWEEN THE UNITED STATES AND MEXICO.

Mr. Trist—(*Very firmly*)—My Government, Gentlemen, will take "nothin' shorter."

Opposition to the Mexican War often took the form of pungent humor.

DILEMMAS OF DISSENT:
CONGRESS & OPPOSITION
TO THE MEXICAN WAR

by

John H. Schroeder

Domestic opposition to wars waged by the United States spans the nation's history. From the War of 1812 to Vietnam, anti-war movements have been characterized by intensity and diversity. Although the opposition has always included small minorities of radical pacifists, religious zealots, and political extremists, dissent has not been confined to them. Sizeable and "respectable" groups of Republicans and Democrats have criticized American wars in the 20th century, as did large numbers of Federalists in the War of 1812, Whigs in the Mexican War, and Democrats in the Civil War. In addition, the record of American history abounds with the anti-war speeches, writings, and activities of numerous prominent intellectual figures, social reformers, clergymen, labor leaders, and businessmen.[1]

Such persistent anti-war dissent is largely attributable to the controversial nature of the conflicts in which the United States has been involved. With few exceptions, American wars have evoked serious questions of necessity, morality, wisdom, and goals. Only President Franklin D. Roosevelt, in

[1]Among the historical studies dealing with various anti-war movements in American history are the following: Samuel Eliot Morison, Frederick Merk, and Frank Freidel, *Dissent in Three American Wars* (Cambridge, Mass., 1970); John H. Schroeder, *Mr. Polk's War; American Opposition and Dissent, 1846–48* (Madison, Wis., 1973); Wood Gray, *The Hidden Civil War; The Story of the Copperheads* (New York, 1942); Frank L. Klement, *The Copperheads in the Middle West* (Chicago, 1960); Robert L. Beisner, *Twelve Against Empire; the Anti-Imperialists, 1898–1900* (New York, 1968); Daniel B. Schirmer, *Republic or Empire; American Resistance to the Philippine War* (Cambridge, Mass., 1972); Harold C. Peterson and Gilbert C. Fite, *Opponents of War: 1917–1918* (Madison, Wis., 1957); Thomas Powers, *The War at Home* (New York, 1973).

15

Originally published in *Capitol Studies*, 3 (Fall, 1975). Reprinted by permission of the United States Capitol Historical Society.

World War II, was able to mobilize a united home front. For, although differences on foreign policy existed prior to the end of 1941, the Japanese attack on Pearl Harbor unified the nation. After December 7, 1941, there seemed no choice but to confront and defeat the Axis powers.

Despite their persistence and size, opposition movements have rarely succeeded. Dissenters outside Congress have usually failed to translate public disillusionment and anti-war sentiment into direct pressure on an administration to reverse its policy. For example, a majority of Americans were exasperated, at one point or another, during the Civil War and the Korean War. But this general public frustration never generated formidable opposition. Though disillusioned, most Americans saw no alternative to continued, if sullen, support for the war policy. Only two conflicts offer notable exceptions. In the War of 1812, strong opposition in New England contributed to the failure of American military strategy. In addition to the many New England citizens who openly assisted and supplied the British, the states of that region withheld numerous well-trained militia units from the American invasion of Canada. In the Vietnam War, widespread dissent and public disillusionment, compounded by an unsuccessful military policy based on a questionable rationale, eventually reversed the American strategy of escalation.

130

Congressional opponents of wars have been particularly ineffective. Not only have they consistently been unable to prevent declarations of war, but congressional critics have also generally failed to curtail military conflicts. Political opponents of the Mexican War well exemplify this tradition of failure. From 1846 to 1848 a small group of Calhoun Democrats joined with virtually the whole Whig party in denouncing "Mr. Polk's War." Like their counterparts in other American wars, these critics confronted, but failed to resolve, several basic problems. First, despite widespread congressional aversion to the idea of war with Mexico, opponents were unable to prevent Congress from voting overwhelmingly to support the administration's war bill. Second, once the war commenced, congressional opponents could find no way of forcing the president to modify his war policies and goals. Third, anti-war forces could never unite on one realistic alternative to the existing policy.

Although these basic problems are representative of American congressional anti-war dissent, several singular characteristics distinguish the Mexican War experience. First, a bipartisan coalition of supporters of the administration's war policy never materialized. During the war, the intense partisanship which characterized the politics of the 1840's was aggravated by President Polk's partisan conduct of the war. Winning the support of most Democrats, he incurred the wrath of virtually every Whig in Congress. Second, virtually all war critics shared, to some extent, Polk's general war goal of territorial expansion. Whigs readily acknowledged the desire for continued expansion, especially the desirability of acquiring California.

However, they sought a controlled expansion. They argued that expansion should result not from war, but from natural growth, negotiation, or purchase. This situation contrasted sharply with later wars, in which critics opposed the objectives themselves, whether they were overseas possessions in the Spanish-American War or the confused, unclear aims in the Korean and Vietnam conflicts.

Finally, congressional opponents had an opportunity to effect significantly the course of the Mexican War. Unlike their counterparts in other conflicts, they were not hopelessly outnumbered.[2] Democratic control of both houses rendered a complete reversal of Polk's aggressive war policy impossible, but a united opposition could have pressed him to modify his goals and curtail the military effort. In the Senate, the Democrats maintained a slim five vote majority during the Twenty-ninth Congress. But Democrats John C. Calhoun and his followers held the balance of power.[3] If these Democrats chose to vote consistently with the Whigs against administration war measures— and the president feared such a Whig-Calhounite coalition—Polk would be forced to alter his policies.[4] In the House, the Democrats held an unbeatable 144 to 77 majority during the Twenty-ninth Congress. But in the Thirtieth Congress, which convened near the end of the war, the Whigs gained a slim 115 to 108 majority, which they might well have used to win concessions from the president. However, the Whig majority made no substantive effort to oppose the administration, and continued to vote needed war supplies. Thus, if the Mexican War does not provide a precise model for congressional opposition to other American wars, it does present the dilemmas which anti-war dissenters in Congress have sought to overcome in almost every war.

In May 1846, when word arrived in Washington that Mexican forces had attacked American soldiers along the Rio Grande, a large number of congressmen believed war with Mexico to be unwise and unnecessary. Opponents included intensely partisan Whigs who had long opposed the president's policies and distrusted his secretive nature, and such Democrats as John C. Calhoun, Thomas Hart Benton, and the followers of Martin Van Buren.[5]

131

---

[2]For example, the Federalists in the War of 1812 were outnumbered during the Twelfth Congress (1811–13) 108 to 36 in the House and 30 to 6 in the Senate. In the Civil War, the Democrats (some of whom did not oppose the war) were outnumbered during the Thirty-seventh Congress (1861–63) 105 to 43 in the House and 31 to 10 in the Senate; similarly, during the Thirty-eighth Congress (1863–65) the Republican majority was 102 to 75 in the House and 36 to 9 in the Senate. In such conflicts as World War I, Korea, and Vietnam, where partisan lines were not firmly drawn, bipartisan majorities have sustained the war effort.

[3]Calhoun's followers in the Senate included Andrew Butler of South Carolina, James Mason of Virginia, and David Yulee of Florida.

[4]*The Diary of James K. Polk, 1845–1849,* ed. by Milo M. Quaife (4 vols., Chicago, 1910), II, 347, 371–72, 377, 378.

[5]Benton quickly overcame his initial reluctance and became one of the war's strongest congressional supporters. Despite their bitter resentment, the Van Burenites consistently sustained the war. They realized that an open break with the administration would injure their hopes of winning control of the party in 1848. At the same time, they sought to qualify their support for a war of conquest in the Southwest by proposing and supporting the attachment of the anti-slavery Wilmot Proviso to vital war measures.

Calhoun later estimated that not a "tenth-part" of Congress supported the president's Mexican policy and, furthermore, that the vote on the war bill "would have been two to one against it," if sufficient time for debate had been allowed.[6] In spite of this, Congress was unable to prevent, or even postpone, the declaration of war. Within a day after the president's war message, Congress overwhelmingly approved the call for war by a vote of 174 to 14 in the House, and 40 to 2 in the Senate.[7]

The ease with which Polk was able to overwhelm a reluctant Congress was largely attributable to the president's power in foreign affairs. For the first time in the history of the republic, the president had utilized his prerogatives as commander-in-chief to help create a situation which virtually guaranteed the outbreak of hostilities, and thereby forced Congress to declare war. Critical here was Polk's order advancing American troops to the Rio Grande. Because Mexico considered the territory above the Rio Grande to be her own, violent retaliation was assured. In his war message, Polk claimed the Rio Grande as the true border, and justified the advance of American troops as a necessary precaution to prevent a threatened Mexican invasion of Texas. He emphasized that the United States had endured a long series of "insults" and "injuries" from its southern neighbor. Not only had Mexico consistently defaulted on several million dollars in damage claims owed American citizens, but had also refused to recognize the annexation of Texas, and had recently rejected the special American diplomatic mission headed by John Slidell. And now Mexican forces had crossed the Rio Grande and "shed American blood upon the American soil." Having exhausted the "cup of forbearance," Mexico had to be chastised quickly and decisively. To this end, Polk requested that Congress recognize a state of war and appropriate the requisite men, money, and supplies.[8]

In the weeks and months following this message, numerous observers discredited the distortions and falsehoods of Polk's war message.[9] In Congress critics of the war readily admitted Mexico's poor deportment but argued that these grievances hardly justified war. Indeed, they continued, Polk himself was responsible for the conflict. Basic to their position was the border question. For if the Rio Grande were not the true border of Texas, the president had ordered the invasion of Mexican soil, thus provoking hostilities. Calhoun Democrats and Whigs emphasized that the Rio Grande had never been the

132

[6]John C. Calhoun to H. W. Conner, 15 May 1846, Library of Congress, H. W. Conner Papers.

[7]For the votes on the war bill see U. S. Congress, *Congressional Globe*, 29th Cong., 1st sess., vol. 15, pt. 1, 795, 804. In the House, all fourteen negative votes were cast by anti-slavery Whigs. In the Senate, only Whigs John W. Davis of Massachusetts and Thomas Clayton of Delaware voted no, but John C. Calhoun abstained, and Whigs John J. Crittenden of Kentucky and William Upham of Vermont voted "ay, except the preamble."

[8]*A Compilation of the Messages and Papers of the Presidents, 1789–1902*, ed. by James D. Richardson (10 vols., Washington, 1903), IV, 437–43.

[9]A sampling of these 1846 speeches appears in the *Congressional Globe*, vol. 15, pt. 1, Appendix, 641–45, 683–86, 763–67, 809–12, 826–29, 812–20, 934–35, 946–50, 952–56, 1115–18.

rightful border, nor had it traditionally been recognized as such by any American president prior to Polk. Rather, they asserted, the true border was the Nueces River, some 150 miles to the north. At best, the desert area between the two rivers was disputed territory, historically inhabited and controlled by Mexican citizens.[10] Accordingly, war critics concluded that responsiblity for the war was "justly chargeable upon Mr. Polk."[11]

Whatever their initial doubts, and despite their subsequent ability to refute Polk's explanation for war, congressional opponents had little choice but to meet the crisis. American blood had been shed, an American army was in apparent danger, the American flag was under attack, and American honor was at stake. In such an emotionally charged atmosphere time was not available for a full and deliberate examination. Yet the actual war bill went far beyond what the emergency required. Not only did it authorize 50,000 volunteers and appropriate $10 million, it was amended to affirm Polk's explanation for the conflict, and to allow him to conduct the war for any goals he desired. The preamble, which loyal Democrats added to the war bill, recognized that a state of war already existed "by the act of the Republic of Mexico," and authorized the president to prosecute the war to a "speedy and successful termination."[12]

133

Significantly, the war bill thereby integrated the issue of immediate military reinforcements and the question of the war's causes. In the Senate, Calhoun quickly made distinctions between "hostilities" and "war." Although the Congress should vote reinforcements for General Zachary Taylor without delay, Calhoun argued that it would only "make war on the Constitution by declaring war to exist . . . when no war had been declared, and nothing had occurred but a slight military conflict between a portion of two armies."[13] Congressional critics in both houses frantically attempted to separate the questions of reinforcements and war. Failing in that effort, they sought to restrict the president's use of the reinforcements. In both houses, they introduced amendments authorizing the president to relieve Taylor's army and prevent any invasion of Texas, but not to invade Mexico or escalate existing hostilities. These amendments, however, were consistently rejected.

Even more infuriating to the dissidents than their failure to modify the war bill was the dilemma which this failure created for them as they voted on the bill. In order to affirm their patriotism by voting reinforcements for an embattled American army in the field, they had to endorse what they believed to be the manifest falsehoods of the president's war message. The war bill,

[10]The president's critics argued that if the Rio Grande were the rightful border, then the capital of the Mexican province of New Mexico, Santa Fe, would definitely be part of Texas since it was located east of the Rio Grande, near its headwaters. Such an assertion was, of course, absurd.
[11]Alexander H. Stephens to Linton Stephens, 13 May 1846, Purchase, N.Y., Manhattanville College of the Sacred Heart, Stephens Papers. (Microfilm copy).
[12]*Congressional Globe*, 29 Cong., 1 sess., vol. 15, pt. 1, 792.
[13]*Ibid.* 796–97.

John C. Calhoun was a rallying point for war opponents in the Senate.

then, purposefully denied dissenters the option of rejecting war on Polk's terms while demonstrating their patriotism.

The fourteen Whigs in the House and two Whigs in the Senate who voted against the war bill drew charges of disloyalty, and even allegations of treason. Understandably, most Whigs and dissident Democrats hesitated to subject themselves to such attacks on their patriotism. In order to defeat or postpone the war bill, they would have had to deny reinforcements to General Taylor. If they did manage to reject or delay the war bill and tragedy should befall General Taylor and his army, they would be held fully liable by their Democratic opponents before the electorate.

The outbreak of the Mexican War thus established a precedent. No one understood this more clearly than John C. Calhoun. Writing several days after the passage of the war bill, he noted the historical importance of Polk's decision, and accurately predicted its future consequence. "It sets the example, which will enable all future Presidents to bring about a state of things, in which Congress shall be forced, without deliberation, or reflection, to declare war, however opposed to its convictions of justice or expediency."[14] Here Calhoun exposed a serious weakness in the system of constitutional checks and balances. Although the Constitution delegated power to declare war to Congress, this prerogative was virtually meaningless in situations such as the one in 1846.

135

Once war was formally declared, a new problem confronted the opposition. Dissidents in Congress now faced the task of ending the conflict through their opposition. In doing so, they addressed a nation overwhelmingly in support of the war during its early months. For the outbreak of fighting in 1846 coincided with the rising fever of Manifest Destiny.[15] This nationalistic ideology combined pride, energy, confidence, and a long-standing sense of national mission with the doctrine of territorial expansion. Scores of expansionist editors and politicians clamored for the United States to realize its territorial destiny by immediately establishing an empire on the Pacific. Expansionists quickly endorsed the war as a way of acquiring the Southwest, as well as a means of uplifting and civilizing the region's "lesser inhabitants." And, whatever their views on expansion, most Americans agreed with President Polk that Mexico, having exhausted the patience of the United States, had to be chastised. From Lansingburgh, New York, Herman Melville described the "military ardor" and "delirium" of the moment. "Militia colonels wax red in their coat facings—and 'prentice boys are running off to the war by scores.—Nothing is talked of but the 'Halls of Montezumas'. . . ."[16]

---

[14]Calhoun to Conner, 15 May 1846, Conner Papers.
[15]The best descriptions and analyses of Manifest Destiny are *Manifest Destiny,* ed. by Norman Graebner (New York, 1968); Frederick Merk, *Manifest Destiny and Mission in American History; A Reinterpretation* (New York, 1963); Albert K. Weinberg, *Manifest Destiny: A Study of Nationalist Expansionism in American History* (Baltimore, 1935).
[16]Herman Melville to G. Melville, 29 May 1846, in *The Letters of Herman Melville*, ed. by Merrell R. Davis and William G. Gilman (New Haven, 1960), 29.

But this initial enthusiasm—manifested by support for the military effort and celebrations of American victories—did not translate into sustained or intense support for the president's war policy. Polk's personal popularity was never exceptional, and his war policy was always criticized. The heavy losses suffered by the Democrats in the congressional elections of 1846–47 indicated widespread voter disfavor with a variety of their positions including, in some areas, administration war policy.[17] Perceptible disillusionment with the war began to grow by the spring of 1847, after a series of American military victories failed to bring peace. Public frustration approached alarming proportions when a prompt settlement did not follow General Winfield Scott's occupation of Mexico City in September. Disillusionment, however, did not bring about overwhelming anti-war sentiment. While opposition grew, so did demands for military escalation. During the fall of 1847, a host of expansionist politicians and editors urged the subjugation of all Mexico as the only means of ending the war and realizing the nation's territorial destiny.

136

This national climate of opinion dictated that congressional opponents of war reverse administration policy without deserting the military effort or disgracing the nation's honor. Assuming correctly that President Polk would not heed their verbal criticisms, warnings, and recommendations, opposition members had to find a means of forcing the president to alter his course. The obvious constitutional power available for this purpose was Congress' control over the authorization of manpower and appropriation. Theoretically, Congress could refuse to vote the money and men necessary to sustain war, thereby forcing Polk to withdraw American troops and make peace. In reality, however, this constitutional power was virtually useless. Once Congress had passed the war bill, it was extremely difficult to withhold money and men, that is, to abandon a war it had sanctioned. And whatever their individual views of the war might be, most politicians believed that American troops committed to the field of battle had to be fully supported. Alexander Stephens, of Georgia, spoke for the great majority of his fellow Whigs in June 1846, when he declared that "all hands to the rescue would be my motto . . . now [that] the fires of war are raging on our frontier, all good citizens should render their willing aid, as I most cheerfully do."[18] "When a House is on Fire," wrote Whig Representative James Graham of North Carolina, "the first duty of every good citizen is to exert himself to extinguish the Fire. . . ."[19]

[17]In these elections, state issues as well as Democratic party factionalism weakened Democratic candidates. In addition, administration policy on the tariff, government fiscal policy, internal improvements, and the Oregon question proved troublesome to the Democrats in various congressional districts.

[18]*Congressional Globe,* 29 Cong., 1 sess., vol. 15, pt. 2, Appendix, 949.

[19]James Graham to William A. Graham, 10 Jan. 1847, in *The Papers of William Alexander Graham,* ed. by J. G. de Roulhac Hamilton (4 vols., Raleigh, 1960), III, 171.

Those who dared to vote against war supplies were subjected to sharp attacks on their loyalty and patriotism. For example, in February 1847, when Calhoun and several other Democrats joined with Whigs in the Senate to defeat a bill providing for additional troops, an administration newspaper, the Washington *Daily Union*, quickly announced that "the Mexicans [had] achieved another victory."[20] Administration supporters further attempted to defame the anti-war faction by linking it, in spirit, to the Federalists who supported the Hartford Convention during the War of 1812. The Whig Party was particularly vulnerable to be thought of as the party of opposition, and to suffer the same fate as the Federalists some thirty years earlier. In his message to Congress in December 1846, the president set the tone when he warned of the danger of anti-war criticism. "A more effectual means," charged Polk, "could not have been devised to encourage the enemy and protract the war than to advocate and adhere to their cause and thus to give them 'aid and comfort'. . . ."[21]

137

Beyond the political risk involved, anti-war politicians questioned whether the withholding of supplies would actually end the war. Mexico was a willing, if outclassed, enemy and much preferred fighting to negotiating with the hated Americans. Even were the president denied war support and forced to withdraw American troops, a peace settlement might not follow. "It takes two to make a peace," wrote Representative James Graham, of North Carolina, in early 1847, "and I do not know that Mexico is willing to make peace. They are a faithless, perfidious people. If we were now to bring our troops on this side of the Rio Grande, she might pursue and prosecute the War on the East side of that River. . . ." In such an instance, "those who oppose the prosecution of the War *now*, will take the responsibility from the shoulders of the Administration and *shoulder* it themselves."[22] Robert Winthrop, of Massachusetts, noted the same difficulty on the question of war supplies.

If Mexico . . . would give the slightest indication of a willingness to enter into negotiations, the case would be clearer. But when she persists in breathing nothing but threatenings & slaughters, & has an army of 30,000 men in martial array, it is rather a delicate matter to take ground for disbanding our own armies or bankrupting the Treasury from which they are to be paid.[23]

The response of most congressional critics, given this untenable situation, was predictable. However they might assail the administration and its war, most opponents consistently voted for war measures. Robert Winthrop well summarized the Whig position when the Twenty-ninth Congress reconvened, in December 1846, by agreeing with his friend Edward Everett that the "true

---

[20]*The Daily Union* (Washington), 9 Feb. 1847, as quoted in Charles M. Wiltse, *John C. Calhoun: Sectionalist, 1840–1850* (Indianapolis, 1951), 299.

[21]Richardson, *Messages and Papers of the Presidents,* IV, 473.

[22]Graham to William Graham, 10 Jan. 1847, *Papers of William Graham,* III, 171.

[23]Robert Winthrop to Mrs. Gardiner, 2 Feb. 1847, Boston, Massachusetts Historical Society, Winthrop Family Papers.

policy of the Whigs" should be "to protest against the war in its causes or rather its pretexts," while saying to the administration that "it is necessary to get honorably out of it:—take as many men and ships and as much money as you please."[24]

Closely related to the problem of forcing President Polk to reverse his war policy was the problem of offering a realistic alternative which would gain peace with honor. Complicating their situation was the fact that opponents of the war did not agree on what the legitimate war goals should be. And this disagreement was reflected in the various alternatives proposed in Congress. A few radical anti-slavery Whigs simply demanded immediate, unilateral withdrawal. They reasoned that because the United States was the agressor, the war would end when the invasion of Mexico was terminated. Basic to the withdrawal plan was the assumption that Mexico would willingly negotiate outstanding grievances through regular diplomatic channels. A second alternative was the "No Territory" strategy devised and endorsed by the conservative majority of Whigs in early 1847. These Whigs attempted to amend various war appropriation bills with the following stipulation: "provided, always, and it is hereby declared to be the true intent and meaning of Congress in making this appropriation that the war with Mexico ought not to be prosecuted by this Government with any view to the dismemberment of that republic, or the acquisition, by conquest, of any portion of her territory. . . ."[25] Supporters of "No Territory" argued that if the United States would explicitly disavow all designs on Mexican soil as a war goal, the enemy would be convinced by this display of good faith, and negotiate an end to the war. In an effort to satisfy expansionist demands for Mexican territory, conservative Whigs denied that their strategy would preclude continued expansion. Once the war ended, they argued, Mexico would probably be willing to sell upper California.

A third, and probably the most realistic, plan was John C. Calhoun's defensive line strategy. In February 1847, with American forces occupying a large portion of northern Mexico and an invasion of central Mexico imminent, Calhoun recommended that Amerian forces assume a "defensive position," claiming a boundary running along the Rio Grande to the southern border of New Mexico, then due west along the thirty-second parallel to the head of the Gulf of California, and finally south through the Gulf to the Pacific Ocean. As an alternative to a possible unlimited war of subjugation against Mexico, this plan envisioned limited territorial acquisition, including New Mexico and upper California. Such a strategy, according to Calhoun, would end the fighting, establish the Rio Grande as the border of Texas, and secure a limited territorial indemnity for war expenses. More important, it

[24]Edward Everett to Winthrop, 5 Dec. 1846, Winthrop Papers; Winthrop to Everett, 12 Dec. 1846, Massachusetts Historical Society, Edward Everett Papers.

[25]*Congressional Globe*, 29 Cong., 2 sess., vol. 16, pt. 1, Appendix, 297.

138

would provide the basis for a permanent peace because the line represented a natural geographic border, and the area north of the line was of little value to Mexico. Calhoun argued that once Mexico was no longer threatened with complete subjugation, and clearly understood the great difficulty involved in any attempt to dislodge American forces from their position, she would promptly end the war.[26]

Inherent in each of these alternative plans, however, were a variety of basic flaws. For example, proponents of unilateral withdrawal and "No Territory" clearly underestimated the intensity of Mexican antipathy toward the United States, and the eagerness of Mexico to wage war against her. This long-standing animosity ran deep. Mexico felt that, not only had the United States arrogantly annexed Texas, it had even failed to apologize for the injury. In short, Mexico was unlikely to terminate hostilities simply because American troops were withdrawn, or the United States disclaimed further designs on Mexican soil. Any Mexican regime negotiating the sale of any territory courted its political demise.

Furthermore, the "No Territory" plan was virtually meaningless, diplomatically. American troops already occupied New Mexico, California, a large part of northern Mexico, and were about to strike into the heart of the nation. With American forces occupying this vast area, "No Territory" amendments were without substance unless they were tied to congressional demands for troop withdrawal. But conservative Whigs, many of whom wanted San Francisco Bay, never supported, or even seriously contemplated, such action. Administration critics also found serious objections to Calhoun's defensive line plan. Most important was the fact that Calhoun's plan would have added much more territory than they wanted. Although most would accept a portion of upper California, they wanted no part of the vast area between Texas and the Pacific coast. None of the proposed alternatives promised success, all contained serious shortcomings. Further, the opposition's disunity made policy alternatives impossible of realization. Never was the opposition able to agree upon, or unite in support of, one anti-war strategy.

This lack of unity resulted directly from the distinct composition and conflicting objectives of the three main anti-war factions. Moreover, each faction tended to view the war as secondary to other issues and to partisan political concerns.

The largest anti-war faction was the conservative wing of the Whig party. Consisting of a large majority of the party's adherents, this faction included illustrious politicians from every section of the nation. Among them were Daniel Webster and Robert Winthrop of Massachusetts, John Berrien and Alexander H. Stephens of Georgia, Henry Clay and John J. Crittenden of

[26]*Ibid.*, 323–27.

Kentucky, and Thomas Corwin of Ohio. Essentially, they addressed the war as a partisan political question rather than as a moral issue. Although they wanted to end the war as quickly as possible, they were more determined to make political capital from it. Because these dual goals were not always compatible, the conservative Whigs compromised their opposition. On the critical queston of war supplies, the Whigs attempted to discredit the administration without damaging the military effort. Accordingly, they sought to frustrate Polk's conduct of the war by delaying, tabling, and amending his military recommendations. However, once these war measures reached a final vote, conservative Whigs voted their support. Likewise, in congressional debate, the Whigs tirelessly assailed the injustice of the war and censured the president's conduct of it. At the same time, they identified with the military triumphs and glory. In both houses, the party extolled the services of American soldiers, and eagerly supported resolutions expressing appreciation to Whig Generals Zachary Taylor and Winfield Scott.[27]

140

The "No Territory" plan of the conservative Whigs also demonstrated the expediency of their position. Meaningless diplomatically, but sound politically, their proposed "No Territory" amendments to war bills enabled Whigs to support the military effort while denouncing Polk's war of conquest. Demanding an end to the war, they could continue to extoll American military achievements. It was, then, an anti-war strategy designed to strengthen the Whig party in anticipation of the 1848 presidential campaign. Conservative Whigs understood that the addition of new territory would precipitate an acrimonious debate over the status of slavery in those areas. They shied from such a struggle. Politicians who loved their party and the Union dearly, Henry Clay, Thomas Corwin, Daniel Webster, and others, wanted to avoid the slavery question because it would shatter the national unity of the Whig party as well as endanger the Union. "No Territory" achieved their purpose during the Mexican War.

Seeking to confront the issue assiduously evaded by the conservative Whigs was a second group of congressional war opponents, the radical anti-slavery Whigs. Known variously as the Conscience Whigs, the "ultras," or the Young Whigs, this small faction of 15 to 20 men was centered in the House. Most prominent was John Quincy Adams but, because of the former president's advancing age and faltering health, fiery Joshua R. Giddings, of Ohio, became its effective leader and spokesman. The war, as the radicals viewed it, was the transparent scheme of the slave power to extend the immoral and criminal institution of slavery into the Southwest. While the

[27]In the congressional elections of 1847, Whig candidates and editors also used Taylor's fame in an attempt to elect Whigs. By booming Old Rough and Ready's name, Whigs could identify themselves with the successful military effort, and foil Democratic attempts to impugn Whig loyalty on the war issue. For an excellent analysis of these elections, see Brian G. Walton, "Elections for the Thirtieth Congress and the Presidential Candidacy of Zachary Taylor," *Journal of Southern History,* XXV (May 1969), 186–202.

conservative Whigs, ever sensitive to the politics of the war issue, maintained their moderate position, the radicals opposed virtually every war measure. They argued that those who supported the war effort only implicated themselves in the crime. "In the murder of Mexicans upon their own soil, or in robbing them of their country," asserted Giddings, "I can take no part either now or hereafter. The guilt of these crimes must rest on others—I will not participate in them. . . ."[28]

Initially, the radical Whigs demanded the unilateral and immediate withdrawal of American troops. When the futility of this demand became obvious, they settled on a more ingenious strategy, which advocated the attachment of the Wilmot Proviso to essential war measures. This proviso provided that slavery was never to exist in any territory acquired from Mexico in the war. Here the radical rationale was both consistent and direct. Because the war was a scheme of the slave power, the anti-slavery Whigs argued that once the possibility of slavery in any new territory was removed, southern incentive for the war would disappear. They felt that southern politicans would immediately demand that the war cease, loath as they were to expend another drop of southern blood, or another southern dollar, to prosecute a war adding free territory to the Union. Men like Joshua Giddings believed that this proviso strategy had a chance of success. Northern politicians of both parties might well vote in support of the proviso, rather than risk the disfavor of their increasingly anti-slavery constituencies.[29] In fact, the proviso was doomed to failure. Clearly, the radicals' view of the war as a slave plot, and their resulting anti-war strategy, prevented any strong coalition with either the conservative Whigs or the pro-slavery Calhoun Democrats.

The third congressional anti-war faction was that of John C. Calhoun and his small group of southern adherents. Both politics and principle motivated the opposition of Calhoun who, by 1846, was resentful of the Polk administration. The South Carolinian believed that high-minded and independent criticism of the war would enhance his stature as a formidable presidential candidate in 1848. At the same time, Calhoun sincerely believed that the war promised to harm the nation's political system and the special interests of the South. Polk's provocation of the war had violated the Constitution by usurping the war-making power of Congress. Moreover, the president's war of invasion and conquest would aggrandize the power of the executive branch of the federal government. This, Calhoun argued, could only injure the southern states, because their political and domestic security relied on a strict

141

---

[28]*Congressional Globe,* 29 Cong., 1 sess., vol. 15, pt. 2, Appendix, 644.

[29]See for example, Joshua R. Giddings to Oran Follett, 26 Jul. 1847 in "Selections from the Follett Papers, III," ed. by Belle L. Hamlin, in *Quarterly Publication of the Historical and Philosophical Society of Ohio,* X (Nov. 1915), 30-33; Giddings to Charles Francis Adams, 12 Aug. 1847, Massachusetts Historical Society, Adams Family Papers.

142

Despite strong opposition, President James K. Polk accomplished most of his war aims.

interpretation of the Constitution and on the doctrine of state rights. Finally, Calhoun was alarmed because he believed that the war would reverse what he called the trend of "reform" in national politics, by renewing calls for a high protective tariff, by strengthening the spoils system in government appointments, and by elevating a Whig to the presidency.[30]

In an attempt to maintain the "reform" trend and to curtail what he believed was becoming an unlimited war of conquest, Calhoun introduced his defensive line strategy. To deal with the slavery question in the territories to be acquired, Calhoun also introduced a resolution declaring that Congress had no power to prohibit American citizens from migrating with their property into any territory of the United States. Despite the fact that Calhoun's plan was probably the most realistic one, it received little Whig support. Similarly, Calhoun refused to contemplate demands for withdrawal made by anti-slavery Whigs, or "No Territory" amendments proposed by partisan-oriented conservative Whigs. Most conservative Whigs refused to budge from their "No Territory" position, and radical Whigs judged Calhoun's positions on the war and slavery to be unconscionable.[31]

143

Failing to unite on one anti-war strategy, the congressional opponents of the Mexican War were doomed to the ineffectiveness which has traditionally marked American anti-war movements. They were unable to end, limit, or even shorten the conflict. What the opposition did accomplish, was to discredit the Democratic administration politically, while frustrating the president personally. From 1846 to 1848, the war issue was one of several which combined to weaken the Democratic party and prepare the way for a Whig victory in 1848. The opposition also angered Polk by delaying, tabling, endlessly debating, and occasionally defeating Polk's war measures. During the Twenty-ninth and Thirtieth Congresses, Polk complained bitterly about the lack of patriotic activity on Capitol Hill. At one point in early 1847, he became so exasperated that he contemplated sending a special message to Congress "calling for action upon the War measures which I have recommended, and which are indispensible to maintain the honour and rights of the country."[32] Ultimately, Polk's perseverence surmounted the weak opposition and secured passage of the war measures he requested.

Probably the most significant achievement of the opposition occurred in February 1848, when Polk submitted a peace settlement to the Senate. The president had serious doubts about the treaty, which had been negotiated in January by Nicholas Trist, a diplomat whom the president had officially

---

[30]See for example, Calhoun to T. G. Clemson, 30 Jul. 1846, in *"Correspondence of John C. Calhoun,"* ed. by J. Franklin Jameson, *Annual Report of the American Historical Association for the Year 1899* (2 vols., Washington, 1900) II, 703; Calhoun to J. E. Calhoun, 12 Dec. 1846, *ibid.,* 714; Calhoun to Mrs. T. G. Clemson, 17 Feb. 1847, *ibid.,* 718; Calhoun to H. W. Conner, 14 May 1847, Conner Papers.

[31]Among the very few Whigs who did endorse Calhoun's strategy were Senator Joseph R. Underwood, of Kentucky, and Representative Caleb Smith, of Indiana.

[32]*Diary of James K. Polk,* II, 368–69.

recalled. Most important, it ceded less territory to the United States than Polk desired. Despite his misgivings, the president finally decided to accept the treaty because it conformed to Trist's original instructions, and because Polk feared that his original territorial goals might be lost if the war continued. For, with the Whigs now in control of the House, Polk feared that Congress would not grant the requisite men and money. "Should this be the result, the army in Mexico would be constantly wasting and diminishing in numbers, and I might at last be compelled to withdraw them, and thus loose [*sic*] the two Provinces of New Mexico & California, which were ceded to the United States by this Treaty."[33] Whatever the validity of Polk's reasoning, and there is reason to believe that Congress would have continued to sustain the war, by 1848 the intensity of the opposition was a factor in ending the conflict. This, then, was the reward for nearly two years of effort.

144

[33]*Ibid.*, III, 348.

THE ATTEMPT TO IMPEACH DANIEL WEBSTER

by

Howard Jones

In retrospect, it is difficult to understand how, short of sheer politics, charges of misconduct in office could have been made against Daniel Webster in 1846. Four years earlier, when he was secretary of state under Whig President John Tyler, Webster helped negotiate a treaty with Great Britain which included settlement of the northeastern boundary of the United States. Uncertainty about the border had existed since the Paris peace negotiations of 1782–83, which ended the Revolutionary War. The disagreement over this issue varied in intensity, lasting until the ratification of the Webster-Ashburton Treaty. The boundary agreement of 1842 had met with much criticism on both sides of the Atlantic—most of it clearly politically inspired. Though the treaty passed both Senate and Parliament by comfortable margins, an investigatory committee in the House of Representatives set out, in 1846, to determine whether Webster, by then Whig senator from Massachusetts, had committed offenses serious enough during the negotiations to justify the unusual procedure of retroactive impeachment.

The background of this impeachment attempt was complex. One element was the unstable political situation in the 1840s. Tyler, soon to be without a party, became the first vice president to assume the presidency as a result of the death of the chief executive. After a bitter power struggle within the Whig party, all members of the cabinet resigned except Webster, who stayed on, he said, because he wanted to continue the northeastern boundary negotiations with Great Britain. Complicating matters was the belief of some

31

Originally published in *Capitol Studies*, 3 (Fall, 1975). Reprinted by permission of the United States Capitol Historical Society.

Americans that the Webster-Ashburton Treaty was a questionable document. It was, after all, a compromise with the British. There was the involvement of Webster himself. He had an almost insatiable need for money, he aspired to the presidency, and for some time he coveted the appointment as American minister at the Court of St. James's in London. Some wondered if he would sell out his country to achieve these objectives.

Democratic Representative Charles Ingersoll, an Anglophobe from Pennsylvania, served as the catalyst for those who personally and/or politically opposed Webster, distrusted Great Britain, or disliked the treaty. The long, bitter Webster-Ingersoll rivalry became public in February 1846 when Ingersoll, Chairman of the House Committee on Foreign Affairs, and Daniel Dickinson, a Democratic senator from New York, accused Webster of promoting federal interference in the case of Alexander McLeod in 1841. McLeod, a Canadian sheriff, was arrested by New York authorities in 1840 for allegedly taking part in the destruction of the privately owned American steamboat *Caroline* in December 1837, an affair involving murder and arson during the Canadian rebellions against the British crown. The Tyler administration had tried—and failed—to remove McLeod's case from the state's courts, while Foreign Secretary Lord Palmerston and others in Great Britain warned that the Canadian's execution would lead to war. McLeod was acquitted but, in 1846, Ingersoll and Dickinson accused Webster of three separate actions: trying to prevent the trial, warning Governor William Seward that unless McLeod was released, New York City would be "laid in ashes," and paying McLeod's defense counsel from government funds.[1]

The affair then took a peculiar twist. Sometime between late February and early April, Ingersoll found that he had been "misinformed" about Webster's actions. His search of the State Department's archives failed to uncover evidence that the Tyler administration had paid McLeod's attorney's fees, and he did not locate the letter allegedly showing that Webster had told Seward that the British would attack New York if McLeod went to trial. The congressman, therefore, prepared to withdraw his charge in the House. He asked his Democratic colleague from Pennsylvania, Henry Foster, to intercede, and offered to retract the allegation of "improper transactions" by the State Department in 1841. Foster told two of Webster's Whig friends in the House, Thomas King of Georgia, and Robert Schenck of Ohio, that Ingersoll planned to withdraw the charge because his information had been "erroneous." But there was a condition: Webster was to withdraw remarks he had made earlier about Ingersoll. Webster, however, had Ingersoll in an embarrassing position and would not let the matter drop. Twice he refused the

[1] U. S. Congress, House, *Congressional Globe,* 29th Cong., 1st sess., vol. 15, pt. 1, 344, 419, 422; Alastair Watt, "The Case of Alexander McLeod," *Canadian Historical Review,* XII (Je. 1931), 145–67; Seward to Richard Blatchford, 23 Mar. 1846, Charles M. Wiltse, ed., Daniel Webster Papers, Dartmouth College (Film 20/26798). Hereafter the Wiltse film collection will be cited as WP.

arrangement. He later explained to a friend that under no conditions would he grant "some soft words" about Ingersoll.[2]

On April 6 and 7, 1846, in the midst of debates over Oregon and Mexico, Webster unleashed a blistering attack against both Ingersoll and Dickinson. He first praised the northeastern boundary settlement, then challenged them to prove "direct and palpable interference by the federal government" in the McLeod case. Ingersoll's speech, Webster declared, was not fit to come out of a "bar-room anywhere." Every statement deserved the label of that "expressive monosyllable which some people are base enough and low enough to deserve to have thrown in their teeth, but which a gentleman does not often like to utter." The only note he exchanged with Seward before summer of 1841, the senator asserted, was dated March 11. In it, he thanked Seward for intimating that, as governor, he would recommend that the state of New York enter a *nolle prosequi* in the McLeod case. Ingersoll's allegations, Webster concluded, originated from "moral obtuseness," the inability to discern truth from falsehood. His mind, Webster bitterly remarked, was "grotesque—*bizarre*." Usually one says "there is a screw loose somewhere," but in "this case the screws are loose all over."[3]

147

Ingersoll, of course, could not let this attack go unanswered. In an effort to save face, he brought a new series of charges—this time on matters relating to the Webster-Ashburton Treaty. In April, on the floor of the House, he three times lashed out at Webster. He accused the senator of "corrupting" the party press in New England by circulating newspaper editorials calling for a boundary settlement. The money for that action, the congressman asserted, came from Webster's unauthorized use of the president's secret service fund, set aside for matters involving foreign relations. To his "great amazement," Ingersoll proclaimed, he discovered this new evidence in the State Department's secret archives. When some House members expressed concern about how he had gained access to these documents, Ingersoll explained that an unidentified subordinate of Secretary of State James Buchanan had granted him entrance because of his position as Chairman of the House Committee on Foreign Affairs. Ingersoll quickly added that he supposed any House member had authority to examine the archives. There was no "conspiracy" against either Webster or the Whig party, he assured his colleagues. His motive was "vindication" of character against the recent personal attack by Webster in the Senate. Ignoring his friends who urged him not to pursue the

---

[2]"Statements of Thomas Butler King & Robert Cumming Schenck re Ingersoll charges," Apr. 1846, WP (20/26877); Webster to Edward Curtis, 15 Apr. 1846, WP (20/26842). Neither Webster nor Tyler could recall the note to Seward which Ingersoll claimed had existed—see Webster to Tyler, 5 Mar. 1846, WP (20/26763) and Tyler to Webster, 12 Mar. 1846, WP (20/26772).

[3]Senate, *Cong. Globe,* 29th Cong., 1st sess., vol. 15, pt. 1, 609–12, 616–20. See Webster's "Notes on Mr. Ingersoll's charges," Apr. 1846, WP (20/26869); Webster to Curtis, 1 May 1846, WP (20/26883); Webster to Fletcher Webster (son), 5 May 1846, WP (20/26901); Webster to Fletcher Webster, 20 May 1846, WP (20/26969). A *nolle prosequi* is a formal notice by the prosecutor that prosecution in a criminal case would be ended.

matter, Ingersoll called upon the House to investigate three charges: (1) un-lawful use of the president's secret service fund; (2) improper deployment of the money to "corrupt party presses"; (3) leaving the State Department in default of some of the money.[4]

Before detailing the charges, Ingersoll explained the purpose of the president's contingency fund. Congress had established it in 1810 "for the contingent expenses of intercourse between the United States and foreign nations." It provided an annual appropriation of nearly $30,000, which the president could use according to his discretion. If the chief executive thought it inadvisable to publicize expenditures, he was to fill out a certificate or voucher indicating the amount spent and deposit it in a secret file in the Treasury Department. On the requisition of his secretary of state, the president could authorize withdrawals through a "disbursing agent" who credited the sum to the State Department's account. The first check drawn during the Tyler administration, Ingersoll showed, was for $1,000, payable to Attorney General John Crittenden for service in New York during the McLeod controversy. During his tenure, Webster withdrew a total of $17,000, none of which, Ingersoll declared, the president had authorized. Tyler, in fact, had been unaware of his secretary's activities until fourteen months after the first withdrawal. At that time, Ingersoll claimed, the president refused to approve such actions.[5]

148

Ingersoll then said that part of the money went for Webster's personal use. A memorandum in the State Department archives showed that Webster, on June 23, 1842, returned $5,000 to the fund, ten days after negotiations had begun with Lord Ashburton, Great Britain's special minister to the United States. Though Webster eventually procured vouchers for several of the other expenditures, a balance of $2,290 remained against him. The secretary left office on May 8, 1843 in default of this amount, Ingersoll concluded.[6]

As for Webster's alleged corruption of the party press in Maine, Ingersoll explained that, in the months preceding the northeastern boundary settle-ment, Webster had deployed secret agents, led by a former state legislator from Maine, Francis Smith, to persuade the state's citizens to accept a compromise line. Such procedure, Ingersoll declared, was financed by the secret service fund. A letter dated August 12, 1842, written by Smith to the secretary, called on the Washington government to "fulfill certain assurances" to persons in Maine who had directed the "party presses." In it Smith said he would accept whatever compensation Webster considered appropriate, but reminded him that they had agreed on an amount in June of the previous

[4]House, *Cong. Globe,* 29th Cong., 1st sess., vol. 15, pt. 1, 636, 699, 729–30. It seems that Ingersoll was correct in his assurances about access to the State Department.
[5]*Ibid.,* 729–30; 2 U. S. *Statutes at Large,* 1810, XLIV, 609; "Copy of a Memorandum," by disbursing agent of State Department of 24 Aug. 1842, but in Webster's handwriting, in "Select Committee on Charges against Mr. Daniel Webster made by C. J. Ingersoll," in WP (40/55375).
[6]House, *Cong. Globe,* 29th Cong., 1st sess., vol. 15, pt. 1, 730.

year. Fair payment to the other agents in Maine—three in number—was $100 or $125 each. Enclosed in the August letter was a bill left blank, which Webster was to fill with fair payment for Smith's services. The secretary eventually remitted $2,000 to Smith, in addition to $500 given him in May 1841, at the outset of their arrangement. Smith's assistants in Maine received $500. All expenditures, Ingersoll noted, came from the secret service fund.[7]

Ingersoll's third charge was a reiteration of the alleged defaults. State Department records, he said, showed that, during the two years following Webster's departure from the State Department, President Tyler sent several letters to him which urged payment. All elicited evasive replies. Only when threatened with public exposure did Webster reimburse the fund, but this was not until February 1, 1845, a month before the inauguration of James Polk. At that time, Webster produced additional vouchers. Despite these returns, Ingersoll declared, the former secretary still owed $1,200 to the fund.[8]

Ingersoll's purpose, it was clear, was the retroactive impeachment of Webster, the first so threatened to a high official in the United States government. Asking Congress to censure Webster for "misconduct" while secretary of state, he urged a House resolution calling on the president to furnish State Department materials which would prove "misdemeanors in office." The question was whether Webster's "malversation, corruption, and delinquency . . . will be deemed impeachable misdemeanors in office, and disqualify him to hold any office of honor, trust or profit, under the United States." That same day, the House moved, by a vote of 136 to 28, that the president furnish State Department documents relating to money drawn from the secret service fund during Webster's tenure as secretary of state. On April 27, it passed the following resolution presented by John Pettit, Democrat from Indiana: ". . . a select committee of five be appointed, to inquire into the truth of the charges this day made in this House by Mr. C. J. Ingersoll against Mr. Daniel Webster, with a view to founding an impeachment against said Daniel Webster. . . ."[9]

Despite the House's understandable unfamiliarity with the impeachment process, several members made insightful comments. Thomas Bayly, Democrat from Virginia, raised a key question (which remained unanswered at least until the 1870s and, more than likely, would be a major source of contention today if it were raised again). Can the House impeach a man no longer in office? Though Ingersoll dismissed the issue as unimportant, Bayly doubted that it was possible, because the Constitution provided for the impeachment of an "officer," not a man. In addition, the House could not impeach Webster in his present position because, like a representative, Bayly shrewdly pointed out, a senator was not an "officer of the United States"; he was an officer of

149

[7]*Ibid.*, 730; Smith to Webster, 12 Aug. 1842, WP (40/55197).
[8]House, *Cong. Globe,* 29th Cong., 1st sess., vol. 15, pt. 1, 730.
[9]*Ibid.*, 636, 643, 735.

150

CREDIT CITY OF BOSTON

Daniel Webster makes his famed reply the Senator Robert Hayne, some sixteen years before the move to impeach him.

the state he represented in Congress. Bayly could not approve of Ingersoll's resolutions to secure evidence "with a view to an impeachment." If the charges seemed warranted, he undoubtedly was implying, the Senate could censure him or expel him from that body. Such right, of course, rested in the Constitution, for it provides that each house determines the qualifications of its members. Webster's case then could go to civil courts of law.[10]

Bayly's remarks drew an immediate rebuttal from former president and current Whig representative, John Quincy Adams. A public officer, Adams assured the House, was always subject to impeachment. The Constitution provides that: "Judgment in Cases of Impeachment shall not extend further than to removal from Office, and disqualification to hold and enjoy any Office of honor, Trust, or Profit under the United States: but the Party convicted shall nevertheless be liable and subject to Indictment, Trial, Judgment, and Punishment, according to Law." Thus there were two provisions for punishment, Adams reminded Bayly: removal from a present position, and disqualification from further public office in the United States. If the House at any time decided to impeach him (Adams) for acts committed while he was president, he was answerable to those charges. If found guilty, he said, it could expel him from Congress.[11]

151

Adams then challenged Ingersoll. Since only the President of the United States could authorize expenditures from the secret service fund, Ingersoll's motion should call for the impeachment of former President Tyler. Until the resolution was revised in this manner, Adams refused to consider impeachment. Ingersoll made no reply.[12]

That same day, Democratic supporters of Ingersoll exchanged some fiery remarks with Whig defenders of Webster, and the House moved for an additional resolution proposed by Schenck, a Whig from Ohio: that a committee of five determine how Ingersoll broke the "seal of confidence" in gaining entrance into the secret archives. Sitting on the committee were three Whigs and two Democrats; on the committee investigating the advisability of impeachment were two Whigs and three Democrats.[13]

Testimony before the committee investigating Ingersoll's charges was given privately, some of it later becoming public. It began with the appearance of the disbursing clerk of the State Department, Edward Stubbs, who underwent careful examination for ten days, from May 9 through May 18. His statements, all supported by documents he produced from State Department archives, conclusively defended Webster's conduct. Every part of the $17,000 withdrawn from the fund, Stubbs showed, was approved by a direct written order of either President William Harrison or President Tyler. Before

[10]*The Constitution,* Art. I, sec. 5, cl. 2; House, *Cong. Globe,* 29th Cong., 1st sess., vol. 15, pt. 1, 638.
[11]*The Constitution,* Art. I, sec. 3, cl. 7; House, *Cong. Globe,* 29th Cong., 1st sess., vol. 15, pt. 1, 641.
[12]*Ibid.*
[13]*Ibid.,* 637, 639–40, 643, 648, 650, 653, 708–709, 731. For the House resolution, see *ibid.,* 734.

Webster left office in May 1843, Tyler wanted to close the accounts, and directed Stubbs to request payment or vouchers from the secretary which would verify the expenditures. Almost three months later, Webster prepared to make payment from personal funds for vouchers not yet received. Tyler, Stubbs explained, had preferred the money immediately, but had allowed Webster to adjust his account when new vouchers arrived. On February 1, 1845, Webster paid the State Department $1,250, leaving $1,050 due, which he later paid. Thus, at the present time, Stubbs emphatically declared, there was nothing outstanding against Webster in public funds.[14]

Stubbs's favorable testimony surprised Webster. The former secretary, convinced that the "original mover of the mischief" was Stubbs, believed that the clerk had gone first to Ingersoll with information relating to the McLeod case. Perhaps he had not intended for the congressman to see secret papers but, once access to the archives was granted, Ingersoll was "let loose among all the vouchers & papers touching secret service money." Though President Tyler doubted that Stubbs had been the one, Webster thought that if Secretary of State Buchanan had "any sense of justice," he would remove the clerk from the archives.[15]

The committee investigation continued with the appearance of Francis Smith, whose four-day testimony reconstructed an elaborate tale of how the Tyler administration, through Webster, engineered Maine's assent to the boundary settlement. In a meeting with Webster, Smith had advocated convincing influential members of both the Democratic and Whig parties in Maine of the necessity of a compromise line. The president, he had argued, should appoint an agent to visit Maine and New Brunswick to determine acceptable terms. A petition would urge the legislature in Augusta to start proceedings. Meanwhile, the state's newspapers would publish unsigned editorials calling for action. The federal government, Smith had suggested, should finance his proposals.[16]

Webster, Smith testified, showed immediate interest. On June 7, 1841, Smith assured him by letter that Maine would cede land to allow a compromise line if it received "equivalents" in land or money. The person advancing this program should be committed to a compromise solution from a "per-

---

[14]Deposition of Stubbs, 9–18 May 1846, in "Unpublished Testimony of the Select Committee," WP (40/55279).

[15]Webster to Fletcher Webster, 17 May 1846, WP (20/26954); Tyler to Webster, 21 Apr. 1846, WP (20/26855); Webster to Fletcher Webster, 20 May 1846, WP (20/26969); Webster to Fletcher Webster, 31 May 1846, WP (20/27013).

[16]Smith to Daniel Webster, 30 Apr. 1846, WP (20/26864). For Smith's background, see Frederick Merk, *Fruits of Propaganda in the Tyler Administration* (Cambridge, Mass., 1971), 9, 59–62; Henry S. Burrage, *Maine in the Northeastern Boundary Controversy* (Portland, 1919), 315. "Official Misconduct of the Late Secretary of State," U. S. Congress, *House Report,* 29th Cong., 1st sess., Serial 490, No. 684, 11–13. Smith had unsuccessfully urged President Martin Van Buren to adopt the same plan in 1837. Smith to Van Buren, 7 Dec. 1837, with enclosure: "Instructions proposed to be given to an agent on the ne boundary & c.", Library of Congress, Martin Van Buren Papers.

sonal, political, and national point of view." Smith volunteered his services. Compensation would be $3,500 a year, in addition to expenses. In the event of success, he expected a further "liberal commission" on whatever monetary exchanges took place during negotiations with Great Britain. President Tyler, Smith emphasized carefully, agreed that the plan might work, and advanced him $500 from the contingency fund.[17]

Having the approval of Tyler, Smith and Webster proceeded with the plan. Smith first circulated a petition in Maine which, after being signed, was forwarded to the legislature in Augusta. Entitled "Settlement of the Northeastern Boundary," it exhorted political leaders to compromise on the boundary dispute before war resulted with Great Britain. Three editorials appeared in the Portland *Christian Mirror*, on November 18 and December 2, 1841, and on February 3, 1842. All signed by "Agricola" and entitled "Northeastern Boundary—Why Not Settle It?", they repeated that the most likely alternative to compromise was war. Finally, Smith and Webster tried to persuade the legislature to appoint commissioners to the negotiations in Washington between Webster and Ashburton. To emphasize the international importance of such an act, Smith accepted the advice of state legislators who recommended that he urge the governor to call a special session. This, they hoped, would underline the gravity of the boundary problem. It also would leave the impression that the movement for compromise with the British had not originated among legislative members themselves.[18]

153

Webster, perhaps without Smith's knowledge, secretly sent Harvard professor of history, Jared Sparks, to Maine in May 1842 to convince its lawmakers of the need for a settlement. He took two maps, which apparently proved the British case for the land in dispute. Sparks's purpose was to persuade the Augusta legislature to act before the maps' publication led to a boundary unfavorable to Maine. His arrival probably caused the legislature to respond to the governor's plea for immediate action. By an almost unanimous vote—177 to 11 in the House, and 29 to 0 in the Senate—the legislature agreed to compromise the dispute, and appointed four delegates —two Democrats and two Whigs—to attend the negotiations in Washington.[19]

[17]"Official Misconduct of the Late Secretary of State," 11; Smith to Webster, 7 Je. 1841, WP (40/55251); Tyler to Webster, 25 Aug. 1842, WP (40/55376).

[18]Petition enclosed in Smith to Webster, 2 Jul. 1841, WP (40/55256); Smith's articles reprinted in "Official Misconduct of the Late Secretary of State," 26–35. On the attempt to secure commissioners to the negotiations, see Francis Smith to Jonathan Smith, 14 Feb. 1842, WP (40/55263); "Official Misconduct of the Late Secretary of State," 14; Webster to Reuel Williams, 2 Feb. 1842, WP (16/21475); Peleg Sprague to Webster, 17 Feb. 1842, WP (16/21606).

[19]Webster to Sparks, 14 May 1842, WP (17/22449); Webster to Sparks, 16 May 1842, WP (17/22464); Herbert B. Adams, *The Life and Writings of Jared Sparks: Comprising Selections from His Journals and Correspondence* (2 vols., Boston, 1893), II, 400; Maine Legislature, *Journal of the Maine Senate,* 22nd Legislature, special session, 26 May 1842, 33–34.

Smith's testimony revealed no sinister motives by the Tyler administration. The campaign in Maine, Smith assured the committee, was a "worthy act," which did not involve bribery or "party purpose." He pointed out that, on the basis of his August 12 letter to Webster, he asked for a commission of only $375 after the signing of the Webster-Ashburton Treaty. If there was anything illegal or questionable about the government's activities in Maine, he remarked to the committee, certainly the pay scale was small. It seemed logical that if there had been "venal motives" involved, he would have pressed Webster for the rest of the money asked for in his June 7, 1841 letter. Smith trusted that Ingersoll's allegations were "an error of temporary passion, and not of the heart," and hoped he would withdraw them.[20]

154

The decisive point in Webster's defense probably came with the appearance before the committee of former President Tyler. In addition to helping disprove Ingersoll's allegations, Tyler's presence no doubt suggested the importance of the presidential office and might have had a psychological effect on members of the committee. Officially summoned by the committee, he began with a long statement of how dangerous Anglo-American relations had become by the time he took office in the spring of 1841. He then corroborated Stubbs's testimony by declaring that he had authorized Webster to draw upon the secret service fund in hiring agents to gather information about the border disputes. Because there was no pro-Tyler newspaper in the state, the president had followed Smith's suggestion to make known the administration's view in the Portland *Christian Mirror*. Without Maine's concurrence, he asserted, there could have been no boundary settlement. Use of the secret service fund had had his knowledge and approval. Besides, employment of agents by the executive office had been accepted practice since the presidency of George Washington. As for the claim of default, Webster had deposited enough personal funds to balance the account, with the understanding that when he presented the other vouchers the government would refund his money.[21]

There could be little doubt of the outcome. The House committee on June 9, 1846, by vote of four to one, exonerated Webster of all charges. The chairman stated the majority opinion: The law committed the secret service fund to exclusive jurisdiction of the president, who could disburse the money himself, or appoint an agent to do so. The committee found no evidence that Webster had used public money to "corrupt the party presses," a decision which suggests that such claim was virtually incapable of proof. As for the president's use of confidential agents, the committee refused to "inquire into the propriety of employing agents for secret service" within the United States.

[20]"Official Misconduct of the Late Secretary of State," 12–17.

[21]Tyler's full testimony, including the expurgated section, is in WP (40/55212). James K. Polk, *The Diary of James K. Polk: During His Presidency, 1845 to 1849*, ed. by Milo M. Quaife (4 vols., Chicago, 1910), I, 430–31.

On the final charge of default, there was little to debate after both Stubbs and Tyler testified that there was nothing outstanding in the account against Webster by the time Tyler left office in 1845. The committee concluded that there was no evidence "to impeach Mr. Webster's integrity or the purity of his motives in the discharge of the duties of his office."[22]

Three days later, June 12, the committee investigating how Ingersoll gained access to the State Department's secret files presented its report. The committee concluded that it could not identify the "one or more of the subordinate officers of the State Department" who had cooperated with Ingersoll. Consequently, it presented the testimony gathered "without any expression of . . . opinion in regard to what is established by it."[23]

There was an effort in the House, a week afterward, to print all testimony gathered in the investigation. The motion was defeated (77 to 57) for the reason set forth in the majority report: The investigation had uncovered facts about America's foreign affairs which, if publicized, could be detrimental to government policy. Members of the committee agreed with President Polk's recent Congressional message, in which he said that the only justification for turning over the documents was in the event of impeachment. Polk explained that if the House believed an inquiry necessary to determine whether there had been improper use of public funds, "all the archives and papers of the Executive departments, public or private, would be subject to the inspection and control of a committee of their body, and every facility in the power of the Executive be afforded to enable them to prosecute the investigation." The committee concurred that government secrecy was secondary to bringing "great public delinquents" to justice. Webster admitted that there might come a time when publication of secret government documents was necessary to bring "high handed offenders to justice," yet he could not foresee such a case arising in America. The House accepted the committee's recommendation that the sections of Tyler's and Stubbs's testimonies dealing with secret agents should be sealed, labeled confidential, and deposited in the national archives.[24]

The basic reason for the attempt to impeach Daniel Webster lies in the intense political atmosphere of the early 1840s, and in the hatred for Webster. When former President Tyler testified in Webster's behalf, he undermined the credibility of the only piece of "evidence" Ingersoll had—Smith's August 12 letter to Webster. Unfortunately for Webster, it was easy to believe charges of misuse of funds because of his notorious lack of thrift, and because of his usual inattention to administrative details in the Department of State. His

155

---

[22]"Official Misconduct of the Late Secretary of State," 1–4.

[23]House, *Cong. Globe,* 29th Cong., 1st sess., vol. 15, pt. 1, 966.

[24]*Ibid.*, 999–1000; "Official Misconduct of the Late Secretary of State," 4; James D. Richardson, ed., *A Compilation of the Messages and Papers of the Presidents* (11 vols., N.Y., 1910), IV, 431–36; Webster to Robert Winthrop, 2 May 1846, WP (20/26885); Webster to Winthrop, 6 May 1846, WP (20/26924).

laxity in securing vouchers for all money drawn from the contingency fund, his carelessness in paying the agreed amount to Smith, his failure to balance the department's accounts before leaving office—all made it appear that he was trying to hide criminal acts by inept bookkeeping.[25]

Another factor making Ingersoll's accusations seem plausible was Webster's employment of Francis Smith as a secret agent. Having the appearance of a shady, underworld character—he was nicknamed "Fog"—Smith was known as a political maverick guided solely by self-interest. The most difficult obstacle in reaching an objective assessment of these events is to view them independent of the motives often attributed to both Smith and Webster. The editorials placed in the Portland *Christian Mirror* simply called for members of both political parties in Maine to state conditions suitable for a boundary compromise. If there was something unethical, immoral, or illegal about the Tyler administration's use of Smith and the newspapers in Maine, it is not clear to this writer.

There can be little argument that Webster's New England campaign was instrumental in bringing about resolution of the boundary. It was a common sense approach to a complex problem, a method sorely needed since the decade of the 1780s. The secretary's use of the secret service fund was defensible because of the effect the boundary dispute had on Anglo-American relations. Further, partisan use of the press was common in American politics. Finally, the Tyler administration's activities may have stretched the statute establishing the contingency fund, but they were not illegal.

The majority report had significance beyond the immediate issue. It drew strong conclusions about proper behavior in public office. One was that government officials could refuse to disclose documents considered detrimental to the public interest. Another—perhaps the most striking—was that the federal government had no right to withhold evidence in proceedings which could lead to impeachment. Questions of public delinquency in office, to the committee and to President Polk, took precedence over appeals to secrecy in the name of public interest. Only after Tyler's testimony absolved Webster of guilt did the committee expurgate from the published documents any references to government employment of secret agents in Maine. Such information, its members reasoned, could damage the public interest.

It seems likely that most House members had no idea of the complex questions involved in the attempt to impeach Webster. Since he was no longer secretary of state, it was questionable, as Congressman Bayly argued, that impeachment proceedings could take place. In 1876 the secretary of war, William Belknap, resigned office two hours before he was to face impeachment by the House. Despite this, he was impeached, and the Senate acquitted him 37 to 25, just five votes short of the necessary two-thirds majority. It is especially interesting that 23 of the 25 senators who voted for acquittal

---

[25]Webster, for example, had not kept a record of the compensation made by the government to Sparks and others for their services in Maine. Webster to Fletcher Webster, 25 May 1846, WP (20/26987).

explained that they did so in the belief that the Senate had no jurisdiction over a civil officer who had resigned. As the Constitution divided the functions of impeachment and trial between the House and the Senate, so did the two bodies differ on whether Belknap was subject to impeachment. On April 15, 1970, Gerald Ford, then Minority Leader of the House, remarked about the attempt to impeach Supreme Court Justice William Douglas that "an impeachable offense is whatever a majority of the House of Representatives considers it to be at a given moment in history." In a similar fashion, it seems that the question of whether a resigned civil officer is subject to impeachment depends on what a majority of the House decides. In the same manner, his guilt appears partly dependent upon whether two-thirds of the Senate agree that the trial is just.[26]

On the basis of the Belknap case, the noted authority on the United States Constitution, Edward Corwin, declared that a civil officer's resignation does not give immunity from impeachment for acts committed while in office.[27] It perhaps is arguable that the incident established the precedent—but not until thirty years after the Webster case. If this is so, it seems that there would be no time limitation placed upon the bringing of charges. John Quincy Adams had argued that if he were found guilty of House charges relating to his presidency, he could be disqualified from holding public office. Yet he did not explain what procedure could have removed him from the House. That body could have expelled him because of its power to determine its members' qualifications. But this step is not part of the impeachment process. In the same way, the Senate could have expelled Webster by a two-thirds vote. Again, however, this is not part of the impeachment process.

There are several unanswered questions about the attempt to impeach Webster. Since, in 1846, the precedent for impeaching a resigned civil officer had not been set, could the House legally have gone ahead with impeachment? Since the Constitution makes it clear that the impeachment process does not apply to members of Congress—they are not "civil officers"—could supporters of Webster have construed the move as simply an effort to remove him from his Senate seat, as Ingersoll indiscreetly suggested? Could one have interpreted the Constitutional provision for punishment to mean that the disqualification from further office was predicated on removal from his present office? In other words, does removal have to precede disqualification, thus making judgment one continuous, inseparable process? If so, Adams was wrong and Bayly was right. Finally, could one assume that if a person could

---

[26]C. Herman Pritchett, an authority on the Constitution, believes that the Belknap case established the precedent that a civil officer can be impeached after he has left office. See his *The American Constitution* (2nd edition, N. Y., 1969), 204. Historian Irving Brant, noncommittal on the matter, concludes that Belknap "escaped conviction on a technicality that lay well within the bounds of legitimate differences of opinion." See his *Impeachment: Trials and Errors* (N. Y., 1972), 4, 155–61. U. S. Congress, House, *Congressional Record,* 91st Cong., 2nd sess., vol. 116, pt. 9, 11913.

[27]Edward S. Corwin, ed., *The Constitution of the United States of America: Analysis and Interpretation* 2nd ed., (New York, 1964), 556. In citing the Belknap case as precedent, Corwin wrote that "resignation of an officer does not give immunity from impeachment for acts committed while in office."

not be impeached after leaving office, he therefore could not be penalized by disqualification from future public office? This penalty, after all, is specifically for someone impeached and found guilty. Whatever the outcome, it seems that Webster's accusers could have explored two avenues of punishment: one, secure his removal from the Senate on the basis of the disqualification clause or, failing that, raise the necessary two-thirds vote in the Senate to expel him; two, eventually bring him to trial in the civil courts. In neither case, of course, could the House of Representatives have been involved.

More than likely, the House members urging impeachment used the term erroneously, as Bayly suggested. They, of course, had the right to accuse Webster of malfeasance in office, but instead of referring to impeachment they would have been wiser to have moved merely for investigation of criminal charges—with no mention of impeachment. Had a House investigation substantiated Ingersoll's allegations, the Senate could have expelled Webster, and the matter then could have gone to the civil courts.

There is real significance to the outcome of this case. Ingersoll's basic charges were that Webster had been guilty of misdemeanors. But, in addition to the secretary's alleged misuse of secret service funds—which, if proved, was a criminal act—the representative posed a moral-ethical issue about employing secret agents to implement government policy. Ingersoll, inadvertently perhaps, had raised the question of whether noncriminal "offenses," as he seemed to define Smith's activities in New England, were also acts which constituted grounds for Webster's impeachment.[28] Article II, section 4 of the Constitution is vague because it does not specify the misdemeanors justifying impeachment. Consequently, if Ingersoll failed to prove illegal use of the contingency fund, his recourse could have been to convince the House committee that the campaign in Maine involving secret agents and newspaper editorials was a misdemeanor. The problem lay in the meaning of the act establishing the president's contingency fund. In a narrow sense, its provisions limited use of government money to America's relations with other countries; in a broad view, however, its use seemed justified because what happened in Maine directly affected Anglo-American relations. The latter interpretation admittedly adds breadth to the act; yet, stretching a statute does not necessarily comprise an offense. On the question of using secret agents, the House committee wisely refused to comment on what essentially was a value judgment. In its simplest terms, Ingersoll's accusations were political and were recognized as such by the committee. Whether its members did it consciously or by accident, their report warned that allowance of noncriminal conduct as an impeachable offense could set a precedent for the almost uncontrolled removal of unpopular public figures from office.

[28]For the argument that framers of the Constitution intended for civil officers to be impeached for noncriminal conduct, see Raoul Berger, *Impeachment: The Constitutional Problems* (Cambridge, Mass., 1973), 55–56, 58–59, 78–93.

John C. Calhoun and the Limits of Southern Congressional Unity, 1841-1850

~~~~

Joel H. Silbey *

JOHN C. Calhoun of South Carolina holds a secure place in current American historiography. Statements abound in the literature of the antebellum period attesting to his importance as a political philosopher and his influential role as a sectional and national leader during a pivotal era of American history.[1] Certainly no one can deny the pre-eminence of the author of the *Disquisition on Government* in many areas of American political life in the first half of the nineteenth century.

On the other hand, there was a major sphere of political life in which Calhoun's attempts to assert leadership failed despite all of his undoubted gifts and subsequent reputation. Throughout much of his long public career Calhoun sought some effective means of protecting the South from the dangers he feared from an increasingly unfriendly North. In his last decade of activity in particular he repeatedly attempted to unite the Southern representatives in Congress

* The author is Associate Professor of History at Cornell University.

[1] Charles Wiltse, his pre-eminent biographer, has called Calhoun "one of the brilliant leaders of American Democracy," while Professor Robert Meriwether suggested that "the sheer power of his mind and the force of his character put him always in an important if not commanding position." Charles Wiltse, *John C. Calhoun, Sectionalist, 1840-1850* (Indianapolis, 1951), 11; Robert L. Meriwether (ed.), *The Papers of John C. Calhoun* (Columbia, 1959), I, xvii. See also the description of Calhoun's role in such important works as Gerald M. Capers, *John C. Calhoun — Opportunist* (Gainesville, Fla., 1960); Avery O. Craven, *The Growth of Southern Nationalism, 1848-1861* (Baton Rouge, 1953); Frederick Jackson Turner, *The United States, 1830-1850, The Nation and its Sections* (New York, 1935).

Originally published in *The Historian*, 30 (November, 1967). Reprinted by permission of *The Historian*.

John C. Calhoun

as well as the Southern people generally into a cohesive political bloc capable of withstanding any overt hostile actions. As he wrote to his son in 1848, "I do hope our present danger will bring about union among ourselves. . . . In Union lies our safety."[2] Consequently, he repeatedly called upon his colleagues to drop all divisive questions between them, put an end to party distinctions, and accept the need for sectional unity.[3] But all of his efforts were in vain; Calhoun was never able to weld these congressmen or their constituents into the united force he desired. His efforts were continually frustrated by the force and intensity of the very partisan divisions between Whigs and Democrats which he asked the Southerners to forget.[4] Despite his leadership ability, strengths, and talents in other fields, Calhoun could not succeed in his drive for sectional unity because of the existence and vitality of a national political structure which, unlike himself, most Southerners accepted.[5]

To Calhoun, as Professor William Freehling has recently pointed out, political parties were the refuge of the scoundrel and spoilsmen and something to be disdained by the right-thinking patriot interested in accomplishing what was best for the country.[6] Unfortunately for the South Carolinian, however, few of his contemporaries considered parties in the same light, and his constant, often violent, opposition to "party hacks" and their organizations placed Calhoun in a weakened political role at the very time that

160

[2] John C. Calhoun to James Edward Calhoun, July 9, 1848 in J. Franklin Jameson (ed.), "Correspondence of John C. Calhoun," *Annual Report of the American Historical Association for the Year 1899* (Washington, 1900), 759.

[3] *Ibid.;* John C. Calhoun to Andrew Pickens Calhoun, July 24, 1849, in *ibid.,* 769.

[4] See the speech of Representative Howell Cobb of Georgia, "The Necessity for Party Organization," July 1, 1848 in *Congressional Globe,* 30th Congress, 1st Session, *Appendix,* 775-77.

[5] The evolution of this party system is well traced in Richard P. McCormick, *The Second American Party System* (Chapel Hill, 1966).

[6] William Freehling, "Spoilsmen and Interests in the Thought and Career of John C. Calhoun," *Journal of American History,* LII (July, 1965), 25-42.

he saw increasing danger to his section.[7] As several historians have recently demonstrated, the 1840's were a period of a highly developed national party system in which two great political coalitions had become significant forces in the politics of every state.[8] Calhoun's problem in the face of the strength of this national party system can be most clearly seen in the response of the congressmen of his section to the issues they confronted in the 1840's and their reactions to his attempts to unify them as a sectional bloc. In both cases Southern congressional behavior dashed Calhoun's hopes by straying far from his ideal of sectional political unity.

161

The most striking thing about the nature of congressional voting behavior in the first half of the 1840's was the amount of party cohesion demonstrated and the notable absence of sectional unity or sectional blocs on the overwhelming number of issues considered. These ranged in subject matter from financial and tariff questions to expansion, land policy, and foreign affairs.[9] Well over eighty per cent of the congressmen from each party voted together in positions clearly opposite to the mass of the members of the other party. Party unity percentages from the Twenty-seventh Congress through the first session of the

[7] John C. Calhoun to H. W. Conner, February 2, 1849, H. W. Conner Papers (photostats), Manuscript Division, Library of Congress.

[8] McCormick, *The Second Party System;* Charles Grier Sellers, "Who Were the Southern Whigs?," *American Historical Review,* LIX (January, 1954), 335-46.

[9] The full range of these issues is spelled out and discussed in Joel H. Silbey, *The Shrine of Party, Congressional Voting Behavior, 1841-1852* (Pittsburgh, 1967). All of the available roll-call votes were brought together and analyzed in a Guttman Scalogram, a statistical device widely used in legislative voting analysis which makes it possible to take a great number of voting responses and readily rank each congressman in relation to every other. The result is a precise definition of all of the different voting blocs on each set of issues. See George Belknap, "A Method For Analyzing Legislative Behavior," *Midwest Journal of Political Science,* II (November, 1958), 377-402; Duncan Macrae, Jr., *Dimensions of Congressional Voting. A Statistical Study of the House of Representatives in the Eighty-first Congress* (Berkeley, 1958).

John C. Calhoun

Twenty-ninth Congress ranged downward from the absolute of 100 per cent on questions of financial policy to a low of 65 per cent on occasional matters of internal improvements.[10] On the other hand, sectional voting blocs were notably absent. The sections divided on almost every issue at about the 50 per cent level, which, of course, is no unity at all.

Southern (slave state) delegations were usually closely divided politically. In the Twenty-seventh Congress, for example, the 98 slave-state congressmen included 50 Democrats and 48 Whigs in the House. Eleven Southern Democrats and fourteen Southern Whigs sat in the Senate.[11] Their voting behavior resembled that of their non-Southern colleagues: They split along party lines. An example of this can be seen in the voting on the tariff bill of 1846. Congress passed the low Walker Tariff bill in mid-summer after months of considering a variety of amendments designed to raise or lower rates, revise the various rate schedules, and otherwise change the dimensions of the bill. Generally, the Congressmen split along party lines on the legislation with only a few dissenters from either party position. More significantly perhaps, the Southerners tended to vote with their Northern and Western party colleagues rather than with their fellow sectional representatives.[12]

[10] There were, of course, some dissenters from the party position on each issue but they varied from issue to issue and did not constitute, apparently, any particular set of regional blocs. Such dissenters are interesting phenomena in their own right and should be studied further, but their presence does not detract from the main point: the high degree of party unity in Congress.

[11] Party membership was drawn from the *Congressional Globe* and the *Biographical Directory of the American Congress, 1774-1960* (Washington, 1961). The South, of course was not always this closely divided, the Whigs, for example, losing heavily there in 1844, but there was always sufficient division within the section to bolster the point being made here.

[12] This put the Southern Whigs in a protectionist position on these votes since they supported efforts to keep tariff duties fairly high.

The Historian

Table One
Congressional Voting, Tariff Issue
Southern Congressmen Only

Position	House				Senate			
	Democrats		Whigs		Democrats		Whigs	
	no.	%	no.	%	no.	%	no.	%
Low-Tariff	62	81.2	—	—	13	86.7	—	—
Moderate	3	9.4	1	5.0	1	6.6	1	8.3
High-Tariff	3	9.4	19	95.0	1	6.6	11	91.7

Calhoun's position on the tariff legislation as well as in other areas of legislative concern reflects the previous point concerning his frustration. To him the tariff was "the most vital of all questions,"[13] and was one which he saw in sectional terms.[14] The debates on the matter did occasionally contain some quite pointed sectional overtones and challenges (as well as denials that there was a sectional aspect to the legislation).[15] The crucial thing is that in voting on the issue, Northerners and Southerners united under party banners for or against protection in general and forsook any alleged sectional advantage. Calhoun himself voted with the Democrats in favor of a low tariff policy. But this naturally placed him in a position against the large body of Southern Whigs in the Senate who supported a high tariff policy. This pattern held on other issues as well. Calhoun usually voted with the Southern Democrats and was therefore opposed by a significant number of others from his section — the Whig congressmen.

[13] John C. Calhoun to James Hammond, November 27, 1842, in Jameson (ed.), "Calhoun Correspondence," 520-21.

[14] See, for example, James Seddon to Robert M. T. Hunter, August 19, 1844, in Charles Ambler (ed.), "Correspondence of Robert M. T. Hunter, 1826-1876," *Annual Report of the American Historical Association for the Year 1916* (Washington, 1918), 68-69.

[15] See the Washington party organs, the *Union* for the Democrats and the *National Intelligencer* for the Whigs, during the tariff debates of 1846 for examples of these views.

John C. Calhoun

Nor was there anything atypical about the degree of party cohesion on the tariff issue in 1846. Other matters considered in these years revealed relatively similar consistencies of national party unity and the lack of sectional voting behavior.[16] Both houses, for example, concerned themselves with Texas and Oregon in 1844 through 1846, issues which historians have usually considered to have had a high sectional content. Actual voting revealed, however, the continuation of partisanship, not the growth of sectionalism. Both Southern and Northern congressmen split on these issues into Whig and Democratic blocs.[17] There had been some discussion about slavery in the territories during these debates but apparently general or particular attitudes toward expansion played a greater role in determining voting than did attitudes toward slavery.[18] Calhoun, himself, vented his anger at this constant division and announced himself as "disposed to believe that the only chance for reformation is to break up the present party organization . . . that is the only way, in which the South can be united, and thereby avert the calamity impending over it."[19] But such pronouncements did little to overcome the strong attachment to the national parties manifested by most Southerners at the time.[20]

There was a crucial legislative area in which party lines did weaken significantly during the decade, but even here

[16] The other issues and their voting patterns are analyzed in some detail in Silbey, *Shrine of Party*, chapters 4-5.

[17] *Ibid.*, 60-62.

[18] The *Cleveland Plain Dealer*, a Northern Democratic newspaper, in supporting the admission of a slave state, put the expansion issue into perspective by saying that the United States could "better endure the evils of slavery for a season than British domination forever." July 18, 1845.

[19] John C. Calhoun to Joseph W. Lesesne, July 19, 1847, quoted in Ralph Draughon, Jr., "George Smith Houston and Southern Unity, 1846-1849," *Alabama Review*, XIX (July, 1966), 192.

[20] The House of Representatives did consider one issue of a sectional nature in this period, a series of votes involving attitudes towards Negroes and slavery such as the question of the gag-rule, the treatment of freed Negro seamen in Southern ports, diplomatic relations with Haiti, etc. On this

Calhoun was not to lead a united Southern political bloc. When Congress considered the Administration's Mexican War policy in 1846-48, the prevailing voting patterns in the Senate continued, the Democrats uniting in support of the Whigs generally against the Administration's war policy. While most of the Southerners split along party lines, Calhoun broke with his Democratic colleagues and joined several of the Whigs in a moderate position.[21] In the House of Representatives, on the other hand, party alignments weakened and Southern unity increased because, regardless of party, most representatives of the slave states voted in favor of a vigorous war policy.[22] As before, this sectional unity was confined to only one issue in one House and is difficult to view as an indication of a wide-ranging growth of sectional unity. Moreover, and significantly, most Southern representatives took a position on this issue different from that taken by Calhoun in the Senate.

165

As the debate over slavery-extension, signalized by the introduction of the Wilmot Proviso in the House, grew in intensity in the years after 1846, Calhoun received for the first time in the decade much warm support for his ideal of sectional political unity. Many newspaper editors and state legislators, several congressmen and other leaders of Southern life now agreed that "their condition is hopeless unless we should become far more united than we are at present. With union we could certainly save ourselves and possibly *the Union.* . . ."[23] In Congress as well, there was

issue there was a high degree of sectional unity, with 91 per cent of all Southern congressmen voting together. Nevertheless, it should be noted that this was the only one of the six issue areas considered in the 27th Congress in which there was a sectional content. Furthermore, even with such a high degree of sectional unity, a few Southerners reacted to this issue in partisan terms and refused, therefore, to vote sectionally.

[21] He was joined by his South Carolina colleague, George McDuffie. See Silbey, *Shrine of Party.* 76-78.

[22] *Ibid.*

[23] John C. Calhoun to Wilson Lumpkin, September 1, 1848. John C. Calhoun Papers, Manuscript Division, Library of Congress.

John C. Calhoun

a sharp increase in Southern sectional voting and a break-down of national party lines when the Senators and Representatives voted on the matters raised by the question of the extension of slavery into the territories. Whereas in the years between 1841 and 1846 the percentage of Southerners voting together had averaged in the fifty to sixty range on all of the issues considered, the situation now dramatically changed. In the voting on a group of issues involving various aspects of slavery in the territories and in the District of Columbia, well over 90 per cent of all Southerners who voted joined in defense of the right to carry slaves into the new territories and against the abolition of slavery or the slave trade in the nation's capital.[24]

Judging by such voting patterns, it appears that the combination of a keenly divisive issue between North and South and a definite drive by Calhoun and his supporters to achieve sectional unity had affected the normal political processes in the United States Congress. But, despite the increase in leadership support and sectional voting, the growth of Southern unity behind Calhoun was still limited. For years the people of this section had fought among themselves over economic and political questions, dividing into partisan blocs because of these questions. Although the issue of slavery had now become vitally important, it did not drive out all vestiges of previous divisions. Southerners continued to divide in the years between 1846 and 1848 when they voted on a group of non-territorial issues.[25] Once again party unity generally averaged in the 75 per cent and above range among the congressmen from all parts of the Union.

These partisan divisions point up the Southern hesitancy to discard traditional behavioral patterns in favor of sectional responses to political issues despite the growth of the debates over slavery-extension. John C. Calhoun placed protection

[24] Silbey, *Shrine of Party*, Chapter Six.

[25] These issues included such questions as land policy, the tariff, internal improvements, and Mexican War policy once again.

of Southern institutions against outside threats first in his scale of values and therefore wanted his colleagues to put aside their differences on all other matters for the larger goal of unity. But most of the political leaders did not respond to alleged sectional dangers with the same intensity as did Calhoun. They wished to continue, where possible, politics as before, despite all pleadings to the contrary. They believed that only through the Democratic or Whig parties could they achieve the policies and programs they desired on the large mass of social, economic, and political matters that concerned them in addition to the slavery issue.[26] So committed to the agency of party were so many of them that some insisted that if, indeed, the South had to be defended from outside pressures, sectional unity, despite Calhoun's arguments, was not the best means of defense. Southerners were in a numerical minority nationally and their best course, therefore, was to maintain close ties with Northerners within the traditional party coalitions. Northerners who were not avidly committed against slavery would prevent anything from hurting the South while joining in pursuit of solutions to other issues.[27] As John Y. Mason of Virginia wrote to Lewis Cass in 1848, "All reflecting men . . . must see, and do see, that the association of the Democratic party, is now the only hope of the Union. The fidelity of Northern Democrats to the compromises of the Constitution . . . will defeat all the base sectional maneuvers of fanatics and knaves."[28]

167

Many Southerners also distrusted the leaders of the sectional unity movement, particularly the Senator from

[26] See the resolutions of the Democrats of the 6th Congressional District of Georgia in the *Washington Union*, June 17, 1847; the resolutions of the Alabama state Democratic convention, February, 1848, in *ibid.*, February 25, 1848; Athens, Georgia, *Southern Banner*, April 6, 1847; Montgomery *Tri-Weekly Flag and Advertiser*, June 22, 1848.

[27] *Southern Banner*, September 30, 1847; *Flag and Advertiser*, March 30, 1847.

[28] John Y. Mason to Lewis Cass, September 25, 1848, Lewis Cass Papers, William E. Clements Library, Ann Arbor, Michigan.

John C. Calhoun

South Carolina. Since the nullification controversy of the early 1830's, there had been Calhoun and anti-Calhoun factions within the Democratic party of many Southern states.[29] Furthermore, his attitude and actions against the Polk administration generally, and the Mexican War particularly, angered the many Southern Democrats who supported the policies of the national Democratic administration.[30] Of course the Whigs of the area also suspected Calhoun. They had considered him an untrustworthy and ambitious political renegade since his break with their party in the late thirties. They thought that he was now probably calling for sectional unity only to promote his own interests, not the South's, and certainly not theirs.[31] Obviously, then, many Southerners in both political parties saw good reason to ignore the suggestions of a man who acted outside their conception of normal political behavior.

Nothing, perhaps, demonstrates this more clearly than Calhoun's failure in 1849 to forge a sectional political bloc in response to a particularly hostile Northern move. In December, 1848 a Northern Whig congressman, Daniel Gott of New York, introduced a resolution to end the slave trade in the District of Columbia. The resolution passed the House of Representatives, leading Calhoun to call a meeting of all Southern congressmen to consider their course of action.[32] He hoped that they would now strongly assert their unity and demonstrate to the North that they could

[29] Charles Wiltse, *John C. Calhoun, Nullifier, 1829-1840* (Indianapolis, 1949), and Wiltse, *Calhoun, Sectionalist,* contain frequent references to the tensions within the Democratic party in the South.

[30] *Washington Union,* April 5, 1847; *Southern Banner,* May 18, 1848; Milledgeville, Georgia, *Federal Union,* May 30, 1848; *Nashville Union,* February 23, June 5, 1847.

[31] Robert Toombs commented about Calhoun that "treachery itself will not trust him." Toombs to John Jordan Crittenden, September 27, 1848, in Ulrich B. Phillips (ed.), "The Correspondence of Robert Toombs, Alexander H. Stephens, and Howell Cobb," *Annual Report of the American Historical Association for the Year 1911* (Washington, 1913), 129.

[32] *Congressional Globe,* 30th Cong., 2nd Sess., 83; Wiltse, *Calhoun, Sectionalist,* 378ff.

act together when endangered.[33]

Despite a great deal of editorial support, the meeting failed. Only 69 of 121 Southern congressmen attended the first meeting.[34] And Calhoun and his supporters could not control the caucus. A moderate Kentucky Whig, Thomas Metcalfe who was an avowed opponent of sectional action, was elected chairman.[35] Other anti-Calhoun moderates joined Metcalfe at the meeting to prevent any rash action.[36] They denied that there was any justification for holding the meeting and reiterated previous arguments against sectional political divisions. Furthermore, with a new Whig President about to enter the White House, many of the members of that party apparently felt that the President should be allowed to deal with the territorial issue without the South forcing his hand.[37] President Polk also intervened to convince Southern Democrats not to be a party to the movement. He deplored agitation on the slavery question and asserted that to him the whole sectional unity movement was "ill-advised."[38]

Because of the opposition to sectional unity, Calhoun

169

[33] Editorial support for the meeting can be seen in the *Charleston Mercury*, November 21, December 19, 20, 1848; Raleigh *Standard*, December 27, 1848; *Federal Union*, January 9, 1849; *Flag and Advertiser*, February 17, 1849.

[34] The proceedings of the meeting may be followed in the *Richmond Enquirer*, January 30, February 9, 1849; *Flag and Advertiser*, January 27, 1849.

[35] Thomas Metcalfe to John J. Crittenden, January 14, 1849, Crittenden Papers, Manuscript Division, Library of Congress.

[36] Robert Toombs to John J. Crittenden, January 22, 1849, in Mrs. Chapman Coleman (ed.), *The Life of John J. Crittenden* (Philadelphia, 1873), I, 335-336; Howell Cobb, *et al.*, "To Our Constituents," February 26, 1849, in Robert P. Brooks (ed.), "Howell Cobb Papers," *Georgia Historical Quarterly*, V (June, 1921), 51ff.

[37] Leslie Coombs to John Clayton, January 22, 1849, John M. Clayton Papers, Library of Congress. Some of the bitter anti-Calhoun feeling at the caucus can be followed in George Badger to John J. Crittenden, January 13, 1849, Robert Toombs to Crittenden, January 22, 1849, Crittenden Papers; Howell Cobb to Mrs. Cobb, February 8, 1849, in Brooks, "Howell Cobb Papers," 38.

[38] Milo M. Quaife (ed.), *The Diary of James K. Polk During His Presidency, 1845-1849* (Chicago, 1910), IV, 249-50, 281, 283.

John C. Calhoun

could not achieve his purpose in the caucus. He prepared an address listing the South's grievances against the North, but many of those attending considered the document too strong. After bitter debate and attempts to substitute a more conciliatory message, they modified the draft considerably.[39] Even then, only 48 of 121 Southern congressmen signed the published address. Many of the most prominent Democrats refused to sign and only two Southern Whigs of 34 in Congress supported the message.[40] Once again, the Southern congressmen had failed to unite and had demonstrated that they would not work together even behind John C. Calhoun and in the face of challenges to their section.[41] Howell Cobb, one of those who had refused to sign the Southern Address, wrote shortly afterwards that "[my] opinion is that my course will ultimately meet with the approval of a large majority of the Southern democracy. And I entertain no doubt that the true interest and policy of the South requires the preservation of the democratic party of the Union, which is hopeless under the lead of Mr. Calhoun."[42]

Despite his repeated setbacks, Calhoun continued to press for the formation of a Southern bloc during the last year of his life. He accomplished little, however. Although the debates over slavery in the territories became even more bitter in early 1850, anti-sectionalist leaders of the two national parties were able to gain the initiative and settle the disruptive territorial problem. Encouraged by the

170

[39] Footnotes Number 36 and 37 above are also applicable here.

[40] There is a list of signers in R. K. Cralle (ed.), *The Works of John C. Calhoun* (Charleston and New York, 1851-1856), VI, 312-13. Among the Southern Democrats who did not sign were Howell Cobb, Sam Houston, Thomas Hart Benton, Andrew Johnson, and many of the congressmen from Georgia, Tennessee, and North Carolina. The two Whigs who did sign were Patrick Tompkins of Mississippi and John Gayle of Alabama.

[41] "The antipathies of Whig and Democrat are too strong in Washington, and their exercise forms too much the habit of men's lives there. . . ." *Charleston Mercury*, January 22, 1849.

[42] Howell Cobb to Robert J. Walker, June 2, 1849, Robert J. Walker Folder, Miscellaneous Manuscripts, New York Historical Society.

growing nation-wide support for a peaceful solution, congressional leaders were able to push through a series of
compromise proposals in 1850 despite the opposition of
Calhoun and his supporters.[43] In his Fourth of March
speech, Calhoun bitterly attacked the proposals, warned that
they were a defeat for the South, and called for a rejection
of the pending bills in favor of clearer guarantees for slavery
in the territories.[44] Southerners in both houses, however,
responded to this speech as they had on previous occasions:
most of them rejected Calhoun's leadership and voted for
the compromise.[45]

The final blow to all that Calhoun had sought to
accomplish came in the immediate aftermath of the crisis
of 1850 when his opposition was still fresh in Southern minds.
Although it has been suggested that from his grave Calhoun
"still molded the thought and partisan feelings of millions,"
the South itself accepted the compromise, party lines
reformed, and many of the Southern rights men who had
endeavored to defeat the compromise found themselves
moving back into their old party groupings lest they become
completely impotent in public affairs.[46] In the two sessions
of Congress immediately after 1850, Southerners were once
more badly divided among themselves on the matters
considered, ranging from foreign affairs, land policy, and
government operation of several services to the question of
internal improvements. On only one issue was there any
sectional unity. Over 80 per cent of the Southerners voted
together against any further agitation on the slavery issue.

171

---

[43] See Silbey, *Shrine of Party*, Chapter Eight.
[44] *Congressional Globe*, 31st Cong., 1st Sess., 451-55.
[45] Silbey, *Shrine of Party*, Chapter Eight.
[46] Allan Nevins, *Ordeal of the Union* (New York, 1947), I, 314. James
Seddon of Virginia when he returned to the Democratic party in 1852, wrote
that the "cursed bonds of party paralyzed our strength and energy when
they might have been successfully exerted, and now as some partial compensation must sustain and uphold us from dispersion and prostration."
Seddon to R. M. T. Hunter, February 7, 1852, in Ambler, "Hunter Correspondence," 137.

John C. Calhoun

They were joined by most Northerners.[47]

In the last ten years of his life, therefore, regardless of his qualities as an articulate spokesman for a particular viewpoint or his contributions to the world of political thought, Calhoun was unable to dominate the behavior of the Southern congressmen or to carry through the revolution necessary to assert such dominance. The roots of his failure and his frustration lay in the nature of the political situation during the last ten years of his life, the nature of which Calhoun apparently never appreciated completely and often rejected. In this period his commitment to sectional political coalitions was abhorrent to most of the political leaders of the South as well as to their constituents. Given the strength of the national party system, someone who worked outside of it as Calhoun did, or who sought to emphasize problems which others did not consider either primary or alone in importance, could not hope to be an effective leader. People who believed that the party spirit — the "foul spell of party" — should be done away with, were in a very decided political minority in the 1840's.[48] Calhoun may have been a far-seeing statesman and a great political theorist, and the intensity of the sectional rhetoric in the late forties and fifties may point up the importance of his ideas, but while he lived his was an independent voice unable to command the allegiance of the millions he called "party hacks" operating in the South and elsewhere.[49]

[47] In the two sessions of Congress immediately after the crisis of 1850 the voting patterns showed a return to Southern internal disunity on the matters considered: foreign affairs, land policy, government operations, and internal improvements. See Silbey, *Shrine of Party*, 121-36.

[48] William L. Yancey used this in an address to a Whig meeting in July, 1847. Quoted in Ralph Draughon, Jr., "The Political Transition of William Lowndes Yancey, 1816-1848," (M. A. Thesis, University of North Carolina, 1963), 160.

[49] I have previously tried to deal with the dangers of over-emphasizing the sectional aspect of pre-Civil war politics. See Joel H. Silbey, "The Civil War Synthesis in American Political History," *Civil War History*, X (June, 1964), 140-50.

The Elections for the Thirtieth Congress and the Presidential Candidacy of Zachary Taylor

By Brian G. Walton

The study of the political events of the years from 1846 to 1848 has revolved primarily around the impact of the Mexican War and the Wilmot Proviso and the complex maneuverings within the Whig and Democratic parties for the 1848 presidential nominations. A full understanding of what was happening in these years requires consideration of a number of other factors. Among these are the nature and significance of congressional elections at that period. This electoral process did considerably more than merely reflect the impact of the major issues of the day upon the electorate and the parties; the institutional framework influenced and shaped the course of politics. This paper examines the elections to the Thirtieth Congress, which met in December 1847, and the effect of those elections upon the national parties and, in particular, upon the promotion by the Whigs of Zachary Taylor as a presidential candidate for 1848.

Today congressional elections are held at the same time across the nation—on the first Tuesday after the first Monday in November in even-numbered years. Mid-term congressional elections are those which fall midway between two presidential elections. Before the Civil War, however, congressional seats were not all filled at the same time.[1] The mid-term elections to the House of the Thirtieth Congress were spread over a fifteen-month period. In August 1846, even before the end of the first session of the Twenty-ninth Congress, Illinois chose its representatives to the Thirtieth. Not until November 1847, just one month before the

[1] In the Constitution (Art. I, Sec. 4) regulations for the election of representatives were left to the state legislatures, but Congress was authorized to make or alter these regulations. By an act of March 3, 1875, Congress specified the first Tuesday after the first Monday in November as the date for congressional elections. *United States Code, 1964 Edition* (14 vols., Washington, 1965), I, xlii, 10.

Mr. Walton is assistant professor of history at Western Carolina University.

Originally published in *The Journal of Southern History*, 35 (May, 1969). Copyright 1969 by the Southern Historical Association. Reprinted by permission of the Managing Editor.

first session of the Thirtieth Congress met, did Louisiana and Mississippi make their choices. Holding these elections over such a long period of time created significant problems for both major parties and had an appreciable effect upon their actions.

Most historians have been surprisingly unappreciative of the importance of the protracted elections to the Thirtieth Congress.[2] Many have entirely omitted all discussion of the congressional elections of 1846-1847, even when their topics made the elections significant.[3] This tendency persists in contemporary writing. For example, the most recent work on the general party politics of the Mexican War period, Chaplain W. Morrison's study of the controversy over the Wilmot Proviso, ignores this subject. Morrison makes no mention at all of the elections for either 1846 or 1847, and at no point does he indicate an awareness that substantial numbers of seats were still being filled in 1847.[4]

Since the beginning of this century a number of historians have erred by stating explicitly that the elections to the House of the Thirtieth Congress occurred together in the fall of 1846. Thus Glyndon G. Van Deusen, in his book on the Jacksonian era, wrote: "The Whigs had had a marked resurgence in the November [1846] elections, and the Democrats had lost the House of Representatives."[5] Most of those who have fallen into this error,

174

[2] A notable exception to this generalization is Charles Sellers, *James K. Polk, Continentalist, 1843-1846* (Princeton, 1966), 310, concerning the elections of 1844-1845 to the Twenty-ninth Congress. This lack of awareness is particularly strange, since the nature of the electoral process in the 1850's has been clearly examined in such well-known works as Roy Franklin Nichols, *The Disruption of American Democracy* (New York, 1948) and Don E. Fehrenbacher, *Prelude to Greatness: Lincoln in the 1850's* (Stanford, 1962).

[3] See, for example, Arthur Charles Cole, *The Whig Party in the South* (Washington, 1913); Justin H. Smith, *The War with Mexico* (2 vols., New York, 1919); Albert K. Weinberg, *Manifest Destiny: A Study of Nationalist Expansionism in American History* (Baltimore, 1935); John Douglas Pitts Fuller, *The Movement for the Acquisition of All Mexico, 1846-1848* (Baltimore, 1936); George Rawlings Poage, *Henry Clay and the Whig Party* (Chapel Hill, 1936); Glyndon G. Van Deusen, *The Life of Henry Clay* (Boston and Toronto, 1937); Charles M. Wiltse, *John C. Calhoun, Sectionalist, 1840-1850* (Indianapolis and New York, 1951); William N. Chambers, *Old Bullion Benton, Senator from the New West: Thomas Hart Benton, 1782-1858* (Boston and Toronto, 1956).

[4] Chaplain W. Morrison, *Democratic Politics and Sectionalism: The Wilmot Proviso Controversy* (Chapel Hill, 1967). In his second chapter, Morrison does examine "the election campaigns held in the fall of 1846" (p. 22), mentioning Massachusetts, Pennsylvania, New Hampshire, New York, and Ohio, but he does not indicate that these included any congressional elections (pp. 22-26). The same disregard may be found in Joel H. Silbey, *The Shrine of Party: Congressional Voting Behavior, 1841-1852* (Pittsburgh, 1967).

[5] Glyndon G. Van Deusen, *The Jacksonian Era, 1828-1848* (New York, 1959), 240-41. See also Elbert B. Smith, *Magnificent Missourian: The Life of Thomas*

thinking that the Democrats lost control of the House at that time, have reasoned that the Democratic defeat was attributable to substantial popular disenchantment with the war in the last months of 1846. Edward G. Bourne, in his article on "The Proposed Absorption of Mexico in 1847-48," which appeared in 1899, wrote: "The opening of Congress [in December 1847] gave an opportunity for the rising feeling for all of Mexico to show its strength. Yet it must not be forgotten that the new House had been elected over a year earlier, when the opposition to the war was perhaps at its height and not yet counterbalanced by the excitement of the victories of 1847."[6] The thesis that popular revulsion against the war in 1846 was replaced by proannexation sentiment in 1847 has often been reiterated since Bourne's day.[7] The logical corollary of this thesis is that congressional elections held in 1847 would have benefited the Democrats.

The thesis, however, has not gone unchallenged. Some writers have questioned the view that the serious defeats suffered by the Democratic party in the fall of 1846, particularly the New York and Pennsylvania congressional elections and the defeat of Silas Wright in his bid for a second term as governor of New York, were the result of antiwar sentiment favorable to the Whigs.[8] In

---

Hart Benton (Philadelphia and New York, 1958), 216; Charles Winslow Elliott, *Winfield Scott: The Soldier and the Man* (New York, 1937), 434-35; Pearl Olive Ponsford, *Evil Results of Mid-Term Congressional Elections and a Suggested Remedy* (Los Angeles, 1937), 11-12; Charles A. McCoy, *Polk and the Presidency* (Austin, 1960), 220; Kinley J. Brauer, *Cotton Versus Conscience: Massachusetts Whig Politics and Southwestern Expansion, 1843-1848* (Lexington, 1967), 219; Frank Otto Gatell, *John Gorham Palfrey and the New England Conscience* (Cambridge, 1963), 143.

  6 Edward G. Bourne, "The Proposed Absorption of Mexico in 1847-48," *American Historical Association, Annual Report, 1899* (2 vols., Washington, 1900), I, 162-63; also William E. Dodd, "The West and the War with Mexico," *Illinois State Historical Society, Journal*, V (July 1912), 159-72; George Lockhart Rives, *The United States and Mexico, 1821-1848* (2 vols., New York, 1913), II, 293-95; Frederick Merk, *Manifest Destiny and Mission in American History: A Reinterpretation* (New York, 1963), 96-97.

  7 Both Fuller, *Movement for the Acquisition of All Mexico*, and Merk, *Manifest Destiny*, stress this change in popular sentiment in 1847. See also Dodd, "The West and the War with Mexico," *passim*.

  8 Neither John Arthur Garraty, *Silas Wright* (New York, 1949), 334-39, 355-56, 362-63, nor Charles McCool Snyder, *The Jacksonian Heritage: Pennsylvania Politics, 1833-1848* (Harrisburg, 1958), 196-98, considers the war a major cause of the Democratic defeats in 1846. Otis A. Singletary, *The Mexican War* (Chicago, 1960), 111, however, does attribute the Democratic defeats in these states to popular dissatisfaction with the war. See, however, Washington *Daily Union*, September 2, 1847, quoting a letter by the Whig senator John M. Clayton of Delaware, which attributed the Whig victories of 1846 to popular revulsion against the Democratic tariff of 1846.

addition, New York and Pennsylvania were the only states in which the Democrats suffered very severe reverses in late 1846, so that emphasis upon them tends to distort the picture.⁹ Such concentration, however, has been typical of a substantial body of the historical literature on the period, probably because these are the only states mentioned in James K. Polk's diary in connection with the elections to the Thirtieth Congress.¹⁰

Other writers have questioned whether popular dislike of the war did abate in 1847. Thus Allan Nevins in 1947 argued that antiwar and anti-Democratic sentiment continued to flourish in 1847: "It was another ironic fact that even while the war covered the army with laurels and gained the republic such rich additions of territory, the party which had made the conflict lost strength, and the party which had opposed it gained ground. One State election after another, while the voters were celebrating the news of victory, ended in Whig successes. Polk's own Tennessee in April [1847] chose a Whig governor in place of a Democrat, and so did Connecticut in July."¹¹

A careful examination of the extended elections to the Thirtieth Congress can make a substantial contribution to an understanding of the impact of the war upon the electorate and of the responses of the political parties to the developing situation. Such elections are much more than simple indicators of electoral preference or party stance and, particularly when held over an extended period of time rather than simultaneously, tend to form as well as reflect public opinion and to shape as well as identify the positions taken by the parties. Present-day sequential presidential

⁹ In Illinois in August 1846 the Democrats had scored substantial victories in the congressional and gubernatorial elections. See Theodore Calvin Pease (ed.), *Illinois Election Returns, 1818-1848* (Springfield, 1923), 153-61. Representative William Sawyer (D.-Ohio) argued that, as a prowar candidate opposed to all agitation of the slavery question, he had increased his majority in Ohio in the fall of 1846. See *Congressional Globe*, 29 Cong., 2 Sess., 89-91 (December 28, 1846).

¹⁰ Milo Milton Quaife (ed.), *The Diary of James K. Polk During His Presidency, 1845 to 1849* (4 vols., Chicago, 1910), II, 217-18. See, for example, Bernard DeVoto, *The Year of Decision: 1846* (Boston, 1943), 276; Eugene I. McCormac, *James K. Polk, a Political Biography* (Berkeley, 1922), 680; Ivor Debenham Spencer, *The Victor and the Spoils: A Life of William L. Marcy* (Providence, 1959), 159; Norman A. Graebner, *Empire on the Pacific: A Study in American Continental Expansion* (New York, 1955), 171; James P. Shenton, *Robert John Walker: A Politician from Jackson to Lincoln* (New York and London, 1961), 99-101; Singletary, *Mexican War*, 111.

¹¹ Allan Nevins, *Ordeal of the Union* (2 vols., New York, 1947), I, 5. Nevins incorrectly places the Tennessee election in April, rather than August, and the Connecticut election in July, rather than in April.

primaries have a similar effect upon public opinion and the candidates.

At the end of 1846 ninety House seats in the Thirtieth Congress remained to be filled (see Table 1). These constituted 39.5 per cent of all seats. The Democrats had lost more than a score of seats in the elections held in the second half of 1846, but they had not lost control of the next House. Had they managed to avoid any further loss of seats in 1847, they would have retained control of the House in the Thirtieth Congress by a margin of almost twenty seats. In other words, the Whigs had to win additional seats in 1847 to control the next House. The year 1847, therefore, witnessed a drawn-out battle between the parties. At the beginning of the year both sides were confident of victory. The administration's organ, the Washington *Daily Union*, predicted a final Democratic majority of fourteen, and James Gordon Bennett's New York *Herald* looked to a Democratic majority of eighteen. The Whig press was equally sanguine: Horace Greeley's New York *Tribune* thought that Whigs would finish five ahead, and the New York *Express* expected a majority of fourteen.[12]

The congressional elections of 1847 were heavily concentrated in the slave states (see Table 1). Of the 90 seats involved, 66 (or 73 per cent) were located in slave states. At the end of 1846 Indiana, with 10 seats, was the only large Northern state still to elect representatives to the Thirtieth Congress. All the other Northern states had chosen their representatives, except New Hampshire, 4 seats; Connecticut, 4 also; and Rhode Island, 2 seats. Maine still had 4 of 7 seats to fill because no candidate for these seats had obtained the required absolute majority. Thus, only 24 (18 per cent) of the 137 free-state seats remained unfilled at the beginning of 1847. The situation was very different in the South. At the end of 1846 a total of 66 of the 91 slave-state seats had not been filled (72 per cent). These 66 seats constituted nearly 30 per cent of all House seats. Not only did the Whigs have to win seats in 1847, but they had to win them in the South, the area of greatest Democratic strength. Of the 90 seats at stake in 1847, the Democrats had held 62 in the Twenty-ninth Congress.

---

[12] Washington *Daily Union*, March 20, 24, 26, 31, April 2, 6, 13, 1847; New York *Herald*, March 5, 14, April 1, 2, 3, 4, 6, 7, 13, 1847; New York *Tribune*, April 1, 2, 3, 7, 10, 1847; New York *Express*, April 1, 6, 1847. Democrats had outnumbered Whigs almost two to one (143 to 77) in the Twenty-ninth Congress. See *Historical Statistics of the United States: Colonial Times to 1957* (Washington, 1960), 691.

178

TABLE 1
ELECTIONS TO THE THIRTIETH CONGRESS HELD IN 1847

Date Held	State in Which Held	Number of Seats Involved	Number of Seats Held by Democrats:		Democratic Gain or Loss in 1847
			In 29th Congress	In 30th Congress	
March 1847	New Hampshire*	4	4	2	−2
April 1847	Rhode Island*	2	0	1	+1
April 1847	Connecticut	4	0	0	0
April 1847	Virginia	15	14	9	−5
August 1847	Kentucky	10	2	4	+2
August 1847	Tennessee	11	6	6	0
August 1847	Alabama	7	6	5	−1
August 1847	North Carolina	9	6	3	−3
August 1847	Indiana	10	9	6	−3
September 1847	Maine*	4	4	4	0
October 1847	Maryland	6	4	2	−2
November 1847	Louisiana	4	3	3	0
November 1847	Mississippi	4	4	3	−1
	Total Slave States	66	45	35	−10
	Total Free States	24	17	13	−4
	Total All States	90	62	48	−14

* When the New Hampshire and Rhode Island elections were first held in the spring of 1847, a number of seats were not filled because no candidate obtained the required absolute majority (two in New Hampshire, one in Rhode Island). Subsequently, these seats were filled, the Democrats winning the Rhode Island seat and losing both the New Hampshire seats. The four Maine seats were also held over from previous elections in which no candidate had obtained the necessary absolute majority.

The Democrats were happy to rely on the war issue to bring them victory in the elections of 1847. They continued to profess a belief in the popularity of the war, and they presented it throughout the year as the major showpiece of the Polk administration. In January 1847 the *Daily Union* declared that the war "is clearly and undeniably popular" and that "the opposition to the war seems to be fast dying away."[13] Their rhetoric combined an emphasis upon military success and substantial territorial gains with appeals to the moral righteousness of the American cause and a heavy stress upon the ceaseless search for peace. The predicted contrast between the territorial gains to be won and the sacrifices necessary to achieve them was relied upon to bring certain victory at the polls. From Polk downward most Democrats believed that the American public entertained few moral qualms about the war, and they saw no reason to try to keep the war "out of politics."[14] This emphasis upon the war served to distract attention from other, perhaps more divisive, issues.

In contrast, the position of the Whigs in 1847 was curiously ambivalent. Even in the South the party generally continued to adhere to a strong antiwar stand. This amazed and elated the Democrats, who considered it a gross strategic error. Louis McLane, formerly Polk's minister in London, asserted that "intoxicated by their accidental victories in Penna. & New York, they are blindly rushing on to defeat more signal and overwhelming than ever."[15] Although this antiwar position did serve as a common bond among Whigs across the nation, it also showed that many Whigs ignored their party's need to win votes in the South in 1847. Many Northern Whigs and much of the Whig press in the nonslave states continued in 1847 to attack the Polk administra-

179

---

[13] Washington *Daily Union*, January 12, February 23, April 2, May 25, October 11, 1847; Henry Horn to Polk, March 24, 1847; J. G. M. Ramsey to Polk, January 29, 1847, in James K. Polk Papers (Manuscript Division, Library of Congress).

[14] In his message to the second session of the Twenty-ninth Congress in December 1846 Polk had applied the constitutional definition of treason to the opponents of the war (the Whigs). See James D. Richardson (comp.), *A Compilation of the Messages and Papers of the Presidents* (10 vols., [New York], 1903), IV, 473. Senator John Davis of Massachusetts was clearly aware of the Democratic strategy. *Cong. Globe*, 29 Cong., 2 Sess., 506–509 (February 25, 1847). See also James N. Jeffreys to Polk, February 18, 1847; "Alabama" to Polk, February 18, 1847 in Polk Papers.

[15] McLane to Polk, December 13, 1846, in Polk Papers; see also Washington *Daily Union*, December 17, 29, 1846; January 3, 1847; Richard Rush to Polk, December 13, 1846; Alfred Balch to Polk, December 18, 1846; J. George Harris to Polk, December 28, 1846, in Polk Papers.

tion as unduly pro-Southern, thereby cutting the ground from under their colleagues in the South. On the other hand, it was evident in the second session of the Twenty-ninth Congress, which met from December 1846 to March 1847, that many Whigs were anxious to avoid any prolonged debate on topics calculated to offend the South seriously. As Salmon P. Chase subsequently characterized it, "At the next session [1846-1847], the Sentiment in favor of the [Wilmot] proviso had visibly lost strength."[16] This remained true throughout the year and was frequently noted.

180

The major Whig response to the crucial role of the South in the congressional elections of 1847 was the promotion of the presidential candidacy of Zachary Taylor, a slaveholder, a military hero, and an alleged victim of the Polk administration. The use of Taylor's name was a natural reaction of Whig editors and leaders below the Mason-Dixon line to the needs and possibilities of the day.[17] With his potent appeal to Southern Democrats, Taylor embodied almost everything the party could desire for its immediate purposes. His name might enable the Whigs to win the seats they needed in the South in 1847 if his personal popularity could be translated into actual votes. As a serious, long-range presidential prospect for 1848 Taylor aroused considerable discord in the party, but as an immediate embarrassment to the opposition he was magnificent party material.[18]

In particular, the use of Taylor's name enabled the Whigs to develop highly ambiguous positions on the war in 1847. Throughout the year, although the Southern Whigs generally retained a distinct antiwar and antiexpansion stance, their promotion of Tay-

[16] Chase to Charles Sumner, December 2, 1847, in *Diary and Correspondence of Salmon P. Chase*, American Historical Association, *Annual Report, 1902* (2 vols., Washington, 1903), II, 125; Washington *Daily Union*, September 24, 1847; New York *Herald*, August 8, 9, September 19, 23, 1847. Morrison, *Democratic Politics*, *passim*, agrees that the proviso was less prominent in 1847 than in 1846, but Poage, *Henry Clay and the Whig Party*, 150, disagrees.

[17] Neither Brainerd Dyer, *Zachary Taylor* (Baton Rouge, 1946), 265-82, nor Holman Hamilton, *Zachary Taylor: Soldier in the White House* (Indianapolis and New York, 1951), 38-44, discusses the elections of 1847, although Hamilton (p. 40) does refer to a letter of Taylor's of late 1846 in which, according to Hamilton, the general rejoiced "at Whig control of the House of Representatives." Hamilton's book will hereafter be cited as *Soldier in the White House.*

[18] J. B. Mower to Willie P. Mangum, July 21, 1847; James E. Harvey to Mangum, June 3, 1847; N. P. Tallmadge to Mangum, July 24, 1847; F. H. Davidge to Mangum, August 1, 1847, in Henry Thomas Shanks (ed.), *The Papers of Willie P. Mangum* (5 vols., Raleigh, 1955), V, 73-74, 65-66, 74-76. See also Henry Clay to Daniel Ullmann, May 12, 1847, in Calvin Colton (ed.), *The Private Correspondence of Henry Clay* (New York, 1855), 541-43.

lor permitted them to rival the Democrats in protestations of national pride and delight in military glory. By eulogizing Taylor and the men in the field they could largely nullify Democratic assaults on their patriotism. Whigs in the South spoke freely against the war, but they hoped to reap some portion of the possible political benefits of military success. By using Taylor's name they could both oppose the war and support it. In addition, Northern hostility to Taylor, while certainly far from universal, served usefully throughout the year to authenticate his credentials as a Southerner.

Taylor's prominence in 1847 also undermined the position of John C. Calhoun, who was potentially a major focus for political discontent in the South, having considerable strength in several states outside South Carolina, particularly Virginia and Alabama. Calhoun shared the attitudes of many Southern Whigs toward the war and territorial expansion, and in the absence of an acceptable Whig candidate he might draw toward himself or toward local candidates identified with him the votes of Democrats disenchanted with the war. Taylor's name attracted such Democrats directly into the Whig ranks and effectively cut Calhoun off from most Southern Whigs by offering them the possibility of party victory.[19]

The Taylor boom got fully under way after the news of the Battle of Buena Vista reached the Atlantic seaboard in early April 1847.[20] Taylor's name, therefore, was already figuring prominently in Whig propaganda when the congressional elections took place in Virginia at the end of April. These first important Southern state elections in 1847 resulted in substantial gains for the Whigs. The Democrats, who went into the elections holding fourteen of the fifteen seats involved, came out holding only nine (see Table 1). Bennett's New York *Herald* attributed the Democratic reverses specifically to the appeal of Taylor's name to men of both parties.[21] Although it was true that the Whigs had made extensive use of Taylor's name, it is far from clear what effect this had on the results. Calhoun had also played a substantial role in Virginia. Calhounite Democrats had stayed away from the polls or in

181

[19] Quaife (ed.), *Diary*, II, 371; Morrison, *Democratic Politics*, 38-51, 110-11.
[20] New York *Evening Post*, March 29, 31, April 5, 1847; New York *Herald*, April 1, 2, 3, 4, 5, 1847; New York *Tribune*, April 1, 2, 3, 7, 1847; Washington *National Intelligencer* April 15, 1847; Joseph Howard Parks, *John Bell of Tennessee* (Baton Rouge, 1950), 229.
[21] New York *Herald*, April 26, 27, 1847; New York *Tribune*, April 26, May 3, 4, 7, 12, 17, 22, 26, 1847.

some places had run independent Democrats against the regular party candidates.[22] Clear patterns of electoral preference could not be discerned, but the results at least emphasized the value of Taylor's name to prevent Calhoun's exploitation of voter discontent for his own benefit.

Even after the Virginia defeat the Democrats could still expect to control the House in the Thirtieth Congress if they held their own in the remaining elections. The Whigs still needed to win seats and therefore continued to build up Taylor through the late spring and early summer. Since they needed above all to attract Democratic votes in the South, they emphasized Taylor's aloofness from party ties. At the same time, however, they did insist that he was a Whig. A reflection of this Whig need to draw all possible benefit from the use of Taylor's name was demonstrated by their efforts to prevent his dubious attitude on the Wilmot Proviso from becoming a major issue in the South in 1847. Even his letter of May 18, 1847, to the editor of the Cincinnati *Signal*, in which he appeared to give his support to the Wilmot Proviso, did not upset many Southern Whigs, for they dwelt almost exclusively upon those portions of the letter in which Taylor expressed his independence of party ties.[23] On this point at least the Whigs were largely successful. Democrats had great difficulty in portraying Taylor as an enemy to Southern interests.[24]

Both sides were optimistic as they approached the elections of August 1847, the largest group of elections of the year. North Carolina, Tennessee, Kentucky, Alabama, and Indiana all chose their congressmen in that month. Forty-seven seats were involved (20.6 per cent of all House seats). "The elections which take place this week may decide the political complexion of the House

182

[22] James M. Crane to Mangum, April 28, 1847, in Shanks (ed.), *Mangum Papers*, V, 63-64; New York *Tribune*, April 19, 23, May 6, 7, 26, 1847. In the last week of March James A. Seddon, an able and attractive young Democratic representative, had declined renomination in his Virginia district specifically because the convention which nominated him attacked Calhoun by name. See Washington *Daily Union*, March 26, 1847; "A Democrat" to Polk, April 3, 1847; A. Atkinson to Polk, April 4, 1847, in Polk Papers.

[23] Nashville *Whig*, June 17, 1847; John Norvell to Polk, July 19, 1847, in Polk Papers. Both Hamilton, *Soldier in the White House*, 44-45, and Dyer, *Zachary Taylor*, 271-72, stress the anti-Southern views expressed in the letter. In many cases this was not the aspect stressed by the Whig press in the South.

[24] Even the *Signal* letter was not exploited by the Democrats as might have been expected. See Nashville *Daily Union*, May 24, 25, 26, 27, 28, June 5, 14, July 13, 14, 19, 22, 24, 31, August 3, 1847; Memphis *Daily Appeal*, July 29, 31, 1847; Joseph Ficklin to Polk, May 1, 1847; Alfred Balch to Polk, May 5, 1847, in Polk Papers; Washington *Daily Union*, April 22, 28, 1847.

of Representatives in the next Congress," said the New York *Evening Post* at the beginning of August. "A year since the whig party regarded it as certain that there would be a whig majority in the next House of Representatives; now they think it only probable."[25] The election campaigns took place during General Winfield Scott's march on Mexico City, and the press by July was filled with rumors of Mexican overtures for peace.

The Democrats went into the elections holding twenty-nine of the forty-seven seats at stake (see Table 1). They lost five altogether, but party lines generally held tight. The Whigs gained three seats in North Carolina to double their representation, but the victory was the result of a reapportionment of the congressional districts by the previous Whig-controlled state legislature and came as no surprise to anyone. The loss of three seats in Indiana (the Democrats had entered the race holding nine of the state's ten seats) was also largely due to Democratic factional disputes in the southern part of the state. Democrats were happy to note that their candidates had actually gained a little ground in the northern districts of the state, where anti-Southern sentiment might have been expected to be strongest.[26] Elsewhere there was little change. The Whigs picked up a seat in Alabama, but lost two in Kentucky. The Tennessee House delegation remained unchanged, but the incumbent governor Aaron V. Brown, a Democrat and a personal friend of Polk, was unseated in an upset.[27]

To each party the August elections brought some cause for happiness and some cause for grief. While the issue of the control of the next House was still technically in doubt, the gain of five seats had gone far toward ensuring ultimate Whig success. The Whig New York *Tribune* acknowledged that the Whigs would still lack a majority when the session opened in December unless there were further Democratic losses, but this seemed very probable,

183

[25] New York *Evening Post*, August 4, 1847.

[26] New York *Tribune*, April 10, September 15, 23, 1847; New York *Herald*, August 1, 12, 14, 16, 17, 18, 27, 1847; New York *Evening Post*, September 3, 8, 1847; Washington *Daily Union*, August 12, 1847.

[27] New York *Evening Post*, August 4, 1847; New York *Herald*, August 1, 14, 16, 1847; George S. Houston to Polk, April 26, May 18, 24, 1847; W. W. Payne to Polk, May 14, 1847, in Polk Papers; Lewy Dorman, *Party Politics in Alabama from 1850 Through 1860* (Wetumpka, 1935), 27-33. Although the Democrats lost the gubernatorial race in Tennessee, the losing margin was only 914 in a total vote of 114,650. See Nashville *Daily Union*, August 7, 1847; Nashville *Republican Banner*, August 13, 27, 1847.

particularly in Maryland and New Hampshire.[28] At the same time, however, the Democrats could view the August elections as at least a limited vindication of their party and its conduct of the war. If the public was tiring of the war, its dissatisfaction was not shown at the polls. The Democratic loss in August 1847 was substantially below the rate of loss in 1846 or in Virginia earlier in the year. On these grounds, there was at least some justification for the claim that the war was becoming more popular in the country and that the Democratic party would benefit politically from adopting a harsh attitude toward Mexico. Certainly, the elections augured well for Democratic chances of holding the party together in 1848.

184

For the Whigs the future was more uncertain. Even if they were finally in a position to secure control of the next House, it had also become unpleasantly clear that neither the war nor Taylor's name was capable of effecting significant changes in electoral preferences in the South. Taylor's name may have helped to win a few seats, but it had not worked the desired magic, for there had been no clear swing to the Whigs. It was also obvious that the Whig party was holding its own in the South despite its continuing opposition to the war and the anti-Southern reputation of its Northern wing. Consequently, it was possible to argue that the Whigs no longer had to tolerate Taylor and his doubtful allegiance to their party's traditional principles, since a regular Whig candidate now appeared to stand a good chance of success in 1848, given the continuing strength of party allegiances.

It was natural that Taylor should suffer substantial setbacks as 1847 drew to a close, regardless of his reluctance to identify himself openly as a Whig or his failure to effect sweeping victories for the party. He had entered the field early, and his star was bound to dim as the novelty of his name wore off and other candidates came into the reckoning. Even the military headlines were dominated after April 1847 by Scott.[29] Aware of these developments, the Washington *Daily Union*, which had shown a keen appreciation of the purposes of the Taylor boom, concluded that the general was no longer of any real use to the Whig party. The Whig

[28] New York *Tribune*, September 23, 1847; New York *Evening Post*, September 8, 1847, predicting a tie in the next House.

[29] Clay to Ullmann, August 4, 1847, in Colton (ed.), *Private Correspondence of Henry Clay*, 544-45; James E. Harvey to Mangum, August 17, 1847, in Shanks (ed.), *Mangum Papers*, V, 77-79; Hamilton, *Soldier in the White House*, 42; New York *Tribune*, May 5, August 6, 9, 12, 1847; New York *Evening Post*, June 8, July 1, 2, 3, 8, 27, 30, 1847.

aim, said the paper, had been "merely to use his name for a season"—for the congressional elections. The *Daily Union* gave Taylor almost no hope of the regular Whig nomination in 1848 and offered the opinion that the Whigs would swing back toward Henry Clay. By the end of August the New York *Herald*, itself quite partial to Taylor, could assert that the general "cannot be reckoned any longer as the candidate of the Whigs."[30]

Under such circumstances the Clay boom in the fall of 1847 came as no surprise. Clay was by far the most prominent of the regular Whig candidates and was certainly capable of polling the party's regular strength. His visit to the Northeast was heavily publicized, and his name dominated newspaper headlines in the last months of the year. His most serious problem was the need for a viable platform, particularly on the war and expansion. The *Daily Union* correctly predicted that Clay would stress a strong opposition to all territorial acquisitions, since this would permit him to appeal to both North and South while avoiding the difficulties inherent in the Wilmot Proviso. In a speech at Lexington on November 13, 1847, which placed him squarely before the public as an aspirant to his party's nomination, Clay did in fact endorse the proviso, but he concentrated most of his remarks upon the need to avoid any territorial acquisitions.[31]

Clay was benefited at this time by a number of developments within the Democratic party. In the fall of 1847 Polk decided to recall Nicholas P. Trist from Mexico and committed himself to an enlarged war. At the same time Secretary of State James Buchanan radically altered his attitude and came out in favor of an increased war effort. The more vigorous measures advocated by the administration presumably implied greater territorial compensation from Mexico.[32] This switch by the administration and

185

[30] Washington *Daily Union*, June 21, July 1, 6, 8, 9, 14, 28, September 17, 1847; New York *Herald*, August 20, 24, 27, 1847; New York *Evening Post*, August 9, 20, 1847. The *Herald* thought Taylor unacceptable to Southerners because he supported the Wilmot Proviso; the *Evening Post* objected to Taylor because he opposed the proviso. See also J. B. Mower to Mangum, September 21, October 18, 1847; H. H. Clements to Mangum, October 8, 1847, in Shanks (ed.), *Mangum Papers*, V, 81-85.

[31] Washington *Daily Union*, September 7, 8, 24, 25, October 11, November 4, 15, 16, 17, 18, 19, 23, 24, 26, 29, December 1, 2, 3, 14, 15, 21, 29, 1847; New York *Herald*, August 13, 18, 19, 22, 24, 25, 26, November 9, 12, 13, 15, 16, 17, 23, 24, 25, 29, December 15, 1847; Leonidas Jewett to John McLean, December 7, 1847, in John McLean Papers (Manuscript Division, Library of Congress).

[32] Quaife (ed.), *Diary*, III, 215-18, 226-27, 256, 275-76, 313-15, 350, 358-60, 403; New York *Herald*, August 10, 11, 12, 29, September 1, 2, 1847; New York *Evening Post*, August 10, 11, 17, 30, 31, September 15, October 3, 1847; New

the wild forecasts of doom for Mexico which dotted the Democratic press gave added emphasis to Northern Whig warnings of a Southern "plot" and made Clay's no-acquisition platform more attractive to the free states than it would otherwise have been.[33]

Clay also gained by the death of Silas Wright of New York in August 1847 and by the subsequent "Old Berks" letter of Buchanan, in which he endorsed the proposal to extend the Missouri Compromise line to the Pacific as a solution to the problem of the territory to be acquired from Mexico. Wright's death removed the only prominent contender for the 1848 Democratic presidential nomination not strongly opposed to the Wilmot Proviso. Buchanan's letter emphasized the impact of Wright's death.[34] It was now extremely unlikely that Clay would face an antislavery Democrat in 1848, and he was therefore in a stronger position to withstand those Whigs who considered him too "soft" on sectional issues. The success of the Clay boom is indicated by the polls which a number of newspapers took on presidential preferences among members of Congress at the opening of the first session of the Thirtieth Congress in December 1847. These polls varied greatly in their findings, but all showed Clay to be far ahead of all other Whig prospects, including Zachary Taylor.[35]

Clay's hopes began to dim, however, as the results of the elections toward the end of 1847 became known. As was expected, the Democrats lost a few further seats in the House (see Table 1)—two in Maryland in October, one in Mississippi in November, and the two held-over elections in New Hampshire—so that the Whigs did have a small majority when the Thirtieth Congress convened in December despite Democratic successes in Maine

186

York *Tribune*, August 10, 11, 14, 16, September 11, 14, October 2, 14, 1847; Washington *Daily Union*, August 28, September 14, October 4, 11, 1847. McCormac, *Polk*, 528, does not consider that Polk changed the administration's policy at this time.

[33] See, for example, the great inconsistencies of opinion on the fate of Mexico in the New York *Herald*, August 11, 13, 25, October 1, 2, 4, 5, 7, 8, 10, 19, 24, 28, 30, 1847.

[34] Washington *Daily Union*, August 31, October 16, November 3, 1847; New York *Evening Post*, August 31, September 7, 8, 13, 14, October 7, 1847; New York *Herald*, August 31, September 11, 19, 1847.

[35] New York *Evening Post*, December 29, 1847; New York *Herald*, December 25, 1847; New York *Tribune*, December 30, 1847. See also Poage, *Henry Clay and the Whig Party*, 167; Harriet A. Weed (ed.), *Autobiography of Thurlow Weed* (Boston, 1884), 575-76; Clay to General Combs, February 18, 1848, in Colton (ed.), *Private Correspondence of Henry Clay*, 555; J. B. Mower to McLean, August 17, September 6, 13, October 4, 11, 25, December 13, 1847, in McLean Papers.

and Rhode Island.[36] But otherwise the Democrats scored a series of impressive victories in important state elections in late 1847. The most widely noted of these was the re-election of Francis R. Shunk in the Pennsylvania gubernatorial race in October.[37] In the same month the Democrats won the gubernatorial elections in Maryland and Georgia, both victories being gains. The Georgia success appeared particularly significant because the state was the only remaining important stronghold of the Whig party in the deep South. The Democrats followed up these successes by winning the New Jersey gubernatorial election at the beginning of November, again a clear gain.[38] The Democratic party was clearly back on its feet in many parts of the nation on both sides of the Mason-Dixon line. This was obvious despite the quarrel which tore apart the New York Democratic party in the fall of 1847 and brought the severe Democratic defeat in that state's elections in November.[39]

187

The Democratic resurgence of late 1847 did much to keep Taylor's name alive. As the Whig electoral surge lost most of its impetus and as the Whigs failed to expand their victories of late 1846 into a general rout of the Democrats in 1847, it became in-

[36] Washington *Daily Union*, August 23, October 1, 5, 15, 19, 1847; New York *Herald*, October 7, 8, 9, 12, 14, 16, 1847; Robert M. McLane to Polk, October 28, 1847, in Polk Papers. The Democrats won the four held-over elections in Maine and picked up one seat in Rhode Island. Washington *Daily Union*, September 2, 18, 1847; New York *Tribune*, September 2, 11, 13, 16, 17, 18, 20, 23, 27, 1847.

[37] Washington *Daily Union*, October 15, 16, 1847; New York *Evening Post*, October 11, 15, 16, 19, 20, 26, 28, 1847; Daniel T. Jenks to Polk, October 25, 1847; Robert M. McLane to Polk, October 28, 1847, in Polk Papers; New York *Herald*, October 16, November 9, 1847. Shunk, however, gained only 51 per cent of the total vote, and only some 60 per cent of the electorate went to the polls, a low figure for Pennsylvania at this time.

[38] Washington *Daily Union*, August 23, October 1, 5, 1847; New York *Herald*, October 7, 8, 9, 12, 14, 16, 1847; New York *Tribune*, October 8, 9, 16, 19, 22, 1847; New York *Evening Post*, November 3, 4, 5, 1847; Edward Harden to Polk, August 21, November 2, 1847, in Polk Papers. See also Richard H. Shryock, *Georgia and the Union in 1850* (Philadelphia, 1926), 140, 151, and Richard P. McCormick, *The History of Voting in New Jersey: A Study in the Development of Election Machinery, 1664-1911* (New Brunswick, 1953), 131-39. The race in New Jersey was the second in that marginally Whig state after the office of governor was made subject to popular election in 1844. The Democratic share of the total vote rose from 49 per cent in 1844 to 51.5 per cent in 1847 in a contest notably unaffected by any strong third-party challenge.

[39] For details of the split in the New York Democratic party, see Morrison, *Democratic Politics*, 75-85; New York *Evening Post*, September 29, 30, October 1, 2, 4, 11, 13, 15, 18, 19, 21, 26, 27, 28, 29, 30, 1847; Washington *Daily Union*, October 5, 15, 16, 22, 30, November 1, 6, 15, 16, 17, 18, 19, 23, 24, 26, 29, December 1, 14, 1847; New York *Herald*, November 3, 6, 9, 19, 1847; New York *Tribune*, September 24, October 1, 4, 11, 13, 18, 29, 1847.

creasingly clear that it would be perilous for the Whigs to nominate in 1848 a man with Clay's record as a loser. Ability to deliver the regular Whig party vote did not guarantee national success at the polls. Even though Taylor's name had failed to produce sweeping Whig victories in the South in 1847, the general appeared to be a more reliable vote-getter than Henry Clay. There was no doubt that he could run better than Clay in the South, and the election of 1848 might well be won or lost there.[40] At the same time the administration's new war policy and Buchanan's support of the plan to extend the Missouri Compromise line to the Pacific benefited Taylor as much as Clay.

In fact, judged from the viewpoint of those who seriously supported Taylor as a candidate for 1848 the relative stalemate which had generally characterized the elections of 1847 turned out to be the best possible development. Had the Whigs continued to win very substantial successes in the 1847 congressional and state elections, this might have been taken as an indication of continuing regular party strength in the South rather than as a demonstration of the effectiveness of Taylor's name.[41] Serious Whig failures in 1847 would certainly have been regarded as evidence of his lack of political appeal. The indecisiveness of the results of 1847 suited the general's needs admirably. It was apparent that there would be few uncommitted voters in 1848 despite all the controversy surrounding the war and the Wilmot Proviso, and it could be predicted that Taylor was more likely to attract those few than Clay. Thus, even at the end of 1847, when Clay seemed to be the coming man, the name of Zachary Taylor was presenting itself with irrepressible political logic as the most sensible choice for the Whig party in 1848.

This study of the Taylor boom of 1847 in the light of the extended elections for the Thirtieth Congress demonstrates the

[40] Clay had had a difficult time in 1844 trying to convince the South that he was not an abolitionist candidate. His tergiversations and equivocations in that year are, of course, almost legendary. See Poage, *Henry Clay and the Whig Party,* 143-47, and Sellers, *James K. Polk, Continentalist,* 145-49, 160-61. By the end of 1847 the two most prominent contenders for the Democratic presidential nomination in 1848 were Buchanan and Lewis Cass of Michigan. Buchanan was still supporting the proposal to extend the Missouri Compromise line to the Pacific, while Cass was a leading advocate of "popular sovereignty," so that both were occupying a very moderate position on the sectional issue. See Washington *Daily Union,* December 28, 29, 1847. For expressions of Taylor's popularity in the South, see Alfred Balch to Polk, September 13, 1847; Aaron V. Brown to Polk, September 17, 1847, in Polk Papers.

[41] The Democratic press was well aware of this fact. See Washington *Daily Union,* July 28, August 12, 1847.

shift in historical emphases which close study of other congressional elections in the 1840's may reveal. Only when viewed in the perspective of the sequential nature of those elections can the Taylor boom be seen for what it essentially was, at least in its inception: an answer to the pressing, temporary need of the Whig party for a candidate whose name could win support in the crucial congressional elections in the South in 1847. The Taylor candidacy may possibly be representative of a number of historical problems of these years in that it emphasizes the desirability of renewed research within the framework of a correct appreciation of the congressional election process.

189

Democratic Senate Leadership and the Compromise of 1850

By Holman Hamilton

In approaching the Compromise of 1850, the modern historian is likely to find himself on ground previously and even repeatedly traversed. The last appearance of Clay, Calhoun, and Webster in the Senate spotlight, the shadow of the second Fugitive Slave Law, the growing prominence of William H. Seward and Salmon P. Chase — these and similar landmarks make the usual roads to the Compromise familiar terrain.[1]

Yet one wonders whether the old historical highways can lead to a successful reappraisal of an oft-accepted story, which the eloquent triumvirate of "America's silver age" has all but monopolized. A number of facts project reasonable doubt. Despite the repeated emphasis which writers have placed on Daniel Webster's "Seventh of March Speech," only one northern Whig senator, James Cooper of Pennsylvania, supported Webster as long as President Zachary Taylor lived. Owing to Henry Clay's prominence in the debates, readers are disposed to assume that Whigs provided most of the votes for Clay's "Omnibus Bill." Actually, it was a Whig, James A. Pearce of Maryland, who spiked Clay's efforts on July 31, 1850; nearly all the Whigs then deserted Clay,[2] and the bulk of the backing given first to Clay and later to Stephen A. Douglas stemmed from Democratic ranks. It is known, of course, that John C. Calhoun died when the "Great Debate" was barely under way. But the role of another southern senator, Henry S. Foote of Mississippi, from the mild winter days of early 1850 through the steamy Washington summer, has been obscured — perhaps by Calhoun's reputation and death.

[1] This article received the Mississippi Valley Historical Association's Pelzer Award for 1954.
[2] *Cong. Globe*, 31 Cong., 1 Sess., Appendix, 1473-79.

Originally published in *Mississippi Valley Historical Review*, 41 (December, 1954). Reprinted by permission of the Organization of American Historians.

Although such truths as these have been touched upon by a number of writers,[3] there has been no documented synthesis of the detached parts of the picture puzzle. Some of the fragmentary parts have but recently been discovered. Others, large and small, remain missing today. Still, the major outlines of the picture can be re-created through a point-by-point analysis of aims, methods, votes, and contributions of Senate Whig and Democratic leaders. Such an analysis provides a key or clue to precisely what was going on behind the spectacular façade of rhetoric and drama.

192

Albert Bushnell Hart, Albert J. Beveridge, and Charles A. and Mary R. Beard are only a few of the numerous authors who have magnified Clay's and Webster's influence far beyond the limits of the facts. According to Hart, in early 1850 "the Compromise was already decided, since the agreement of Clay and Webster meant the effective coalition of Southern Whigs and Northern 'Cotton Whigs'." Also, said Hart, Webster's Seventh of March Speech "was virtually an announcement that the Senate would vote for the Compromise." [4] Actually, President Taylor's death in July and Millard Fillmore's accession — together with the switch from Clay's methods to Douglas' methods — provided the deciding factors, and none of these things could have been foreseen in March.

Beveridge went into considerable detail to do justice to the remarks of Jefferson Davis, Seward, Douglas, and Chase. For this he deserves commendation. But, in the pages of his second volume on Abraham Lincoln, his lucid discussion suddenly breaks down. The importance of Taylor's death is slighted. Beveridge seems satisfied to say: "So opposition disintegrated and, one after another, the measures suggested by Clay were enacted." [5] A poorly informed reader of Beveridge's book is at a loss to know how and why the Compromise finally survived.

Charles A. and Mary R. Beard, in *The Rise of American Civilization*, have no doubt influenced students by the tens of thousands.

[3] There is no adequate, full-scale study of the Compromise of 1850. Perhaps the clearest picture of what the present writer considers the correct story may be derived from two sources: Frank H. Hodder, "The Authorship of the Compromise of 1850," *Mississippi Valley Historical Review* (Cedar Rapids), XXII (March, 1936), 525-36; and George F. Milton, *The Eve of Conflict: Stephen A. Douglas and the Needless War* (Boston, 1934). See also George D. Harmon, "Douglas and the Compromise of 1850," *Journal of the Illinois State Historical Society* (Springfield), XXI (January, 1929), 453-99.

[4] Albert B. Hart, *Salmon Portland Chase* (Boston, 1899), 124.

[5] Albert J. Beveridge, *Abraham Lincoln, 1809-1858* (2 vols., Boston, 1928), **II**, 118-30.

Yet the Beards declared: "Once more, as in 1820 and 1833, Clay was to prevail. But he won this time only through the aid of Webster." [6] Still another facet of the same fallacy was later presented by Burton J. Hendrick, who wrote that Howell Cobb "deserted his Democratic party in 1850 and joined forces with the antislavery Whigs in upholding the Compromise measures of that year." [7] In other words, we are asked to believe that the Democratic party opposed the Compromise; that the antislavery Whigs were outstanding in its support; that Clay pushed through the Compromise, but only with the aid of Webster; and that an effective coalition of northern and southern Whigs spelled success for the Compromise as early as March. With each and all of the allegations, the facts themselves take issue.

Lest it be objected that most of these scholars belonged to a past generation, it may be instructive to look into Allan Nevins' *Ordeal of the Union.* Published as recently as 1947, the *Ordeal* contains much that the specialist should value. Nevins does not fall into Edward Channing's error in terming the pro-Compromise position of Cobb a "marked overturn" in the Georgian's sentiments.[8] Nor does he say with James Ford Rhodes that "Webster's influence was of the greatest weight in the passage of the compromise measures," or that "Clay's adroit parliamentary management was necessary to carry them through the various and tedious steps of legislation." [9] But the *Ordeal* does describe Clay's influence as "unrivalled," and the Seventh of March Speech as 1850's "great turning point." [10]

The record shows that the speech of March 7 was not nearly as great a "turning point" as President Taylor's death or the subsequent adoption of the Douglas strategy. The votes demonstrate that Clay's influence was not only rivaled but surpassed by that of the Douglas-Cass Democrats. An equally pertinent criticism lies in the area of Nevins' emphasis. He mentions aspects of the Compromise tangle to which the Beards, Beveridge, and the others

[6] Charles A. and Mary R. Beard, *The Rise of American Civilization* (2 vols., New York, 1927), I, 715.

[7] Burton J. Hendrick, *Statesmen of the Lost Cause: Jefferson Davis and His Cabinet* (New York, 1939), 96.

[8] Edward Channing, *A History of the United States* (6 vols., New York, 1905-1925), VI, 80-81.

[9] James Ford Rhodes, *History of the United States from the Compromise of 1850* (7 vols., New York, 1893-1906), I, 157.

[10] Allan Nevins, *Ordeal of the Union* (2 vols., New York, 1947), I, 266, 296.

appeared oblivious. The irony is that, time and again, he relegates significant material to mere footnote status and neglects to integrate it with his text and conclusions.

In one footnote, Nevins cites Orlando Brown's reference to Lewis Cass's broaching a compromise on January 11, nearly three weeks before Clay's first compromise proposal. In a second footnote, he quotes Robert C. Winthrop's luminous prediction that "any other course" than Taylor's "will kill Whiggery at our end of the Union." In a third footnote, he gives a little space to the contribution of Foote and Thomas Ritchie in forming the Committee of Thirteen.[11] These happen to be a few of the vital links in the chain, but the chain as a whole remains to be forged.

Among the papers of William M. Meredith is a letter written on June 1, 1850, by Whig Senator John H. Clarke of Rhode Island. Clarke was anti-Compromise, as was Secretary of the Treasury Meredith. Reporting to the secretary, Clarke expressed his belief that "from the North & West we can safely depend upon" Senators John Davis, Samuel S. Phelps, William Upham, Albert C. Greene, Truman Smith, Roger S. Baldwin, William H. Seward, William L. Dayton, Jacob W. Miller, Thomas Corwin, and Clarke (Whigs); Hannibal Hamlin, James W. Bradbury, Alpheus Felch, Isaac P. Walker, and Henry Dodge (Democrats), plus John P. Hale and Salmon P. Chase (Free Soilers). When Clarke wrote "we," he referred to the anti-Compromise people who followed President Taylor and Senator Thomas H. Benton. Of the Delaware senators, John Wales was a pro-Taylor and anti-Compromise Whig; Presley Spruance wavered, but Clarke expected him to vote against Clay's Omnibus Bill.[12]

Clarke's summation is echoed, in almost every detail, in a revealing document written by Senator Lewis Cass twelve days later, and addressed to his son-in-law, Henry Ledyard. Cass was pro-Compromise and anti-Taylor, which lends special credence to his assertion that his own Michigan colleague, Felch, was deserting him and lining up with Taylor and Benton.[13]

A third manuscript, until recently in private hands, was sent by Illinois Senator Douglas to the two Democratic journalists

---

[11] *Ibid.*, I, 264 n., 268 n., 285 n.

[12] John H. Clarke to William M. Meredith, June 1, 1850, William M. Meredith Papers (Historical Society of Pennsylvania, Philadelphia).

[13] Lewis Cass to Henry Ledyard, June 13, 1850, Lewis Cass Papers (William L. Clements Library, Ann Arbor, Michigan).

responsible for his paper in Springfield. Dated August 3, 1850, the Douglas communication disclosed some of the reasons for the failure of Clay's attempt to pass the Compromise in what was known as the "omnibus" form, even after the death of Taylor. From the first, Douglas and Clay had seen eye to eye respecting the Compromise end-product in which each was interested. The "Little Giant," however, wanted component parts of compromise legislation voted on separately, one at a time. Clay, on the other hand, was determined to rush the program through Congress at one swoop. Realizing that he could not bring Clay around to the methods he himself preferred, the younger man gave way to the elderly Kentuckian in the late winter and spring (when Taylor was living), and even as late as the end of July (when Fillmore occupied the White House). Douglas did this although, as chairman of the Senate committee on territories, he had at least as good a claim to the authorship of the Compromise as anyone else.[14]

195

The certainty that Clay's "Omnibus Bill" would have failed with Zachary Taylor in the Executive Mansion is indicated by its recorded failure when the favorably disposed Fillmore resided there, with the patronage power ranged on Clay's side. After Clay saw his measure vanquished, the exhausted old Whig beat a retreat to Newport's beaches, while Douglas captained Compromise forces and succeeded where he had failed. Douglas did exactly what he had thought he could do at the outset, masterfully promoting piecemeal, instead of combined, legislation. Douglas' letter of August 3 to Charles H. Lanphier and George Walker accurately prophesied that what did happen would happen.

The ultimate passage of the Compromise, under Douglas' guidance, raises the question as to the nature of the strength behind it. It also leads to inquiry concerning the origin of the parts of the compromise arrangement, which from 1850 to 1854 was thought to have settled the sectional controversy.

An analysis of the Senate votes on the integral portions of the Douglas-sponsored Compromise, between August 9 and September 16, shows only four senators supporting all five bills. These were Augustus C. Dodge, Democrat of Iowa; Sam Houston, Democrat of Texas; Daniel Sturgeon, Democrat of Pennsylvania; and John Wales, Whig of Delaware. Eight other senators voted "yea" on

[14] Stephen A. Douglas to Charles H. Lanphier and George Walker, August 3, 1850, Patton Papers (Illinois State Historical Library, Springfield).

four occasions and abstained from casting ballots on a fifth. With the exceptions of Dodge, Houston, Sturgeon, and Wales, these men came closest to giving the Compromise their complete backing in August and September. The eight were Jesse D. Bright, Democrat of Indiana; Lewis Cass, Democrat of Michigan; Stephen A. Douglas, Democrat of Illinois; Alpheus Felch, Democrat of Michigan; Moses Norris, Democrat of New Hampshire; James Shields, Democrat of Illinois; Presley Spruance, Whig of Delaware; and James Whitcomb, Democrat of Indiana. Of the twelve senators who lent the Compromise the greatest strength under Douglas' sponsorship, ten were Democrats and two were Whigs.[15]

196

For the individual bills, Democrats likewise provided the greatest share of needed support. On August 9, sixteen Democrats and fourteen Whigs approved the Texas boundary measure.[16] On August 13, seventeen Democrats joined fourteen Whigs and two Free Soilers in voting statehood to California.[17] Two days later, nineteen Democrats and only eight Whigs supplied the winning total for New Mexico's territorial legislation.[18] The *Congressional Globe* does not contribute a yea-and-nay breakdown on the fugitive slave bill, but August 23 found eighteen Democrats and nine Whigs assenting to its engrossment for a third reading — virtually tantamount to passage.[19] Finally, on September 16, the abolition of the slave trade in the District of Columbia was due to eighteen Democrats, thirteen Whigs, and two Free Soilers.[20] In every one of the five tests, the Democratic part of the pro-Compromise majority was larger than the Whig part. For the fugitive slave and New Mexico measures, the ratio was at least two to one.

By the same token, when three sections of Clay's Omnibus Bill had been defeated on July 31, only five of the Kentuckian's fellow-Whigs sustained him on the New Mexico question while sixteen Democrats followed his "lead." On the Texas boundary, Clay and ten other Whigs went down with seventeen Democrats in an extremely close vote. And on the California statehood issue, Clay had only six Whigs in his camp together with sixteen Democrats and two Free Soilers. Senators siding with Clay on all three tests

15 *Cong. Globe*, 31 Cong., 1 Sess., 1555, 1589, 1647, 1830.
16 *Ibid.*, 1555.
17 *Ibid.*, 1573.
18 *Ibid.*, 1589.
19 *Ibid.*, 1647, 1660.
20 *Ibid.*, 1830.

were Daniel S. Dickinson of New York, George W. Jones of Iowa, Bright, Cass, Augustus C. Dodge, Norris, Spruance, Sturgeon, and Whitcomb.[21] Eight of the nine were Democrats. In defeat as in subsequent victory, under Clay's aegis as well as Douglas', Democrats stood for the Compromise more consistently and faithfully than Whigs.

It will be observed that there were shifts of sentiment on the part of some members of the Senate between the dates of Clarke's and Cass's letters and the critical votes of July 31, August, and September. Most of these changes involved Whigs. Spruance, whose position had been uncertain in June, was pro-Compromise in July and August. Wales had been correctly considered an anti-Compromise man by Clarke;[22] and even Clay characterized him as such.[23] Yet in August, Wales took new ground. Clarke himself and his fellow Rhode Islander, Albert C. Greene, supported Douglas' Texas boundary bill; Clarke did not vote on three of the August trials, and Greene voted "nay" on two of them. But the approval given the Texas boundary on August 9 by Clarke, Greene, John Davis, Phelps, Smith, Spruance, and Wales (together with the absence of Dayton and Miller)[24] made the difference between defeat and victory.

A case might be made that Whig deviations from anti-Compromise to pro-Compromise positions were of transcendent importance in the reckoning. Admittedly, last-minute additions to the Compromise forces transformed disaster into triumph for the compromisers. These additions also demonstrated the effect of Taylor's death and Fillmore's succession on Whig late-comers whose votes were sorely needed by the Douglas high command. There also is no gainsaying the fact that, even as some Whigs favored the Compromise first under Clay and then under Douglas, not a few Democrats were ranged in opposition before and during Clay's seashore

197

[21] *Ibid.*, Appendix, 1479, 1481, 1483. In providing these summaries the Utah territorial bill has not been included because of the peculiar nature of its passage as a truncation of the "Omnibus Bill." As in the case of the fugitive slave bill, the *Congressional Globe* gives no yea-and-nay breakdown on the Utah bill's passage. *Ibid.*, 1504. If the votes of July 31 favoring the Utah bill's engrossment for a third reading were part of the text summaries, the total Democratic preponderance would be still more impressive. Twenty-four Democrats and eight Whigs supported engrossment; three Democrats, thirteen Whigs, and two Free Soilers opposed it; six Democrats and four Whigs did not vote. *Ibid.*, Appendix, 1485.
[22] Clarke to Meredith, June 1, 1850, Meredith Papers.
[23] *Cong. Globe*, 31 Cong., 1 Sess., 1332.
[24] *Ibid.*, 1555, 1573, 1589, 1647, 1830.

vacation. But both the hard core and the greater number of Compromise votes in the dramatic and decisive contests were Democratic in origin. This fact is fundamental in gaining a clear comprehension of the story as a whole.

It is equally imperative, in clarifying political attitudes and votes of senators, to determine the connection between legislative instructions and the Compromise of 1850. Over fifty years ago, William E. Dodd observed that in the second quarter of the nineteenth century the principle of state legislatures instructing United States senators was "accepted fully by one party and partially by the other."[25] Although Dodd and other scholars have stressed the importance of the practice during the Jackson-Van Buren period,[26] no comparable studies of the 1850 scene have been printed. From 1846 to 1850, fourteen northern legislatures sent resolutions to Washington, and southern capitols lagged but little.[27] All this was done on the theory that since the state legislators elected the senators they had a right to tell them what to do. Whereas Whigs had been the chief victims of instructions from 1834 to 1840,[28] now Democrats were impaled on their own precedents; this was especially true of Northwesterners. No one resigned from the Senate on account of instructions in 1850, but Cass threatened to do so unless Michigan withdrew its instructions — whereupon Lansing at once complied.[29] Douglas was embarrassed by instructions, while John P. Hale made light of the instructions idea.[30] Generally, instructions showed that politicians at home were less inclined to compromise than were a majority of the men they had elected to the Senate.[31]

Ever since the annexation of Texas and the onset of the Mexican

[25] William E. Dodd, "The Principle of Instructing United States Senators," *South Atlantic Quarterly* (Durham), I (October, 1902), 331.

[26] *Ibid.*, 327-32; George H. Haynes, *The Senate of the United States: Its History and Practice* (2 vols., Boston, 1938), II, 1025-34; Clement Eaton, "Southern Senators and the Right of Instruction, 1789-1860," *Journal of Southern History* (Baton Rouge), XVIII (August, 1952), 303-19.

[27] *Cong. Globe*, 31 Cong., 1 Sess., 1085-87. Research guideposts are available in Herman V. Ames (ed.), *State Documents on Federal Relations: The States and the United States* (Philadelphia, 1906), 241-62.

[28] Eaton, "Southern Senators and the Right of Instruction, 1789-1860," *Journal of Southern History*, XVIII (August, 1952), 305-18.

[29] Floyd B. Streeter, *Political Parties in Michigan, 1837-1860* (Lansing, 1918), 115-17.

[30] *Cong. Globe*, 31 Cong., 1 Sess., 1114; Appendix, 1652.

[31] This conclusion is based on an unpublished study of the subject by the writer. It is buttressed by more than forty pertinent state legislative resolutions.

War, extremist and moderate arguments and plans of settlement had been advanced and presented in Washington. The ill-starred Clayton Compromise of 1848, which Clay stated he had never read, proved no model two years later.[32] Extension of the Missouri Compromise line to the Pacific, advocated by such Southerners as Jefferson Davis and Hopkins L. Turney,[33] held no attraction for Clay or the Douglas Democrats. The new fugitive slave bill was primarily sponsored by James M. Mason of Virginia, a Calhoun-Davis Democrat;[34] in its final form, it contained harsher provisions (in northern eyes) than the ones Daniel Webster desired.[35] California statehood had been promoted in the Thirtieth Congress by the Democrat Douglas and the Whig William B. Preston.[36] Yet the boundaries of the California state envisioned by Douglas and Preston were far from those defined in the Compromise of 1850, and the California picture had been altered economically and politically by the discovery of gold. The Texas boundary solution of 1850 was premised on ideas backed by successive Texas governors.[37] Abolition of the slave trade in the District of Columbia, frequently broached in the past, commanded the assent of many northern Whigs and Democrats.[38]

199

If California statehood and ending the slave trade in the District were predominantly northern measures in 1850, and if the fugitive slave and Texas boundary bills derived most of their support from Southerners, two other parts of the Compromise had a different appeal. Designed to dispose of the New Mexico and Utah problems, they gave territorial governments to those western regions, with a proviso that states formed from them would be admitted with or without slavery as their constitutions should provide.

The New Mexico territorial bill was the issue which wrecked Clay's omnibus plan, and perhaps it ought to be remembered that about three fourths of the Senate Whigs contributed to its fate.[39]

[32] *Cong. Globe*, 31 Cong., 1 Sess., 1145, 1155, 1157.

[33] *Ibid.*, 249, 1133.

[34] *Ibid.*, 99, 103, 171, 233-36.

[35] *Ibid.*, 1111; Fletcher Webster (ed.), *The Private Correspondence of Daniel Webster* (2 vols., Boston, 1857), II, 402.

[36] *Cong. Globe*, 30 Cong., 2 Sess., 21, 190-93, 319, 477-80, 607-608; Milo M. Quaife (ed.), *The Diary of James K. Polk during His Presidency, 1845 to 1849* (4 vols., Chicago, 1910), IV, 194-96.

[37] Edmund T. Miller, *A Financial History of Texas* (Austin, 1916), 118.

[38] *Cong. Globe*, 30 Cong., 2 Sess., 83-84, 105-108, 211-16; *ibid.*, 31 Cong., 1 Sess., 79-84.

[39] *Ibid.*, 31 Cong., 1 Sess., Appendix, 1479.

When Douglas took control, he did not promote the New Mexico bill until after the Texas boundary and California statehood measures had been passed. With a considerable show of skill he then directed the adoption of the New Mexico measure.

In achieving his New Mexico aim, Douglas was aided directly by eighteen Democrats and eight Whigs, and indirectly by twenty-three absentees. Only three Democrats — Hamlin, Walker, and Henry Dodge — spoiled the Democratic record.[40] When one realizes that these three were also the only Senate Democrats out of thirty-three to oppose the Utah bill of July 31,[41] it is evident that Democrats had the key role with regard to both New Mexico and Utah.

200

This was no accident. For upwards of two years, the majority or national element of the Democratic party had initiated and repeated the "non-intervention" or "popular sovereignty" doctrine embodied in this territorial plan. As far back as December 14, 1847, Dickinson, the New York Democrat, had introduced resolutions specifying that territorial legislatures should decide all questions of domestic policy within the territories.[42] Ten days later, Lewis Cass addressed his famous "Nicholson Letter" to Alfred O. P. Nicholson of Tennessee. Cass's position, comparable to Dickinson's, was summarized by the injunction: "Leave to the people who will be affected" by the slavery issue "to adjust it upon their own responsibility and in their own manner."[43] The Nicholson letter became Cass's personal platform in his campaign for the 1848 Democratic presidential nomination.[44] Dickinson, who publicly enunciated the idea before Cass did, served as the Michigan Democrat's lieutenant both in that contest (which Cass won handily) and in the post-convention canvass.[45] The Democratic national platform was vague, but was capable of being interpreted along the lines of the Dickinson resolutions and the Nicholson letter. In fact, it was thus interpreted by Jefferson Davis

[40] Ibid., 1589.
[41] Ibid., Appendix, 1485.
[42] Ibid., 30 Cong., 1 Sess., 21. Two months later, Dickinson agreed to the amending of his second resolution by the addition of the phrase, "in subordination to the Federal Constitution and reserved rights of the States and people." Ibid., 773, and Appendix, 306. This was more in line with the Calhoun position.
[43] William L. G. Smith, Fifty Years of Public Life: The Life and Times of Lewis Cass (New York, 1856), 607-16.
[44] Frank B. Woodford, Lewis Cass, the Last Jeffersonian (New Brunswick, 1950), 251-57.
[45] Cong. Globe, 36 Cong., 1 Sess., Appendix, 302.

and by the host of northern Democrats loyal to Cass in his presidential quest.[46]

Historians have commented on the antipodal contrast between what Cass and Dickinson seemed to mean by non-intervention and what John C. Calhoun certainly did mean. Before Cass said a word on the subject, Calhoun had employed the same label to mark a radically different doctrine. Calhoun's non-intervention was designed to permit Southerners to take their slaves into the western territories, without interference by the federal government or by the territories themselves.[47] During the Taylor-Cass-Van Buren struggle of 1848, most southern Democrats said that Cass's non-intervention was the same as Calhoun's. Davis suspected that this was not the case at all. Cass himself in 1850, becoming more candid than in 1847 or 1848, verified the Davis suspicion. According to Cass's remarks in the "Great Debate," territorial legislatures could sanction or prohibit slavery as they preferred.[48]

Regardless of whether Cass's 1850 contention was justified or consistent, not a few of the southern Democratic senators went along with the New Mexico and Utah arrangement in the Compromise of 1850, just as most northern Democratic senators did. At various stages, Foote, Houston, William R. King of Alabama, and others joined Northerners along the non-intervention route. A single phrase in the bills, "consistent with the Constitution," [49] made it possible for Southerners to put their own gloss on the Compromise keystone. Anomalous or hazy as the territorial provisions were, they were Democratic provisions. Created by Democrats and supported by Democrats from both the sections, they were championed late and secondarily by Henry Clay and Daniel Webster.

Whether Webster would assent to what tradition has termed "Clay's plan" remained in doubt until March 7, 1850.[50] How late Clay was can best be illustrated by an exchange of views between Foote and Clay on February 14. Foote had first presented a plan closely resembling what came to be the Compromise. He had

[46] *Ibid.*, Appendix, 456; Milo M. Quaife, *The Doctrine of Non-Intervention with Slavery in the Territories* (Chicago, 1910), 76. Quaife's study was overlooked by several recent writers —but not by Channing, who leaned rather heavily on it.

[47] Richard K. Crallé (ed.), *The Works of John C. Calhoun* (6 vols., New York, 1853-1855), IV, 339-49.

[48] *Cong. Globe*, 31 Cong., 1 Sess., 398-99.

[49] Quaife, *The Doctrine of Non-Intervention with Slavery in the Territories*, 118.

[50] Robert C. Winthrop, Jr., *A Memoir of Robert C. Winthrop* (Boston, 1897), 109-14.

called for a select committee of fifteen, to pass upon the sectional problems and united most or all of them in a single bill. Foote said he made this move on the assumption that Clay favored just such strategy in his remarks of February 5 and 6, supporting his own resolutions of January 29.[51] Clay, however, denied that this was his aim. In fact, the Kentucky Whig disparaged the Democrat's "omnibus speech, in which he introduced all sorts of things and every sort of passenger, and myself among the number."

202

"My desire," Clay explained, "was that the Senate should express its sense upon each of the resolutions in succession, beginning with the first and ending with the eighth. If they should be affirmatively adopted, my purpose was to propose the reference of them to appropriate [standing] committees. There are some of the subjects which may be perhaps advantageously combined. . . . But never did I contemplate embracing in the entire scheme of accomodation and harmony . . . all these distracting questions, and bringing them all into one measure." Foote, on the contrary, "certainly thought that all or most of these matters could be embraced in one bill, at least so far as positive legislative action was concerned. I think so yet; and, acting upon this opinion, I have actually embraced them in the bill introduced by me." The Mississippian went on to charge Clay with "playing the game of political power with our neighbors of the North in a manner decidedly unskillful. He is throwing into the hands of his adversaries all the *trump cards* in the pack." [52]

Whoever may have held the trump cards in 1850, evidently by 1852 it was the Democratic party that benefited from the Compromise. Although its platform was scarcely less ambiguous than in 1848, Franklin Pierce rode confidently to the White House on the magic carpet of the most important letter of his life, in which he pronounced himself a Compromise Democrat.[53] In 1854, another twist of the popular sovereignty doctrine resulted in the Kansas-Nebraska Act.[54] In 1856, James Buchanan's banner proclaimed a variety of non-intervention,[55] and the 1850's saw Douglas making

[51] *Cong. Globe*, 31 Cong., 1 Sess., 356, 365-69.

[52] *Ibid.*, 368-69.

[53] Roy F. Nichols, *Franklin Pierce: Young Hickory of the Granite Hills* (Philadelphia, 1931), 201-202.

[54] Quaife, *The Doctrine of Non-Intervention with Slavery in the Territories*, 98-124; Milton, *Eve of Conflict*, 108-10.

[55] George T. Curtis, *Life of James Buchanan, Fifteenth President of the United States* (2 vols., New York, 1883), II, 176, 180.

popular sovereignty his political steed.[56] Thus what was done on Capitol Hill in August and September, 1850, was in line with Democrats' policies — enunciated in 1847, 1848, and 1852, and often echoed by leading Democrats in the post-Compromise decade.

Both the Democratic and the Whig spokesmen and leaders most intimately identified with the Compromise of 1850 then and thereafter gave proof of this interpretation. Just as the Democrats produced most votes, such Democratic stalwarts as Douglas, Cass, Foote, Houston, Dickinson, and King were on Clay's side in successive tests.[57] Were they siding with him? Or was he siding with them? Here another question of emphasis confronts the historian.

203

Douglas asserted in the Senate, without Whig denials, that nearly all the omnibus measures advanced by Clay's Committee of Thirteen had previously been considered and approved by the territorial committee, which had a Democratic majority and of which Douglas was chairman.[58] What Clay did was to connect old bills, change some of them slightly, and cause the enactment of one to depend on the enactment of all.[59] This was a procedure Clay lifted from Foote, and one Douglas' committee had decided against. Clay was less the originator and more the improviser. Incorporated in his recommendations, indeed the epitome of them, was the non-intervention theory of Dickinson and Cass.

Several persons claimed the role of originator of the compromise settlement. One, on the Senate floor, was Foote, who said "without egotism" (his own words) that "the report of the Committee on Territories was based upon bills introduced by myself." [60] Jefferson Davis' response to this sally was a relaxed "Oh, yes, I am willing to give you all the credit for that." Referring to the Compromise itself, however, Davis added: "If any man has a right to be proud of the success of these measures, it is the Senator from Illinois." [61] Years afterward, Foote traced popular sovereignty's inception back past his own contribution and Cass's Nicholson letter to Dickinson's resolutions.[62] Without subtracting an inch from the Little Giant's

[56] Milton, *Eve of Conflict*, 97 ff.
[57] *Cong. Globe*, 31 Cong., 1 Sess., *passim*.
[58] *Ibid.*, 1830.
[59] Douglas to Lanphier and Walker, August 3, 1850, Patton Papers.
[60] *Cong. Globe*, 31 Cong., 1 Sess., 1830.
[61] *Ibid.*
[62] Henry S. Foote, *War of the Rebellion; or, Scylla and Charybdis* (New York, 1866), 71-74.

stature, credit must also be given to Cass, Foote, and Dickinson — Democrats all — as well as to Douglas.

The Whigs' point of view, and especially that of Webster and Clay, should be borne in mind. Daniel Webster was in a tiny minority where opinion of Senate Whigs from the North was concerned as long as President Taylor lived.[63] Webster hoped to obtain the presidential nomination in 1852.[64] But the Whig delegates rebuffed Webster and Fillmore, bestowing the worthless palm on Winfield Scott. Webster died on October 24, 1852. His biographer, Claude M. Fuess, has written: "If Webster had lived and had been able to go to the polls, he would undoubtedly have cast his ballot for Franklin Pierce." [65]

Clay, who died on June 29, 1852, had favored Fillmore, in opposition to Scott and Webster, for the Whig nomination.[66] Because of his death at that particular time, no one can say with precision what he would have done on November 2. Possibly he might have taken the road which Webster had begun to follow. Clay's statement in Frankfort, Kentucky, in the autumn of 1850,[67] strongly suggests that he could not have voted for the Whig ticket two years later — with Scott running under the aegis of William H. Seward and Thurlow Weed. Earlier in 1850, Clay insisted that he was not the least interested in parties, party maneuvers, or party statutes;[68] and in 1851, he was brought forward as a Democratic or Union presidential possibility, with Cass for vice-president.[69] Throughout the 1850 controversy, Clay's speeches emphasized the placing of national interests ahead of party interests.[70] This has been interpreted as a sure proof of statesmanship. Yet could it not as logically mean abandonment of allegiance to the majority element within the Whig party, and adherence to the non-intervention program of the Democrats?

Dickinson's resolutions of 1847, Cass's Nicholson letter of 1847,

[63] Clarke to Meredith, June 1, 1850, Meredith Papers.

[64] Claude M. Fuess, *Daniel Webster* (2 vols., Boston, 1930), II, 277, 280-89.

[65] *Ibid.*, II, 358. In October, 1850, at Franklin, New Hampshire, Webster and Pierce "fraternized and joined in commending the recently enacted laws." Nichols, *Franklin Pierce*, 181.

[66] Glyndon G. Van Deusen, *The Life of Henry Clay* (Boston, 1937), 421, 424.

[67] *Ibid.*, 414-15.

[68] *Cong. Globe*, 31 Cong., 1 Sess., 1097.

[69] Nevins terms the movement to nominate a Union ticket of Clay and Cass "curious and absurd." Nevins, *Ordeal of the Union*, II, 4 n. Again he relegates an item of some significance to a footnote.

[70] *Cong. Globe*, 31 Cong., 1 Sess., *passim*.

the territorial aspect of Cass's candidacy in 1848, and Foote's proposals of late 1849 were Democratic contributions. The majority of Douglas' committee on territories was Democratic, as were most of the Compromise leaders on the floor. If Douglas the Democrat guided the Compromise through to success, if Democrats supplied most of the votes, and if Democrats were far more consistent than Whigs in underwriting component parts, small wonder that in 1852 the Democrats ran a pro-Compromise nominee — and that the Whigs went down to party defeat and party death.

Two other matters merit mention. One is the likelihood that the Whig party was hopelessly split on the sectional question, in 1850 and even before. Unable to elect one of their seasoned statesmen to the presidency, the Whigs had to rally their faltering forces and appeal to independents behind the glamor of military heroism; this mirrored intrinsic weaknesses. During Taylor's lifetime, the bulk of the Whig senators stoutly opposed the Compromise. After his death, Clay's "omnibus" was halted despite the push Democrats gave it. Even under Fillmore, and with Douglas in command in the Senate, the piecemeal measures could not have passed if many Whigs had not absented themselves when the yea-and-nay roll was called. Thus opposition, followed by negation, should be highlighted in accounts of the Compromise and integrated with the decline of Whiggery.

The second vital corollary is related to the first. Why the underscored prominence of Clay and Webster in virtually every version of the debates? Why the exaggerated emphasis on what they are presumed to have contributed? True, Clay returned to the Senate from retirement and for months did take charge of the Compromise efforts in the public gaze. Webster delivered one of the most brilliant speeches in American annals under circumstances loaded with drama. Such facets certainly deserve to be taken into account. Yet on the basis of many another fact developed here, from the standpoint of strength, of votes, of practical influence, the Clay-Webster contribution was merely secondary and supplemental alongside the major and primary Democratic backing of the Compromise.

Democratic senators and representatives, Democratic newspapers, Democratic party chieftains did much to play up Clay's and Webster's co-operation with them. It was not unlike what we have seen in our own era, in connection with Democratic foreign policy

— to which such Republicans as the late Arthur H. Vandenberg, the present Henry Cabot Lodge, and other senators gave allegiance. Who loomed largest during the 1940's in the internationalist phase of Senate foreign policy? Was it Alben W. Barkley of Kentucky, James E. Murray of Montana, Brien McMahon of Connecticut, Elbert D. Thomas of Utah, or one of the numerous other Democrats who were steadfast in this regard? Or was it Vandenberg of Michigan? The popular interpretation appears to favor Vandenberg. There is something so sensational about a man who bucks the majority element within his minority party, to join the majority party on a fundamental issue, that this seems to insure a certain kind of immortality.

According plenty of credit to Clay and Webster, as also we give it to Vandenberg and Lodge, should not historians take a closer look at what the protagonists represented? Are men who deliver two or eight votes more significant than those who speak for twenty? By what strange alchemy was Douglas long relegated to a really negligible part in the Compromise achievement? Did the relationship of Daniel Pomeroy Rhodes to the Douglas estate have anything to do with James Ford Rhodes's assigning Douglas to the limbo in 1850? [71] Is the prominence of Republicans among historical writers from 1865 to 1920 to be equated with Clay-Webster Whig emphasis? [72] These questions are packed with possibilities, warranting thorough investigation.

Nearly forty years ago, in the *Mississippi Valley Historical Review*, St. George L. Sioussat emphasized the need of re-exploring the Compromise of 1850.[73] Not all that Sioussat found wanting has yet been supplied. The evidence is never all in. But benefiting from the discovery of old manuscripts penned by Senators Cass, Clarke, and Douglas, and from a rereading and perhaps a more extensive reading of the *Congressional Globe* and kindred sources, it is possible to come closer now to the realities of 1850, and to view the true structure behind the façade.

[71] Frank H. Hodder, "Propaganda as a Source of American History," *Mississippi Valley Historical Review*, IX (June, 1922), 10-12.
[72] This is another aspect of some questions discussed in Howard K. Beale, "What Historians Have Said about the Causes of the Civil War," *Theory and Practice in Historical Study: A Report of the Committee on Historiography* (Social Science Research Council, *Bulletin 54*: New York, 1946), 55-102.
[73] St. George L. Sioussat, "Tennessee, the Compromise of 1850, and the Nashville Convention," *Mississippi Valley Historical Review*, II (December, 1915), 347.

'The Cave of the Winds' and the Compromise of 1850

By HOLMAN HAMILTON

IF AEOLUS HAD FORSAKEN HIS CAVE OF THE WINDS TO VISIT Washington in late 1849, he would have felt thoroughly at home in the United States House of Representatives. Never before, in six decades under the Federal Constitution, had congressional chaos been more evident. Wordiness emanated from men who under normal conditions would have busied themselves with organization. For three hectic weeks the House could not organize because there was no Speaker on the dais, and none could be elected. House rules called for a majority decision, but there was no majority. And so, during most of December, orators tore passions to tatters and members voted ineffectually while the mere clerk of the previous session presided and sought a modicum of order. Often at night, when adjournment came, caucuses met in that same chamber—and southern, northern, western, and eastern partisan and factional storms continued as before. The House of December 1849 was truly a cave of political winds.

Capable men were members, people of past or future prominence. Horace Mann of Massachusetts and Henry W. Hilliard of Alabama were educators and men of literary skill. Thaddeus Stevens of Pennsylvania and Jacob Thompson of Mississippi represented extremist elements. The roster of able congressmen included Robert Ward Johnson of Arkansas, John A. McClernand and William A. Richardson of Illinois, Albert G. Brown of Mississippi, and James L. Orr of South Carolina. Thomas L. Clingman and David Outlaw of North Carolina rubbed elbows with Joshua R. Giddings of Ohio, James X. McLanahan of Pennsylvania, Frederick P. Stanton of Tennessee, and Volney E. Howard

Originally published in *The Journal of Southern History*, 23 (August, 1957). Copyright 1957 by the Southern Historical Association. Reprinted by permission of the Managing Editor.

of Texas. In the large New York delegation were James Brooks, William Duer, and Preston King. Georgia had sent three gifted men in Howell Cobb, Alexander H. Stephens, and Robert Toombs. From Massachusetts came the scholarly Robert C. Winthrop, Speaker of the Thirtieth Congress; from Kentucky, the resourceful Linn Boyd who (like Orr) was a future Speaker; from New Jersey, the wealthy businessman James G. King; from Ohio, the irrepressible Free Soiler, Joseph M. Root; from Tennessee, a future president, Andrew Johnson of the Greeneville district; and from Virginia the devoted Richmond Democrat James A. Seddon.

208

Although these and other representatives measured up to standards of previous Congresses, they and their chamber soon would be overshadowed by a Senate of unusual brilliance. For the Thirty-first Congress was the one in which John C. Calhoun, Henry Clay, and Daniel Webster met for the final time. Thomas Hart Benton was a senator, too, and the tall Texan, Sam Houston of Huntsville, joined veterans like Alabama's William R. King and relative newcomers like Henry S. Foote in the senatorial drama. Leaders of the younger generation, Salmon P. Chase, Jefferson Davis, Stephen A. Douglas, William H. Seward, stood ready to challenge older senators' prominence.

At the start of the Thirty-first Congress, the contrast between the two houses seemed rooted less in personalities than in voting alignments. If the Senate Democracy's nationalistic and sectionalistic blocs were at odds on policy fundamentals, the large Democratic paper majority presented a united front for organizational purposes. Vice President Millard Fillmore was a Whig, but Senate Democrats experienced no difficulty in dominating the committees.[1] Meeting and adjourning from day to day with no extensive debate, the Senate at the outset marked time while the House wrangled. Though some representatives like Meredith P. Gentry and George W. Julian reached Washington late, nearly all of the 231 House seats were occupied from the beginning. Of the members answering the roll call on the first ballot and the last, 108 were Democrats, 103 Whigs, and nine Free Soilers— while a single congressman (Lewis C. Levin) belonged to the Native American party. The principal candidates for Speaker

---

[1] *Cong. Globe*, 31 Cong., 1 Sess., 40-41, 44-45.

usually were Cobb the Democrat and Winthrop the Whig. In the course of 62 ballots over the three-week span, the total vote ranged from a high of 226 to a low of 217, of which the Georgian's maximum was 103 and the Bostonian's 102. At various times, on their own responsibility or as a result of pressure, both Cobb and Winthrop withdrew their names to give ambitious colleagues a chance for preferment. But, with one exception, no other aspirant surpassed the Cobb-Winthrop crests. Not only was a House majority lacking, but a group of Southern Whigs refused to back Winthrop, some Southern Democrats declined to support Cobb, and the Free Soilers had their own candidate and with the dissident Southern Whigs held the balance of power.[2]

209

On the sixty-third ballot, the impasse ended. The winds in the cave spent themselves momentarily. Conflicting elements bowed to reason, finding a way out of their blind alley by resorting to a plurality decision.[3] When Howell Cobb thus won the speakership and named the committees' personnel, the Democratic party found itself in control of both House and Senate organizations.[4] Still, the fact that the lower chamber had to fall back on a plurality procedure suggested troubles that would develop as soon as the House tried to legislate.

Could House majorities ever be attained in the course of the 1850 debates? Sober onlookers were frankly pessimistic, for the speakership election reflected schisms within each of the major parties, not only in Washington but in the United States as a whole. According to many a Northerner and Whig, the annexation of Texas in 1845 had caused most of the problems now vexing Congress. Annexation had been followed swiftly by the Mexican War, the Wilmot Proviso, the acquisition from Mexico of a vast amount of western soil, and then the forty-niners' gold

[2] *Ibid.*, 2-39, 41-44, 46-48, 51, 61-67; Holman Hamilton, *Zachary Taylor: Soldier in the White House* (Indianapolis, 1951), 247-52. Winthrop felt the Whigs erred in shifting votes from himself to other candidates. He believed that, if he had received 102 votes on the forty-first ballot, his supporters "would have made me Speaker." Robert C. Winthrop to John P. Kennedy, December 16, 1849, in Kennedy Papers (Peabody Institute, Baltimore).

[3] Frederick P. Stanton took credit for this, and stated that the solution was reached despite 48-28 opposition in the Democratic caucus. Stanton to James Buchanan, December 24, 1849, in Buchanan Papers (Historical Society of Pennsylvania, Philadelphia).

[4] *Cong. Globe*, 31 Cong., 1 Sess., 66-67, 88-89.

rush to the Sacramento Valley. Were Southerners entitled to own slave property in the new American West? *Or* should the Proviso be passed and slavery excluded from that area? *Or* was the popular sovereignty principle feasible and fair? *Or* did the solution lie in projecting to the Pacific Ocean the Missouri Compromise line of 36°30′, with slavery admitted below and forbidden above it? Intraparty Whig weaknesses and Whigs' want of accord on these questions had been symbolized in 1848 by General Zachary Taylor's presidential nomination. Taylor had been given no platform by the Whigs, and his personal statements on the issues of the hour invited conflicting views. His election, in turn, had been due in great measure to a split in the northern Democracy with particular reference to New York. Thus the Taylor of the White House was a minority President, just as Cobb was a minority Speaker. The Whig Administration of 1849 and early 1850 lacked the mandate, experience, and cohesion essential to first-rate executive leadership.

The General in the Mansion, however, was not slow in making his influence felt. In the spring of 1849 Taylor had sent Representative Thomas Butler King of Georgia to the West Coast as his special agent. King in June informed the Californians of the "sincere desire of the Executive" to protect them "in the formation of any government, republican in its character, hereafter to be submitted to Congress, which shall be the result of their . . . deliberate choice." Before many months passed, California adopted a free-state constitution and applied for admission to the Union. In August at Mercer, Pennsylvania, Taylor asserted that "the people of the North need have no apprehension of the further extension of slavery." In November, an army officer left Washington for Santa Fe with a directive that "if the people of New Mexico desired to take . . . steps toward securing admission as a state, it would be his duty . . . 'not to thwart but to advance their wishes.' " The President's intent was unmistakable. If his hopes were realized, neither popular sovereignty nor projection of the 36°30′ line could apply to California or New Mexico, and the free- and slave-state balance in the Senate would be permanently destroyed. Was the White House slaveholder a Wilmot Proviso man, an enemy of the South in Southern

210

Whig clothing? The thought was appalling to many Southerners.[5]

With this as the background for the Thirty-first Congress, it might be supposed that Taylor would have drawn Northern accessions to his banner. His annual message in December ended on a ringing Union note, and a special message the third week in January underscored statehood in the West. The Free Soilers in the House, however, were not content with the Proviso's end-product; they demanded the letter of the law. Most Northern House Democrats, better disciplined than Whigs, maintained their records as party regulars. It is true that Northern Whigs were impressed, but, as subsequent trends unfolded, some veered away from the Administration to pursue a less drastic course. The unpopularity of Taylor's cabinet, inept distribution of federal patronage, and Whig losses in recent congressional races did not constitute the raw materials of which majorities are composed. Southerners, on the other hand, quickly sensed that Taylor personified danger to their interests. Southern Democrats favored popular sovereignty or the 36°30' plan. Such original Taylor-for-President boosters as Stephens, Toombs, and other Southern Whigs had turned thumbs down on Winthrop for Speaker and now would fight Taylor to the bitter end.

211

If the dilemma of December was not to be repeated during 1850, much would depend on Howell Cobb and his comrades of the Democratic high command. Chairman Boyd of the Committee on Territories proved to be the Speaker's right arm and presided over most of the debate as chairman of the Committee of the Whole. A third key figure was Douglas's lieutenant, chairman McClernand of the Committee on Foreign Affairs who, despite the title, would devote nearly all his energies to domestic problems. Still another was Virginia's Thomas H. Bayly, head of the Ways and Means Committee. The role of Cobb has been the subject of a scholarly monograph,[6] but a statistical study of House speeches and votes can add a great deal to the story, and Boyd's, McClernand's, and Bayly's contributions certainly enter into the reckoning.

Most of the initiative for the Compromise of 1850 had its origin

[5] Hamilton, *Zachary Taylor: Soldier in the White House, passim.*
[6] Robert P. Brooks, "Howell Cobb and the Crisis of 1850," in *Mississippi Valley Historical Review* (Cedar Rapids, 1914-), IV (December 1917), 279-98.

in the Senate. In the course of the next three-quarters of a century, almost every historian treating the topic gave a lion's share of credit to Clay and Webster[7] In more recent times emphasis has been placed on Douglas and the Senate Democratic majority.[8] Latterly, too, a distinctive effort has been made to depart from vague or inaccurate remarks about the Compromise per se, and carefully to define the slavery provisions of the acts organizing New Mexico and Utah Territories.[9] In addition to establishing the two Western territories, with legislatures which could prohibit or establish or regulate slavery, the Compromise admitted California into the Union as a free state; settled the Texas-New Mexico boundary controversy; assured Texas that the United States would assume the Texas debt; included a fugitive slave law designed to plug loopholes in the old law of 1793, and abolished the slave trade in the District of Columbia.[10]

Bills incorporating the several parts of the Compromise were passed by Congress in July, August, and September. In the preceding December and January, outbursts of sectional pride and passion evoked general concern in and out of Congress. The New York Whig diarist, Philip Hone, compared representatives in Washington with the Jacobins of the French Revolution. The nation "trembles at its base," Hone brooded, and "for the first time in our history" men did not hesitate "openly to threaten a

212

[7] James Ford Rhodes, *History of the United States from the Compromise of 1850* (7 vols., New York, 1893-1906), I, 120-95; James Schouler, *History of the United States under the Constitution* (6 vols., New York, 1880-99), V, 159-98; George P. Garrison, *Westward Extension, 1841-1850* (New York, 1906), 320-31. Of the older "standard" multi-volume histories, John B. McMaster, *A History of the People of the United States from the Revolution to the Civil War* (8 vols., New York, 1883-1913), VIII, 12-42, is in several ways the most satisfactory on the Compromise. In Edward Channing, *A History of the United States* (6 vols., New York, 1905-25), VI, 75-85, many of Rhodes's and Schouler's fundamental errors are avoided, but details are slighted, and the work is marred by numerous minor mistakes.

[8] Frank H. Hodder, "The Authorship of the Compromise of 1850," in *Mississippi Valley Historical Review*, XXII (March 1936), 525-36; George F. Milton, *The Eve of Conflict: Stephen A. Douglas and the Needless War* (Boston, 1934), 50-78; George D. Harmon, "Douglas and the Compromise of 1850," in *Journal of the Illinois State Historical Society* (Springfield, 1908-), XXI (January 1929), 453-99; Holman Hamilton, "Democratic Senate Leadership and the Compromise of 1850," in *Mississippi Valley Historical Review*, XLI (December 1954), 403-18.

[9] Robert R. Russel, "What Was the Compromise of 1850?", in *Journal of Southern History* (Baton Rouge, 1935-), XXII (August 1956), 292-309.

[10] 9 *U. S. Stat.* (69 vols., Boston, 1845-1955), 446-58, 462-68.

dissolution of the Union." Congressman McLanahan agreed that the slavery question had reached a dangerous crisis. "A lion is in the path of our Country's glory," the Pennsylvania Democrat reported privately. "May Heaven shield us from impending danger." "The issue between the South and the North is the all absorbing subject here," the sick but alert Senator Calhoun wrote his son from Washington. ". . . The Southern members are more determined and bold than I ever saw them. Many avow themselves to be disunionists."[11]

To William B. Ogden, who was soon to make a fortune in the city of Chicago, "the prospects ahead" were "not cheering in any way"; Calhoun was bent on the "dissolution of the Union," and "if a rupture does take place the North will have to unite" in rallying to Taylor and "aiding him to put it down."[12] The Whig Senator Webster and the Democratic Senator Lewis Cass later looked back on the situation as one of the most dangerous in American annals.[13] The junior senator from Illinois, a Democrat, saw "the extreme Southern men . . . in a state of excitement which prepares them for the most desperate resolves." A North Carolina Whig in the House feared that "armed men might be admitted into this Hall, and . . . this place might become a scene of bloodshed." Shortly before Christmas, one of the most conservative Northern Democrats found "more bad feeling" on Capitol Hill "than can be well conceived unless by those present." Over in Philadelphia an aristocratic Whig was pessimistic: "No one can say how soon we may be involved in the dangers & calamities of disunion. The house is not yet organized & parties are becoming inflamed." Slavery and related topics were being used "as the cloak of the ambitious designs of demagogues & to delude & excite the people—who . . . are victims & tools." An ex-congressman and ex-governor of the Bluegrass State warned a prominent Missourian: "You can hardly conceive of the irritation

213

[11] Philip Hone, manuscript diary, December 15, 1849, and January 7, 1850 (New-York Historical Society, New York City); James X. McLanahan to Buchanan, December 2, 1849, in Buchanan Papers; J. Franklin Jameson (ed.), *Correspondence of John C. Calhoun,* American Historical Association *Annual Report . . . for the Year 1899* (2 vols., Washington, 1900), II, 780.

[12] William B. Ogden to E. A. Russell, December 31, 1849, in Ogden Papers (Chicago Historical Society).

[13] Lexington *Kentucky Statesman,* October 30, November 23, 1850.

and bad feeling . . . excited in this northern border of Kentucky" by abolitionists and other Northern radicals. In mid-January, the Whig publisher of the Washington *National Intelligencer*, conversing with a Marylander when they met in the House, voiced alarm "in reference to the Southern movement on the Slave question, threatening a dissolution of the Union."[14]

Events in the House during most of January substantiated the forebodings. While in the Senate moves were being made for pacification, Clingman, Howard, Seddon, and Brown, irked by Free Soilers and also by the President, delivered fiery orations to their fellow representatives. Jeremiah Morton of Virginia and Samuel W. Inge of Alabama carried on in February the sharp Southern criticism of Taylor, King, the cabinet, the Proviso, statehood for California, and, in general, Northern attitudes toward the South. Stanton, though more moderate, joined in the attack. From January 22 through February 13, not a single Northern member made a set speech in the chamber. Seven Southern representatives delivered set speeches, each lasting approximately an hour, and one of these Southerners twice took the floor. All eight efforts, with the partial exception of Stanton's, were saturated with grievances and studded with threats. In mid-February, the balance began to be redressed by the calmer remarks of Hilliard the Alabama Whig and Marshall J. Wellborn the Georgia Democrat, the non-sectionalistic but intensely partisan observations of the Indiana Democrat, Graham N. Fitch, and the characteristic Wilmot Proviso slants of Root the Ohio Free Soiler and Mann the Massachusetts Whig. Of the forty-four formal, hour-long addresses heard in the House during the sixty-nine day period preceding April 1, nineteen were Northern in origin and twenty-five Southern, despite the fact that Northerners constituted a three-fifths majority of the total membership.

The temper of the House in early 1850 could also be gauged

14 James Shields to Buchanan, December 8, 1849, in Buchanan Papers; David Outlaw to Mrs. Outlaw, January 14, 1850, in Outlaw Papers (Southern Historical Collection, University of North Carolina, Chapel Hill); Daniel Sturgeon to Buchanan, December 22, 1849, in Buchanan Papers; Sidney G. Fisher, manuscript diary, December 16, 1849 (Historical Society of Pennsylvania); Thomas Metcalfe to David R. Atchison, December 26, 1849, in Atchison Papers (Western Historical Manuscripts Collection, University of Missouri, Columbia); John P. Kennedy, manuscript diary, January 19, 1850, in Kennedy Papers.

by protracted corollaries of the battle between Winthrop and Cobb. Representatives voted twenty times before managing to elect a clerk. Three ballots were taken to choose a chaplain; eight were necessary for a sergeant-at-arms, and none of the fourteen candidates for doorkeeper could win that lofty office after fourteen trials.[15] Already Richard K. Meade of Virginia had rushed gesticulating at Duer of New York, when the latter branded Meade a liar. In February, an Illinoisan's comments in the House brought a challenge to a duel from Jefferson Davis. The first week in March, during a debate, Edward Stanly of North Carolina flung the charge of disgraceful rudeness at a fellow Whig from Alabama.[16] Moreover, the normal House routine, memorials, petitions, pensions, patent laws, the Seventh Census, the coastwise trade, and a contested election in Iowa, cluttered up the agenda and contributed to the delay. Concurrently, the Senate had its own moments of frustration and sectional wrath. But Foote, Cass, Douglas, Clay, and others were bent on achieving a compromise. And, six days after Clay introduced his resolutions in the Senate, there came the first of four important moves that helped somewhat to tranquilize the agitated House.

215

The first step involved the House's reaction to Root's resolution that the Proviso be applied to the region acquired from Mexico, with the exception of California. On February 4, the resolution was tabled 105-75—eighteen Northern Democrats and fourteen Northern Whigs siding with the South against the Proviso. Cobb did not vote; his vote was not needed. Especially significant was the presence of McClernand and Richardson in the majority, joining as they did Bayly and Boyd and other Southern Democrats like Baltimore's Robert M. McLane.

The following Sunday, February 10, an even more meaningful victory was scored for the compromise cause in a Washington hotel. Thomas Ritchie, now editor of the Washington *Union* and Nestor of the Democratic party, in his young manhood had been

[15] *Cong. Globe*, 31 Cong., 1 Sess., *passim*. The speech of Oregon Delegate Samuel R. Thurston has been excluded from the statistical survey.

[16] *Ibid.*, 27, 467; Washington *National Intelligencer*, March 6, 1850; Outlaw to Mrs. Outlaw, February 24, 27, 28, 1850, in Outlaw Papers; Donald F. Tingley, "The Jefferson Davis-William H. Bissell Duel," in *Mid-America* (Chicago, 1918-   ), XXXVIII (July 1956), 146-55.

a warm friend of Henry Clay. Then for years they were opponents, Clay dominating the Whigs and running for president while Ritchie bossed the Virginia Democracy. Now, at last, they were reunited. After James W. Simenton of the New York *Courier & Enquirer* had taken part in the preliminary arrangements, Ritchie with Bayly at his side called on the Kentuckian at his quarters. No other Democratic journalist had more influence than white-haired "Father" Ritchie. No other Whig senator had more prestige than the venerable "Harry of the West." When the tall, fair, thirty-nine-year-old Bayly brought what Ritchie described as "ingenuity and learning" to the discussion, he was contributing "ways and means" of enormous value to House and Senate compromisers. Several days before, Ritchie criticized Clay in the columns of the *Union*. Henceforth, partisans would rub their eyes at the quantity and fervor of Democratic tributes to the Democratic party's traditional archfoe. That Clay-Ritchie handclasp at the National Hotel, as the shadows lengthened on a Sunday afternoon, symbolized the coalescing of compromise strength.

Then, on the 18th, there came the third test of the House leaders' control or ingenuity. Five days before, Taylor had submitted a four-line message transmitting the California constitution, and James D. Doty of Wisconsin sought to capitalize upon it. A free-soil Democrat, Doty proposed that Boyd's Committee on Territories report a California statehood bill unconnected with other legislation. This, of course, was a red flag to Southerners, a signal for leaders to enter the fray. There were twenty-eight roll calls, and tactics of delay were dexterously employed, for it was clear that if Doty succeeded debate on California would be halted. With Bayly demanding resistance "at all hazards," Southerners and Northern Democrats stalled and dodged—their motions and maneuvers sustained by Cobb in the chair from early afternoon till midnight. Finally, Cobb decided that the day had expired; the resolution went over, and for the first time the full force of the speakership was unmistakably felt.[17]

[17] *Cong. Globe*, 31 Cong., 1 Sess., 276, 375-85; Henry S. Foote, *A Casket of Reminiscences* (Washington, 1874), 24; Charles H. Ambler, *Thomas Ritchie: A Study in Virginia Politics* (Richmond, 1913), 281-82; Richmond *Enquirer*, September 10, 1852.

The next night, Speaker Cobb's house on Third Street was the scene of a conference almost as significant as the one attended by Ritchie, Clay, and Bayly. With Douglas acting as a *deus ex machina*, McClernand invited Stephens and Toombs to join in a private discussion of objectives and methods with John K. Miller (an Ohio Democrat), Boyd, Cobb, Richardson, and McClernand himself. The four Southerners and three Northerners, five Democrats and two Whigs, agreed to a Douglas-McClernand plan of action. What McClernand proposed was that he should sponsor bills for the territorial organization of New Mexico and Utah on a popular sovereignty basis, with the understanding that California would be admitted as a free state and slavery retained in the District of Columbia. McClernand also promised that Douglas would follow a similar procedure in the Senate.[18] The fact that these Southern Whigs were willing to underwrite the Democrats' program of adjustment was encouraging not only to McClernand but to his Southern confreres, Cobb, Boyd, and Bayly.

217

Although each of these occurrences logically heartened the compromise men, three other facts were most discouraging. The first was the attitude of Calhoun, who set his face sternly against such adjustments. The second was President Taylor's opposition, for reasons diametrically opposed to Calhoun's. But even the combined influence of these two determined men, together with the votes of the Free Soilers, could never have prevented a compromise had it not been for a third consideration, a surprising tactical shift by Clay. It is ironic that Clay, who originally favored keeping all parts of a compromise separate and taking up bills one at a time, was persuaded by Foote and Ritchie in February and March that several of the measures ought to be combined.[19] While Clay was undergoing his fateful conversion congressional oratory continued and observers reacted variously to developments on the Hill.

Hone wished that Clay's February 5 speech would calm the "rage of contending factions," but concluded "I fear not." Senator

[18] Alexander H. Stephens, *A Constitutional View of the Late War Between the States* . . . (2 vols., Philadelphia, 1868-70), II, 202-204.

[19] Foote, *A Casket of Reminiscences*, 24; *Cong. Globe*, 31 Cong., 1 Sess., 365-69.

James M. Mason of Virginia, on the other hand, believed in early February that "the danger of dissolution, once imminent, is diminishing every day."[20] On the 9th, Speaker Cobb looked "sanguinely to the period when all patriotic hearts will and can unite in saying 'all is well.'" Yet, four days later, Representative Stephens confessed: "I see very little prospect of future peace and quiet in the public mind." While Daniel Webster waxed optimistic ("The clamor about disunion rather abates"),[21] Calhoun declared: "The excitement . . . continues on the increase. I see no prospect of any satisfactory adjustment." Burgeoning confidence was mirrored in Representative James Gore King's report: "No reasons exist for any uneasiness on account of the angry discussions. . . . Of course some compromise will be found." A single violent speech from either side would ignite a flame, Outlaw felt on the first of March; still, the Whig congressman thought that "most of the steam is blown off by this time and that those who wish to speak, may be cool and temperate." Perhaps the best proof of growing moderation in both House and Senate is contained in one of Calhoun's letters. Writing on March 10 (six days after his own address had been read for him by Mason, and three days after Webster's Seventh of March Speech), the Carolinian considered it possible that the slavery question might be "patched up for the present, to brake [*sic*] out again in a few years."[22]

During March and April, the Senate was the setting for so much memorable political drama that there has been an understandable tendency to slight the House in most accounts. Not only Senators Calhoun and Webster but Thomas J. Rusk, Hannibal Hamlin, Seward, Douglas, and others reflected all shades of public opinion in their formal orations. Calhoun died the last

218

[20] Hone, manuscript diary, February 8, 1850; James M. Mason to William C. Rives, February 4, 1850, in Rives Papers (Manuscripts Division, Library of Congress).

[21] Ulrich B. Phillips (ed.), *The Correspondence of Robert Toombs, Alexander H. Stephens, and Howell Cobb*, American Historical Association *Annual Report . . . for the Year 1911* (2 vols., Washington, 1913), II, 183-84; Fletcher Webster (ed.), *The Private Correspondence of Daniel Webster* (2 vols., Boston, 1857), II, 355.

[22] Jameson, *Correspondence of John C. Calhoun*, 782-84; James G. King to Baring Brothers & Company, February 28, 1850, in Baring Papers (Public Archives of Canada, Ottawa); Outlaw to Mrs. Outlaw, March 1, 1850, in Outlaw Papers.

morning in March and in mid-April the Senate created a Select Committee of Thirteen with Clay as chairman. In the latter part of April and the first week of May, while the committee's report was in the making and with numerous senators at home mending their fences, a greater share of attention was turned to recent and current trends in the House.

April's fifteen set speeches in the House were delivered by eight Southerners and seven Northerners, eight Democrats and seven Whigs. In May, two Free Soilers joined six Whigs and four Democrats, the sectional division of the orators being eight from the North and four from the South. Linn Boyd, as chairman of the Committee of the Whole, presided when most of the remarks were made. In June, one Southern Democrat complained that he had tried unsuccessfully for two months to win recognition from the dais. The fact that Southern Democrats controlled the machinery, and that Whigs and Democrats alternated in the spotlight, suggests that Boyd was exceedingly fair in recognizing the speakers. In June everyone who wished to speak had a chance, and the floor went begging more than once.[23] Each of forty-seven representatives was allotted his hour in the first June fortnight—26 Southerners, 21 Northerners, 29 Democrats, 12 Whigs, and six Free Soilers addressing themselves to the House and their constituents.

At times, the procedure verged on the ludicrous. In an effort to give each congressman his due, sessions often were held at night, so sparsely attended that on one occasion only twenty-eight members were present, and on another thirty-two. This was in June when, once again, senatorial jockeying had a greater appeal. Indeed it grew clear, as the late spring advanced, that many members of the House were more interested in defining their own stand for Buncombe or home appraisal than in debating colleagues' views or even determining what they were. One evening after the dinner recess, Cobb and Boyd were two of only eight men in the chamber when time came for the House to return to work, and no more than sixteen were on hand when at last the House did come to order and the orations were resumed.[24] Some of the speeches printed in the *Congressional Globe* never

219

23 *Cong. Globe*, 31 Cong., 1 Sess., 1110, 1123, 1171.
24 *Ibid.*, 1123, 1151, 1167.

were delivered at all. Others were dressed up for the record, following informal "ad lib" remarks punctuated by laughter or boredom.

One hundred and eleven representatives held the floor between late January and mid-June. Forty-two were Southern Democrats, 17 Southern Whigs, 24 Northern Democrats, 20 Northern Whigs, and eight Northern Free Soilers. More significant ideologically is the breakdown which shows 10 Southerners in favor of an extension of 36°30'; 21 Northerners and Southerners backing Taylor's plan; 32 members from both sections preferring the popular sovereignty solution, and 11 speaking out clearly for the Wilmot Proviso. Some representatives did not say precisely what they were for, but stated pointedly what they were against. This was particularly true of South Carolinians Daniel Wallace and William F. Colcock. Williamson R. W. Cobb of Alabama lamented Congress' failure to create a joint Senate-House committee, with all sectional issues referred to it. Most atypical of their states were Meredith P. Gentry of Tennessee, Thomas S. Haymond of Virginia, and Edward Stanly of North Carolina (who followed President Taylor's lead) and Pennsylvania's Thomas Ross (who predicted "dissolution" of the Union, if "aggressions upon the domestic institutions of the South are persevered in").[25] Some representatives did not fully develop their positions. Others advocated California statehood, without identifying themselves either with Taylor or with the Proviso men. Still others apparently failed to hand in their speeches for publication in detail. Eight representatives spoke more than once. Over half the House membership sat silent or made the briefest comment, but the desire of almost 50 per cent to give utterance to their convictions or to awareness of expediency's benefits suggests the impact of the 1850 crisis.

So much for rank-and-filers' speeches. A few words of leaders at critical moments and parliamentary maneuvers later in the year would transcend most of them in importance. For many weeks, however, except on such matters as the Root and Doty moves heretofore mentioned, the pro-compromise chieftains made

[25] *Ibid.*, Appendix, 336-45, 429-33, 459-64, 598-600, 646-49, 684-87, 832-36. Haymond hailed from the Wheeling district, part of the future state of West Virginia.

little headway. Back in March, the bills on which the conferees agreed at Cobb's house were reported in the Senate by Douglas. Still, it was noteworthy that the Senate chose to base its debate from May through July not on the methods favored by Douglas but on the "Omnibus Bill" and other parts of the report of Clay's Committee of Thirteen. The House, moreover, gave McClernand no opportunity from early spring well into the summer to go even as far as Douglas had gone. McClernand in April did announce a précis of the measures he stood ready to sponsor, if and when he got the chance.[26] But the long House debate was premised on Taylor's February 13 message and a bill of Doty's for California statehood. New Mexico, Utah, the Texas boundary, the Texas debt, fugitive slaves, and the slave trade in the District entered into the discussion only indirectly or inferentially. Wretched acoustics in the hall of the House brought echo and confusion there, and the buzz of conversation in front of the dais resulted in frequent raps for order. Yet the verbosity persisted. Amendments were offered, and amendments to amendments, and provisos altering amendments' amendments. But, aside from the speechmaking, nothing substantial was done by the House, and no key legislation was passed, when, with little warning, on July 9 death came to President Zachary Taylor.

221

Millard Fillmore, the new President, looked with favor on compromise. But Taylor's death and Fillmore's accession met with less rapid political reaction in the House than in the Senate. Armed with Fillmore's co-operation, Clay pressed forward in the hope of gaining passage for the Omnibus Bill, the territorial part of which was successively amended by John Macpherson Berrien of Georgia, James W. Bradbury of Maine, and William C. Dawson of Georgia. The tinkering led on July 31 to the destruction of the New Mexico territorial provision in its entirety. The Texas dollars-for-acres arrangement was also cut out, as was California statehood. Nothing but Utah Territory remained, a tragic remnant, in Clay's eyes, of the bill on which he had set his heart.

After Clay's final defeat in the Senate, the tired old Kentucky Whig left the capital for a rest and young, dynamic Stephen A. Douglas came from the wings to the center of the stage. Taking

26 *Cong. Globe*, 31 Cong., 1 Sess., 592, 628-29.

up measures one at a time, Douglas within a fortnight rushed two bills through to Senate passage. In less than a month, the total was four. With Utah previously approved, all that remained when Clay returned from his seashore respite was the District slave trade's abolition. This last compromise provision met approval on September 19, under the personal guidance of Clay.[27] Meanwhile, all Washington and much of the nation turned from the Senate to the House to concentrate on developments there.

Wednesday, August 28, marked a striking change in the tone and tempo of the House of Representatives. No longer did California speeches virtually monopolize the members' time. No longer did discussion of land titles in Oregon, Revolutionary War pensions, Indian depredations, railroad right of ways, or even governmental appropriations delay action on the compromise. The General Appropriations Bill had been passed. California statehood had been shunted aside, and routine business for the most part postponed. Now, with the Senate example before them, Boyd and McClernand demanded decision as the Texas debt-and-boundary measure was taken up on the floor of the House. Straightway Boyd offered an amendment, combining this bill with the one providing for New Mexico's territorial organization. Granting doubt as to whether it was better to "consider the bills in a connected or in a separate form," Boyd hoped to test the sense of the House in relation to the establishment of territorial governments on the popular sovereignty principle. "We have . . . been listening to speeches for nine long months," the Democrat from western Kentucky exclaimed. ". . . I am astonished at the patience with which our constituents have borne our procrastination. I think we have talked enough—in God's name let us act."

Act the House did. On September 3, the combined bill or "little omnibus" became the special order of the day.[28] Immediately the question of Texas bonds, bondholders, and lobbyists cropped up. Senator Robert W. Barnwell believed that the "whole difficulty about the boundary of Texas was gotten up

<hr>

[27] Hamilton, "Democratic Senate Leadership and the Compromise of 1850," 407-12.
[28] *Cong. Globe*, 31 Cong., 1 Sess., 1696-97, 1727, 1736.

by . . . Clay . . . and others interested in the Bonds of Texas." Barnwell "never could at all understand the matter" until the New England men, "almost in a body," voted for the Senate Texas boundary-and-debt bill. Similar suspicion was felt in the House concerning the "corruption of the 10,000,000" dollars,[29] with reference to Northern representatives and Northern holders of Texas securities. Congressman Giddings had already said that "the payment of this ten millions" was intended "to raise Texan stocks from fifteen cents on the dollar to par value, to make splendid fortunes in little time. To take money from the pockets of the people and put it into the hands of stock-jobbers, and gamblers in Texas scrip." On September 4, Preston King likewise raised the issue of Texas bonds. Two days later, as the House neared a vote, Representative Jonathan D. Morris of Ohio, noting the lobbyists on the floor, demanded their expulsion and opined, "If there are any Texan bondholders in here, they can see and hear as well in the galleries."

223

Although Speaker Cobb replied to Morris that the seventeenth rule of the House (keeping lobbyists off the floor) "would be enforced," Brown of Mississippi later said it had "not been done." On that same September 6, the House approved the engrossment of the bill for a third reading—a highly consequential step which may be regarded as the pivot not only for the "little omnibus" but for the whole compromise in the House. The *Globe* for the 6th contains an unusual statement: "The announcement of the result was received with manifestations of applause of various kinds, the most peculiar and attractive of which was a sort of unpremeditated *allegro* whistle, which the Reporter does not remember to have heard before (certainly never in the House of Representatives). The other tokens of glorification were of a less musical order. It was evident that the greater portion of the applause, especially at the outset, was on the floor of the Hall itself." Cobb now interposed "vigorously" to check the noise. Cries of "Order!" were met with shouts of "Let them stamp! It is all right!" The chamber was "in an uproar."[30]

[29] Robert W. Barnwell to James H. Hammond, August 14, 1850, in Hammond Papers (Manuscripts Division, Library of Congress). On June 24, Barnwell of South Carolina succeeded Franklin H. Elmore, who had been appointed to Calhoun's Senate seat and died May 29, 1850.

[30] *Cong. Globe*, 31 Cong., 1 Sess., 1562, 1746, 1763-64.

Passage of the "little omnibus" followed a few minutes later by a margin of 108 to 97 . A debate of less than a single day was needed before the House officially approved of California's entrance into the Union. Here the vote was 150-56, and that on the Utah territorial bill 97-85, both on September 7. September 12 saw the fugitive slave measure triumph by 109-76. On September 9, by 31 to 10, the Senate ratified the House's union of the Texas and New Mexico bills, something that might have been impossible had Douglas first presented them there in combination. Abolition of the slave trade in the District carried in the House, by 124-59, on September 17. On September 9, 18, and 20, President Fillmore's signature translated the component parts of the Compromise into law. Then, on the last day of the month, the first session of the Thirty-first Congress came to an end. The House and the Senate adjourned sine die, after Speaker Cobb and President Pro Tem William R. King spoke briefly and let their gavels fall. At last the Compromise of 1850 was an actuality.[31]

224

Reviewing the record in the House, it is instructive to discover that twenty-eight members cast their ballots for every one of the five measures. Twenty-five of these were Democrats, and three were Whigs. Twenty-five were Northerners, and three Southerners. Only two were Southern Whigs. Only one was a Southern Democrat, and only one a Northern Whig. Such House statistics demonstrate that wholehearted backing of the Compromise was predominately Democratic and almost exclusively Northern. It was rooted principally in the Northwest, the extreme Northeast, and Pennsylvania.

A further analysis of the tallies shows how the Whigs came into the picture. Nine representatives supported the first four bills but conveniently absented themselves on the District slave trade test; all nine hailed from the slave states of Kentucky, Missouri, Tennessee, North Carolina, or Delaware—and two-thirds of them were Whigs. All eight who voted affirmatively four times but were not recorded on the Fugitive Slave Bill represented New York, Pennsylvania, or Ohio districts—four Whigs, three Democrats, and one Native American. Alexander W. Buel

[31] *Ibid.*, 1764, 1772, 1776, 1784, 1807, 1837, 2072, 2074; 9 *U. S. Stat.*, 447-58, 462-68.

of Michigan failed to vote on the Utah bill, and William H. Bissell of Illinois on the Texas-New Mexico measure, but with these exceptions both stood with the majority. Sixteen members answered "yea" four times and "nay" once. Of all the thirty-five congressmen who cast affirmative ballots in four instances and either opposed or abstained in the fifth, 20 were Whigs, 14 Democrats, and one was a Native. Nineteen were Southerners, and sixteen Northerners. At this point, it becomes obvious that border-staters in general were willing to move along Compromise lines, provided they did not have to endorse abolition of the District slave trade; that a number of Compromise-minded Northerners could not see their way clear to underwriting the Fugitive Slave Bill, and that even some moderate representatives were absent when embarrassing showdowns came. Of the sixty-three men who backed at least four of the bills, 39 were Democrats, 23 Whigs, and one was a Native. Forty-one were Northerners, and twenty-two Southerners. The contrast between Democrats and Whigs on one hand, and between Northerners and Southerners on the other, is not as extreme in this larger category as where only the twenty-eight consistent yea-voters were involved. Still, the fact that the Compromise was primarily Democratic- and North-supported is borne out by both sets of figures.

225

Additional evidence respecting House sentiment may be obtained from the voting on particular measures. The Texas-New Mexico bill was supported by 59 Democrats, 48 Whigs, and one Native American; it was opposed by 42 Democrats, 45 Whigs, and 10 Free Soilers. Approval for California statehood came from 57 Democrats, 82 Whigs, 10 Free Soilers, and one Native American; opposition from 45 Democrats and 11 Whigs. The Utah bill passed thanks to 61 Democrats, 35 Whigs, and one Native; ranged against it were 28 Democrats, 47 Whigs, and 10 Free Soilers. Eighty-two Democrats and 27 Whigs voted in favor of the Fugitive Slave Bill, while 16 Democrats, 50 Whigs, and 10 Free Soilers composed the minority. When 50 Democrats, 66 Whigs, seven Free Soilers, and the single Native American supported the District of Columbia bill, 44 Democrats and 15 Whigs were opposed. Recapitulating, more House Democrats than Whigs gave aid to the Texas-New Mexico, Utah, and fugitive slave portions of the Compromise by margins of 11, 26, and 55 votes. Only 25 fewer Democrats than Whigs voted affirmatively on California, and only 16 fewer on the District bill. On all five of the measures taken together, there were 309 Democratic and 258 Whig "yea" votes, as against 175 Democratic and 168 Whig "nay" votes. Not only were Democrats chiefly responsible for the passage of a majority of the five bills, but also a larger proportion of Democrats than Whigs cast affirmative ballots in the aggregate. Projections on a percentage basis are even more impressive. When the numerical superiority of the Democrats and the Whigs' greater inclination to duck or dodge are taken into consideration, the percentage analysis reinforces conclusions contained in this article.

In some ways, those figures may seem less significant than the study of ballots on the basis of sections. Fifty-six Northern representatives and 52 Southerners voted affirmatively on Texas; 123 Northerners and 27 Southerners on California; 41 Northerners and 56 Southerners on Utah; 31 Northerners and 78 Southerners on rendition of fugitives, and 120 Northerners and four Southerners on abolishing the District slave trade.[32] The 1850 North-South division and the nature of future sectional differences thus are mirrored. It is scarcely a surprise to anyone familiar with House speeches that Southern members provided most of the votes for the Fugitive Slave Bill, or that Northerners strongly favored a free California and the ending of the trade in the District. More interesting are the nearly equal South-North strength behind the touchy Texas-New Mexico plan and the slightly less even backing for Utah Territory. The District bill was extremely unpalatable to the South.

On the Sunday morning after the "little omnibus," California, and Utah bills were passed by the House, one of James Buchanan's intimate friends privately described the "almost universal rejoicing" in Washington on Saturday night. Bonfires, processions, serenades, speeches, suppers, drinking, and cannon salutes marked that delirious September weekend. Buchanan was informed that "Mr. Foote has diarrhea from 'fruit' he ate—Douglas has headache from 'cold' &c. No one is willing to attribute his illness to drinking or frolicking—Yet only last evg. all declared it was 'a

---

[32] *Cong. Globe*, 31 Cong., 1 Sess., 1764, 1772, 1776, 1807, 1837.

night on which it was the duty of every patriot to get drunk.' I have never before known so much excitement upon the passage of any law. There were more than 1000 persons in the procession which in turn visited Cass, Webster, Foote, Clay (out of town)[,] Douglas[,] Cobb[,] Linn Boyd &c—each of whom, excepting Clay, gave a speech. Webster it was said 'was very happy and very eloquent because he was drunk' having had a dinner party."

On Monday, President Fillmore sighed his relief to Governor Hamilton Fish of New York: " 'The long agony is over.' . . . Though these several acts are not in all respects what I could have desired, yet, I am rejoiced at their passage, and trust they will restore harmony and peace to our distracted country." Charles Francis Adams disagreed. From Quincy, Massachusetts, he wrote an Indiana representative: "The consummation of the iniquities of this most disgraceful Session of Congress is now reached—I know not how much the people will bear. My faith in their *moral* sense is very much shaken. They have been so often debauched by profligate politicians that I know not whether a case of breach of promise will lie against their seducers." The future minister to Great Britain called for a "naked history of the events of the Session," leaving interpretation of them to the judgment of "honest people."[33]

227

Other Americans of 1850 shared Adams's reliance on the historical approach. "Over the main entrance to this Hall," declaimed Congressman David S. Kaufman of Texas in June, "we see represented Clio, the Muse of History, with pen in hand, mounted upon the chariot of Time, taking note of the events which daily transpire here. She seems to be averting her face from the page of the present!—Oh! may it not be ominous of events, *unworthy of record,* about to transpire in this sacred hall of freedom! But may our action be such that she will be enabled, out of the events of this session, to fill the brightest page of human history—that which records the triumph of a free people over themselves, their passions, and their prejudices." The mor-

---

[33] J. M. Foltz to Buchanan, September 8, 1850, in Buchanan Papers; Millard Fillmore to Hamilton Fish, September 9, 1850, in Fish Papers (Manuscripts Division, Library of Congress); Charles F. Adams to George W. Julian, September 14, 1850, in Giddings-Julian Papers (Manuscripts Division, Library of Congress).

dant Senator Benton of Missouri made this classical allusion: "Homer made a mistake when he thought he was writing history, and attributed to the pale-faced lady—about as pale as the moon, and about as cold—the labor of unraveling every night what she had woven during the day; and my opinion is, that instead of writing history, he had a vision, and saw the American Senate legislating on the compromise bill."[34]

What Benton said of the Senate was at least equally true of the House. According to Robert Toombs of Georgia, writing in March, "The present Congress furnishes the worst specimens of legislators I have ever seen here, especially from the North. . . . We can have but little hope of good legislation." In May, Webster observed: "It is a strange and a melancholy fact, that not one single national speech has been made in the House of Representatives this session. Every man speaks to defend himself, and to gratify his own constituents. That is all." Concurrently, a breakup of parties was seen by the discouraged Levi Woodbury: "I am heartily sick of staying here—. The democratic party seems quite disorganized & split into fragments & I look to no satisfactory settlement of their difficulties this session if ever." From Boston, in June, Charles Sumner wrote: "The old parties seem now, more than ever, in a state of dissolution. The cry will soon be

Mingle, mingle,
Ye that mingle may."[35]

Despite all the Cassandra-like prophecies, which continued to the very eve of September 6, somehow the necessary votes were mustered—somehow majorities were formed. How and why? Success can be fairly explained only in terms of multiple causation.

President Taylor's death was extremely important. On July 29, a New York congressman wrote that Fillmore's agents "are here every day in the Ho of Reprs & busy." Northern Whigs "caved in" and joined the Democrats, and Charles E. Clarke told of one who "laughs over his shame & admits it." The Texas bond lobby

---

[34] *Cong. Globe*, 31 Cong., 1 Sess., Appendix, 940, 1484.

[35] Phillips, *The Correspondence of Robert Toombs*, II, p. 188; Webster (ed.), *The Private Correspondence of Daniel Webster*, II, 369-70; Levi Woodbury to Mrs. Montgomery Blair, May 1, 1850, in Woodbury Papers (Manuscripts Division, Library of Congress); Charles Sumner to Julian, June 6, 1850, in Giddings-Julian Papers.

was hard at work. The sergeant-at-arms who failed to keep lobbyists off the floor of the House on the most critical day of the year was the same functionary to whom two of the wealthiest Texas bondholders loaned large sums; he, in turn, made a practice of loaning money to congressmen. The Free Soil Representative Julian charged that "slaveholding influences are . . . buying up one after another northern men, who are as mercenary in heart as they are bankrupt in moral principle."[36]

Sheer weariness certainly was a cause. "Let us at least try the strength of this bill," Representative George Ashmun urged, ". . . instead of longer trying the strength of our lungs and the patience of the House and the country." "Our debates . . . have degenerated into colloquies," said Benton; they "have run down to dialogues and catechisms." Clay and Webster probably were more influential in the country at large than on Capitol Hill. Foote, in his account of the crisis, stressed the big public meetings favorable to compromise which were held "in every part of the republic" and for which Clay was primarily responsible.[37] Thus the force of public opinion was brought to bear on the legislators.

That both major parties and numerous leaders shared in some degree the credit for the Compromise is readily demonstrable. That the achievement was more Democratic than Whig is substantiated not alone by the votes but by the source of the popular sovereignty emphasis. "We stand where we stood in 1848," Stephen A. Douglas proclaimed in the Senate, and Boyd, Mc-Clernand, and other Democrats echoed the rallying cry in the House. Whigs finally flocked to the Democrats' banner when a Higher Will aided human skill. And it was with relief that representatives journeyed home to their wives and children on those October days of 1850, released from what one congressman described as "not a Hall" but "a cavern—a mammoth cave, in which men might speak in all parts, and be understood in none."[38]

229

---

[36] Charles E. Clarke to Thurlow Weed, July 29, 1850, in Weed Papers (University of Rochester); Adam J. Glossbrenner to Corcoran & Riggs, September 27, 1850, in Riggs Family Papers (Manuscripts Division, Library of Congress); *Cong. Globe*, 31 Cong., 1 Sess., Appendix, 578.

[37] *Cong. Globe*, 31 Cong., 1 Sess., 1664, 1698; Henry S. Foote, *War of the Rebellion; or, Scylla and Charybdis* (New York, 1866), 147; Henry Clay to Leslie Combs, December 22, 1849, in Louisville *Journal*, July 21, 1860.

[38] *Cong. Globe*, 31 Cong., 1 Sess., 1118, 1425.

DEAN L. YARWOOD
University of Missouri

Legislative Persistence: A Comparison of the United States Senate in 1850 and 1860

It is suggested in this paper that students of legislative systems might gain much valuable information by studying persistence of legislatures. In this connection, the Senate of 1849-1850 is compared to that of 1859-1860 on the basis of voting patterns. Such variables as the arrangement of cleavages, the proportion of brokers, and the cohesion of various types of units such as brokers, sections, and legislative parties are analyzed for their relevance to this problem.

I

DAVID EASTON, in his recent volume, *A Framework for Political Analysis*, has called attention to the necessity of studying the "life processes" of political systems.[1] His book consists of a clarion call to the study of how political systems are able to ward off stresses which continually threaten to bring about their doom. In a very useful distinction, he separates "persistence" from "equilibrium" (self-maintenance), thus unravelling a troublesome source of confusion in one of the most time-honored concepts utilized in the study of politics. The latter concept, as usually employed, poses problems for Easton because it is ". . . weighted with the notion of salvaging the existing pattern of relationships and directs our attention to their preservation."[2] In short, it is used to denote a set of relationships that indicate a "business as usual" systemic condition and it limits our focus to this type of condition. "Persistence," on the other hand, is used by Easton to refer to the ability of the system to endure; i. e., the ability to make authoritative allocations of values and to secure their acceptance regardless of the amount of change involved.[3] The focus of persistence is on systemic survival, pure and simple, rather than on the "business as usual" conditions. Other than calling our attention to a different order of problem, the distinction between "persistence"

[1] David Easton, *A Framework for Political Analysis* (Englewood Cliffs: Prentice-Hall, 1965).
[2] *Ibid.*, p. 88.
[3] *Ibid.*, pp. 96-97.

Originally published in *Midwest Journal of Political Science*, 11 (May, 1967). Reprinted by permission of the University of Texas Press.

and " equilibrium " is also useful because it facilitates the integration of concepts developed by conflict theorists into systems theory and hence promises a synthesis of these two bodies of theory.[4]

Easton's concern with the concept of persistence is to direct attention to the problem of the survival of political systems regardless of the particular types of structures involved. It is proposed here that the concept also can be employed usefully in a more limited sense to extend our understanding of legislatures. The study of persistence of legislative systems is a proper concern taken by itself if only because it suggests different types of problems than those associated with equilibrium to scholars of the legislative process. Other than their heuristic value, the results of such studies should be useful for those who feel it is desirable that legislatures survive as meaningful political institutions. Moreover, in crises in which the legitimacy of legislative structures as such is not called into question, it is most likely that their decisions and nondecisions will be important for the survival of the political system. Where the latter condition holds true, to study legislative persistence is simply to study a portion of the mechanisms that play a part in the authoritative allocation of values for the political system. This paper attempts to shed some light on the problem of legislative survival by employing the concept of persistence to analyse two sessions of the United States Senate which met in the decade prior to the Civil War.

The Senate of the First Session of the Thirty-first Congress, which met from December 3, 1849 until September 30, 1850, satisfies the criteria of persistence—it was able to make authoritative allocations of values that were accepted. Though stresses from its environment weighed heavily on this Senate, it actively sought to influence its environment in order to secure the persistence of the larger system and itself along with it. The notion of dynamic interaction, of mutual influence if you will, between the Senate and the larger system in the face of a major crisis, is important to understanding this session. Its major product, the Compromise of 1850, would have to be judged by most standards to have been a creative effort to solve the extremely difficult problems that threatened the survival of the system. The evidence suggests that it was accepted by the dominant factions of the country, at least until after the passage of the Kansas-Nebraska

---

[4] See, for example, Easton's treatment of the consequences of political cleavages in *A Systems Analysis of Political Life* (New York: John Wiley & Sons, Inc., 1965), esp. Chapter 15.

232

Act.[5] Our data will make clear, however, that the various conceptions of equilibrium would not offer fitting descriptions of this Senate. It was clearly a legislature under stress, the outcome of which hung in the balance.

The other session selected for examination is the Senate of the First Session of the Thirty-sixth Congress, which met during the seven months between December 5, 1859 and June 25, 1860. This Senate failed at the task of persistence. While forces from the outside battered it, internal conditions were such that the Senate could not respond in a manner to reduce the stresses threatening the nation. It is entirely reasonable that its internal conditions actually exacerbated strains in the larger system. In any case, while this Senate was in session, delegates from most of the Southern states bolted the Democratic National Convention first at Charleston and again when it was later rescheduled at Baltimore. It seems plausible that effective secession can be dated from this time since, when the South left the Democracy, it gave up its privileged access to the United States government. South Carolina was to formally secede from the Union on the 20th of December, 1860, and most of the states of the Old Confederacy would follow suit in the first two months of 1861. What was left unresolved in conflict on the legislative terrain was to continue on the field of open military encounter.

233

II

Four hypotheses were formulated to orient research for this study. They are:

(1) In the Senate of the First Session of the Thirty-sixth Congress there were fewer lines of cleavage than in the Senate of the First Session of the Thirty-first Congress.

(2) The proportion of the Senate's membership that could reasonably be classified as broker decreased in the 1859-1860 session as compared to the 1849-1850 session.

(3) In the 1859-1860 session two sectional blocs emerged each of

[5] See, for example, Holman Hamilton, *Prologue to Conflict* (New York: W. W. Norton & Co., 1964), pp. 185-186. Hamilton notes that the Fugitive Slave Act was the cause of some violence even in the years immediately following its passage. However, complete acceptance is not a criterion for persistence. Of more significance to the problem of persistence is that moderates gained ground in several state elections in the South following the Compromise of 1850; that in 1852, both major political parties pledged support in their platforms to the Compromise; and that the popular support of the Liberty party dropped from the 12.5% it had garnered in the 1848 election to just over 6% in 1852.

which had much greater cohesion than any rival voting units in the 1859-1860 session or any voting units in the 1849-1850 session.

(4) These blocs tended to cut across the membership of the Democratic party.

Taken together, these hypotheses suggest that the arrangement of the cleavages, the proportion of the Senate's membership that is composed of brokers and the voting unity of the various blocs and parties are important to our investigation of the problem of legislative persistence.

One of the most recurring themes of the social sciences, especially among conflict theorists, is the belief that superimposed cleavages may result in nonpersistence.[6] It is to this theme that the first hypothesis speaks. According to this concept, the arrangement of the cleavages that results from the great issues brought before a legislature should have considerable importance for the attainment of its functional goal. If the cleavages that result from policy formation are superimposed, that is if they result in a division of the legislature substantially into two strongly partisan groups which oppose each other on all issues, it is improbable that acceptable conflict resolution will result. One problem with this arrangement is that it allows for the ready identification of hostile and friendly interests; they are the same regardless of the issue. Another is that antagonisms that result from a single issue have added to them the antagonisms that result from all other issues. In extreme circumstances it is possible for a legislature to spawn a permanent set of victors and losers, assuming consistency in electoral outcomes.

By way of contrast, when many lines of cleavage result from public policy, systemic persistence is the likely result. Tensions are not allowed to accumulate because policy is the result of constantly shifting coalitions. Antagonists on one issue become allies on the next and enter into still other combinations as other issues come to the

---

[6] This concept is presented in several sources. Among them Ralf Dahrendorf, *Class and Class Conflict in Industrial Society* (Stanford: Stanford University Press, 1959), pp. 213-215; Lewis Coser, *The Functions of Social Conflict* (Glencoe: Free Press, 1956), pp. 72-81; E. E. Schattschneider, *The Semi-Sovereign People* (New York: Holt, Rinehart and Winston, 1960), pp. 62-77; and Seymour Martin Lipset, *Political Man* (New York: Doubleday & Company, Inc., 1959), pp. 83-92. Though it is phrased in terms of memberships rather than cleavages, the term "overlapping membership" relates to the same phenomenon. See David B. Truman, *The Governmental Process* (New York: Alfred A. Knopf, 1958), pp. 164-167. Coser finds the concept in one form or another in the writings of Georg Simmel, E. A. Ross, and James Madison.

fore. The possible combinations in a legislative body are myriad. And, of course, the losses sustained on any particular issue are compensated for by gains on other issues.

Guttman scale analysis provides a convenient technique for testing the first hypothesis.[7] Its ability to isolate attitudinal dimensions allows us to discover the cleavages that existed on matters of public policy in these two sessions. It seems reasonable that in a legislature characterized by a lack of superimposed cleavages we could expect to find a large number of scales; it would not be unusual to find from 5-7 scales in legislatures with as limited populations as the Senates

[7] The scale analysis was conducted, with minor modifications, according to the techniques utilized by Duncan MacRae in his study, *Dimensions of Congressional Voting: A Statistical Study of the House of Representatives in the Eighty-first Congress*, with the collaboration of Fred H. Goldner (University of California Publications in Sociology and Social Institutions, Vol. I, No. 3. Berkeley: University of California Press, 1958).

Briefly, the technique involved the identification of preliminary universes based upon the researcher's understanding and insights relevant to legislative politics of this period. Twelve such preliminary universes were identified for the 1850 session and 13 were identified for the 1860 session. Roll calls were assigned to the various universes, multiple assignments being made where it seemed reasonable to do so. Roll calls with positive marginals of greater than .90 or less with .10 were not assigned. The items in each universe were arranged in an array from the one with the smallest positive marginal to the one with the largest positive marginal. An exponential model was employed to determine scalability; each item in an array was scaled against the next five items.

When the items that were scalable were separated from the nonscalable ones, an intensive effort was made to determine whether or not the nonscalars would scale in some other relationship. First, the nonscalar items in each universe were inverted (i. e., the negative marginals were made positive and vice versa) and another effort was made to scale them in their original preliminary universes. Then their scalability was tested in other universes where it seemed reasonable to do so. Again, marginals were inverted as a final test of possible scalability of the remaining nonscalars. Last, the number of roll calls that were scalable in more than one scale suggested that the scales themselves might be mutually scalable. This insight was tested and the result was the two sectional scales.

Once the scales were identified, conventional methods were employed to assign senators to scale positions. In case of errors and absences, the average of alternatives method was used to determine scale positions. When this method resulted in an average half way between scale positions, these cases were rounded toward the median scale position. If the possible assignments included half or more of all scale positions, no assignment was made. Similarly, when there was more than one error in a senator's voting record, no assignment was made. Finally, the estimated reproducibility of each scale was calculated by dividing the number of errors (counting one error per nonscale type) by the number of correct responses. Ambiguous patterns were not counted for the purposes of estimating reproducibility.

with which we are dealing. Moreover, the correlations between the scales that are identified should be low—each should represent clearly different alliances. Last, in a legislature characterized by a lack of imposed cleavages, the individual scales should contain only a moderate number of roll calls, perhaps 10-20. To the extent that these conditions are not met, it seems reasonable that a legislature can be characterized as tending toward a condition of superimposed cleavages.

The results of scale analysis (shown in Table 1) provide several

TABLE 1

CUMULATIVE SCALES OF SENATORIAL VOTING, 1850 AND 1860

Date	Scale	No. of Roll Calls	Estimated Reproducibility
1850	Sectional Scale	101	.99
1850	Compromise Scale	11	1.00
1850	Legislative Tactics Scale	10	.97
1850	Land Policy-Railroad Scale	7	.97
1860	Sectional Scale	109	.97
1860	Reject Scale	10	.99

surprises.[8] The first is the paucity of scale dimensions, a characteristic that strongly suggests that Hypothesis (1) has only limited validity. Scale analysis of the 1849-1850 session resulted in the identification of only four scales; a sectional scale, a compromise scale, a legislative tactics scale and a land policy-railroad scale. This is a smaller number than had been anticipated. However, the fact that only two scales, a sectional scale and a reject scale, were found in the Senate session of a decade later partially substantiates the hypothesis.

Rank order correlations between the scales of each session support the inference that the first hypothesis is only slightly verified by our data.[9] These are presented in Table 2. Particularly noteworthy is the correlation of −.75 between the 1850 sectional scale and the compromise scale of that session. This suggests that the items of these scales, though they do not meet the Guttman scale criteria for mutual

[8] A copy of the various scales showing the ordering of the senators will be provided on request to the author.

[9] The rank order correlation utilized for this section was the Kendall rank order correlation coefficient with a correction for tied pairs. A discussion of this measurement is contained in Sidney Siegel, *Nonparametric Statistics for the Behavioral Sciences* (New York: McGraw-Hill, 1956), pp. 213-219.

scalability, are nonetheless very closely related. The content of the items in these scales further indicates their relatedness. The 1850 sectional scale is composed of roll calls of the various portions of what later became known as the Compromise of 1850.[10] The core items of the compromise scale are roll calls on the question of whether or not to submit the proposals of Clay, Bell, and others to a special committee of thirteen senators. Added to these are some roll calls related to the organization of the territories of Utah and New Mexico and to

TABLE 2

RANK ORDER CORRELATIONS BETWEEN CUMULATIVE SCALES, 1850 AND 1860

	Compromise Scale 1850	Tactics Scale 1850	Land Policy-Railroad Scale 1850	Reject Scale 1860
Sectional Scale 1850	−.75	.18	.11	—
Compromise Scale 1850	—	−.30	−.07	—
Tactics Scale 1850	—	—	−.17	—
Sectional Scale 1860	—	—	—	.66

the Texas boundary dispute that did not scale with the items of the sectional scale. Though the correlation coefficients between the sectional scale and the compromise scale on the one hand and the legislative tactics scale on the other are not very high (.18 and −.30 respectively), inspection of the peculiar groups ranked together on the legislative tactics causes one to suspect that all three scales resulted

[10] That is, it is composed of roll calls related to the organization of the territories of Utah and New Mexico, the admission of California to statehood, the payment of a sum of money to Texas in return for its allowing its boundary to be changed, the Fugitive Slave Act, and the abolition of the slave trade in Washington, D. C.

Perhaps it would be helpful to suggest some secondary sources that discuss these sessions in some depth. Sources which contain good discussions of the proceedings of the Senate of the First Session of the Thirty-first Congress are Hamilton, *op. cit.*, esp. Chaps. III-IX, and Allen Nevins, *Fruits of Manifest Destiny*, 1847-1852 (Vol. I of *Ordeal of the Union*, 4 Vols.; New York: Charles Scribner's Sons, 1947), pp. 253-345. For similar treatments of the Senate of the First Session of the Thirty-sixth Congress see Allen Nevins, *The Emergence of Lincoln: Prologue to Civil War*, 1859-1861 (Vol. IV of *Ordeal of Union*. 4 vols.; New York: Charles Scribner's Sons, 1950), pp. 112-131, 188-201; and Roy F. Nichols, *The Disruption of American Democracy* (New York: Macmillan Company, 1948), pp. 323-333.

from a single concern—the sectional issues then before the Senate. In point of fact, the roll calls that make up the tactics scale were items that were salvaged while rummaging through the nonscalar items from the sectional scale. The bulk of the roll calls contained in the tactics scale occurred on July 31, 1850, and all of them were rejected from the sectional scale because the most avid abolitionists joined with the most stalwart defenders of "the peculiar institution," both with the purpose of crippling the Omnibus bill.[11] The fourth scale of the 1849-50 session, the land policy-railroad scale, does represent a clearly separate type of concern. It is composed of a series of roll calls making a land grant to Illinois for railroad construction and others dealing with the acquisition and sale of western land. The low correlations between this scale and the other scales (.11 with the sectional scale, $-.07$ with the compromise scale, and $-.17$ with the legislative tactics scale) along with the particular content of its items, show beyond doubt that this scale taps an entirely different dimension from the other three. Taken collectively, the import of these correlation coefficients is to lay bare the fact that the degree of superimposition of cleavages in the 1849-1850 session is only partly evidenced by the small number of cleavages. The severity of the imposition becomes even more apparent when one considers that three of the four scales identified deal with the same set of concerns.

The story is much the same in the 1859-1860 session. Here two scales were identified, a sectional scale and a reject scale. The 1860 sectional scale contains almost every conceivable type of item for its day—items dealing with homestead legislation, internal improvements, slavery, the Davis Resolutions, army and navy appropriations, government contracts, post office concerns, and patent right legislation. The rank order correlation between this scale and the reject scale is high, .66. This strongly suggests that they are part of the same dimension. The reject scale resulted from a search through the items that were rejected from the 1860 sectional scale. However, unlike the legislative tactics scale of the previous session that resulted from a similar search,

---

[11] "Omnibus bill" was the name given by President Taylor to S. 225. See Nevins, *Fruits of Manifest Destiny, op. cit.,* p. 338. This bill proposed to deal with the admission of California, the organization of the territories of Utah and New Mexico and the Texas boundary dispute with a single act, as recommended by the Committee of Thirteen. However, though the hopes of its proponents were high in late July, on July 31st all of the provisions of S. 225 except those dealing with the organization of the territory of Utah were unceremoniously defeated. The defeated portions of the bill were passed piecemeal in August and September of 1850.

this scale appears to have no meaning. The 10 roll calls contained in this scale came from seven different preliminary universes.[12] The time span in which the roll calls of the 1850 tactics scale occurred told us something about its meaning; this is not true of the 1860 reject scale. Though most of the roll calls of the reject scale took place within a five week period between May 25, 1860, and June 23, 1860, the timing seems to be coincidental. The only possible interpretation of the reject scale is that it is composed of a series of items, each scalable within themselves, that share a quasi scale relationship to the 1860 sectional scale. The fact that they form a scale is in all probability a matter of pure chance. Hence, for all intents and purposes, the Senate of the First Session of the Thirty-sixth Congress can be considered a unidimensional legislature! The unidimensional character of the 1859-1860 session, as compared with at least two dimensions in the session of a decade earlier, again, tends to lend some credibility to Hypothesis (1).

239

Perhaps the most astounding characteristic about these scales is the large number of roll calls contained in the two sectional scales. Typically one would expect to find a maximum of 15-20 roll calls in a single Senate scale. By way of contrast the 1850 sectional scale contains 101 roll calls and the sectional scale of 1860 is composed of 109! Something of the magnitude of these scales can be grasped through a comparison of their number to the total number of roll calls on public measures in each session. The 1850 sectional scale includes about 45 per cent of all roll calls taken on public bills during the Senate of the First Session of the Thirty-first Congress. The 1860 sectional scale contains 52 per cent of the roll calls related to public measures taken in the First Session of the Senate of the Thirty-sixth Congress. The slightly larger number of roll calls included in the 1860 sectional scale, along with the fact that they constitute a greater percentage of the total number of roll calls, tends to verify the first hypothesis, but as with the other features of our data, they do so only to a slight degree.[13]

With unusual data, it can usually be anticipated that the importance

[12] These include roll calls on homestead legislation (1), administration bills (3), postal bills (2), army bills (1), navy bills (1), a bill to take an agricultural census, and a roll call pertaining to the Davis Resolutions.

[13] The limited validity of Hypothesis I is also evidenced by the percentage that the scalable roll calls in all scales in each session is of the total number of roll calls in each session. In both of these sessions 57 percent of all roll calls taken scaled in one dimension or another. If the cleavages were superimposed in one session but not in the other, we could expect the session with superimposed cleavages to produce a greater percentage of scalable roll calls.

of unexpected conclusions will overshadow that of the expected ones. This generalization holds true here. The overriding feature about our data is that they provide clear evidence that the cleavages on public policy were superimposed in *both* sessions. Everything about our scales—their small number, their relatedness, and their extreme size—supports this interpretation. The rigidity that was manifested in 1850 was not anticipated when Hypothesis (1) was formulated. Its presence has deep-running ramifications for this study. The arrangement of cleavages in the 1850 session provides us with a dramatic illustration of the importance of distinguishing between " persistence " and " equilibrium." This session does not fit any of the equilibrium definitions; it was clearly not a time of " business as usual " or anything approximating that condition. It was an unusual time when the major cleavages of the day were forged together into a single compromise measure intended by its proponents to save the Union. The question of whether to enact the Compromise and the form it would take was the major preoccupation of the 1850 session. This preoccupation with the Compromise helps account for the comparability of the 1850 sectional scale relative to the 1860 sectional scale. Yet, the overriding significance of the Compromise was that an action was taken, in which the Senate played its part, that was aimed at nothing less than securing survival. Thus it was able to perform its functional role even though it was confronted with a crisis of the first magnitude. To analyse this condition is to get at the problem of survival itself rather than the conditions typical of systemic operation. A further point of importance needs to be made. The mere occurrence of sharply superimposed cleavages taken by itself is not a sufficient condition for nonpersistence. Cleavages accumulated along the same lines in the 1850 session as well as in the 1860 session. To get at the problem of nonpersistence we must ask, "What characteristics are associated with sharply imposed cleavages in a legislature which has failed to secure persistence that are not associated with such cleavages when found in a legislature that is able to persist? "

Our data provide us with some tentative answers. They suggest that there is an exaggerated tendency to seek intrabloc consistency on issues by conflict units in a legislature that has failed to persist. Manifestations of this process can be found by comparing the sectional scales of the two sessions. In 1850 the question of the disposition of western lands was an entirely separate dimension; by 1860 the roll calls on the homestead bill scaled with the items of the sectional scale. Thus, the process of superimposition of cleavages seems to have run its course so far as scalable items were concerned. It seems plausible that this characteristic, when present, is associated with nonpersistence in legislatures.[14]

Further analysis of the two sectional scales suggests other insights into our problem. It seems likely that the following occurrences are associated with nonpersistence in legislatures: (1) large numbers of usually insignificant issues become congruent (scalable or nearly so) with controversial ones and (2) questions related to the organized means of force become congruent with controversial issues. Taking the former point first, intensive efforts were directed at discovering scales and clusters of scalable items in the 1850 session on such miscellaneous concerns as administration bills, government economy bills, bills that related to the economy, and a bill to provide for the taking of the seventh census. Though two clusters of four items each were uncovered, these neither scaled with each other, nor with the sectional scale, nor with either of the scales closely related to it. In 1860, however, 29 roll calls of a miscellaneous nature scaled with the sectional scale of that year, and another 6 scaled with the reject scale. These included roll calls related to postal concerns (16), abolition of the franking privilege (7), government contracts other than postal contracts (4), patent right legislation (3), administration bills (3), a bill to incorporate a U. S. Agricultural society (1), and a bill proposing an agricultural census (1).

241

Similarly, an effort was made to isolate army and navy scales among the roll calls of the 1849-1850 session. Again, though two clusters of scalable items were found, one containing 4 roll calls and the other one 3, the two did not scale together. However, 2 of the roll calls from one of the clusters did scale with the sectional scale. These roll calls both related to the abolition of flogging in the U. S. Navy. In the 1860 session as many as 28 roll calls, 4 from naval bills and 24 related to army bills, scaled with the sectional scale and another 2 scaled with the reject scale. The thrust of these data is to support the proposition that the exaggerated tendency for congruency between controversial issues on the one hand, and miscellaneous and military

---

[14] However, it should be noted that the degree of superimposition of cleavages (though not the tendency toward such a condition) evidenced in the 1860 Senate is probably partially the result of the small universe. It seems reasonable that if one were to compare the 1850 session of the House of Representatives with the 1860 session of the House employing scale analysis that the tendency would be the same though the cleavages would not be superimposed to the same degree.

issues on the other, is a phenomenon associated with nonpersistence in legislatures.

The remaining hypotheses also suggest some tentative answers to be explored in our search for characteristics associated with superimposed cleavages in legislatures that have failed to survive that are not present in legislatures that have persisted with such cleavages. The second hypothesis states:

> The proportion of the Senate's membership that could reasonably be classified as broker decreased in the 1859-1860 session as compared with the 1849-1850 session.

242

The role structure of a legislature can be conceptualized in a simple schema as consisting of partisans and brokers. Each has important consequences for the persistence of a legislature. The partisans take extreme positions on the issues in conflict and in this manner define the outer limits of debate. Their roles are those of advocacy and defense, liberal partisans bearing the banners of new causes and conservative partisans defending the *status quo*. It is between their positions that equilibrium is established, if indeed it is established.

The brokers occupy positions between these extremes. We can conceive of two types of brokers, issue-oriented and professional brokers. The former move in and out of the ideological center as the issues change while the latter remain in the center almost regardless of the issue. Whether they are issue-oriented or professionals, the brokers have great consequences for legislative durability. From their middling positions they explore alternatives within the limits set by the partisans in order to forge compromises. Since the partisans typically do not have enough power to elect one of their own to positions of power, the choice often devolves upon brokers. Uncertainty about the brokers' vote makes them the object of assiduous cultivation by both partisan groups and thus enhances their power. Their middling position also places them at the center of a network of communication, a resource that further augments the power of the brokers and helps to secure legislative persistence.[15]

In a legislature that fails to survive we can expect certain processes to take place. We can expect that as the issues become more superimposed, the ranks of the brokers will become depleted and those of the partisans will swell. As the ratio of brokers to partisans decreases,

---

[15] For a perceptive discussion of a modern Senate which parallels some, but not all of these points, see David B. Truman, *The Congressional Party: A Case Study* (New York: John Wiley & Sons, Inc., 1959), esp. Chapter IV.

the possibilities for compromise will also dwindle. Those who remain in the middle develop greater cohesion as the reasons for remaining there decrease. Concomitantly, the votes of the brokers become more predictable and the power that they usually derive from the uncertainty over their vote is lost. At the same time, the communications function that they usually perform is performed less well as the partisans interact more within their own groups and identify more strongly with them.[16]

TABLE 3

Brokers in the Senate, 1850 and 1860

Year	No. of Senators	% of Senate Membership
1850 Brokers	34	57
1860 Brokers	24	37

Though our data do not allow us to trace and thus validate all parts of this process, they do allow us to establish crucial portions of it.[17] If the second hypothesis is correct, the percentage of the membership of the 1849-1850 session that is classified as broker should exceed the percentage of the membership of the 1859-1860 session that is so classified. Table 3 shows the percentage of senators from these two sessions classified as brokers.[18] This classification includes 57 per cent

[16] See James A. March and Herbert A. Simon, *Organizations* (New York: John Wiley & Sons, Inc., 1958), p. 66. Two hypotheses are presented by these authors that are particularly suggestive to our discussion. They are: "The more *frequent the interaction* between an individual and the members of a group, the stronger the propensity of the individual to identify with the group; and vice versa" and "The greater the *number of individual needs satisfied in the group*, the stronger the propensity of the individual to identify with the group; and vice versa" (emphasis in the text).

[17] It should be emphasized that our data do not allow us to test all parts of the theory pertaining to the stabilizing functions of the brokers. However, in as much as our statements about the brokers are interrelated and some of them are demonstrated to be valid, the others take on added plausibility by that fact. This would seem to be warranted, at least in the absence of empirical evidence tending to disprove the untested portions of the theory.

[18] In the 1850 session, senators were classified as brokers if they ranked in the middle quartiles of groups on the 1850 sectional scale or, alternately, if they ranked in the middle quartiles on any two of the other three dimensions. In 1860, they were classified as brokers if they ranked in the middle two quartiles of groups on the sectional scale of that session. The 1860 reject scale was not

of the membership of the 1850 Senate while only 37 per cent of the 1860 Senate membership is included. Thus, the second hypothesis is validated.

Another part of this theory can be tested. When discussing the process of nonpersistence, we suggested that the cohesion of the

TABLE 4

COHESION OF VOTING UNITS IN THE SENATE, 1850 AND 1860 [a]

Unit	Indices of Cohesion	
	1850	1860
Whigs (1850) Republicans (1860)	32.4	90.4
Democrats	30.7	74.7
South	81.4	80.6
North	53.9	36.5
Brokers	42.2	54.2

[a] The indices for 1850 are the average indices of cohesion on the roll calls contained in all scales of that session. The indices of cohesion for 1860 are computed only on the roll calls contained in the 1860 sectional scale. The roll calls of the 1860 reject scale were not included because of the apparent lack of meaning of this scale. If the roll calls of the reject scale had been included, no group's average cohesion would have varied more than a point from those presented.

brokers would become stronger as the legislature approached the condition of nonpersistence. Evidence which supports this expectation is presented in Table 4. The index of cohesion for the brokers during the 1849-50 session was 42.2; during the 1859-60 session it increased

---

used as a basis of classification since it is difficult to visualize what moderating consequences could result from behavior relative to a number of apparently unrelated roll calls. These standards of classification offer two advantages: (1) they tend to weight the sectional scales which were the objects of such great concern to contemporaries and (2) of the standards that were theoretically reasonable, these least tended to prove the hypotheses correct.

A word of emphasis is in order. The inclusion of senators as brokers does not necessarily mean that they were moderates on the sectional scale of 1850, which includes the matters of major concern to historians. Two senators classified as moderates, Jefferson Davis and Hannibal Hamlin, were close to the opposite poles on that scale. However, the fact that they were moderate on two other dimensions does suggest that their behavior relative to these dimensions did contribute to the persistence of the 1850 session. Of particular interest in this regard is that they shared the same classification on the 1850 land policy-railroad scale.

to 54.2. This supports the inference that the votes of the brokers became more predictable in 1860 than in 1850. It is likely that public policy in 1860 was less the result of an intricate web of power and influence spun by their actions, a web that can usually be expected to augment legislative persistence.

The third and fourth hypotheses can be discussed together. They are as follows:

> In the 1859-1860 session two sectional blocs emerged, each of which had much greater cohesion than any rival voting units in the 1859-1860 session or any voting units in the 1849-1850 session.
>
> These blocs tended to cut across the membership of the Democratic party.

245

The data unmistakably show that these hypotheses are inaccurate and misleading. An assumption that was made in formulating them was that sectionalism increased between 1849-50 and 1859-60. It seemed to be no more than common sense that the sectionalism evidenced in the voting patterns of the senators would increase in a time of profound sectional strife. Yet, this did not happen. (See Table 4.) The cohesion of the South was substantially the same in both sessions; in 1849-50 it was 81.4 and in 1859-1860 it was 80.6. The cohesion of the Northern senators actually decreased quite markedly between these sessions. In the 1849-1850 session it was as high as 53.9, but by 1859-1860 it had decreased to 36.5.

There are other shortcomings about these hypotheses also. One of their major inadequacies is that they fail to identify the combat units properly. The expectation that a substantial number of Northern Democrats voted with Republicans and against their Southern brethren on a substantial number of roll calls logically followed from the assumption about increasing sectionalism. However, the deduction was as erroneous as the assumption on which it was based; these sectional associations did not develop to the degree anticipated. An inspection of the scale positions of the Northern Democrats on the 1860 sectional scale illustrates this point. While all Republicans were placed in the first five scale positions, no Democrat placed higher than the ninth scale position. An analysis of the roll calls on which the 1860 sectional scale is based produces much the same result. No Senate Democrat voted with the Republican majority on as many as one-third of the roll calls contained in the 1860 scale. This suggests that all members of the Senate Democratic party were much more like other Democrats, regardless of section, than they were like Republicans. The sectional division such as it did develop within the Senate Democratic ranks encompassed only a minority of the roll calls and a minority of the Senate party. The small size of the defecting group is evidenced by the fact that six, or about one-half, of the Democratic senators from the North who were placed on the 1860 sectional scale voted with their party colleagues from the South on all but 13 roll calls (about 12%) contained in the 1860 scale.[19] Six of the 13 items were on miscellaneous topics such as postal matters and the question of replacing the professors at West Point while the remaining seven were on issues of some consequence. Of the latter group, four were procedural roll calls aimed at weakening or defeating the Homestead Act, two dealt with the return to Africa of victims of the illegal slave trade, and the other one would have asserted the duty of Congress to protect slave property in the territories.

The conflict units of 1860, properly identified, were political parties substantially or entirely controlled by opposing sections. It is important to note that this description delineates two characteristics of the conflict units. Neither cohesive parties nor sectionalism taken alone seems to be a sufficient condition for legislative nonpersistence. It will be recalled that sectional conflict as evidenced by Senate voting patterns was even greater in 1850 than it was in 1860. Yet, the 1850 Senate was able to persist while the 1860 one was not. This supports the contention that sectionalism, of itself, is not a sufficient condition to be a sign of legislative nonpersistence.

The increase in party unity that developed between these sessions was nothing short of spectacular. In the 1849-1850 session the Whig

---

[19] Included in this group are senators from the border states of Maryland, Kentucky and Missouri and Senator Lane of Oregon. The latter was a North Carolinian by birth and Southerner by sympathy. Five Northern Democratic senators were not placed in the 1860 sectional scale because of their large number of absences or because of scale errors. One, Senator Haun of California, was only a member of the Senate from December, 1859 to March, 1860, and hence he can be ignored. The partial voting patterns of two of the remaining senators, Bayard (Del.) and Thomson (N. J.) indicates that they were most in sympathy with the half of the Northern Democrats who were most pro-Southern. The other two, Douglas (Ill.) and Pugh (Ohio), had partial voting patterns that suggest they were most in sympathy with the half of the Northern Democratic delegation that was most pro-Northern. Particularly noteworthy is the partial voting record of Senator Douglas, which suggests that he was the most pro-Northern of all the Senate Democrats. However, Douglas' absences were so numerous as to limit the validity of any generalization based on his voting pattern.

party cohesion was 32.4 and that of the Senate Democrats was about the same at 30.7. The cohesion of the Republican party in the 1859-1860 session, however, was a remarkable 90.4, while the unity of the Democrats had increased to 74.7.[20] Still, in spite of these dramatic increases in party cohesion between the sessions, party unity alone cannot be interpreted as indicative of legislative stress. Though British parliamentary parties have long been characterized by strong cohesion, no responsible observer has doubted the ability of Parliament to persist. Moreover, the party cohesion of the Senate Democrats in 1860 was not much greater than it has been among both Democrats and Republicans in the U. S. House of Representatives in some 20th Century Congresses.[21] Hence, strong party cohesion by itself does not presage legislative nonpersistence either.

It is probable, however, that the combination of party unity and sectionalism in the Senate contributed to nonpersistence in 1860, both of the Senate and of the larger system. In 1860 the legitimate associations for organizing the Senate—the legislative parties—were themselves controlled sectionally. This meant that national unity was no longer necessary for the harmony of the two major political parties in the Senate as had been true in 1850.[22] No longer did the Republican

[20] In view of recent studies of legislative behavior which suggest that the majority party, especially when it controls the executive, is the more cohesive, it might be well to point out that in 1860 the Republican minority was the more cohesive even though the Democrats controlled the White House. In 1850, the cohesion of the two parties was about the same even though the Democrats were a truncated majority. See Truman, *The Congressional Party, op. cit.,* pp. 93, 308-316; and John Wahlke, Heinz, Eulau, William Buchanan, and LeRoy Ferguson, *The Legislative System: Explorations in Legislative Behavior* (New York: John Wiley and Sons, Inc., 1962), p. 344.

[21] Julius Turner, *Party and Constituency: Pressures on Congress* (Johns Hopkins Studies in Historical and Political Science, Vol. LXIX, No. 1, Baltimore: Johns Hopkins Press, 1951), pp. 23-29.

[22] The difference between the complexion of the Senate Democratic party and the National Democratic Convention is of interest here. While the Senate Democratic party had a distinctly Southern hue and was very cohesive, the National Convention was weighted toward the Northern point of view but was to split sectionally. Indicative of this discrepancy, the preconvention favorite for the nomination, but one who was opposed bitterly by the South, was none other than Stephen A. Douglas. Two factors seem to account for these differences. First, the ranks of the pro-Northern Democrats in the Senate seem to have been decimated by the elections of the 1850's and in some cases, as a result of members changing parties. Second, representation in the National Convention was based on the electoral college. Hence, there was a more genuine clash between sectional interests within the Democratic party at the Convention than there was

247

abolitionists have to deal with the slave interests within their own party as the Whigs had had to do a decade earlier. Nor, for that matter, did the slave interests of the Democratic party need to concern themselves much with the protestations of their northern colleagues. When sectionally superimposed cleavages include among them political parties as was the case in 1860, one result for a legislative body is that the social gulf between members of opposing political parties is widened because sectional antipathies are added to those of political origin. At the same time, the amount of meaningful social traffic between members of the same party is likely to increase because of the convergence of the goals, values, and symbols, of party and section. In the circumstances of 1860, the intricate adjustments of the brokers were no longer necessary to maintain party harmony. The Senate was organized by efficient combat units capable of conducting sectional warfare, not by instruments of sectional compromise and accommodation. Thus, our discussion of the third and fourth hypotheses supports the generalization that legislative nonpersistence is encouraged when issues become superimposed along sectional lines, if at the same time legislative parties are substantially controlled by the opposing sections.

III

This paper suggests that the separation of the concept of "persistence" from "equilibrium" is a worthwhile operation. These concepts relate to two clearly different systemic problems, the former focusing on crisis conditions, the latter on normal relationships. If they are used interchangeably, the cost is the blurring of important theoretical distinctions. The strategy adopted in this paper was to compare a legislature that was able to persist under great stress with one that was not able to persist in an effort to identify structural conditions associated with these two systemic states. This strategy is useful, but naturally conclusions that result from it must be accepted in the light of its limitations. It is reasonable that all conditions necessary to persistence will not become apparent in a single case or again, that not all factors thought to be relevant in a single situation will be found to be relevant from the perspective of a large number of cases. Other studies of a similar nature are needed to establish that the relationships identified here are indeed regularities.

The data marshalled to test Hypothesis (1) resulted only in a

among Senate Democrats. On the matter of representation in the National Convention during this period, see V. O. Key, *Politics, Parties and Pressure Groups* (5th ed., New York: Thomas Y. Crowell, 1964), p. 405.

qualified validation of it. The small number of scales discovered, the high correlation between most of the scales of each session and the extremely large number of roll calls contained in the sectional scales of both of these Senates all suggested that the cleavages were sharply superimposed in 1850 as well as in 1860. These features of the data supported the inference that the presence of sharply imposed cleavages is not by itself evidence of legislative nonpersistence. Hence, we were led to search for characteristics in addition to sharply imposed cleavages that were associated with legislative nonpersistence but not with legislative persistence. Two generalizations were offered. First, the continuation of the process of superimposition so that all scalable roll calls of the Senate were included in a single scale was associated with nonpersistence. Second, our data suggested that it is indicative of legislative nonpersistence when an exaggerated desire for congruency causes (1) large numbers of usually insignificant issues to become congruent (scalable or nearly so) with controversial ones and (2) questions related to the organized means of force to become congruent with controversial issues.

249

Hypothesis (2) was supported by our data. In this hypothesis it had been predicted that the proportion of the Senate's membership that could be classified as broker decreased in 1860 as compared to the proportion so classified in 1850. In addition, it was deemed to be a mark of the inability to persist that the cohesion of the brokers increased substantially in 1860 over what it had been in 1850. These findings suggest that brokers play vital roles in securing persistence in legislatures.

The third and fourth hypotheses proved to be based on a false assumption. When they were formulated it was assumed that the amount of sectional voting in the Senate increased between 1850 and 1860. This assumption was not supported by our data; the cohesion of the South was about the same in both of these sessions while that of the North actually decreased markedly in 1860 as compared to what it had been in 1850. Though the increase in party unity of both parties between 1850 and 1860 was phenomenal, it did not seem that this taken by itself is necessarily associated with legislative nonpersistence. Our discussion of the data gathered for these hypotheses led to the generalization that legislative nonpersistence is encouraged when the issues are superimposed along sectional lines, if at the same time the legislative parties are also controlled by opposing sections. With the merging of these two features, legislative parties are transformed from institutions with powerful integrative consequences into institutions with explosive disintegrative capabilities.

BLACK SLAVES, RED MASTERS, WHITE MIDDLEMEN: A CONGRESSIONAL DEBATE OF 1852

by JAMES E. SEFTON*

A list of the most noteworthy congressional debates over slavery would include those on the Compromises of 1820 and 1850, the Gag Rule, the slave trade, and the Kansas-Nebraska Bill, among others. Sometimes, however, debate on a comparatively minor episode of a large issue can be highly illuminating. In the spring of 1852, the House of Representatives devoted perhaps ten hours to a bill which brought to a close a bizzare story that had begun sixteen years earlier during federal efforts to remove the Seminole Indians from Florida. Ever since the United States acquired Florida from Spain in 1819, white residents had clamored for removal of the Indians. Desultory guerrilla warfare increased, reaching a climax between 1835 and 1842 in the Second Seminole War.[1] General Thomas S. Jesup, who commanded the United States troops in Florida from 1835 until 1838, saw that the long-standing hostility between the Seminoles and their parent tribe, the Creeks, might be turned to his military advantage. In August 1836 he recruited a regiment of Creeks for federal service. The enlistment contract stipulated that the Creeks were "to receive the pay and emoluments and equipments of soldiers in the Army of the United States, and such plunder as they may take from the Seminoles."[2]

While in federal service the Creeks captured or received the surrender of more than 100 Negroes who had been living with the Seminoles and whom the Indians considered their allies. Most of these were slaves of various Seminole chiefs; some were runaways from white plantations in Florida and Georgia; a

251

---

* Mr. Sefton is associate professor of history at California State College, Northridge.

1. John K. Mahon, *History of the Second Seminole War, 1835-1842* (Gainesville, 1967).
2. *Congressional Globe,* 32nd Cong., 1st sess., 611.

---

small number claimed to have been born free. Those who could be identified as runaways were restored to their white owners by General Jesup, who paid the Creeks $20.00 each for them. The remainder were kept in federal military custody and transferred to Fort Pike, Louisiana, for safekeeping.[3] Jesup, meanwhile, hoping to hasten the final surrender of the Seminoles, realized that one of the major stumbling blocks was the Indians' fear that upon surrendering they would lose their remaining Negroes. On March 6, 1837, certain chiefs signed a document of capitulation at Camp Dade, in which Jesup agreed "that the Seminoles and their allies, who come in, and emigrate to the West, shall be secure in their lives and property; that their negroes, their *bona-fide* property, shall accompany them to the West; and that their cattle and ponies shall be paid for by the United States, at a fair valuation."[4]

Troubles soon multiplied. The Camp Dade cease-fire agreement shortly broke down, due in part to the displeasure of whites with Jesup's apparent policy on Negroes. He did not want planters searching for their runaways (nor slave-catchers looking for any salable black man) to raid Indian settlements, thus jeopardizing the removal project. Nor did he want to expose his troops to danger in the process of aiding the planters, an attitude which to the whites seemed inconsistent with the spirit of the fugitive slave law. But the general came under pressure from many sources. As a result, his policy on Negroes between April and September 1837, was a crazy-quilt of orders and statements which attempted to do the impossible: sort the Negroes into several categories according to individual histories. Those who ran away from white owners were to be returned; those whom the Seminoles captured from whites might or might not have to be returned depending on the date of capture; those whom the Seminoles purchased and still possessed, or who had surrendered, could go west with the Indians in accordance with the Camp Dade agreement; those captured by the Creeks were their property; the few who insisted they were free were mentioned least and left in a kind of limbo.[5]

3. *House Executive Documents*, 25th Cong., 3rd sess., no. 225, 4-5.
4. *Ibid.*, 52.
5. *Ibid.*, 2-5, 8-22, 51-57; Mahon, *History of the Second Seminole War*, 201-06.

252

Even if the elaborate documentation needed for such a policy had been available, nobody would have been satisfied. Planters, press, and territorial legislatures nagged; slave traders defied, and then demanded protection; Creeks pestered for possession of the ones they had captured; Seminoles distrusted; Negroes feared to come into the lines lest they be captured by Creeks. Finally, on September 6, Jesup announced that all captured Negroes would be held at Fort Pike pending orders from the secretary of war.[6] Three days later Jesup ordered that the Creek regiment be mustered out of service, thus precluding further captures under the 1836 enlistment contract. Negroes now surrendered in greater numbers, and since they seemed to possess a strange influence over the Indians, admittedly not common to a slave-master relationship, the Seminoles too came in more speedily.[7]

By the spring of 1838 the Negroes were no longer an impediment to the Indians' removal from Florida, but they were still an impediment to peaceful relocation in Oklahoma. During 1837 General Jesup had been sending Negroes not the property of whites to Fort Pike in groups to get them out of the general theatre of war. New Orleans was also a principal stopover on the journey to the Indian Territory. The government's removal program envisioned the Seminoles and Creeks becoming close neighbors in Oklahoma.[8] By the Camp Dade agreement, the Seminoles expected their slaves to go west with them; by their enlistment contract the Creeks also anticipated possession. Here was the kernel of the matter. The presence of ex-Seminole slaves among the Creeks would be sure to cause friction and perhaps war between the tribes.

Jesup foresaw the danger, and he tried unsuccessfully to preclude it. When he mustered out the Creeks, he offered them $8,000 for the slaves they had captured in hopes that the government would then send them to a Liberian colony. But the Creeks wanted the slaves, and in the spring of 1838 a delegation of chiefs was in Washington clamoring for possession. Through the agency of Joel Poinsett, secretary of war, and C. A. Harris, commissioner of Indian Affairs, a solution was found. James C. Watson, a Georgia slaveowner who was well-known to the war

253

6. *House Exec. Doc.*, no. 225, 4-5.
7. *Ibid.*, 20; Mahon, *History of the Second Seminole War*, 93-94, 128, 205-06.
8. *House Exec. Doc.* No. 225, 2-24; Mahon, *History of the Second Seminole War*, 77, 206.

department as a contractor in earlier Indian removal operations, agreed to purchase the slaves claimed by the Creeks. On May 8, 1838, he signed a contract with the delegation in Washington, agreeing to pay $14,600 for sixty-seven Negroes, the number to which sickness and death had reduced the original contingent. The Creeks, by power of attorney, appointed N. F. Collins to receive the Negroes from federal custody and to turn them over to Watson. The war department provided Collins with orders directing the commanding officer at Fort Pike to release them; Watson gave the money to Major William Armstrong, senior Creek agent and one of the organizers of the agreement, who paid it to the Creeks on July 4.[9]

Tribulations continued. Watson never received the Negroes. Jesup had been sending not only the slaves to Fort Pike but the emigrating Seminoles as well. For some unaccountable reason, officers at the fort permitted the Indians and slaves to be re-united, and once this occurred it was impossible to distinguish slaves the Creeks had captured from ones they had not, let alone separate any of them from the Seminoles. When Collins arrived with the war department's orders, the commanding officer de-clined to obey them since heavy force would have been needed. Instead, the 1,275 emigrés at Fort Pike, red and black, were loaded aboard two transports, and the little flotilla, Marine Lieutenant John G. Reynolds commanding, went chugging up the Mississippi with the remonstrating Collins tagging along. Every time the odyssey presented a chance—at Natchez, Vicks-burg, Arkansas Post, Little Rock, Fort Smith, Fort Gibson— Collins pleaded to debark with Watson's Negroes. Nothing availed. At every menace the Seminoles became more refractory. When Reynolds asked the governor of Arkansas for aid in effec-ting delivery, he was ordered to get the expedition out of the state without delay. General Matthew Arbuckle, federal com-mander in Arkansas, also refused to help. Thus Watson's Negroes and their Seminole masters reached the Indian Territory where they remained. Secretary Poinsett, not wishing to start a new war, rescinded the original delivery orders and recommended that Congress indemnify Watson.[10]

---

9. *House Reports,* 27th Cong., 2nd sess., no. 558.
10. *Ibid.; House Exec. Doc.* No. 225, 28-30, 42-51, 81-82, 91-116; Mahon, *History of Second Seminole War,* 251-52.

That simple suggestion set in motion the legislative machinery which creaked and groaned for fourteen years. Congresses were elected and adjourned; committees sat, reported, and rose; Watson died, and his estate went bankrupt. Congress, in the winter of 1838, received the first petition, but not until the spring of 1852 was an appropriation voted. Occasionally a committee would report a bill.[11] The largest proposed award was $21,604 in 1842: the purchase price, four years' interest, and a little extra to cover the expenses of Watson's agents. But such bills never reached debate. Only in June 1848 did one ignite a spark of controversy, and even that was a little tempest confined to the committee of claims, where four members including David Wilmot had with a full-scale minority report set their faces solidly against any award at all. The minority report was a curious item. In stating the facts of the case, the anti-slavery quartet admitted several key propositions which their ideological successors in the 1852 debate would staunchly deny. And after clearly admitting that the Negroes were both slaves and property, they quoted at length from the Philadelphia Convention, *The Federalist*, and related sources to show that slaves were not property at all. But again the bill failed to reach debate.[12] Finally, on January 29, 1852, John R. J. Daniel of North Carolina, chairman of the committee of claims, submitted the bill that was enacted for the purchase price plus six per cent interest.[13]

Daniel's bill went upon the private calendar for consideration in the committee of the whole. House rules, plus objections by anti-slavery congressmen, resulted in a badly fragmented debate, beginning on February 20, recurring on March 19, and again on April 9, when the bill finally passed.[14] The three-day debate was a very untidy affair due to the complexities of the case and the random assignment of the floor. For clarity, therefore, it has been reorganized according to its main questions, working down from the larger ones to the smaller.

255

---

11. *House Report* 558; *House Reports*, 28th Cong., 1st sess., no. 132; *House Reports*, 29th Cong., 1st sess., no. 535.
12. *House Reports*, 30th Cong., 1st sess., no. 724.
13. *House Reports*, 31st Cong., 1st sess., no. 102; *House Reports*, 32nd Cong., 1st sess., no. 45.
14. *Congressional Globe*, 32nd Cong., 1st sess., 420, 611-16, 650, 791-99, 1035-43.

256

The most basic question of all was whether slavery existed
among the Seminoles. Congressman William Sackett of New
York and other opponents argued that since there was no positive
evidence in "Seminole law" that slavery existed, one must necessarily conclude that it did not.[15] Thomas Bartlett, a freshman
congressman from Vermont, when asked by Georgia's James
Johnson whether slavery might not exist "under customary laws
without statutory laws," merely brushed the embarrassing inquiry aside. Neither the laws of Florida nor the laws of the
Seminole "nation," he said, revealed whether slavery existed
among the Indians.[16] Sackett even invoked international law by
asserting, "The law of nations—the contrary not being shown—
clearly establishes the fact that slavery does not exist there, and
therefore they [the Negroes] were taken as ordinary prisoners
of war."[17] He could not safely elaborate the proposition, however. The Seminoles, and all Indian tribes for that matter, had
a very dubious status as "nations" in spite of the federal government's practice of treating with them as if they were foreign
powers. John Marshall, when it was a matter of deciding whether
the Cherokees were a "foreign nation" within the meaning of
the Constitution, called them a "domestic dependent nation."[18]
Later, when it was a matter of deciding whether Georgia law
had any force in Cherokee country, he exempted the tribe from
all but federal laws.[19] Slavery certainly existed in Florida Territory by an act of its legislative council which the federal government had taken no steps to annul.[20] It was, of course, improbable that the federal government would permit international law
to supercede any domestic law where Indian affairs were concerned.

In the debate of March 19 Sackett rather abruptly introduced
the question of legal existence once again—apparently to avoid
coping with an embarrassment raised by Congressman Daniel—
and noted that whereas the laws of some states made color a
presumptive indicator of slave status, under the Constitution
the presumption was always to be in favor of freedom unless the

15. *Ibid.*, 611, 614, 797, 1036.
16. *Ibid.*, 1036.
17. *Ibid.*, 612.
18. *Cherokee Nation v. Georgia*, 5 Peters 1, 17 (1831).
19. *Worcester v. Georgia*, 6 Peters 515 (1832).
20. Mahon, *History of the Second Seminole War*, 60.

contrary were proved. Herschel Johnson, having in mind the United States Supreme Court's recent ruling in *Strader* v. *Graham*, was here prompted to ask if the court had not established a rule whereunder they would accept as conclusive the ruling of the highest state court on the status of a Negro.[21] Although Johnson's point did narrow the overly-generous conception Sackett was trying to establish, the New Yorker correctly pointed out its present inapplicability since no determination by a state court was involved.[22]

Those who supported payment did not exert themselves to demonstrate the existence of slavery among the Seminoles. They merely asserted what they said everyone knew: that slavery existed among both Seminoles and Creeks and that they carried on a reciprocal slave trade as well.[23] Historians are agreed that the Seminoles, Creeks, Cherokees, Choctaws, and Chickasaws all held slaves prior to the Civil War. Some Seminole chiefs, to increase their prestige, bought slaves and paid for them with livestock. Creeks in search of slaves frequently raided Seminole settlements. The laws of the Creek Nation as written down in 1825 by Chilly McIntosh, the son of the half-Scot Creek chief William McIntosh, clearly recognize the institution of slavery. Quaker missionaries who visited the Creeks in Oklahoma in 1842 confirmed that they had long held slaves and "appear insensible on the subject of this great evil."[24]

Some congressmen, seeking a weakness in the southern case, pointed out that the Seminoles treated their Negroes much better than whites did. These legislators found, in the accumulated military despatches and letters, references to the "influence" the Negroes had on the Seminoles and to the "affection" of the Indians for the blacks.[25] The status of Indian Negroes seemed to be a blend of slavery and the elements of share-cropping. Seminole practice was to permit the Negroes to live in separate villages and to pay their owners periodically a quantity of grain

257

---

21. 10 Howard 82 (1850).
22. *Congressional Globe*, 32nd Cong., 1st sess., 797.
23. *Ibid.*, 612.
24. Sigmund Sameth, "Creek Negroes: A Study of Race Relations" (M.A. thesis, University of Oklahoma, 1940), 2; Edwin C. McReynolds, *The Seminoles* (Norman, 1957), 48; Mahon, *History of the Second Seminole War*, 74; Antonio Waring, ed., *The Laws of the Creeks* (Athens, 1960); Grant Foreman, *The Five Civilized Tribes* (Norman, 1934), 171.
25. *Congressional Globe*, 32nd Cong., 1st sess., 614, 1036.

or livestock as a symbol of their servile status. Seminole society also included other Negroes of every status imaginable. Some were born free, some were West Indian refugees, some were descendants of successful eighteenth-century fugitives from the United States. Intermarriage further complicated the picture. It would, perhaps, be most accurate to say that there was a great diversity of status among the estimated 1,400 Negroes who were associated with the Seminoles in 1835, and that where slavery existed in a chattel form, it was a much less formal institution than the southern plantation version.[26]

The second major question extractable from the 1852 debate was whether the word "plunder," as employed in General Jesup's 1836 enlistment agreement with the Creeks, embraced slaves. Sackett insisted that the agreement had nothing to do with slaves, in part because the word "slaves" was not used, but more fundamentally because of his belief that slaves were not property.[27] John Daniel, James Abercrombie, James Johnson, Charles Stuart, and Josiah Sutherland all took the position that the agreement did include slaves, by virtue of the understanding of the people associated with it. Everyone, they said—Jesup, the Creaks, the commissioner of Indian affairs, the secretary of war—all knew slaves were included. A large body of official correspondence dating from 1836-1840 supported their contentions. It was no trouble (though it was a bit boring) to read it into the record, and doing so seemed to steer the debate away from the wearisome question, now decades old, whether slaves were property.[28] On occasion the debate became narrowly legalistic and focused upon the proper rules of interpreting contracts, with Southerners taking the most latitudinarian view.[29]

Near the end of the third day's debate, Sutherland definitively settled the semantic aspect of the "plunder" question by asserting that the word described the method of acquisition rather than the nature of the thing acquired.[30] But this had been the

26. McReynolds, *The Seminoles*, 23, 48, 244; Joshua Giddings, *The Exiles of Florida: or, The Crimes Committed by our Government against the Maroons, who fled from South Carolina and other Slave States, Seeking Protection under Spanish Laws* (Columbus, Ohio, 1858; facsimile edition, Gainesville, 1964).
27. *Congressional Globe,* 32nd Cong., 1st sess., 611.
28. *Ibid.,* 612, 614, 791, 794, 798-99, 1040. The correspondence, in addition to being in the *Globe,* is also in *House Exec. Doc.,* No. 225.
29. *Congressional Globe,* 32nd Cong., 1st sess., 791, 1037.
30. *Ibid.,* 1041.

less knotty branch of the problem. The question whether slaves were property at all was a continuous thread throughout the debate. But because of the circumstances, it took a specific form. Had the federal government, through the instrument of a contract, any power to recognize property in slaves? That may be considered the third major issue raised in the debate.

Here was a basic question of constitutional interpretation, and a longstanding one. Nor did present issues require any new arguments. Sackett, Bartlett, and the other Northerners, adopting as they had to on such occasions the unfamiliar strict constructionist approach, insisted that the Constitution did not recognize slavery and that the federal government had no delegated power to make contracts involving slaves. Johnson, as Southerners had done while debating the compromise measures two years earlier, used the fugitive slave clause to show that the Constitution not only recognized but guaranteed slave property. He also added that slavery among the Seminoles was a fact and that the government could quite properly make contracts "in reference to existing facts."[31] Just before debate finally closed, John Freeman of Mississippi stated, "I know the fact that the Government of the United States have dealt in slaves, and that they have sold slaves under execution to pay debts due to them. And they have taken slaves in payment of obligations, due upon United States bonds of public officers in the South."[32]

Charles Sweetser, seeking further to weaken the constitutional position of the Southerners, asserted that if the slaves had actually been property, then the United States could only transfer title to the Creeks following a judicial proceeding. A rejoinder, necessarily tardy because house debates were always disorderly, came from Sutherland. He believed the whole question of whether the United States could hold slaves or deal in slave property was irrelevant in this case because the government never had title to the slaves at any time. Title, in his

259

31. *Ibid.*, 612, 792-94, 1037.
32. *Ibid.*, 1039. In March 1848 a resolution had come up in the house directing the judiciary committee to report a bill "to prohibit the sale of persons held as slaves on any precept in favor of the United States," because federal law permitted the type of sale Freeman had referred to. Alexander H. Stephens served notice of his intent to debate the resolution, so it was laid over, and no further action was had. See *ibid.*, 30th Cong., 1st sess., 457.

view, had passed directly from the Seminoles to the Creeks by virtue of capture during wartime.[33] Here was a reference to the fourth major question, and a confusing one indeed: What, according to the laws of war, is the effect of capture upon the legal status of slaves?

Thomas Walsh of Maryland called capture of enemy property a recognized wartime right; others spoke off and on to support that right or to deny its relevance.[34] The truth of the matter, though highly relevant, would have satisfied neither side. There certainly is a right of capture, but its effect is to vest title to the property in the capturing government, not in that government's private soldiers. If slaves were property, this rule would have made the federal government a slave owner, thus bringing the argument back to the third question. And if the slaves were property, they could certainly be plunder, thus bringing them within the scope of Jesup's agreement with the Creeks. Of course, the northern view that the government could in no way recognize slave property would still have left the Negroes slaves of the Seminoles. That outcome was not really desirable to the Northerners, but only less unpalatable than paying a white man for his investment in them. In view of the fugitive slave clause, which convinced Southerners that the Constitution recognized slaves as property, Sackett, Sweetser, and the other Northerners had to search elsewhere for some legal principle that would allow them to classify horses, wagons, and similar things as captured enemy property but captured slaves as prisoners of war.

The appeal was distinctly of the "higher law" variety. Bartlett attacked Jesup's agreement as violating both "the law of nations, that obtains among civilized and Christian nations," and "the law of nature."[35] Sweetser called it "a *barbarism* that even savages would scout as unworthy of even savage warfare."[36] The doubts about whether the Negroes had ever actually been slaves afforded a useful springboard, since there was little doubt that they would have been slaves if either the Creeks or Watson had obtained effective possession of them. Thus in the opening debate of February 20 Sackett called the directive to Watson's

33. *Ibid.*, 32nd Cong., 1st sess., 1037, 1039.
34. *Ibid.*, 1038, 611.
35. *Ibid.*, 1036-37.
36. *Ibid.*, 1040-41.

agent to release the Negroes an unlawful order to make slaves out of prisoners of war. At the end of the second day, March 19, Charles Skelton asked if it were lawful, in America or anywhere else, to sell prisoners of war into slavery. Stuart promptly assured him it was quite legal for the government to go into an area where slavery was a recognized institution and to offer a regiment of Indians all the slaves they might capture.[37]

Discussion of the capture question led the chamber back to the Mexican War in search of precedents, and on April 9 a three-way colloquy pitted Sweetser against Johnson and Walsh. The Southerners wanted to know how the taking of various property from enemy aliens in Mexico differed from the taking of slaves from our own rebellious population in Florida. Sweetser insisted that the cases differed because the Seminoles were under the protection of our flag "to some extent" and so the government was bound to protect their rights as citizens of Florida. He also noted that in Mexico the property did not end up in the hands of individual troops.[38]

Such citings of recent history failed to satisfy anyone. But the general matter of capture led into the fifth major question, a purely factual one: were any of the Negroes in dispute actually captured by the Creeks? Here was a point, surely, on which simple chronology would make an end of cavil. Jesup enlisted the Creeks in September 1836, though they did not get into actual service until late December. The Seminoles signed an instrument of surrender at Camp Dade in March 1837, and the Creeks were mustered out of service the following September. Since the terms of the Camp Dade agreement seemed to preclude further seizure of property belonging to Seminoles who surrendered, and in fact stated that "their negroes, their *bona-fide* property, shall accompany them to the West," Sackett concluded that captures could only have occurred during the brief interim between December 1836 and March 1837. He did not think there was sufficient evidence to show that specific captures had taken place during this period, and that on the contrary, many Negroes either surrendered or had been seized following the Camp Dade agreement.[39]

261

---

37. *Ibid.*, 612, 799.
38. *Ibid.*, 1038.
39. *Ibid.*, 611, 793.

To combat Sackett's position, Johnson merely referred to General Jesup's order of September 9, 1837, mustering the Creeks out of service and paying them for the Negroes they had captured. The instructions were specific: "The chiefs and warriors who were actually in the field, and present at and aiding in the capture of the Negroes, are alone to receive any part of the sum allowed; those who remained in the camp, and did not march, are to receive nothing. Eight thousand dollars will be paid to the captors for the Seminole negroes, and twenty dollars each for those the property of citizens."[40] Moreover, on July 20, 1837, Jesup sent to the adjutant general of the army a list of "the Indian negroes captured during the campaign." Since dates of individual captures are not given in the list, there is no way of knowing whether any of the 103 were taken after the Camp Dade agreement. The list is entitled "Registry of negro prisoners captured by the troops commanded by Major General Thomas S. Jesup, in 1836 and 1837, and owned by Indians, or who claim to be free." Only eight on the list "claimed to be free"; the others all indicated a specific Indian as their owner.[41] In addition, General Jesup's correspondence for the late summer of 1837 shows his intention that since the Camp Dade cease-fire had failed and hostilities were resuming, the policy of awarding property to the capturing units would resume as well.[42] Thus there is clear evidence that the commanding general considered that at least some Negroes fell within the purview of his 1836 agreement with the Creeks, and perhaps he should have been the best judge.

The Camp Dade agreement was central, and Sackett had

262

---

40. *Ibid.*, 792; Thomas S. Jesup to Lieutenant Searle, September 9, 1837, in *House Exec. Doc.* No. 225, 20; Orders No. 175, Headquarters Army of the South, September 6, 1837, in *ibid.*, 4.
41. Jesup to Brigadier General R. Jones, July 20, 1837, in *ibid.*, 65-69. It is interesting to note that every Negro on the list has an English Christian name, which in view of the small number claiming to be free suggests either an original white owner or an aversion on the part of Indians to using Seminole names for non-Indians.
42. There is also a letter to Captain B. L. Bonneville, Seventh Infantry, who commanded a detachment of Choctaw warriors, stating that the Choctaws should have whatever Seminole property they seized, Negroes included. The letter is dated ten days after the Creeks were mustered out. *Ibid.*, 19-21. If any Negroes were in fact captured by the Choctaws, they apparently were sent west without the development of any special controversy.

still another use for it. The very same property which Watson bought from the Creeks had been guaranteed to the Seminoles by Jesup, he said. Hence, if Secretary Poinsett and Indian Commissioner Harris had induced Watson to buy it, they would be liable to imprisonment for "while in the public service, unlawfully and clandestinely trying to violate a solemn treaty of the Government." At this bombshell Daniel merely observed that there were two groups of slaves involved, and that the surrender agreement did not cover ones previously captured. Sackett, the only effective reply having slipped his mind, passed on to something else.[43]

It was just as well that the Northerners not try to make too much out of the Camp Dade agreement. They could not use it against the property rights of Watson without using it in favor of the property rights of the Seminoles. This obvious anomaly sometimes encouraged Southerners to doubt the sincerity of the opposition. As Herschel Johnson remarked on the second day of debate, some members seemed not to care that the Negroes were slaves of Indians as long as they were not slaves of southern whites.

What Sackett should have done when Daniel confronted him with the existence of two groups of slaves was to ask the sixth major question: in view of the confusion at Fort Pike, how could individual Negroes be labelled "captured" or "surrendered"? The Northerners had their share of embarrassing situations; here was one for the supporters of the bill. Johnson met it by asserting that Watson's right to payment rested not on identification of specific individuals but on the fact of the government's possession of his property and its failure to meet its obligation to convey it to him. Responsibility for identification was the government's, he averred, and if the Negroes could not be identified, it was no fault of Watson's.[44] This was a rather shaky position, but it was the only ground available, and there was an element of cleverness about it. In 1852 identification was irrelevant since the issue was only reimbursement of the purchase price, not the full market value or physical possession. Moreover, the contract between Watson and the Creeks did not contain a list of the slaves sold. They had been in con-

263

---

43. *Congressional Globe*, 32nd Cong., 1st sess., 796.
44. *Ibid.*, 615, 793.

tinuous military custody, and the officers in charge had not instituted a system of identification at the outset. Military correspondence shows that the slaves were moved from place to place in Florida in small groups before being sent to Fort Pike, and although some rosters were compiled, the paperwork was not very efficient.[45]

The charge that federal officials had been delinquent in identifying the Negroes lay at the threshhold of the seventh major question: what was the status of the United States with respect to Watson's contract with the Creeks? Clearly the government was not a party to it, and nobody undertook to prove the contrary. The real disagreement came over the extent of knowledge and assent. In a long exchange with Johnson on March 19, Sackett maintained that the government did not regard itself as a participant in Watson's deal with the Creeks, and in fact had no knowledge of it until 1840. Johnson read letter after letter detailing the government's involvement at every stage of the sale proceedings.[46] Sackett was not convinced, whereupon Alexander Evans of Maryland took up the letter-reading task. On the day after the contract was signed, Commissioner Harris asked Major General Alexander Macomb, commanding general of the army, for orders directing the commanding officer at Fort Pike to release the Negroes to Watson's agent. The adjutant general sent the orders out the next day. Evidence of assent to a sale could hardly be stronger, Evans declared.[47]

Some opponents sought stronger ground in the related allegation that whatever the government's role in the case, it had not guaranteed Watson possession of the slaves, but at best had promised only to order their release.[48] Perhaps there could be a difference between promising to give an order and promising to guarantee delivery, but the Southerners could not see it. As Evans insisted, the United States "induced the sale, brought it about, fixed the price, and ordered delivery, and then failed to fulfill the order, and that is the point of the case."[49] One may also reasonably suppose that Watson would have been reluctant to invest borrowed money in a purchase, especially of slave

45. House Exec. Doc. No. 225, 2-28.
46. Congressional Globe, 32nd Cong., 1st sess., 794-96, 613-14.
47. Ibid., 797-98.
48. Ibid., 792.
49. Ibid., 798.

property, without credible assurances that he would actually receive it.

Woven throughout the debate on the government's relation to the contract was a ninth question: was the government to blame for losing the property? The government held the property in trust, Evans said, and then permitted it to be eloigned and carried off. The government thus became responsible for its value. "All else is irrelevant," he said in a fit of piqued fatigue, "and there is no use of lugging in all these things and embarrassing the minds of the committee with such an accumulation of matter."[50] On the final day the debate again became narrowly legalistic, with warnings about possible court actions against the government for failure, as the bailee, to deliver the property to the bailors.[51]

On that note the debate ended rather abruptly. Some of the nine major questions had been answered, others had not. Some were unanswerable, either from lack of evidence or from presence of conflicting and confused evidence. The house recognized the futility of further debate and so after defeating, seventy-five to forty-seven, a move by Thaddeus Stevens to adjourn, the chamber approved the measure by a vote of seventy-nine to fifty-three.[52] Senate action was perfunctory. The bill came over from the house on April 12, and on July 26, after trading a few aspersions and jibes about delaying tactics, courtesies, rights, and perquisites, the senators agreed to take it up. They hurried it through without debate and without a roll call.[53] President Fillmore signed it, apparently without question.[54]

The debate had been a curious one, not just for specific legal intricacies but for broader points as well. For twenty-five pages of the *Congressional Globe*, legislators attacked and defended slavery while debating a bill that would not alter the status of a single individual. The Negroes had remained with the Indians all along and were the subject of numerous tribal difficulties. Kidnappers carted some of them off to be sold to white planters. Some set out with Wild Cat, a renegade Seminole chief, to

265

---

50. *Ibid.*
51. *Ibid.*, 1038, 1041-42.
52. *Ibid.*, 1043.
53. *Ibid.*, 1047, 1115, 1651-52, 1922-23.
54. 10 Statutes, 734.

settle in Mexico during the winter of 1849, but only reached
Cow Bayou, Texas, before they decided to return. Their second
such odyssey ended in capture by the Comanches who held them
for ransom, which the Creeks decided to pay as a means of
getting possession of more Negroes. Territorial separation of
the Creeks and Seminoles by the treaty of 1856 brought some
degree of quiet, and the Emancipation Proclamation finally gave
the Negroes their freedom. Their descendants, as well as those
of slaves belonging to the other southeastern tribes, still live in
Oklahoma.[55]

Notwithstanding that all the rhetoric would not free a single
Negro, the debate was nonetheless a classic encounter on one of
the most sensitive elements of the slavery system. States rights,
local option, treatment of slaves, and other things were probably
side issues. Money was changing hands, and that was the heart
of it. Furthermore, Watson's motive for the purchase seemed
to be pure speculation since the 1838 market value was considerably more than he paid. The debate may well have gained in
intensity by coming along just two years after Congress had
ended the slave trade in the District of Columbia as part of the
Compromise of 1850. Therein lies another point. Statesmen
hailed the 1850 measures as closing up all of the slavery questions still outstanding. Yet the Watson case showed how the
subject would not down. No matter what laws were passed, it
seemed there was always a need for one more.

55. Foreman, *The Five Civilized Tribes*, 243, 256-57, 262-70.

266

The Issues in the Congressional Struggle
Over the Kansas-Nebraska Bill, 1854

By ROBERT R. RUSSEL

I T IS THE PURPOSE IN THIS ARTICLE TO DISCUSS ONLY THE PUBLIC issues in the congressional struggle over the Kansas-Nebraska bill. It is not proposed to discuss the personal or political motives of Stephen A. Douglas, Salmon P. Chase, Franklin Pierce, Jefferson Davis, and other central figures. It is intended to imply, however, that one can not write satisfactorily on these latter matters unless he understands what the public issues were, what the provisions of the Kansas-Nebraska bill were in its successive versions, and how those provisions were calculated to affect the resolution of the issues involved.

The struggle over the Kansas-Nebraska bill involved other important matters besides slavery in the territories, namely, territorial government in general, public lands policy, Indian policy, and the choice of a route or routes for railroads to the Pacific coast. But here we shall be concerned only with the paramount matter of slavery. On the final passage of the bill probably not as many as five votes in both houses together turned principally or even largely on the bearing the bill might be expected to have on any issue other than slavery.

All of the territory proposed to be organized by the Kansas-Nebraska bill lay north of the parallel of 36° 30′, and nearly all of it lay within the limits of the Louisiana Purchase.[1] And by the eighth section of the Missouri Enabling Act of 1820, commonly called the Missouri Compromise, slavery had been "forever prohibited" in all the Louisiana Purchase north of the parallel of 36° 30′ except within the limits of the contemplated state of Missouri. The general issue in the Kansas-Nebraska struggle was, accordingly: Should the Missouri Compromise settlement be disturbed and, if so, what other provisions with regard to slavery should be substituted?

The debates and the voting in Congress on the Kansas-Nebraska bill make it abundantly clear who in that body wanted what with regard to slavery in the territory involved and why. And, as a

[1] The southwest corner west of the 100th meridian and south of the Arkansas River was not a part of the Louisiana Purchase.

Originally published in *The Journal of Southern History*, 29 (February, 1963).

matter of fact, Douglas and every other knowledgeable politician knew in advance what various leaders, factions, and groups wanted, for they had all been through the long struggle over slavery in the Mexican Cession, the bitter contests over whether the Compromise measures of 1850 should be accepted in various parts of the country, and more recently the Presidential campaign of 1852.

Southern state rights Democrats and a considerable faction of Southern Whigs had come to hold what may, perhaps, best be denominated the common-property doctrine of the powers of the federal government in the territories. This doctrine or view was briefly as follows: The territories are the common property of the several states, not of the United States as an entity. The federal government necessarily governs the territories but only as agent of or trustee for the common owners, the states. As agent or trustee, it may not discriminate among the states and, accordingly, must allow citizens of the several states to enter the territories freely and on equal terms and take with them any property —slaves, for example—of which they had been lawfully possessed in the respective states from which they had come and must afford such property owners due protection in their property while in the common territories. People who subscribed to the common-property doctrine considered the slavery prohibition of the Missouri Compromise and all similar restrictions to be unconstitutional. They also considered it unconstitutional to leave the decision as to slavery to the territorial governments, for, as they pointed out, a principal—the federal government in this case— could not delegate to its creature, a territorial government, a power of which it was not itself possessed. The only power with regard to slavery Congress might confer upon territorial governments was the power, indeed the obligation, to protect slaveowners in their property rights.[2]

[2] Among the best reasoned statements of the common-property doctrine in the Thirty-Third Congress were those of Senators Robert M. T. Hunter of Virginia and Andrew P. Butler of South Carolina and of Representative William T. S. Barry of Mississippi. *Congressional Globe*, 33 Cong., 1 Sess., app., 221-26, 232-40, and 612-19. In an earlier article (to which I intend this to be a sequel), I denominate the doctrine, the "property-rights doctrine." That term now seems ill-chosen, for it suggests reliance on the protection of property under the due-process-of-law clause of the Fifth Amendment. See R. R. Russel, "What Was the Compromise of 1850?" *Journal of Southern History*, XXII (August 1956), 292-309. See also Arthur Bestor's critique of the common-property doctrine—which he calls "the extra-jurisdictional principle"—in "State Sovereignty and Slavery: A Reinterpretation of Proslavery Constitutional Doctrine, 1840-1860," Illinois State His-

If Southern state rights senators and representatives could have had their way entirely, they would have written into the Kansas-Nebraska Act and into every other territorial measure a declaration of the validity of the common-property doctrine and a requirement that the territorial courts and legislatures afford slaveowners due protection in their property. Such a provision, if enforced in the territories, for, say, ten or twenty years, might well have resulted in several of them developing into slave states. The common-property doctrine was no mere abstraction. As has been true with many constitutional contentions, it had no doubt been invented because of the practical advantages that might follow its application.[3] Strongly proslavery people had been striving to get new slave states into the Union so as to maintain strength enough in the United States Senate to ward off the passage of legislation inimical to the peculiar institution.

269

Southern Jacksonian Democrats, of whom there were still many left, especially in the Upper South, did not accept the common-property doctrine. But such had been the shifts and fortunes of politics in recent years that of the large Democratic delegation in the Thirty-Third Congress only one senator, Sam Houston of Texas, was a Jacksonian, and only one representative, Thomas Hart Benton, now in the House after thirty years in the Senate, can be clearly recognized as belonging to that faction. Of thirteen Southern Whig senators at least three, Archibald Dixon of Kentucky, Robert Toombs of Georgia, and John M. Clayton of Delaware, held constitutional views difficult to distinguish from those of the state rights Democrats, and of the twenty-three Southern Whig representatives at least one, John R. Franklin of Maryland, was of the same persuasion.[4]

Not one Northern senator or representative who spoke on the Kansas-Nebraska bill accepted the common-property doctrine or was willing to write it into a piece of legislation. All but a few from the North took the position that Congress had the power to legislate for the territories in all matters and accordingly to

torical Society, *Journal*, LIV (Summer 1961), 117-80, and also published separately.

[3] The doctrine had first been clearly stated by Robert Barnwell Rhett of South Carolina in the House of Representatives, January 5, 1847; and John C. Calhoun had presented it in a set of resolutions in the Senate, February 19, 1847. *Congressional Globe*, 29 Cong., 2 Sess., app., 244-46, 455.

[4] So was Thomas L. Clingman of North Carolina who had long been a Whig but now claimed to belong to no party. *Ibid.*, 33 Cong., 1 Sess., app., 489. The party affiliations in the Thirty-Third Congress are taken from *ibid.*, 33 Cong., 1 Sess., 1-2.

delegate to a territorial legislature the power to legislate on slavery and other rightful subjects of legislation.[5] Senator Lewis Cass of Michigan was one of the exceptions. He argued with much learning that Congress had no power whatever to legislate for the territories in matters of local concern except to give each a frame of government and start it on its way.[6] A few other Northern Democrats in Congress, of whom Douglas was not then one, agreed with Cass.[7] All that Cass's view and the common-property doctrine had in common was that according to each the slavery prohibition of the Missouri Compromise was unconstitutional; they differed widely in supporting reasoning. Senator Salmon P. Chase of Ohio presented but did not press the idea, later popular with the new Republican party, that it would be a violation of the due-process-of-law clause of the Fifth Amendment for the federal government to permit slavery in any of the territories.[8]

The large majority of Southern Whigs agreed with the great majority in the North in their view as to the constitutional powers of Congress over slavery in the territories, although they agreed with their state rights colleagues in wanting the Missouri Compromise repealed and the territories opened to slavery.

Next to congressional acceptance and implementation of the common-property doctrine the state rights people wanted most the repeal of the slavery restriction in the Missouri Compromise; and in wanting this they were joined by nearly all other Southerners. The debates on the Kansas-Nebraska bill make it starkly clear that a principal reason Southerners wanted the restriction repealed was that they had come to regard it as an insult and a reproach to their section, a stigma implanted on their institutions by an act of the Congress of their own country. Southerners' denunciations of the Missouri restriction in 1854 were as bitter as their denunciations of the Wilmot Proviso had been in its time. Senator Andrew P. Butler of South Carolina termed it "a festering thorn" in "the side of the South."[9] Senator David R. Atchison of

[5] The best statement of the majority view was that of Senator John Pettit of Indiana, a former judge. *Ibid.*, app., 212-21.

[6] *Ibid.*, 33 Cong., 1 Sess., 456-58; app., 270-79.

[7] Senators Augustus C. Dodge of Iowa, Moses Norris, Jr., of New Hampshire, and Isaac Toucey of Connecticut took the same line. *Ibid.*, 375-83, 305-310, 313-21. Lewis Cass said Jesse D. Bright of Indiana, who was absent because of illness, also agreed. *Ibid.*, 279.

[8] *Ibid.*, 138. Those familiar with Chief Justice Roger B. Taney's opinion in *Dred Scott v. Sanford*, 19 U. S. 393 (1856) will remember that Taney also relied on the due-process clause but used it to protect the master in his "property" rather than the Negro's "liberty," as Chase would have done.

[9] *Congressional Globe*, 33 Cong., 1 Sess., 1309; app., 240.

Missouri called it "infamous"[10] and Representative Philip Phillips of Alabama, a "miserable line, containing as it does a congressional imputation against one half the states."[11] Some Northerners could understand the Southern feeling. Cass said that if he were a Southerner he would regard the restriction as "invidious." "And certainly to remove this bar sinister from the national escutcheon," he continued, "may well furnish a more powerful motive of action to a great community jealous of its honor, than any hope or expectation that its accomplishment will lead to the introduction of slavery into these territories."[12] Senator Truman Smith of Connecticut, who made the most powerful speech against repeal, said, "We know that legislation like the act of 1820 has ever been to them a stumbling block and an offense."[13]

271

Those Northern senators and representatives who opposed the repeal of the Missouri Compromise restriction or its weakening in any way also made its proposed repeal a matter of conscience but in the opposite way. Slavery was such a violation of the rights of man, they said, such a moral and social evil, that they could not in good conscience vote to permit it to enter or even vote to give it indirectly a chance to enter a territory in which it was not already established. They further said that slavery was so degrading to the dignity of labor that, if slaves should be taken into the territory, even in comparatively small numbers, free workers from the North and immigrants from Europe would shun it and in effect be excluded.[14] The "Appeal of the Independent Democrats" asserted that opening the territory to slavery would "exclude from a vast unoccupied region immigrants from the Old World and free laborers from our own States, and convert it into a dreary region of despotism inhabited by masters and slaves."[15] Of the many Northern members of Congress who for the sake of

[10] Ibid., 33 Cong., 1 Sess., 1303.
[11] Ibid., app., 533.
[12] Ibid., 278.
[13] Ibid., 173.
[14] Ibid., 155, 162, 262-70. In a long teaching career in Northern colleges I have presented the substance of this and the preceding paragraph to thousands of students. A rough estimate is that half understood how it might be a matter of conscience with many congressmen to vote to exclude slavery from the territories and one in ten could believe that Southern congressmen might regard exclusion by law as an insult and a reproach and understand how and why they could do so. Yet no one who can not understand both of these conflicting attitudes and the reasons why people maintained them can understand the causes of secession and civil war.
[15] Ibid., 281-82. Adequate extracts are in Henry Steele Commager (ed.), Documents of American History (New York, 1934), 329-31.

national and party harmony were willing to make concessions to the South, not one was willing to vote for any provision of law that would *directly* establish or protect slavery in a territory.

The legislative history of the Kansas-Nebraska Act may be characterized briefly as the territorial aspects of the great congressional slavery struggle of 1846-1850 all over again, but compressed into five months and with most of the bargaining and compromising done in closed committee meetings, conferences of leaders, and caucuses instead of on the floors of the Senate and House, as had been true of the Compromise of 1850.

On December 14, 1853, early in the first session of the Thirty-Third Congress, Augustus C. Dodge of Iowa introduced a bill in the Senate to organize a territory of Nebraska embracing all of the then unorganized territory of the United States lying between the parallels of 36° 30′ and 43° 30′ north latitude.[16] The bill made no mention of slavery, and it was assumed that if enacted it would leave the slavery prohibition of the Missouri Enabling Act in force. Dodge's bill was properly referred to the Committee on Territories, of which Douglas was chairman.

On January 4, 1854, Douglas on behalf of the committee reported the Dodge bill back to the Senate with important amendments and submitted a committee report which explained provisions likely to be controversial and gave or purported to give the reasons why the committee had included those provisions.[17] One amendment pushed the northern boundary of the proposed territory up to the forty-ninth parallel, the national boundary. Other amendments gave the bill provisions with regard to slavery that were all but identical with those of the Utah and New Mexico acts of 1850, provisions which, in those acts, embodied a very significant part of the Compromise of 1850.[18] Putting these provisions in the Nebraska bill, of course, represented considerable concessions to the South.

The most significant slavery provision of this first version of the committee Nebraska bill was as follows: "The legislative power of the territory shall extend to all *rightful subjects* of legislation *consistent with* the Constitution of the United States and the provisions of this act . . . ." A few matters were excluded from

[16] For a description of the Dodge bill, see *Congressional Globe*, 33 Cong., 1 Sess., 221-22.

[17] *Report on Nebraska Territory, Senate Reports*, 33 Cong., 1 Sess., No. 15 (Serial 706). An adequate extract is in Allen Johnson (ed.), *Readings in American Constitutional History, 1776-1876* (Cambridge, Mass., 1912), 426-29.

[18] For a description of the bill, see *Congressional Globe*, 33 Cong., 1 Sess., 222.

272

this sweeping grant but slavery was not one of them. This provision remained unchanged in the later versions of the bill.[19] It meant that the territorial legislature would have power to legislate on the subject of slavery, either to establish it, exclude it, or make other provision regarding it, unless perchance such legislation should be held unconstitutional by the courts. That this was the meaning of the provision was made unmistakably clear by an explicit statement to that effect in the committee's report and by another section of the bill itself, the germane portion of which reads as follows:

That in order to avoid all misconstruction, it is hereby declared to be the true intent and meaning of this act, so far as the question of slavery is concerned, to carry into practical operation the following propositions and principles, established by the compromise measures of . . . [1850], to wit: First, that all questions pertaining to slavery in the Territories, and in the new States to be formed therefrom are to be left to the decision of the people residing therein, through their appropriate representatives.[20]

273

The provisions just described, be it noted, would not have repealed or abrogated the slavery prohibition of the Missouri Compromise but would have left it in effect, enforceable in the courts, until the time, if that should ever come, when the territorial legislature should have superseded it with other legislation or the courts should have held it unconstitutional. The said provisions, if enacted, would have left the Missouri Compromise in precisely the same legal position that the Utah and New Mexico acts left the Mexican laws prohibitive of slavery which were in effect in those territories at the time of cession to the United States. These acts left the Mexican laws in effect but gave the territorial legislatures the power to change them and recognized that their constitutionality might be tested in the courts.

The provisions just cited, insofar as they related to territories,

[19] All italics except conventional ones are mine throughout the article. See sections 6 and 24 of the Kansas-Nebraska Act, *ibid.*, 1249-53, or in Francis Newton Thorpe (comp.), *The Federal and State Constitutions, Colonial Charters, and Other Organic Laws* . . . (7 vols., Washington, 1909), II, 1161-76. For the New Mexico and Utah acts of 1850, see *ibid.*, V, 2615-22, and VI, 3687-93.

[20] *Congressional Globe*, 33 Cong., 1 Sess., 222. Section 21 did not appear in the bill as originally printed but did in later printings. As it appeared before the debate began and before any amendments were proposed and did not change the meaning anyway, the reason for the delay need not concern us. See Allan Nevins, *Ordeal of the Union* (2 vols., New York, 1947), II, 94-95. Nevins says, "This significant section gave it [the bill] an entirely new meaning"; but he had overlooked the section on legislative power and its intended meaning.

not states, provided, in short, for squatter sovereignty. The term *squatter sovereignty*, which has come to be respectable, is the most satisfactory term in use to designate the thing it designated for both *popular sovereignty* and *nonintervention* applied to states as well as to territories. Furthermore, nonintervention applied to slavery only, not to all "rightful subjects," as did the other two terms, and, as applied to slavery in the territories, it had in 1854, as we shall see, a different connotation in the South from what it had in the North.

274

Another provision in the committee Nebraska bill relating to slavery was, "and when admitted as a State or States, the said Territory, or any portion of the same, shall be received into the Union, with or without slavery, as their [*sic*] constitution may prescribe at the time of their admission . . . ." This provision did not mean, as so many history books have implied, that the committee was proposing that Congress waive a constitutional power to decide whether a new state should be a free state or a slave state, for only a very few congressmen believed that Congress possessed such a power.[21] Its enactment would simply represent an attempt on the part of the Thirty-Third Congress to pledge future congresses not to refuse to admit a new state from the region involved either because it would be a slave state or because it would be a free state, as the case might be. This provision remained unchanged in the later versions of the bill.[22] It occasioned little controversy.

A third slavery provision in the committee Nebraska bill, copied verbatim from the Utah and New Mexico acts, was designed to insure that any sort of court case that might arise in the proposed territory "involving title to slaves" or "any writ of habeas corpus, involving the question of *personal freedom*" might be appealed to the Supreme Court of the United States; the stock judiciary provision in earlier territorial acts did not insure that a slave case, even though it might involve a constitutional issue, could go any higher than the supreme court of the territory in which it might arise. The more careful appeals provision had been put in the Utah and New Mexico acts to insure that, if the constitutional issue of the powers of Congress over slavery in the territories should be decided in a court, that court would be the highest in

[21] The only identifiable ones are Senator William H. Seward of New York and Representative E. Wilder Farley of Maine. *Congressional Globe*, 33 Cong., 1 Sess., app., 154, 679.
[22] See sections 1 and 19 of the Kansas-Nebraska Act.

the land.[23] This provision also remained unchanged in later versions of the Nebraska bills, and it also occasioned no controversy.[24]

The explanation the Committee on Territories gave in its accompanying report for proposing to disturb the settlement of the slavery question embodied in the Missouri Compromise and substitute the provisions we have just described was to this effect: The "prevailing sentiment" in the South is that the slavery restriction of the Missouri Compromise is unconstitutional and that under the Constitution "every citizen [has] a right to remove to any territory of the Union, and carry his [slave] property with him under protection of the law . . . ." Some "eminent statesmen" in the North hold that "Congress is invested with no rightful authority to legislate on the subject of slavery in the territories" but must leave it to the people of the territories. (This last plainly was a bid for the support of Cass and probably for that of President Pierce.[25]) The prevailing view in the North is that the Missouri restriction is constitutional. "These controverted questions . . . involve the same grave issues which produced the agitation, the sectional strife, and the fearful struggle of 1850." The Compromise measures of that year provided a solution then *and were intended to be applied in similar circumstances in the future.* Both national political parties have endorsed the Compromise of 1850 "with singular unanimity." So let us adopt the slavery provisions of that compromise as the best solution in the present crisis.

If Douglas and his collaborators had ever expected that the committee bill in its original form would be acceptable to a majority in Congress or to a majority of the Democratic members, they were quickly disillusioned. On January 16, Senator Dixon gave notice that he would introduce an amendment providing that the eighth section of the Missouri Compromise Act

shall not be so construed as to apply to the Territory contemplated by this act, or to *any other* Territory of the United States; but that the citizens of the several States or Territories shall be at liberty to take and *hold* their slaves within *any* of the Territories of the United States,

275

[23] Russel, "What Was the Compromise of 1850?" 292-309.
[24] See sections 9 and 27 of the Kansas-Nebraska Act. The bill also contained provision for the return of fugitive slaves. It caused no debate.
[25] Pierce's views seem not to have been well known. Roy F. Nichols gives only a few hints in his *Franklin Pierce, Young Hickory of the Granite Hills* (Philadelphia, 1958), 139 especially. Another eminent Northern statesman who held the Cass view was former Senator Daniel S. Dickinson, leader of the New York Hards, a faction of the Democratic party of the state which at the time was warring on the Pierce administration over patronage matters.

or of the States to be formed therefrom, as if the said act . . . had never been passed.[26]

It is not likely that Dixon had been authorized to act as spokesman for any faction or group. But, it will be noted, except that he did not demand a congressional declaration of the validity of the common-property doctrine, he had voiced the extreme Southern demands. If his proposed amendment had been adopted *in toto* (it was not), it would not only have repealed the Missouri Compromise but would also have nullified the main feature of the committee bill, namely, squatter sovereignty, and the laws of Oregon, Minnesota, Utah, New Mexico, and Washington territories prohibitive of slavery in addition; for it would have estopped any territorial legislature from prohibiting slaveowners to bring their slaves into that territory and hold them there.

Just what other pressures were applied upon Douglas and his committee off the Senate floor by proslavery representatives does not clearly appear. But that such pressures were applied is evident from what happened later, was freely charged at the time by opponents of the Kansas-Nebraska bill, and was more or less frankly acknowledged by Southern leaders. Said Senator R. M. T. Hunter, of Virginia, for one, "Was it not then an inevitable consequence of the course of events I have depicted that the South should make this request for the repeal of the Missouri Compromise?"[27]

At any rate, on January 23, and still before debate on the bill had formally begun, Douglas on behalf of the Committee on Territories reported a substitute for its first bill that was distinctly more favorable to the proslavery views. The substitute would create two territories (instead of one) in the Nebraska region, one, Kansas, lying between the thirty-seventh and fortieth parallels, the other, Nebraska, extending from the fortieth parallel to the forty-ninth. Except for the names and boundaries, the slavery and other provisions relating to the one territory were identical with those for the other. The substitute retained intact, for each of the proposed territories, the slavery provisions already described, including squatter sovereignty. But a new provision stated that the eighth section of the Missouri Enabling Act "was *superseded* by the *principles* of the legislation of 1850, commonly called the compromise measures, and is declared inoperative."[28]

---

[26] *Congressional Globe*, 33 Cong., 1 Sess., 175.

[27] *Ibid.*, app., 221.

[28] For a description of the substitute, see *ibid.*, 33 Cong., 1 Sess., 222.

The inclusion of the provision declaring the Missouri Compromise inoperative was a great concession to the sensibilities of Southern people and an added shock to those of antislavery folk. But with squatter sovereignty left intact, it is highly questionable that the virtual repeal of the Missouri Compromise would in actual practice increase the likelihood that Kansas and Nebraska or the one or the other would become slaveholding. Under the original committee bill, had it been enacted, a slaveowner presumably would have been afraid to migrate into either territory and take slaves along until and unless the territorial legislature first legalized slavery, for otherwise territorial judges might set their slaves free under the eighth section of the Missouri Act. People from the free states, presumably hostile to slavery, and nonslaveholders from slave states, who might prove also to be opposed to the establishment of the institution, would not be taking such property risks in coming to the territory and would, therefore, be less likely to be deterred from coming. This difference in risks would militate against the legalization of slavery by the very important first legislature or by any subsequent one. Under the committee substitute, if it should be enacted, slaveowners might well be just as hesitant about moving into the territory with their property until and unless the legislature should have first legalized slavery; for until then they could have little assurance that the territorial legislature would not prohibit slavery when it should come to act on the subject or that meanwhile the judges would protect them in their property in the absence of any statute law on the subject—as the majority in Congress certainly assumed would be the case. Indeed, the judges might even enforce the common law principle that slavery can not exist where there is no statute positively establishing it. In short, squatter sovereignty with the Missouri Compromise repealed would have about the same practical result as squatter sovereignty without repeal. In either case squatter sovereignty would weight the scales considerably in favor of freedom. However, the creation of the two territories instead of one, as proposed in the first committee bill, whether designed for that purpose or not, would greatly improve the chances that the South would eventually get another slave state. The proposed Territory of Kansas would lie directly west of Missouri, and it might well be that people friendly to slavery would move into the new territory from that state in sufficient numbers to dominate the early legislatures and get slavery firmly established. But, if the district lying west of Mis-

277

souri should be included for a time with that lying west of Iowa in a single territory, that single territory almost certainly would choose to be free. Free state people moving into the upper district from and through Iowa would certainly overbalance any majority of slave state people that might enter the lower portion from or through Missouri, and accordingly the critically important early legislatures would almost certainly have free state majorities.[29]

Formal debate on the Kansas-Nebraska bill, as it now was, began in the Senate on January 30. The next day, William A. Richardson of Illinois, chairman of the House Committee on Territories, introduced in the House of Representatives a Kansas-Nebraska bill almost identical with the one before the Senate.[30] Neither bill came regularly before the House until May 8, but many members managed to speak on the bills while other less exciting measures were technically before the House. The House debates were about as long and as able as those in the Senate.

The debates soon revealed that the provision in the bills that virtually repealed the Missouri Compromise was unfortunately worded to say the least. If declaring the Compromise "inoperative" was equivalent to repealing it, why not say "repealed"? And how could a specific prohibition in an act of 1820 have been superseded by the "principles" of the legislation of 1850? Opponents of disturbing the Missouri Compromise had a field day in showing by long quotations from the speeches of the framers of the Utah and New Mexico acts of 1850 that not one of them had at the time believed or even suggested that anything in those acts would supersede, or render inoperative, or weaken the slavery prohibition of the Missouri Compromise. And the influential Senator Cass and other supporters of the bill were unwilling to countenance what they considered a misrepresentation. Furthermore and more serious, Southern state rights members were far from satisfied with the squatter-sovereignty feature of the bills and the lack of any recognition of the common-property doctrine other than the minor provision for insuring a test in the Supreme Court if a case should ever arise in one of the territories involving the constitutionality of an act of its legislature inimical to slavery.[31]

At this critical juncture, the senators favorable in general to the Kansas-Nebraska bill, both Democrats and Whigs, now caucused

[29] *Ibid.*, 1238; app., 645, 871.
[30] *Ibid.*, 33 Cong., 1 Sess., 294-97.
[31] *Ibid.*, 280-81, 337-45; app., 133-45.

several times and worked out a rewording of the troublesome sections. Douglas moved the revised version in the Senate on February 7, with, so he said, "the general concurrence of the friends of the measure." [32] We know next to nothing of what was said in the caucuses. John Pettit of Indiana and Cass were the chief talkers among the Northern Democrats; Albert G. Brown of Mississippi, state rights Democrat, seems to have talked a lot. [33] But "by their fruits ye shall know them." The caucus amendment bears all the earmarks of having been the product of hard bargaining between Northern Democrats and Southern state rights Democrats and Whigs. Other Southern Whigs probably exercised a moderating influence on their state rights colleagues.

For the clause in the pending bill that ran "which [the Missouri Compromise] was *superseded* by the *principles* of the legislation of 1850, commonly called the compromise measures, and is hereby *declared inoperative*," the caucus amendment would substitute, "which *being inconsistent with* the *principle of nonintervention* by Congress with slavery in the States and Territories, as recognized by the legislation of 1850, commonly called the compromise measures, is hereby declared *inoperative and void*." The caucus amendment did not modify the sections of the pending bill giving the territorial legislatures the power to legislate on "all rightful subjects," slavery included. But for the sections saying it was the true intent and meaning to carry into effect the principle, "that all questions pertaining to slavery in the Territories, and in the new States to be formed therefrom, are to be left to the decision of the people residing therein, through their appropriate representatives," the caucus amendment would substitute the following: "it being the true intent and meaning of this act not to legislate slavery into any Territory or State, nor to exclude it therefrom; but to leave the people thereof perfectly free to form and regulate their *domestic institutions* in their own way, subject *only to the Constitution of the United States.*" [34]

Declaring the Missouri Compromise "inoperative and void" would appear more decisive to Southern minds than "inoperative" alone but still would not grate as harshly on Northern ears as "repeal." Declaring the Missouri Compromise void because it

279

---

[32] *Ibid.*, 33 Cong., 1 Sess., 353.

[33] On caucuses, see *ibid.*, 1310-11; app., 939 ff; New York *Times*, February 4, 6, 1854; and Robert Toombs to W. W. Burwell, February 3, 1854, in Ulrich B. Phillips (ed.), *The Correspondence of Robert Toombs, Alexander H. Stephens, and Howell Cobb* (Washington, 1913), 342.

[34] *Congressional Globe*, 33 Cong., 1 Sess., 353.

was "inconsistent with" the Compromise of 1850 instead of because it had been "superseded by" the Compromise would satisfy the scruples of Cass and others with regard to historical accuracy but would still carry the injunction to the faithful that they were under some sort of moral compulsion to apply the solution of 1850 to the problem of 1854. The assertion in the caucus amendment that the Compromise of 1850 recognized the principle of "nonintervention by Congress with slavery in the States and Territories" was plainly, insofar as it applied to territories, a sop to the state rights wing. While to Northern men and the majority of Southern Whigs "nonintervention in the territories" meant permitting squatter sovereignty—which the Utah and New Mexico acts did plainly permit [35]—to state rights men it meant recognizing a constitutional right of slaveholders to take their slaves into the territories and hold them and to be protected in their property therein. Another concession to the state rights group was the insertion of the phrase, "subject only to the Constitution of the United States," qualifying the grant of squatter sovereignty. This phrase, if enacted, would mean that Congress was admitting that its power to prohibit slavery in the territories or to grant territorial legislatures the power to do so was questionable and that it was not trying to influence a prospective decision of the Supreme Court by asserting or even assuming the constitutionality of its action. No such admission was in the Utah and New Mexico acts.

Northern Whigs and anti-Nebraska Democrats had not attended the caucuses that framed the compromise amendment just described. The Northern Democrats in the caucuses had been outnumbered by Southern Democrats and Whigs approximately two to one. There can be only one reason, therefore, why the Southerners had not forced more concessions, namely, the understanding that to do so would result in the defeat of the bill in the House, if not also in the Senate, and the disruption of the Democratic party. The caucus amendment was approved in the Senate, February 15, 35 to 10.

On the Senate floor, Chase, the most active leader of the opposition, promptly jumped on the principal concession the caucus amendment would make to the South: the qualifying clause, "subject only to the Constitution of the United States." To this he proposed to add, "under which the people of the Territory, through their appropriate representatives, may, if they see fit, *prohibit* the existence of slavery therein." Several Northern Demo-

---

[35] See Russel, "What Was the Compromise of 1850?"

crats and Southern Whigs friendly to the bill indicated a willingness to support Chase's amendment provided the words "or introduce" were inserted after "prohibit." The amendment thus changed would have amounted to an assertion by Congress of its constitutional power to legislate on the subject of slavery in the territories and of the constitutionality of squatter sovereignty. The state rights people would have none of that; those friends of the bill who had indicated an inclination to support the change shied away; and, when Chase's amendment came to a vote, in its original form, caucus lines held and it was defeated 36 to 10.[36]

Even after the caucus agreement, in both houses state rights members continued to expound their common-property doctrine at every turn. Their objects probably were to try to persuade themselves and the public that the Missouri Compromise was being repealed because a majority in Congress believed it to be unconstitutional—which was not so—and to influence the thinking of Supreme Court justices against the day of decision.

281

There was naturally some speculation in the course of the struggle as to how the Supreme Court would decide when and if a case involving the constitutional issue should come before it. A few on each side expressed misgivings.[37] But the remarkable thing is how confident most members seemed to be that the Court would sustain their particular views. Neither faction or group tried to exact a pledge from the others to abide by the expected decision. A few members declared that the bill would pledge Congress to accept the decision whatever it might be, and a few promised to abide by it.[38]

The opponents of the Kansas-Nebraska bill employed as their chief talking point the contention that the substitution for the Missouri Compromise of another settlement of the slavery question was a gross violation of a "sacred" sectional compact. According to that compact, ran the argument, the North was to consent to Missouri entering the Union as a slave state and allow Arkansas to remain open to slavery, and in return the South agreed that

[36] *Congressional Globe*, 33 Cong., 1 Sess., 421-22, 519. Similar amendments were also defeated in the House. *Ibid.*, 1238-39.

[37] Representatives John R. Franklin of Maryland, Laurence M. Keitt of South Carolina, Wiley P. Harris of Mississippi, and Henry Bennett of New York did. *Ibid.*, app., 419, 467, 549, 692.

[38] Taking the position that the bill would pledge Congress to accept the decision were Senator Charles E. Stuart of Michigan and Representatives Laurence M. Keitt and Wiley P. Harris; promising to abide by the decision were Representatives William H. English of Indiana and William T. S. Barry of Mississippi. *Ibid.*, 286, 467, 549, 606, 618.

forever after slavery should be excluded from all of the Louisiana Purchase north of the line 36° 30′ excepting Missouri. The North had lived up to its agreement. Missouri had been admitted as a slave state. Arkansas had remained a slave territory and in due time had been admitted as a slave state. Now that Kansas and Nebraska are ready for settlement and organization as territories, the South demands that the prohibition on slavery be repealed. How can Southern senators and representatives honorably make such a demand?

Southerners were very sensitive to the charge of broken faith, but their spokesmen were at no loss for a reply. One reasoned reply was that the Missouri Compromise had never been a compact between the sections in any proper sense of the term. The South had been forced by a numerically superior North to accept an unconstitutional and discriminatory prohibition of slavery in the remainder of the Louisiana Purchase in order to prevent a palpably unconstitutional limitation from being imposed on the new state of Missouri as a condition of admission, namely, the gradual abolition of slavery. The most effective Southern reply, however, to the charge of broken faith was *tu quoque*. If, ran this reply, division along a parallel of latitude was a fair settlement for the Louisiana Purchase, it was also a fair settlement for the acquisitions farther west. The South had repeatedly offered to extend the line to the Pacific. President Polk had proposed it. Even John C. Calhoun, Jefferson Davis, and the Nashville Convention had been willing to make such a division, in spite of their view that exclusion of slaveholders with their property from the common territories was clearly unconstitutional. But Northerners would not agree. They had insisted for four years on applying the hateful Wilmot Proviso to all the territory acquired from Mexico, that part south of the line 36° 30′ as well as that north of it, and in the end they had forced the South to accept another compromise which admitted all of California as a free state without its ever having gone through the territorial stage and left the South only the barest chance of ever introducing slavery into Utah or New Mexico. Therefore, the South had been released by the actions of the North from any obligation it may ever have had to regard the Missouri Compromise as a binding contract.[39]

---

[39] Good arguments on whether or not the Missouri Compromise was still morally binding were those of Salmon P. Chase and William H. Seward, *pro*, and Senator George E. Badger of North Carolina and Representative Alexander H. Stephens, *contra*. *Ibid.*, 133-40, 150-55, 145-50, 193-97.

It is not likely that the extended arguments as to whether the Missouri Compromise had been a solemn compact or not and, if so, which side had first broken faith changed *directly* a single vote in Congress. But that the South was guilty of a breach of faith certainly gained wide acceptance in the North and contributed powerfully to the outburst of righteous indignation there, and that outburst, in turn, caused many Northern Democrats in Congress, especially in the House, to withdraw their support from the Kansas-Nebraska bill and a small number of cautious Southern members to draw back in dismay.

Another issue in the Kansas-Nebraska debates was, of course, the merits of squatter sovereignty. Few senators or representatives from either section showed any enthusiasm for squatter sovereignty as a proper principle for governing territories. A few supporters extolled it as being in accord with American principles of democracy and contended that the people, native born and foreign born, who would settle the territories were just as capable of choosing their "domestic institutions" as people in the states were and had as good a right to do so.[40] Some Northern Democrats who were supporting the Kansas-Nebraska bill admitted that they were choosing squatter sovereignty only as a way of taking the accursed subject of slavery in the territories out of Congress and, thus, relieving themselves of the necessity of voting for exclusion. To vote for outright exclusion would give deep offense to their Southern brethren and might well result in disrupting the Democratic party and endangering the Union. Douglas added the argument, not very flattering to the efficacy of our federal government, that in our history the people of the several territories had always in actual practice decided the slavery question to suit themselves so Congress might as well give them authority to do so in the first place.[41]

Northern Whigs and free soil Democrats exposed the weaknesses and hypocrisies of squatter sovereignty unmercifully. How would it quiet slavery agitation to transfer the controversy from Congress to territorial legislatures? What would supporters do in the event Utah, or Kansas, or Nebraska should legalize polygamy? Marriage was certainly a "domestic institution." Furthermore, it was only a pretense that the bill granted squatter sovereignty, for

[40] See remarks of Senators Stephen A. Douglas and Lewis Cass and of Representatives Alexander H. Stephens and Christian M. Straub of Pennsylvania. *Ibid.*, 337, 278, 195, 746.

[41] *Ibid.*, 278-79. Those familiar with Douglas' career will recall that he continued to take this line even after the Dred Scott decision.

it contained the stock governmental provisions making the territorial governor, secretary, and principal judges appointive by the President, giving the governor an absolute veto of bills passed by the legislature, requiring that the laws enacted be reported to Congress, and stipulating that legislation disapproved by Congress would be null and void.[42] The supporters of the bill met these sallies in silence for the most part. But they did finally amend the bill by giving the Kansas and Nebraska legislatures power to override governors' vetoes by a two-thirds majority and by striking out the requirement that laws passed by the legislatures be submitted to Congress.[43] Pettit explained that, while Congress could not divest itself of the power to disallow territorial laws, the amendment would "show . . . what our intention is."[44]

284

To state rights Democrats and some of the Southern Whigs, squatter sovereignty was a bitter pill, for reasons already explained. When they were called upon by opponents of the Kansas-Nebraska bill to explain how they could support a measure containing a feature so distasteful to them, they replied variously: The territorial legislatures would recognize their constitutional duty and provide for the protection of slave property (even though Congress was not meeting its obligation!). If the legislatures should fail to meet their constitutional obligation, surely the territorial courts would meet theirs. The bill would give the South a "chance" to get a new slave state. If it would accomplish nothing but the removal of the intolerable stigma of the eighth section of the Missouri Enabling Act, it would be justified.[45] "Our honor is saved," said Senator James M. Mason of Virginia. "Nothing is saved but our honor; and yet we agree to it."[46] After all, said some, we can not press the Northern Democrats too far lest we disrupt the party and endanger the Union. A number of state rights men who were supporting the bill simply refused, in the face of all the evidence, to recognize openly that squatter sovereignty was in it.

The tendency of some Southern senators to refuse to recognize that the squatter sovereignty provisions of the bill meant what they said exasperated some Northern Democrats, and in the last days of the Senate debate Charles E. Stuart of Michigan demanded with some asperity that his Southern colleagues state in

[42] *Ibid.*, 175, 154-55, 662, for examples.
[43] *Ibid.*, 33 Cong., 1 Sess., 423, 520.
[44] *Ibid.*, app., 212.
[45] *Ibid.*, 239-40; 33 Cong., 1 Sess., 1303, 1309, 1311.
[46] *Ibid.*, app., 299.

unequivocal language that they had the same understanding of the provisions that Northern Democrats had.[47] Under catechism most of the Southern leaders admitted, although not all in unequivocal language, that under the bill the territorial legislatures would have the power to exclude slavery.[48] But some, notably Senators Toombs and Dixon, avoided making the unpleasant admission.[49] And in the House a number of members persisted in asserting that, if squatter sovereignty was in the bill, they could not find it.[50]

Apparently because of just such avoidances and intransigencies and because of the efforts of opponents of the bill to take advantage of them to foment dissension in the ranks of the bill's supporters, some historians have concluded that the terms of the bill were understood one way in the North and another in the South and, even, that the terms had been deliberately made ambiguous to maintain unity among the bill's supporters.[51] Now this simply can not be true, in the light of the terms of the bill, the extended debates on the merits of squatter sovereignty, and the admissions of Southern leaders. Even men in the street understood the squatter-sovereignty feature. Witness the well-known fact that even before the final passage of the bill arrangements were being made in the North and in Missouri to contest the control of the first legislature in Kansas.

It is obvious that the votes of members whose consciences were not too strict or principles too doctrinaire might turn on whether they believed that, under the provisions of the bill and other factors which would operate, the territories or the one or the other would more likely become a free state or a slave state. The recorded debates in Congress are about the last place one should look to try to find out what the beliefs of individual members were on this score. When supporters of the bill, Northern and Southern, were appealing to Northern waverers, they argued that

285

[47] *Ibid.*, 285.

[48] Among these were state rights Democrats R. M. T. Hunter, A. P. Butler, Albert G. Brown, James M. Mason, and James A. Bayard and Whigs George E. Badger, John M. Clayton, Thomas G. Pratt of Maryland, John Bell of Tennessee, and William C. Dawson of Georgia. *Ibid.*, 289, 239, 292, 228-32, 299, 776, 286, 291, 937, 939, 303; 33 Cong., 1 Sess., 691.

[49] *Ibid.*, 1311, 240; app., 346-51, 140-45.

[50] At least Representatives W. T. S. Barry of Mississippi and James F. Dowdell of Alabama did so. *Ibid.*, 618, 704.

[51] Allan Nevins, for example, says, "Supporters of the bill were themselves bitterly divided as to the point at which popular sovereignty was to be applied . . . . Only by a sharp suppression of debate on this vital point was unity maintained." *Ordeal of the Union*, II, 101.

both territories would become free states. When they were appealing for the votes of Southern waverers, they asserted that under the bill there was a good prospect that Kansas, at least, would become a slave state. Northern opponents of the bill in appealing for Northern votes against it commonly asserted that, if the bill should pass, the territories would become slave states. But when Northern Whig leaders were trying to persuade Southern Whigs not to vote for the bill, they said, Why violate a compact and arouse antislavery passions when the territories will both become free states anyway? [52] In a more or less unguarded moment Senator John Bell of Tennessee divulged to the Senate that Senator Atchison of Missouri had been assuring Southern colleagues privately that Kansas would become a slave state and that the Southern people were being told that such would be the case.[53] At any rate senators and representatives remained uncertain enough and concerned enough about the outcome in the territories, especially Kansas, that they continued to the end to weigh carefully every proposed amendment that might affect the choice in the territories.

Opponents of the Kansas-Nebraska bill alleged that the Committee on Territories in its second version of the bill had divided the originally proposed Nebraska Territory into two with the deliberate purpose of improving the chances for the South to get a new slave state. They could offer only circumstantial evidence, namely, the fact that division would improve Southern chances. Dodge of Iowa and Douglas in the Senate and Richardson and Bernhart Henn of Iowa in the House explained that the division had been made at the request of the Iowa delegation and with the consent of the Missouri delegation. The former feared, they said, that with only one territory, the valley of the Kaw, being somewhat more accessible than the valley of the Platte, would be settled somewhat earlier and would get the seat of government and these advantages, in turn, would give the Kaw Valley route an advantage over the Platte Valley route in the struggle which was going on over the choice of route for the first railroad to the Pacific. There can be no doubt of the keenness of the rivalry over railroad routes and the extent of the interests involved.[54] But whether the divi-

[52] *Congressional Globe,* 33 Cong., 1 Sess., app., 162, 176.
[53] *Ibid.,* 939-40.
[54] *Ibid.,* 33 Cong., 1 Sess., 221; app., 382, 795, 886-88. See Frank Heywood Hodder, "The Railroad Background of the Kansas-Nebraska Act," *Mississippi Valley Historical Review,* XII (June 1925), 3-22; and Robert R. Russel, *Improve-*

sion into two territories had been made originally for the one purpose or the other or for both we may never know for certain. However, we are certain that every senator and representative understood that the division of the original Nebraska into two would greatly increase the likelihood that the South would get a new slave territory subsequently to become a new slave state; and we can be reasonably certain that, whether a bargain had been made in the first place or not, the friends of the bill who met in the caucuses and conferences at least agreed to support the proposed division. For, when Chase proposed in the Senate to amend the bill by combining the two proposed territories into one, every Southern senator present and every Northern senator present who later voted for the bill voted to retain the division; and every Northern senator present (with two exceptions) who' later voted against the bill voted to combine. When a similar amendment was proposed in the House, the totals *against* and *for* the amendment on a voice vote were so close to the totals *for* and *against* the bill on its final passage that it is reasonable to conclude that practically all the friends of the bill had voted to retain provision for two territories and practically all the opponents had voted for only one.[55]

287

As the Senate debate neared its close, it developed that several Southern senators believed that the abrogation of the Missouri Compromise would have the effect of reviving in the proposed territories the old Spanish laws of Louisiana; and these laws sanctioned slavery. Northern supporters of the bill reacted sharply. They had understood that the abrogation of the slavery restriction of the Missouri Compromise would leave the proposed territories without any law on slavery or on anything else until the legislatures should have filled the void. Revival of the old Spanish laws might give a slight temporary advantage in Kansas to the proslavery people, and, of more concern, it would have put Northern men in the position of having voted positively to legalize slavery in the territories, a position no Northern man dared be caught in. In this minor crisis, George E. Badger of North Carolina, the leader of the Southern Whigs, offered the following amendment: "Provided, That nothing herein contained shall be construed to revive or put in force any law or regulation which may have existed prior to the act of . . . 1820, either protecting,

ment of Communication with the Pacific Coast As an Issue in American Politics, 1783-1864 (Cedar Rapids, Iowa, 1948).

[55] Congressional Globe, 33 Cong., 1 Sess., 520, 1238.

establishing, prohibiting, or abolishing slavery." This proviso was adopted without debate by a vote of 35 to 6, five of the six being state rights Democrats.[56] Later there were bitter recriminations among Southern representatives over the proviso. Badger and some other good Southern lawyers said the provision was no concession to the North, for the repeal of the Missouri Compromise would not otherwise revive earlier laws. Other Southern members disagreed and insisted the proviso was a concession to the North that should not have been made.[57]

On March 2 Senator Clayton of Delaware, up to then a supporter of the bill, moved to amend it by striking out a provision that would give the rights of suffrage and holding office to aliens who had declared their intention of becoming citizens of the United States. Striking this out would leave only citizens eligible. The Senate approved Clayton's amendment 23 to 21 with every Southern senator present voting aye and every free state senator but one voting nay. Although the new Know-Nothing movement may have influenced a few votes, the alignment and the accompanying discussion make it clear that the main consideration was not the proper treatment of immigrants but how the suffrage requirements would affect the slavery question in the first territorial legislatures: Immigrants were predominantly strongly antislavery, and giving them the suffrage would strengthen the free state cause.[58] In the House, where the Northern majority was large, Richardson in moving to substitute the Senate bill for the House bill omitted the Clayton amendment, and no one tried to restore it. After the bill without the Clayton amendment passed the House and was returned to the Senate, a large majority of those who had voted for the amendment now voted against restoring it lest insistence on the amendment kill the bill in the House, where the vote had been very close.[59]

In the Senate the final division on the Kansas-Nebraska bill, counting all who were paired and all who were absent but later indicated how they would have voted had they been present, was 41 to 17. Northern Democrats voted 15 for the bill, 5 against it; Southern Democrats, 15 for to 1 against. Northern Whigs voted none for, 7 against; Southern Whigs voted 11 for, 2 against. The two Free Soilers, of course, voted "Nay." The lone Southern Dem-

[56] *Ibid.*, 520; app., 289-96, 836.
[57] *Ibid.*, 33 Cong., 1 Sess., 686-91; app., 488, 583, 419, 427-28, 549, 618, 796.
[58] *Ibid.*, 33 Cong., 1 Sess., 520, 1300 ff.; app., 297-98.
[59] *Ibid.*, 33 Cong., 1 Sess., 1132, 1300-1309, 1321; app., 765 ff.

ocrat who voted against the bill was Sam Houston of Texas; his principal reason seems to have been that he thought the South was making a grievous mistake in making demands that were rousing antislavery passions while receiving so little practical advantage in return.[60] The two Southern Whigs who voted against the bill were Bell and Clayton. Both had joined with other Southern senators in earlier votes. Bell voted "Nay" at the last because of the rising storm in the North and Clayton, ostensibly, because he could not swallow squatter sovereignty.[61]

The House, counting as above for the Senate, passed the bill 115 to 104.[62] Northern Democrats voted 44 to 44; Southern Democrats, 57 for, 2 against. Northern Whigs voted none for and 45 against; Southern Whigs, 14 for and 7 against. The six Free Soilers voted against, of course. The two Southern Democrats who voted against the bill were John S. Millson of Virginia and Thomas Hart Benton. Millson, a state righter of the strictest sort, could not stomach squatter sovereignty.[63] At least three other Southern Democrats and one Whig who disliked this feature refused to vote.[64] The seven Southern Whigs who voted against the bill in the House gave explanations similar to those of Senators Bell and Houston.[65]

The slavery provisions of the Kansas-Nebraska bill were not the work of any one man or clique. They were a compromise, hammered out with great difficulty in committee, conferences, and caucuses and on the Senate floor, between a majority of the Northern Democratic senators and representatives on the one hand and nearly all the Southern senators and representatives, both Democratic and Whig, on the other. Although quite similar to the slavery provisions of the Utah and New Mexico Acts of 1850, the provisions of the Kansas-Nebraska Act included two new concessions to Southern sensibilities, principles, and interests. They abrogated the slavery prohibition of the Missouri Compromise, whereas the Utah and New Mexico acts did not abrogate

[60] *Ibid.*, 33 Cong., 1 Sess., 520, 521, 550, 1321, 1324; app., 788, 338-42, 550; 33 Cong., 1 Sess., 691-92; app., 383-93.

[61] *Ibid.*, 407-15.

[62] *Ibid.*, 33 Cong., 1 Sess., 1254-55.

[63] *Ibid.*, app., 425-29.

[64] Democrats John McQueen and Laurence Keitt of South Carolina and Wiley Harris of Mississippi and Whig John R. Franklin of Maryland. *Ibid.*, 419-22, 463-68, 547-50.

[65] Robert M. Bugg, William Cullom, Emerson Etheridge, Nathaniel G. Taylor, all of Tennessee, Theodore G. Hunt of Louisiana, and Richard C. Puryear and Sion H. Rogers of North Carolina. *Ibid.*, 434-39, 538-43, 811-16, 830-37.

the Mexican laws prohibitive of slavery; and they admitted that the prohibition of slavery in a territory by Congress or by the territorial legislature was of questionable constitutionality. Considering that the region being organized had long been "dedicated to freedom" by a federal statute, the Northern Democrats who voted for the Kansas-Nebraska bill made great sacrifices of sentiment, interests, principles, and personal political advantage in their states and districts for the sake of party unity and sectional accommodation. But, and this is perhaps the point most frequently overlooked in accounts of the struggle, the Kansas-Nebraska Act fell far short of meeting what the great majority of Southern congressmen thought were the South's just demands.

The Kansas-Nebraska Act: A Century of Historiography

By Roy F. Nichols

The process of federal lawmaking can be very intricate, and correspondingly baffling to the historian. Few acts of Congress have had a passage more difficult to trace accurately than that of Kansas-Nebraska fame, and few have received more attention from historians. The historiography of the measure has been the more difficult because of the sectional conflict in which it was a significant episode. Historical thinking about it has been colored by the emotional overtones produced by the historians, conditioned by their several geographical and cultural backgrounds. Despite the hundred years which have elapsed since the episode occurred, historians are still of several minds about it and there is cause to doubt whether the full story has yet been told. A century of historiography has produced an extensive bibliography, a variety of interpretations, much argument, and certain questions yet unanswered.[1]

Historical thinking and writing about the bill began very shortly after its enactment. The subsequent struggle to make the territory of Kansas into a state, and the political fortunes of Senator Stephen A. Douglas, the sponsor of the bill, called forth frequent reference to the circumstances of its passage in various famous political campaigns involving his senatorial and presidential ambitions.[2] Two very divergent views concerning the nature of the bill and the motivation of its supporters became current almost immediately. The friends of Douglas described the bill in terms of his own committee report as designed to .advance "certain great principles, which

---

[1] This article is a revised version of a paper which was presented at a luncheon session of the annual meeting of the Mississippi Valley Historical Association in St. Louis on April 29, 1955.

[2] The Douglas campaign biographies of 1860 made some of the earliest contributions to the historiography of the bill. A Member of the Western Bar [Henry M. Flint], *Life and Speeches of Stephen A. Douglas* (New York, 1860); James W. Sheahan, *Life of Stephen A. Douglas* (New York, 1860).

Originally published in *Mississippi Valley Historical Review*, 43 (September, 1956). Reprinted by permission of the Organization of American Historians.

would not only furnish adequate remedies for existing evils, but, in all time to come, avoid the perils of similar agitation, by withdrawing the question of slavery from the halls of Congress and the political arena, committing it to the arbitration of those who were immediately interested in, and alone responsible for, its consequences." [3] Another and much more numerous company, including Douglas' foes, found something akin to their views in "An Appeal of the Independent Democrats in Congress," which appeared twenty days after Douglas presented his own statement. These opponents of the measure thundered forth in print: "We arraign this bill as a gross violation of a sacred pledge; as a criminal betrayal of precious rights; as part and parcel of an atrocious plot." [4]

These views, so wide apart in their implications, provided the ideas basic to the two schools of thought which have been dominant ever since, and much of what has been written on the subject has been conditioned either by one of these ideas or by the other. The second view was almost the only one prevalent in the historical literature which appeared during the Civil War. This writing was highly colored by the conflict and when the popular authors who were chronicling the battles and campaigns alluded to the Act they generally characterized it as a move of southern aggression, part of the plot, a thing which was evil, and by statement or implication Douglas was an evildoer. [5]

The next phase of the historiography of the bill was supplied by writers of reminiscences, such as Joshua R. Giddings, Ohio congressman, Horace Greeley, famous editor of the New York *Tribune*, and Henry S. Foote, sometime senator from Mississippi. They supplied some scattered details designed to belittle Douglas and to demonstrate the idea of a southern conspiracy. Practically all of this writing was northern in origin and sympathy. [6] This disparagement of Douglas was soon followed by an effort on the part of his

[3] *Senate Reports*, 33 Cong., 1 Sess., No. 15.

[4] *Cong. Globe*, 33 Cong., 1 Sess., 281.

[5] Thomas J. Pressly, *Americans Interpret Their Civil War* (Princeton, 1954), *passim* and bibliography. See particularly 142 n., 263-64, 298, 315.

[6] Joshua R. Giddings, *History of the Rebellion, Its Authors and Causes* (New York, 1864), 364; Horace Greeley, *The American Conflict* (2 vols., Hartford, 1864-1866), I, 224; Henry S. Foote, *War of the Rebellion* (New York, 1866), 182-84, and *Casket of Reminiscences* (Washington, 1874), 93. Of the very slight amount produced by southern writers, only Alexander H. Stephens, *A Constitutional View of the Late War between the States* (2 vols., Philadelphia, 1868-1870), was much noticed by historians. Stephens accepted Douglas' interpretation of his work and motives. The foes of the Compromise of 1850 were the aggressors. *Ibid.*, II, 241-57.

292

brother-in-law to glorify his leadership in the matter. In a book consisting of a series of statements which he said had been dictated to him by the Senator, J. Madison Cutts presented an extended account of Douglas' efforts to open Nebraska, pointing out the pressure of the population on the frontier and the absolute necessity of making concessions to southern legislators who had the power of blocking the measure indefinitely. Douglas was said to have boasted: "I passed the Kansas-Nebraska Act myself. I had the authority and power of a dictator throughout the whole controversy in both houses. The speeches were nothing. It was the marshaling and directing of men and guarding from attacks, and with a ceaseless vigilance preventing surprise." [7]

293

The climax of this phase of the bill's historiography came with the publication, beginning in 1872, of the *History of the Rise and Fall of the Slave Power in America*, written by Henry Wilson, vice-president under Grant and formerly a leading Free-Soiler. Wilson made an extensive effort to gather facts by consulting his contemporaries. His own viewpoint was well illustrated by the title of his work and by the following quotation:

> No event in the progress of the great conflict stands out more prominently than the abrogation of the Compromise of 1820. As both effect and cause it defies competition and almost comparison with any single measure of the long series of aggressions of the Slave Power. . . . No single act of the Slave Power ever spread greater consternation, produced more lasting results upon the popular mind, or did so much to arouse the North and to convince the people of its desperate character.[8]

Thus the verdict of these participants — practically all of them pro-Union and antislavery — as they penned their memoirs was largely in agreement with the theory that there had been a conspiracy against the best interests of the nation, though there was no clear outline of who had conspired or how. And there was no agreement as to the part Douglas had played or about his motivation. Was he a statesman, a conspirator, or a tool? [9]

[7] J. Madison Cutts, *A Brief Treatise upon Constitutional and Party Questions* (New York, 1866), 122.

[8] Henry Wilson, *History of the Rise and Fall of the Slave Power in America* (3 vols., Boston, 1872-1877), II, 378.

[9] Other accounts by participants continued to appear: Jefferson Davis, *The Rise and Fall of the Confederate Government* (2 vols., New York, 1881); William Cullen Bryant and Sydney H. Gay, *Popular History of the United States* (4 vols., New York, 1876-1881); James G. Blaine, *Twenty Years of Congress* (2 vols., Norwich, Conn., 1884-1886); John A. Logan, *The Great Conspiracy* (New York, 1885); Samuel S. Cox,

At this point a new element entered into the historiography of the bill. This was provided by men who had not participated in the scenes of conflict, but who were now coming forward to examine the records and write from them in a fashion which began to be called scientific. The first of these was a trained German historian, Professor Hermann E. von Holst of the University of Freiburg. During political exile in the United States he had begun thinking about its history and when he returned to Germany he wrote a multi-volume work. That which included the Kansas-Nebraska episode appeared in English in 1885 and in it he devoted some two hundred pages to a very detailed account of the Act.[10] He had read little but the official documents, yet he was the only writer so far to grasp the influence of the complexities of American politics upon the shaping of the bill. Nevertheless, he was content with the simple conclusion natural to a liberal who hated slavery, that the rivalry of Douglas and Pierce for southern support for the presidency was the prime motivation.[11] At the same time, he effectively destroyed the constitutional pretensions of Douglas' arguments,[12] though he failed to grasp the realistic value of the Senator's planning. His work did much to strengthen the current northern or Republican theory of an evil thing done at the behest of the slave power.

While von Holst's volumes were appearing, two wealthy men, turned historians, were engrossed in similarly extensive works. In 1891, the fifth volume of James Schouler's *History of the United States under the Constitution* appeared,[13] and in the next year James Ford Rhodes began the publication of his *History of the United States from the Compromise of 1850*. Both used much more source material than did von Holst but they reached much the same conclusion. The Kansas-Nebraska bill was the reprehensible creation of Douglas, the demagogic aspirant for the presidency.[14]

Three Decades of Federal Legislation (Providence, 1885) ; John G. Nicolay and John Hay, *Abraham Lincoln: A History* (10 vols., New York, 1890) ; Varina H. Davis, *Jefferson Davis: A Memoir* (2 vols., New York, 1890) ; Mrs. Archibald Dixon, *True History of the Missouri Compromise and Its Repeal* (Cincinnati, 1898).

[10] Hermann E. von Holst, *Constitutional and Political History of the United States* (7 vols., Chicago, 1876-1892), IV, 256-461.

[11] *Ibid.*, 314.

[12] *Ibid.*, 375-402.

[13] James Schouler, *History of the United States of America under the Constitution* (7 vols., Boston, 1880-1913), VI, 285.

[14] James Ford Rhodes, *History of the United States from the Compromise of 1850*

Hardly had this canon of Republican interpretation been "scientifically" established by this trio of historians when a measure of reaction set in and efforts were made in the direction of the rehabilitation of Douglas. In 1897, Professor John W. Burgess of Columbia University published a volume entitled *The Middle Period*, which covered the Kansas-Nebraska situation. Professor Burgess was a Tennessee Unionist, veteran of the Civil War. He had the prevailing German concepts of scientific history and was a nationalistic liberal. He was closely associated with his most brilliant student, William A. Dunning, whose father had been a war Democrat. Burgess pictured Douglas as a sincere representative of the West sharing with his fellow citizens a keen sense of the importance of local autonomy. He defended him for declaring his principles and pointed out that men often identify themselves and their ambitions with principles which they believe essential for the peace and welfare of their country.[15]

295

At the turn of the century, younger scholars, products of the burgeoning graduate schools, began to take up the problem. A young Columbia graduate student, Allen Johnson, had been within the range of Burgess's influence although taking his doctorate in European history. When he settled down to teach in Grinnell College, Iowa, he chose as his next work a study of Stephen A. Douglas, who had been waiting forty years for a scholarly and comprehensive biographer. Johnson explored vigorously, turned up a certain amount of new source material including what few fragments the Douglas family then seemed to have preserved, and produced a scholarly, well-written biography which appeared in 1908.

His was a well-rounded account of Douglas and the bill. He had a more comprehensive grasp of the part which the needs of the West played in creating this measure. He discounted the immediate presidential ambitions of Douglas and pictured him as a sincere believer in popular sovereignty as the solution of the problem of the peaceable opening up of new territories. His effort to maintain a judicial attitude is illustrated by his verdict that the effort of the Senator to repeal the Missouri Compromise by "subtle" indirection was the "device of a shifty politician." Douglas, never-

(7 vols., New York, 1892-1906), I, 420-98. For Rhodes's motivation see Frank H. Hodder, "Propaganda as a Source of American History," *Mississippi Valley Historical Review* (Cedar Rapids), IX (June, 1922), 3-18.

[15] John W. Burgess, *The Middle Period, 1817-1858* (New York, 1897).

theless, was the dominant figure, the resourceful statesman to whom the responsibility for the measure was due.[16]

In the next year after the publication of Johnson's *Douglas*, P. Orman Ray's Cornell doctoral dissertation, *The Repeal of the Missouri Compromise*, was published.[17] This work represented an intensive, unprejudiced recanvass of the evidence and the discovery of significant new material. Ray challenged the theory of Douglas' exclusive agency and emphasized the idea suggested by the memoir writers and von Holst that various political situations, particularly the bitterness of Missouri local politics, were the controlling factors.[18] As some reviewers of this book pointed out, probably Ray claimed too much, the evidence which he marshaled was not altogether conclusive, the Missouri question was only one of a series of factors in a complex situation.[19]

One of the reviewers was Professor Frank H. Hodder of the University of Kansas. He had been long at work on the history of the bill, in fact as early as 1899 he had published an almost unnoticed article defending Douglas as a sincere statesman laboring for western development. Hodder was developing a theory regarding the bill, which he presented before the State Historical Society of Wisconsin in 1912.[20]

Hodder's perspective was much broader than Ray's and he played up an idea which he had not advanced in his earlier article. He was impressed by the part played in western development by

---

[16] Allen Johnson, *Stephen A. Douglas* (New York, 1908).

[17] P. Orman Ray, *The Repeal of the Missouri Compromise* (Cleveland, 1909).

[18] John A. Parker, "The Secret History of the Kansas-Nebraska Bill," *National Quarterly Review* (New York), XLI (July, 1880), 105-18, and reprinted as a pamphlet under the title, *The Missing Link. . . . What Led to the War, or the Secret History of the Kansas-Nebraska Act*, with an introductory note by Waldorf H. Phillips (Washington, 1886). John A. Parker to Lyon G. Tyler, June 1, 1889, Tyler Papers (Division of Manuscripts, Library of Congress). Parker was clerk to the House Judiciary Committee in 1854. Parker to James Buchanan, March 29, 1854, Buchanan Papers (Historical Society of Pennsylvania). See also *A Statement of Facts and a Few Suggestions in Review of Political Action in Missouri* (n. p., 1856).

[19] The principal reviews of Ray's book were by Allen Johnson, *American Historical Review* (New York), XIV (July, 1909), 835; by Frank H. Hodder, *Dial* (Chicago), XLVII (September 1, 1909), 120; and by William A. Dunning, *Political Science Quarterly* (New York), XXIV (September, 1909), 527.

[20] Frank H. Hodder, "Stephen A. Douglas," *Chautauquan* (Meadville, N. Y.), XXIX (August, 1899), 432-37, reprinted in *Kansas Historical Quarterly* (Topeka), VIII (August, 1939), 227-37; Hodder, "The Genesis of the Kansas-Nebraska Act," State Historical Society of Wisconsin, *Proceedings*, 1912 (Madison), 69-86. See also James C. Malin, "Frank Heywood Hodder, 1860-1935," *Kansas Historical Quarterly*, V (May, 1936), 115-21.

railroad promoters, particularly those seeking to construct a line to the Pacific.[21] It was Hodder's conclusion that the chief interest at work in opening up Nebraska was the promoters' desire to secure a right of way for this transcontinental line. He saw Douglas as the railroad promoter motivated by this role rather than by his political ambitions. Though he had some complimentary things to say about Ray's work, he brusquely dismissed his main thesis as "untenable."

Ray replied at the annual meeting of the American Historical Association in 1914 by describing Hodder's thesis as unproven and untenable.[22] Some years later, Hodder devoted his presidential address before the Mississippi Valley Historical Association, in 1925, to providing further evidence of Douglas' railroad interest.[23]

297

While we applaud the zeal of these protagonists we may also comment on the inflexibility which controversy develops. The truth probably would have been more nearly attained had each recognized that the other had made a contribution and had they united their points of view. This, in fact, was done by Albert J. Beveridge in his *Abraham Lincoln* in 1928. In this fragment in which interestingly enough Douglas was the hero, Beveridge, in an elaborate account of the Kansas-Nebraska bill, recanvassed all the evidence and brought back Douglas as the glamorous leader dealing with and influenced by the combination of forces developed by Hodder and Ray.[24]

The 1930's produced at least two additions to the growing corpus of analysis and interpretation. The author of this essay and George Fort Milton re-examined the roles of two of the prominent figures in the action, Franklin Pierce and Stephen A. Douglas. Since the work of Henry Wilson, various allusions had been made to the part played by the President under pressure either of ambition or of expediency. Not until the publication of *Franklin Pierce* in 1931 had any comprehensive attempt been made to explain the President's situation and the practical motivation which

[21] This idea had been discussed and discarded by Ray. See *Repeal of the Missouri Compromise*, 237-42.

[22] Ray, "The Genesis of the Kansas-Nebraska Act," American Historical Association, *Annual Report*, 1914 (2 vols., Washington, 1916), I, 259-80.

[23] Hodder, "The Railroad Background of the Kansas-Nebraska Act," *Mississippi Valley Historical Review*, XII (June, 1925), 3-22.

[24] Albert J. Beveridge, *Abraham Lincoln, 1809-1858* (4 vols., Boston, 1928), III, 165-217.

led him to make the bill an administration measure. The factional strife in the Democratic party was explored, and with it the President's need of regaining the support of important elements in his party, particularly in the Senate. The success of his administration depended upon congressional endorsement of his patronage program, his domestic legislative plans, and particularly of his ambitious foreign policy. Without the support of the Senate leaders he would be helpless and discredited. Therefore, when the leading bloc of senators demanded his endorsement of the measure, he felt he must acquiesce.[25]

298

George Fort Milton, in the meantime, had conceived of a comprehensive trilogy of volumes to embrace the whole period from 1850 to 1869. He had finished the last one, *The Age of Hate*, and he then turned to the first. As in the last he had chosen a central figure, Andrew Johnson, so in the first he would concentrate on Douglas. He turned to the problem with great ingenuity and enterprise and shortly discovered what had always been thought to be lost, namely, the papers of Douglas in great quantity. Mining this great treasure and working indefatigably in repositories all over the land he produced a very comprehensive biography. In his consideration of the Kansas-Nebraska bill, he recognized the inadequacy of simple explanations of complex phenomena and brought together in a comprehensive synthesis the fruits of his own labors and of those of his many predecessors. He showed calm judgment and capacity to evaluate many of the controversial factors in the situation. For much of Douglas' career, his work will be definitive. But he did not deal with the chief historiographical problem connected with Kansas-Nebraska, namely, the influences, external and internal, which produced the various drafts of the bill; nor did he provide a systematic reconstruction of what Douglas personally went through in his connection with the legislative process which produced the law. To Milton, Douglas more than ever was the dominant courageous statesman, the master of the

[25] Roy F. Nichols, *Franklin Pierce* (Philadelphia, 1931); Wilson, *Rise and Fall of the Slave Power*, II, 382-83; Jefferson Davis, *Rise and Fall of the Confederate Government*, I, 27-28; Varina H. Davis, *Jefferson Davis*, I, 669; Nicolay and Hay, *Abraham Lincoln*, I, 349-50; Charles E. Hamlin, *Hannibal Hamlin* (Cambridge, 1899), 270; Sidney Webster, "Responsibility for the War of Secession," *Political Science Quarterly*, VIII (June, 1893), 276; John Bach McMaster, *History of the People of the United States* (8 vols., New York, 1883-1913), VIII, 195-96 n.; Henry B. Learned, "Relation of Philip Phillips to the Repeal of the Missouri Compromise in 1854," *Mississippi Valley Historical Review*, VIII (March, 1922), 303-15.

situation. Milton's work, published in 1934, placed the capstone on the structure of Douglas' rehabilitation; von Holst, Rhodes, *et id genus omne* had been revised.[26]

But revision does not stay put and there is ever a yearning for new and more satisfying synthesis and interpretation. Allan Nevins of Columbia determined to rewrite Rhodes completely and in the course of this work made a thorough recanvass of the circumstances attending the enactment of the Kansas-Nebraska bill. In 1947 his first volumes appeared containing his findings.[27] He was impressed by the inadequacy of the various specialized interpretations and prepared an inclusive and complicated narrative designed to retell and resynthesize the story. While he still maintained Douglas in the central position, he took much of the heroic statesman away from him. He showed him as a powerful and ruthless opportunist, playing by ear, with little respect for logic or truth, determined above all things to carry his bill and demonstrate his leadership. Despite his exhaustive studies, Nevins found enigma and mystery in the framing of the bill.[28] Why did a man of Douglas' experience behave in such a curious, complex, and heedless fashion?

299

Six years later, another thoughtful historian, Avery Craven, published the results of his mature judgment. He had given some of his findings in *The Coming of the Civil War* in 1942,[29] but his further thought was presented in *The Growth of Southern Nationalism*, published in 1953.[30] His special contribution was a penetrating analysis of public opinion in the South, tracing in enlightening detail the way in which northern attack changed indifference into united support on the part of the South. This change of opinion in turn gave birth to the northern idea of southern aggression which did so much to furnish the stereotype of an aggressive and wicked South. He painted a most realistic picture of Douglas and showed how his turgid character made him either loved or feared and made him so easy to hate. Like Nevins, Craven alluded to an elusive element. On the question of the motivation for the peculiar

[26] George Fort Milton, *Eve of Conflict: Stephen A. Douglas and the Needless War* (New York, 1934).

[27] Allan Nevins, *Ordeal of the Union* (2 vols., New York, 1947), II, 43-159.

[28] *Ibid.*, 91, 107.

[29] Avery Craven, *The Coming of the Civil War* (New York, 1942).

[30] Craven, *The Growth of Southern Nationalism, 1848-1861* (Baton Rouge, 1953), 172-205.

metamorphosis of the bill, he wrote, "Who and what were responsible for this remains a mystery." [31]

Finally, the latest in the chapters of the historiography of the bill, written by James C. Malin, *The Nebraska Question, 1852-1854*, likewise appeared in 1953.[32] Malin, a disciple of Hodder, returned to the theme of Douglas the great statesman. Douglas, in his opinion, was fighting the tendency toward centralization which the mechanical revolution was advancing. His doctrine of popular sovereignty or local self-government was designed to restore the balance and preserve democracy. Malin has made a minute analysis of as much of public opinion as he could find recorded in western Missouri to show that Douglas was but reflecting ideas current on the Missouri-Kansas frontier. However, as he has not yet fully investigated the problem of the congressional action on the bill, he has not penetrated the depths of its "mysteries."

The fact that both Craven and Nevins made mention of unsolved problems in the historiography of the Kansas-Nebraska bill presents a convenient opportunity to join with them in expressing the belief that something is still lacking in the complete history of the bill. Despite all this great labor and highly intelligent consideration, historians have been studying Hamlet with Hamlet either left out or incorrectly identified. For Stephen A. Douglas was not Hamlet. This situation has arisen because of what appears to be the historian's principal intellectual difficulty. He is, speaking generally, an excellent reporter but he frequently leaves something to be desired as an interpreter. This does not mean that he does not sense the working of the forces that shape events but rather that the nature of the process by which these forces influence human behavior eludes him. He fails to trace adequately the connections between antecedent situations and accomplished fact, the process of becoming.

This is the difficulty with the historiography of the Kansas-Nebraska bill. We now very clearly understand the various forces making it inevitable but we have contented ourselves with thinking of Douglas as the agency through which they worked to shape the bill. This is not an adequate consideration of the extremely

---

[31] *Ibid.*, 180.

[32] James C. Malin, *The Nebraska Question, 1852-1854* (Lawrence, Kan., 1953). See also Robert W. Johannsen, "The Kansas-Nebraska Act and the Pacific Northwest Frontier," *Pacific Historical Review* (Berkeley), XXII (May, 1953), 129-41.

complex process by which the bill took its peculiar shape and was enacted into law. This process of becoming is the Hamlet which has been left out.

This key to the whole matter, this process of becoming, can only be discovered by exploring some of the intricate processes of American political behavior connected with our party system and law-making mechanism. Such an exploration may help to clear up the mystery, to identify Hamlet.

The growth of the nation and the expansion of its population had reached a point in the early 1850's when the passage of a bill opening up the Nebraska territory had become inevitable, and whether Douglas was interested in it or not probably in the end did not much matter. As far as the achievement of the object of the bill was concerned, states were going to be organized between the Missouri and the Rockies regardless of any man or men. In the short session of the Thirty-second Congress, a simple bill organizing a territory called Nebraska had passed the House. The territory was given limits approximately those of the present state of Kansas and no reference was made to slavery. It had failed in the Senate in its last hours for lack of four southern votes.

True understanding of what happened next can be best secured by reference to the disorganized state of American politics of that particular time. In 1853-1854 there was prevalent a feeling of political uneasiness, probably symptomatic of the process of disintegration going on within existing political combinations, an uneasiness which ordinarily precedes the reintegration of a series of political elements into a new party. In the United States in the nineteenth century there were such periods of disintegration and reintegration in politics every twenty years or thereabouts just as there were financial panics. Democrats and Whigs had crystallized about 1834-1836 and now a new combination was about to form as the Republican party in 1854-1856.

The chief indication of this disintegration-reintegration process was the prevalence of a factionalism in both major parties which was producing a growing sense of insecurity among the leaders. This insecurity produced a tendency among politicians to grasp any possible advantage which might arise from current interests and to push it to extreme length. It was above all else a period of political expediency and sometimes of desperate expedients.

301

The factionalism current at the close of the 1840's seemed to have very dangerous implications. A split in the ranks of the Jacksonians had lost them the presidency in 1848. In the fight over the organization of the Mexican Cession both Democrats and Whigs had been so fragmentized in 1850 that it had been extremely difficult to reorganize them for the campaign of 1852. The force of traditional combat and the lure of spoils and power, however, had temporarily restored an uneasy unity within each party. In an election which careful analysis showed to be very close, the Democrats won by only a small margin in the popular vote.[33] They had won only to fall into a more complex factionalism which bore the promise of even greater demoralization than that of 1848, and their executive leadership showed itself incompetent to deal with the situation.

302

The Whig party, which the election returns showed to have a great political voting strength, was plagued by the fact that in combatting the usually victorious Democrats on the state level its two wings had supported policies that nationally were irreconcilable. In the South the Whigs had become very southern, in the North, very northern; so extreme had been their expressions that it was more than ever difficult to get them together on any platform of national agreement. How could they escape this dilemma?

Two other developments added to the disorganized state of politics. During the turmoil over Texas, the Mexican War, and the Compromise of 1850, three resourceful men, John P. Hale of New Hampshire, Salmon P. Chase of Ohio, and Charles Sumner of Massachusetts, had gained places in the Senate by skillful maneuvering in badly divided state legislatures. But without regular party support, these Free-Soilers were now faced with private life. They were men of desperate fortunes and likely to undertake disruptive policies. And a final disturbing force in the politics of the time was a revival of antagonism to foreigners and to Catholicism.

Politics, it can be seen, were thus in such confusion that a maximum number of politicos were disturbed and disorientated by it. An unusual number were uncertain of their proper roles and were confusedly groping for new alignments which would insure some greater security and more certain prospect of victory. Under such circumstances, any legislation which offered opportunity for politi-

[33] Nichols, *Franklin Pierce*, 216.

cal controversy and advantage would be seized upon. For this purpose the Nebraska question was ideal. It was obvious that some bill must be passed and soon, therefore, each faction and individual was alert to gain the greatest possible advantage from the inevitable.

Most observers, including probably Douglas, thought that the chief reason why the Nebraska bill had failed in March, 1853, was because the arbitrary limits of the short session did not give enough time to complete the measure. And there is reason to believe that Douglas thought that in the next session it would go through with little trouble. Certainly no one seems to have foreseen the terrific explosion which developed. The reasons why these unforeseen developments were precipitated in the disturbing fashion which so aroused the nation can be better understood if we examine a series of situations which were cumulating during the summer of 1853 and which had little to do with the ostensible purpose of this legislation, with territorial organization, railroad projects, or anything else but politics.

The first of these were the personal difficulties of Douglas, which were many. In 1852, as a relatively young man, not yet forty, he had challenged his elders and made a strenuous effort to secure the Democratic nomination for the presidency. In doing so, he had stepped out of line and had, therefore, gained the ill will of many of his party associates, particularly those of more advanced years. The friends of Lewis Cass were particularly ill-disposed toward him. Largely as a result of this precocity, Pierce had given him no part or influence in the new administration, a snub which was all too obvious. Added to these political difficulties, he had suffered great personal sorrow in the death of his wife.

Thus beset, Douglas literally fled from the scene of his griefs and disappointments and spent some six months between sessions in Europe. From the middle of May until the end of October he was out of the country and largely out of touch with American politics. He traveled widely and talked with monarchs and statesmen. There were indications that he was planning to take up foreign affairs and to seek a new role in the Senate as a leader in shaping foreign policy.[34] It might enable him to recover lost ground and give him a new means of forging ahead in popular esteem for, as the Demo-

[34] Milton, *Eve of Conflict*, 12-14. New York *Herald*, November 18, 19, 1853.

crats had discovered, foreign affairs were sometimes more effective politically than domestic affairs — and safer.

But while Douglas was far away that summer of 1853, the game of politics in the Democratic party was becoming intense and bitter. The Pierce administration had realized that the Democrats were in power only because the Barnburners, the bolters of 1848, had returned to the fold; and the returning group had been admitted to the patronage. But many party members were not forgiving and bitterly opposed their readmission to good standing. One group in New York who were called Hard-shells, a current term for believers in closed communion, fought this policy of Pierce so hard that the Democrats lost the state in 1853.[35] In the South, radical followers of Calhoun displayed equal bitterness as they battled to regain control of the Democratic party in their section. In several southern states "soft" men had accepted the Compromise of 1850 and had come to power on coalition Union tickets dedicated to sectional peace, a policy endorsed by Pierce in his distribution of patronage.[36] The heirs of Calhoun and the Hard-shells were likely to make trouble when the Senate took up the confirmation of Pierce's Barnburner and "Soft-shell" appointees.

A final issue which created dissension within the party had appeared during the summer, when the President and members of his cabinet made a ceremonial excursion to New York City to open the Crystal Palace Exhibition. On the journey, James Guthrie, secretary of the treasury, and Jefferson Davis, secretary of war, had spoken in support of federal aid for a transcontinental railroad to the Pacific. There were important elements in the Democratic party, notably in Virginia, who were opposed to the exercise of such powers by the federal government as well as to the appropriation of such sums of money.[37] So there was dissatisfaction on this count.

All these tangled relationships increased distrust of Pierce as a political chief. His policies were considered demoralizing, his plat-

---

[35] Roy F. Nichols, *Democratic Machine, 1850-1854* (New York, 1923), *passim*, and *Franklin Pierce*, 241-58, 276-93; Craven, *Growth of Southern Nationalism*, 172-77; Nevins, *Ordeal of the Union*, II, 69-77.

[36] This southern political complex has never been given adequate attention. We are in particular need of a closer analysis of Virginia politics during the 1850's. See New York *Herald*, November 25, 29, 30, 1853; Philadelphia *Ledger*, January 2, 1854; Francis P. Blair to Martin Van Buren, March 4, 1854, Van Buren Papers (Division of Manuscripts, Library of Congress); von Holst, *Constitutional and Political History of the United States*, IV, 314-15 and notes, 318 n.

[37] Nichols, *Franklin Pierce*, 279-80.

form inadequate. The party was thought to be falling apart under his incompetent leadership. Certain influential people became convinced that it had been a mistake to choose a leader so young and untried. Some more experienced party tacticians, it was believed, must come forward to repair the damage before it was too late. They must provide some new platform on which the party might once again unite.

A move in this direction appears to have started rather early that summer in an obscure way in Virginia. The so-called national party organ, the Washington *Union*, had been supporting Pierce's patronage recognition of the rebels of 1848. Its editor, Robert Armstrong of Tennessee, who never wrote a line, had reorganized his staff and had fired a Virginian, Roger A. Pryor, replacing him with John W. Forney of Pennsylvania. This act may not have been unrelated to the next journalistic development. In September, a new Democratic newspaper, *The Sentinel*, appeared in Washington. This sheet was edited by a Virginian, Beverley Tucker, who undertook to combat the "free-soil" tendencies of the Pierce administration.[38]

305

Whether this journalistic venture was a part of a wider plan for supplying the leadership which Pierce had failed to produce is not altogether clear. But it is obvious that as Congress was assembling there was a movement in that direction in the Senate under leadership very definitely southern. The chairmen of the three principal committees — foreign relations, finance, and judiciary — Senators James M. Mason and Robert M. T. Hunter of Virginia and Andrew P. Butler of South Carolina, together with David R. Atchison of Missouri, president pro tempore and acting vice-president, were congenial spirits who kept house together on F Street near the Patent Office. Politically they were the heirs of Calhoun and they were among those who were distressed at Pierce's "weakness" and the seeming disintegration of their party. They liked Pierce personally but they realized that he needed help. They could hardly have been said to approve of his patronage recognition of Barnburners, but they did not want to revolt against him this early by refusing to confirm his "free-soil" appointees. They were the most

[38] *Ibid.*, 279; New York *Herald*, November 12, December 9, 1853; Diary of Edward Everett, December 6-7, 1853 (Massachusetts Historical Society); Washington *Union*, August 19, September 25, 1853.

powerful men in the Senate, but they were burdened by a sense of responsibility and they were looking for a way out.[39]

Atchison's political situation in Missouri may have given them a suggestion as to the means, particularly as events in the early days of the new session were especially irritating to them. When Congress assembled in December, 1853, Forney, of the *Union*, was elected clerk of the House. Hardly had he entered office than he dismissed a Virginian, John A. Parker, the librarian of the House. The clannish and powerful Virginians liked this no better than the dismissal of Pryor. They did not find it difficult, therefore, to join with the Whigs and some Hard-shell Democrats in arranging an obvious snub to the President. They joined in defeating the plan of the administration to assign the Senate printing to Armstrong of the *Union*, and instead chose Beverley Tucker for the contract.[40]

At the same time the members of the F Street Mess were planning a more aggressive step in the direction of taking over party leadership. They seem to have determined to reinterpret the party platform and to prescribe it as a test which the Barnburners must accept before the Senate would approve certain of the President's principal New York appointees. The Hard-shell press mentioned this possibility with enthusiasm.

In the shaping of this new test Atchison's needs could be used as a convenient instrument. The Senate was about to resume consideration of the Nebraska bill which had so nearly passed during the last session. In a bitter campaign which Atchison had been fighting with Thomas H. Benton that summer in Missouri for re-election to the Senate, he had promised to secure the organization of the new territory without the exclusion of slavery or else withdraw. These messmates seemed now to have become convinced that they could use the Nebraska question as a means to prescribe a new test, and incidentally to help their colleague retain his seat in the face of Benton's onslaught. The basic tenet in Pierce's political creed was acceptance of the Compromise of 1850, which prescribed self-government in the territories and popular sovereignty, partic-

[39] Ray, *Repeal of the Missouri Compromise*, 229-33; Blair to Van Buren, August 24, 1854, Van Buren Papers.

[40] New York *Herald*, December 10, 1853; John A. Parker to J. F. H. Claiborne, December 23, 1853, Claiborne Papers (Division of Manuscripts, Library of Congress); *Cong. Globe*, 33 Cong., 1 Sess., Appendix, 44-45; Washington *Union*, December 8, 13, 17, 24, 1853; Everett Diary, December 12, 16, 1853; Washington *Star*, December 13, 14, 17, 1853; St. Louis *Missouri Republican*, December 20, 1853.

ularly regarding the existence of slavery. To this general creed the Barnburners had subscribed. But if popular sovereignty was good for some territories, it must be good for all. Therefore, the logical implication of this policy was that it should be extended to all territories, even those dedicated to freedom by the Missouri Compromise. The party must now recognize this logic by extending popular sovereignty to Nebraska, and the Barnburners must demonstrate their sincerity by accepting it.

Behind this brief for consistency was southern feeling, particularly among those with speculative interests, that if great railroad and real estate operations were to be undertaken, the South must be allowed to participate; its leaders would no longer submit to the humiliation of exclusion.[41] Some among the southern leadership appear to have become convinced that if they could produce a measure which would organize Nebraska along the lines of the Compromise of 1850 and "requiring a distinct vote now either for or against . . . this would compel honorable gentlemen to show their hands and let the country know what they understand by the administration phrase 'acquiesce in the compromise measures.' "[42] They were in truth the heirs of Calhoun.

Douglas, as chairman of the committee on territories, must of course be dealt with. There was no political love lost between the Calhounites and the opportunistic and pushing young Illinoisan. He might be described as a boon companion of Atchison and his name might be coupled with Hunter's in political and business enterprises, but they did not think of him as one of them and his power was frequently a threat to theirs. The Senate managers, who included Jesse D. Bright of Indiana, lieutenant of Cass and Douglas' rival for the dominant role in the Northwest, were busy with a plan to enlarge the membership of the Senate committees by adding another Democrat to each of the major groups. Whether they were ready to deprive Douglas of his cherished post if he proved recalcitrant is not known, though they did take it from him five years later. Bright was busy with this reshuffling and Atchison perhaps found it an opportune time to approach Douglas, who could not fail to recognize him as a member of the Mess.

[41] See notes 18 and 39; also New York *Herald*, January 2, 4, 11, 25, 1854; Baltimore *Sun*, December 21, 1853, January 9, 1854; Philadelphia *Ledger*, January 9, 1854; Washington *National Intelligencer*, February 6, 1854; Washington *Union*, February 18, 1854.

[42] New York *Herald*, January 4, 1854.

Atchison, according to his own testimony, which Douglas never categorically and unequivocally denied, reminded Douglas that he needed at least four southern votes for the Nebraska bill. These he could not have unless some way were found to permit slaveholders to go with their property into the new territory at its opening. The bill of the previous session, which ignored this question, would not do. Atchison further told Douglas that if he did not want to father this new bill, he, Atchison, would resign as vice-president de facto and assume the chairmanship of the committee on territories. Douglas realized he must heed Atchison's "suggestions"; he was helpless and he knew it. Without the votes of the Mess he could secure no bill, and the pressures for its enactment were mounting.[43]

But he would do it in his own way, for he knew he had taken on no easy assignment. He had canvassed the possibility of abandoning the Missouri Compromise a year before this but had discarded it as too hazardous and had nearly succeeded in getting through a bill which ignored the issue. Now he must face the slavery question in some fashion, but under real difficulties. Contrary to the accepted belief, Douglas did not have comfortable control of his own committee. It had been reconstructed by some of his senatorial enemies, either by accident or design, in a way embarrassing to him. He was associated with three Democrats and two Whigs; but one of the Democrats was Sam Houston. The Texas senator had his own ideas about Nebraska, and in the last session he had voted against the simple bill then under discussion. Now he delayed coming to Washington for a month and upon arriving would not attend committee meetings. Douglas could do nothing until Houston agreed, and it turned out that Houston would accept nothing outside the framework of the Compromise of 1850. So in the end Douglas copied the phraseology of the act organizing Utah with an explanatory stipulation that the design of the Nebraska bill was to leave all questions pertaining to slavery in this new territory "to

[43] Everett Diary, December 10, 1853; New York *Herald*, December 10, 1853; Washington *Star*, March 4, 1854; Blair to William Allen, February 10, 1854, William Allen Papers (Division of Manuscripts, Library of Congress). See Ray, *Repeal of the Missouri Compromise, passim*, particularly 274 n. and 276-88. Senator Andrew P. Butler declared on the floor of the Senate: "General Atchison . . . had perhaps more to do with the bill than any other Senator." *Cong. Globe*, 34 Cong., 1 Sess., Appendix, 103. Senator James M. Mason also discussed the subject. *Cong. Globe*, 35 Cong., 2 Sess., 1248.

the decision of the people residing therein, through their appropriate representatives." Nothing was said about the Missouri restriction; it was just ignored. The new bill embraced not the small area of the previous bill but all the remainder of the Louisiana Purchase.[44]

The presentation of Douglas' revision of the 1853 bill on January 4, 1854, gave other interests ideas about political uses to which they might put the measure. Senator William H. Seward, a leader of the Whig party, shrewdly grasped some rather intricate possibilities. He urged some of his northern Whig associates to lead in attacks upon Democrats by encouraging public meetings of protest and sponsoring legislative resolutions demanding that northern senators and congressmen oppose the bill. In after years he described the more Machiavellian role he played. He suggested that southern Whigs place their Democratic opponents at a disadvantage by assailing them for dodging repeal, and at the same time to proclaim the Whigs as true friends of the South by opposing the dodge or by offering a repeal amendment to the act. Beyond this, Seward had an even more subtle intent. He wished to make the bill as obnoxious as possible to northern voters, for this would help northern Whigs discredit the Democrats. Although Whig Senator Archibald Dixon of Kentucky offered the repeal amendment, he claimed many years later that he could not remember Seward's influence.[45]

Dixon's move gave the cue to a third group to engage in the politics of the bill. The Free-Soil senators and representatives moved much more directly than the subtle Seward. Sumner offered an amendment reaffirming the Missouri exclusion and the Ohio men, led by Giddings and Chase, drafted the "Appeal of the Independent Democrats," arraigning the bill as "a gross violation of a sacred pledge." This manifesto was designed to and did set off a chain reaction which gave northern leaders their desired opportun-

[44] Private Letters of Parmenas Taylor Turnley (London, 1863), 104-106. Rhodes, History of the United States from the Compromise of 1850, I, 425 n., says Douglas was the Committee on Territories, but this is questionable. Everett Diary, January 4, 1854.

[45] William H. Seward to Thurlow Weed, January 7, 8, 1854, Thurlow Weed Papers (University of Rochester Library); Dixon, Missouri Compromise and Its Repeal, 457, 591; Nicolay and Hay, Abraham Lincoln, I, 345-50; Member of Western Bar [Flint], Life and Speeches of Douglas, 171-74; James T. Du Bois and Gertrude S. Mathews, Galusha A. Grow (Boston, 1917), 144-45; Thomas L. Clingman, Speeches and Writings (Raleigh, 1877), 335.

ity to mobilize the anti-southern voting strength of the more populous North.[46]

While the Whigs and Free-Soilers were planning these moves, elements in the Democratic party had become increasingly dissatisfied with Douglas' dodge. Some Calhounite lawyers thought it would not admit slavery to Nebraska. Then, too, the repeal amendment of Dixon further embarrassed southern Democrats because it served to expose them to a charge that they were acquiescing in a subterfuge and so gave advantage to their Whig opponents. Simultaneously, doubts were rising in the minds of certain northern Democrats like Cass and members of the administration, none too friendly with Douglas, that the matter was being badly handled in a fashion that might easily split the party again. Therefore, various Democrats, including Pierce and his cabinet, began seeking a new formula which might insure united Democratic support and the passing of the much desired bill.[47]

The Calhounites, Douglas, and the President finally achieved a formula to which they got the rather unstable Pierce committed in writing. They would open Nebraska to slavery by declaring that the Missouri Compromise had been "superseded" by the Compromise of 1850 and "declared inoperative." Also, two territories were created instead of one, one west of a slave state and the other west of a free state. This division, reminiscent of the arrangement of 1820, gave the measure more of an air of compromise, and Pierce agreed to give the bill his support.[48]

The second revision of the bill and the "Appeal" were launched almost simultaneously on January 23 and 24 and they brought immediate results. Such a wave of indignation swept through the

[46] Malin, *Nebraska Question*, 300-302. Chase had been affronted only a few days before when Atchison had excluded him from a select committee on the Pacific Railroad appointed on Chase's motion.

[47] Notes of Philip Phillips, left for his children, Philip Phillips Papers (Division of Manuscripts, Library of Congress); John Wentworth, *Congressional Reminiscences* (Chicago, 1882), 54-55; John Moses, *Illinois, Historical and Statistical* (2 vols., Chicago, 1892), II, 588-89; George M. McConnell, "Recollections of Stephen A. Douglas," Illinois State Historical Society, *Transactions*, 1900 (Springfield), 48-49; Philadelphia *Ledger*, January 13, 14, 1854; George W. Jones to Howell Cobb, February 16, 1854, Robert P. Brooks (ed.), "Howell Cobb Papers," *Georgia Historical Quarterly* (Savannah), VI (June, 1922), 149.

[48] See note 20, and Everett Diary, January 23, 1854; Joseph Robinson to John H. George, January 24, 25, 1854, John H. George Papers (New Hampshire Historical Society); Jefferson Davis to John A. Parker, June 13, 1888, Dunbar Rowland (ed.), *Jefferson Davis, Constitutionalist* (10 vols., Jackson, Miss., 1923), IX, 459; John Bigelow, *Retrospections of an Active Life* (5 vols., New York, 1909-1913), I, 171.

310

North at this blow to liberty that the possibility of support from northern Democrats was threatened; and if there were to be a serious revolt among them, the seemingly overwhelming majorities in the Senate and House might disappear, for in both bodies there were more Democrats from the North than from the South.

A further matter for concern was the discovery by the Calhounites of a great and seemingly unexpected indifference to the measure in the South. Many in that region just did not believe that climate would permit any more slave states, and they were not interested in efforts to open territories that would only create more free states. Furthermore, they did not trust Douglas' popular sovereignty. To many it implied that a host of free state people unhampered by any slave property might move right in and elect a territorial legislature which would immediately exclude slavery. Such a proposition was a tricky device to get more free states with no possible advantage to the South. Many so-called Compromise or Union Democrats in the South held these views.

311

Thus the Democratic strength seemed to be melting away, north and south. The fate of the bill, therefore, hung on selling the idea to the South, particularly by appealing to the southern Whigs, and on whipping northern Democrats into line behind an administration bill. For these purposes, the second revision — the January 23 bill — was proving unsatisfactory, so a series of partisan and bipartisan senatorial caucuses was organized to hammer out another formula which would really insure repeal without using the word and which would overcome southern suspicions of popular sovereignty.

In this series of caucuses in which the leadership was now definitely southern and bipartisan, and in which Douglas by the nature of things could have only a restricted part, a new formula was achieved. The Missouri Compromise was at last specifically declared "void." Recent immigrants were excluded from voting in the territorial elections, an idea attractive to the revived nativism which was becoming popular among southern Whigs. The question of the legality of slave property in the territories was by peculiar language assigned to the Supreme Court. By these caucus actions southern Democrats and southern Whigs were brought to agreement and persuaded to present an almost completely united front. The force behind the caucus procedure was not Douglas but the increasing violence of the attacks against the bill as an act of aggression on the part of the slave power. This insult roused the latent southern nationalism which had been slowly taking shape and for the first time the South presented a united front. Such a combination had a leadership which included not only Douglas, but the members of the Mess and the fiery Whig, Robert Toombs of Georgia. Douglas had the spectacular floor leadership but these others dominated the caucuses that supplied the votes. The bill in this shape finally secured a very comfortable margin in the Senate — 37 to 14. But it still had to pass the House.[49]

312

The heated contest in the Senate had been simple compared with the complex situation that was developing among the representatives. The historian finds that little critical attention has been given over the century to this phase of the struggle and, what is more damaging to the cause of truth, little evidence regarding the contest remains beyond the official record and scattered partisan newspaper comment. Personal correspondence, diary, and memoir material seems not to have survived in any significant quantity. Most historians, absorbed in Douglas and the Senate contest, have expended their pages liberally on that phase of the problem, and have then passed quickly over the struggle in the House. Von Holst, who treated it most extensively, failed to grasp the principal problems of strategy.

The bill ran into trouble in the House from the start. The principal reason was the political hazard which it provided for so many of the representatives. Most members were concerned by the fact that they were in the midst of or on the eve of their re-election campaigns. The rising tide of indignation in the North was frightening to many Democrats who would have to face angry voters, indignant at contrivers or supporters of this measure. Furthermore, the na-

---

[49] New York *Herald*, February 3, 4, 8, 1854; Washington *Star*, February 6, 1854; Baltimore *Sun*, February 7, 1854; Philadelphia *Ledger*, February 8, 1854; Robert Toombs to W. W. Burwell, February 3, 1854, Ulrich B. Phillips (ed.), *The Correspondence of Robert Toombs, Alexander H. Stephens, and Howell Cobb*, American Historical Association, *Annual Report*, 1911 (2 vols., Washington, 1913), II, 342-43; Arthur C. Cole, *The Whig Party in the South* (Washington, 1913), 286; St. Louis *Missouri Republican*, February 23, 1854. The final draft of the bill, written in a clerk's hand, is in the Senate Files (National Archives). That its wording received close attention up to the last minute is illustrated by the fact that in a sentence concerning "The principle of non-intervention by Congress with slavery in the States and Territories, as established by the legislation of 1850 . . . ." the word "established" was crossed out and "recognized," written in another hand, substituted.

ture of the Democratic majority in the House provided a problem. On paper it was so huge, 159 to 75, that there might seem to have been no conceivable trouble. But the difficult hurdle was that 92 of the 159 Democrats, by far the greater part, came from northern constituencies. So there was trouble, even in the House Committee on the Territories. The chairman of this goup was one of Douglas' most loyal associates, William A. Richardson of Illinois, who presided over a committee made up of four southern Democrats, another from Missouri, a second Democrat from a free state — William H. English of Indiana — and two Whigs. The original plan had been to report out a duplicate of Douglas' January 23 version on that day, but English and the Whigs objected and delayed the report until January 31, and with it English then filed a minority pronouncement.[50]

313

The discussion in the House committee defined the strategy of the contest which was to ensue. English represented a large proportion of the ninety-two northern Democrats. These men resented the semantic gymnastics used to deal with the slavery question. They wanted a forthright statement of the doctrine of popular sovereignty, of self-government in the territories, acknowledging the complete control of the slave question by the territorial governments. They felt they would have a chance in the coming election if they were fighting a positive battle to extend democracy, whereas if they were forced on the defensive by charges of destroying the Missouri Compromise they were in grave danger.

The final version of the bill as it came from the Senate put them at the greatest disadvantage. This version — the revision of the January 23 bill — not only declared the Missouri Compromise void, but it gave no specific authority to the territorial governments over the admission of slavery. To make matters worse for some of the congressmen, the bill excluded unnaturalized foreign immigrants from political participation in the organization of the territories. Not only did this provision exclude numerous potential free state voters but it aroused foreign-born voters against the Democrats in various districts.

A group of northern Democrats, therefore, planned some embarrassing strategy which, if successful, would for the time being at least take the bill out of the control of the administration leaders.

[50] English's minority report is in *House Reports*, 33 Cong., 1 Sess., No. 80.

Sixty-six of the ninety-two northern Democrats revolted and successfully completed this maneuver. The administration was defeated, 110 to 95. Of the thirteen delegations which the northern Democrats "controlled," only Pennsylvania, Illinois, and California showed any real loyalty. New England, New York, and New Jersey failed utterly. Even Michigan and Indiana, bailiwicks of Cass and Bright, fell away. Ohio and Wisconsin would have little of the measure.

314

This defeat was a blow which challenged all the ingenuity which the administration, Douglas, and the bipartisan southern coalition could muster. Probably few of the sixty-six wanted to prevent the organization of the territories but many either wanted a different bill or hoped to get something for themselves out of the measure's passage. In fact the revolting northern Democrats were fighting not so much to defeat the bill as to change it. They wanted a return to Douglas' first bill of January 4 or else to have English's popular sovereignty amendment or something like it inserted. Furthermore, they wanted to strike out the immigrant-exclusion amendment.

So three forces girded themselves for final efforts. The opposition sought to enlist the revolting sixty-six Democrats in the final defeat of the bill. The administration and the congressional managers were trying to get them to return to regularity. The revolters themselves were battling to get their terms accepted. Here history draws the curtain. The evidence of what went on in the minds and emotions of these sixty-six still remains hidden, if it exists. What experiences these sixty-six had, what pressures were exerted on them, how they reacted, what they wanted and either got or did not get, whether some reasoned it out or reacted to pressure from home, how many were moved by moral indignation or were swayed by party loyalty, remains hidden. Answers to these questions would supply the real history of this phase of the bill's passage, yet these answers are not known.

It was, of course, obvious that the President and his cabinet made some efforts with patronage promises, offers of administrative favors, and persuasive arguments, but they were handicapped by the fact that much of their patronage had been used up. Furthermore, the unstable President and the administration newspaper, the Washington *Union*, blew hot and cold. Some effort was made to re-form the ranks by appeals to party loyalty, and Douglas sought to persuade, to order, to overawe; in fact he used all the tactics his ingenious mind and dynamic personality could contrive. Who was promised what, and why shifts were made is still almost wholly unknown. We have only the bare results. No change was made in the bill save the restoring of political privilege to unnaturalized settlers and the bill passed.[51]

On one occasion before final passage of the bill, some eighteen Democrats were persuaded to return to the ranks of regularity and on one other strategic roll-call, when a two-thirds vote was required, a second eighteen, who on no other occasion supported the bill, contributed their votes. Even then the final victory was won, not by Douglas and his Democratic cohorts, but by a bipartisan coalition marshaled by the Georgia Whig, Alexander H. Stephens, who devised the slick maneuver which in the end put the bill over. The eighteen Democratic rebels who had been persuaded to change and vote "aye" were not enough. Had it not been for the support of thirteen southern Whigs, the now impotent Democratic majority could not have carried the bill.[52]

Thus the act came into being. It bore little resemblance to the bill for which Douglas had struggled in the short session of the preceding Congress. The Calhoun faction, southern and northern Whigs, Free-Soilers, the administration, and certain Hard-shell Democrats had all made use of this measure in one way or another and the final bill was the work of many hands and the fruit of much strategic planning. Its real history is the analysis of how a bill ostensibly to organize a territory had been made an instrument of the fundamental political reorganization that the disintegration of the old parties had made inevitable. The story of these political

[51] *Cong. Globe*, 33 Cong., 2 Sess., Appendix, 31, 35, 47, 64; Sidney Webster to George, June 5, 1854, George Papers.

[52] Richard M. Johnston and William A. Browne, *Alexander H. Stephens* (Philadephia, 1878), 277. The final affirmative vote was 113 to 100, with only 100 of the 159 Democrats voting aye. Of the northern Democrats who voted, forty-four were favorable and forty-three opposed. Eight southern Democrats and five northern Democrats did not vote; from their own statements and previous votes the last five seem certainly to have been opposed to the measure. Full Democratic support for the bill can be reckoned as 108, which was not enough to carry it. Of the eighteen rebels who finally voted for the bill, eight came from New York, three from Pennsylvania, two from New Jersey, three from Indiana, one from Ohio, and one from Michigan. The other eighteen who "obliged" just once were mostly from New England, Ohio, and Indiana. They supplied the only substantial help the administration got from New England and Ohio in this struggle. Of the thirteen state delegations controlled by the Democrats, only four — Pennsylvania, Indiana, Illinois, and California — remained anywhere near loyal to the party leadership.

maneuvers is the neglected element in the history of the bill; it is the so-called mystery, the Hamlet which has been hitherto either omitted or only very sketchily treated.

In this fateful legislative session a new plank had been added to the Democratic platform, the President and the principal Barnburner and Soft-shell officeholders had accepted it, the appointments had been confirmed. Douglas himself had lost an essential portion of his northern support without improving his position in the South. A significant segment of the northern Democracy had left the party. Likewise, a real anti-southern coalition which could capitalize the voting superiority of the more populous North was insured; the seed of the Republican party had been planted. Finally, and not usually noted, was the fact that in this winter of political discontent, the southern members of Congress for the first time organized and presented a well-nigh solid political front and among them traditional party divisions were largely laid aside. It was but a few steps onward to secession, the Confederacy, and the Solid South.

The great volcano of American politics was in a state of eruption. In the midst of the cataclysm, one sees Douglas crashing and hurtling about, caught like a rock in a gush of lava. When the flow subsided, old landmarks were found to be either greatly altered or obliterated. Two new masses were prominent on the political landscape, the Republican party and the Solid South. Douglas had disappeared.

316

Journal of Interdisciplinary History, xx:1 (Summer 1989), 1–24.

Joel H. Silbey

After "The First Northern Victory": The Republican Party Comes to Congress, 1855–1856

Between its first electoral victories in the congressional races of 1854 and Abraham Lincoln's triumph in the presidential contest six years later, the Republican party grew from one faction among several opposing the dominant Democrats to a majority position within the Northern electorate. Accounts of its rise to political prominence often have the quality of an American morality play. Determined to resist the further expansion of slavery on the American continent, the Republicans proved able to overcome the hesitations and resistance of the indifferent, the hostile, and those with other agenda. Although Republicans themselves disagreed about timing and the reach of their future policies, there was no question that with their victory in 1860, at a minimum, the further expansion of slavery had been checked, a situation which Southern secessionists read clearly, to their ultimate sorrow.

317

The initial symbol of Republican emergence was Nathaniel P. Banks' election as Speaker of the House of Representatives in the 34th Congress. As Harrington suggested almost fifty years ago, this "first Northern victory" was a great triumph. The original Republican bloc in Congress was far from a majority. Republicans shared an anti-Democratic orientation with a number of other groups not necessarily friendly to themselves. At first, when the House met, the party situation was greatly fragmented. There were 79 Democrats, 37 Southern Whigs, and 117 Anti-Nebraskas (or, as the *Tribune Almanac* labeled them, "opposition of all shades"). Only 46 House members called themselves Republicans at that point. Like each of the other anti-Nebraska blocs, the Republicans were not yet a party but a protest movement.[1]

Joel H. Silbey is President White Professor of History at Cornell University. He is the author of *The Partisan Imperative: The Dynamics of American Politics Before the Civil War* (New York, 1985).

1   Fred Harvey Harrington, "'The First Northern Victory,'" *Journal of Southern History*,

Although it took an unprecedented period of time, the Republicans became the ultimate beneficiaries of the political realignment that was underway. In the House, they eventually won the support of enough other Northern anti-Democrats, especially from the anti-immigrant, anti-Catholic American party bloc, to put Banks in the Speaker's chair. It was a crucial victory for them in terms of policy consequences and proved to be a compelling portent of the future course of American politics. As Potter has argued:

318

> Banks personified the link between nativism and antislavery, but also the greater appeal of antislavery. His election meant that a large bloc of congressmen with both nativist and anti-Nebraska associations had, with few exceptions, given its primary allegiance to antislavery and thus to the emerging Republican party. . . . At the same time, the speakership contest compelled the loose anti-Nebraska coalition in Congress to take a long step toward unity and permanent organization.[2]

Potter and others who have written about the growth of the Republican party have been aware of the complications and difficulties inherent in this "long step toward unity and permanent organization." Still, whatever those problems were, historians have often regarded them as temporary. They have brushed aside any that existed after Banks' great triumph. From 1855 onward, all went well for Republican party builders, culminating in their great electoral triumph in 1860. Although no one can deny what the eventual outcome was, the smooth road described from Banks' victory onward gives less attention than warranted to the difficulties posed by the continuing importance of political factors unfavorable to the Republicans and of alternative political channels. These negative factors took much effort to overcome. The party's movement toward success may have been inexorable, but the nature of the political scene and of the particular elements at

---

V (1939), 186–205; *The Tribune Almanac and Political Register for 1856* (New York, 1856), 3. *The Congressional Globe* did not list the party identification of members at the opening of the session as it usually did.

2 David M. Potter, *The Impending Crisis, 1848–1861* (New York, 1976), 256. See also Eric Foner, *Free Soil, Free Labor, Free Men: The Ideology of the Republican Party Before the Civil War* (New York, 1970), 247–248.

REPUBLICANS IN CONGRESS, 1855–1856 | 3

play posed many uncertainties for the Republicans throughout the late 1850s.

The Republicans appeared in the middle of an intensely partisan era—an age dominated by powerful party loyalties expressed rhetorically, at the polls, and on the floors of Congress. Memories, prejudices, and years of battling against each other precluded an easy alliance of the anti-Nebraskas under a new banner. In Congress, Whigs and Democrats had long voted against each other on the traditional questions of tariffs, finances, land, and territorial expansion. Even as the new agenda crystallized in the early 1850s, and many members of these old parties sorted themselves into new, largely sectional, coalitions, the memories of long years in opposition to one another, as well as the survival of many issues which had traditionally separated Whigs from Democrats, continued and posed tricky questions for the emerging Republicans. As the *New York Times'* Washington correspondent wrote at the end of 1855, "it is a difficult matter to harmonize a new party, made of men who have been for a life-time engaged in political strife with each other; and it could scarcely have been expected that the elements of the Republican Party in Congress would fuse at once and without trouble."[3]

319

Equally critical was the fact that the resistance to the Democrats grew out of not one but several new and distinct issues which the old parties did not handle satisfactorily. Although there were areas of ideological and policy agreement among the various anti-Democrats, there were also major differences in emphases and priorities, each having substantial support in the electorate. They were difficult to overcome even after Banks had moved into the presiding officer's chair in the House. The many political groups appearing on the scene as a result of the realignment of the 1850s remained a series of disparate protest movements. Republicans themselves were constantly chagrined by the extent of the "miserable local divisions" in their early years, and the ever present possibility that members of one bloc or another might defect despite their inclination to unite over the Kansas issue.[4]

3 Silbey, *The Shrine of Party: Congressional Voting Behavior, 1841–1852* (Pittsburgh, 1967); *New York Times*, 10 Dec. 1855.
4 Potter, *Impending Crisis*; William Gienapp, *The Origins of the Republican Party, 1852–1856* (New York, 1987); *idem*, "The Crime against Sumner: The Caning of Charles Sumner and the Rise of the Republican Party," *Civil War History*, XXV (1979), 218–246; Francis Fessenden, *Life and Public Services of William Pitt Fessenden. . . .* (Boston, 1907), I, 63.

There were, however, elements working in the Republicans' favor: the widespread hostility to the territorial policies of Franklin Pierce's administration; the continuing relevance of the Kansas dispute as the border war became bloodier; and the determination of many Republican leaders to build bridges to their potential allies and create a powerful coalition. There was no question that the potential for a coherent party existed, but party building was not automatic. It was an art form rooted in the available resources, conscious individual will and energy, and the opportunities offered by events. The process of transforming the originally fragmented anti-Democratic factions into a more coherent and permanent party was still a matter of development, with unpredictable obstacles and consequences, even given the power of the anti-Nebraska commitments that linked many in 1855. As Ohio's John Sherman, serving his first term in the House, later described the situation, "during the first session of the 34th Congress, the opponents of slavery were without a party name or organization. They agreed only in the one demand that slavery should not be established in Kansas. On the other questions they voted on old party lines."[5]

Although historians have studied the emergence of the Republicans with great energy and care, the congressional dimension of party development remains only partially understood. The efforts to organize an effective legislative coalition were as critical an aspect of Republican growth as were the forging of a common ideology and the organization of voters to contest the Democrats at the polls. It merits a close and detailed examination comparable to that traditionally given to the electoral and leadership dimensions of party building. The House of Representatives, the scene of the first Republican victory, witnessed the full dimensions of the battle to build a party in the early stages of its emergence to power.

In the campaign to elect a House Speaker, Republican congressional leaders had to work with, convince, and/or replace the other members who also opposed the ruling Democrats. The Know-Nothing presence, in particular, posed critical problems and opportunities for the Republicans. Nativism was already de-

320

---

5 John Sherman, *John Sherman's Recollections of Forty Years in the House, Senate and Cabinet: An Autobiography* (Chicago, 1895), I, 136.

clining as an independent political force. Nevertheless, Republican party builders had to take its stubborn adherents fully into account in building their majority. The Know-Nothings were powerful in many of the anti-Democratic constituencies of the North and South, and they held a significant bloc of seats in the House. In addition, some representatives, although elected as Republicans, had close ties to the Know-Nothings.[6]

Many party builders considered Banks to be the most effective candidate that the Republicans could offer for Speaker because he could draw support from both Americans and Democrats. Banks was a second-term congressman who, as he himself pointed out on the floor, had originally run not as a Republican but as a Democrat and Know-Nothing. Horace Greeley referred to him as "a Northern American of Republican proclivities." He did receive support from many Northern Whigs and Americans but the problem of continued hostility toward the Republicans from other Whigs and Know-Nothings remained. In the early and middle stages of the speakership contest, votes were cast for seventeen different anti-Nebraska candidates, including Republicans, Know-Nothings, and Whigs. Many Know-Nothings made it clear that their refusal to support Banks rested on principles and policies and their commitment to their own agenda. The "Know Nothing madness," Charles Sumner lamented, was doing much harm to the Republicans. "In the House we are weak, in the Senate powerless." As one Democratic congressman put it during the contest, "there seems to be greater hostility between the different factions of the opposition than there is between either of them and the Democratic party." William A. Howard, a Republican congressman from Michigan, conceded "that we cannot marshal our forces so as to bring every man into the ranks."[7]

It was not for lack of trying to find the elements of a common cause. At the beginning, Greeley had hoped that a call to a legislative caucus when Congress convened would include "all mem-

321

6 Gienapp, *Origins of the Republican Party*, 189–271.

7 New York *Daily Tribune*, 19 Nov. 1855, 3 Jan., 13 Feb. 1856; Frederick Seward, *Seward at Washington as Senator and Secretary of State* (New York, 1891), II, 291; David H. Donald, *Charles Sumner and the Coming of the Civil War* (New York, 1960), 278. Lewis D. Campbell of Ohio, Henry M. Fuller of Pennsylvania, and Alexander Pennington of New Jersey were the most important anti-Nebraska candidates. *Congressional Globe*, 34th Cong., 1st Sess., 27, 147, 227.

bers who believe Kansas ought of right to become a Free State" and not be limited to those who were against the Pierce administration which was "too narrow and paltry[?] a platform." But such a general meeting was not held; nor, in fact, was the "narrow and paltry" one. A correspondent of the New York *Tribune* deplored the fact that "the elements of opposition to the Administration are found to be so discordant that the idea of a simple anti-Administration caucus to nominate a candidate has been entirely abandoned." Some of the Republicans and Know-Nothings did meet before Congress convened. That meeting passed a Republican-sponsored resolution not to support anyone for Speaker who would not make anti-Nebraska men a majority on every committee. But, as Joshua Giddings lamented, "the leading members of the 'Know-Nothings' did not appear at any of the caucuses."[8]

322

Some Know-Nothings and Republicans regretted the failure to hold a general caucus. "Had such a caucus been held, I should all along held myself bound to an acquiescence in its decision," one said. But here, for five weeks, "no such meetings had taken place." An opportunity had been missed. "If the anti-Nebraska men . . . had held a caucus when we first assembled, we should have elected a Speaker on the second, if not the first, vote. We did not hold one, and it is generally known why we did not." Even those who had met in the partial caucus, including the resolutely anti-slavery Joshua Giddings, backed off from their resolution that all committees should have an anti-Nebraska majority when it became clear that no majority for Speaker could be built on that proposal. They supported Banks despite a description of him as "one of the most antisectional individuals" in the North, his recent membership in the Know-Nothings, and his uncertain Republicanism.[9]

There were constant attempts to find a way out of their predicament, wipe out past memories, and reduce the impact of such prejudices and continuing divisions. As one editor told Banks, "I have caused the [Boston] *Atlas* to say that whatever

8 Horace Greeley to Schuyler Colfax, 7 Sept. 1855, Greeley Papers, New York Public Library [hereafter Greeley Papers]; New York *Tribune*, 30 Nov. 1855; Joshua R. Giddings, *History of the Rebellion* (New York, 1864), 383.
9 *Congressional Globe*, 34th Cong., 1st Sess., 231, 245; James Brewer Stewart, *Joshua R. Giddings and the Tactics of Radical Politics* (Cleveland, 1970), 235–236.

seeming affinities the Republican Party may have with parties of the past, it is now a creation sternly summoned out of present exigencies and having its first real being on the 2nd day of February." Greeley was behind an attempt to win over Americans to "the Republican movement" by a policy "to sink the distinction [between Republicans and Know-Nothings] as much as possible."[10]

Initially, there were too many fears, memories, and uncertainties stemming from the realities of the past. "We came here—I speak now of anti-Nebraska men—" one of them said, "entertaining differences of opinion upon some other questions." Or, as a Southern Democrat scornfully summed up, "why cannot you organize your opposition? . . . Because the heterogeneous mass, thrown up by the prejudices of the people, growing out of the legislation of the last Congress, could not act together upon any single question." Fear of Whig domination was particularly strong among those congressmen who had traditionally opposed that party, former democrats, in particular. Many Americans had refused to join the Whigs, as well, and remained hostile to any signs of Whig control of Republican affairs.[11]

Some Republicans saw positive gains from the long contest. "The more votes for speaker the better," one wrote to Banks. "The lines between the Parties will be more firmly consolidated." As William Pitt Fessenden told his son in late 1855, "events are fast bringing the Republicans and Americans from the free states to the conviction that neither can do without the other." And Giddings concurred: "The great hope of our enemies that Know Nothingism would destroy us is growing more and more faint. Our forces are constantly becoming more and more consolidated and our ranks more and more compact and firm."[12]

Others, however, grew increasingly concerned as the weeks passed inconclusively. The New York *Tribune*'s comments and

323

10 _____ Lincoln to Nathaniel P. Banks, 5 Feb. 1856, Banks Papers, Library of Congress, Washington, D.C.; Greeley to Charles Dana, 6 Feb. 1856, in Joel Benton (ed.), *Greeley on Lincoln* (New York, 1893), 116; Greeley to William M. Chase, et al., 9 May 1856, Greeley Papers.

11 *Congressional Globe*, 34th Cong, 1st Sess., 146, 256; James M. Stone to Banks, 8 Dec. 1855, Banks Papers; "H" to Banks, 29 Feb. 1856, *ibid*.

12 Stone to Banks, 25 Jan. 1856, Banks Papers; Fessenden, *Life of Fessenden*, I, 70; Joshua R. Giddings to Joseph A. Giddings, 12 Jan. 1856, Joshua R. Giddings Papers, Ohio Historical Society (microfilm edition, Cornell University Library).

correspondence reflected the anguish that Republican party builders felt and the all but insurmountable problems that they faced.
One day the paper would harshly attack those Northern Know-
Nothings holding out against Banks, and the next it would seek
to calm the waters it had stirred up. With such capriciousness and
bitterness, confusion and pessimism were the common coin of
the Republican leaders. Finally, a breakthrough occurred. As Harrington described it almost fifty years ago, the Southern Know-
Nothings hated the Democrats enough to refuse to unite with
them and elect one of the Democratic candidates. Anger, confusion, and shouting marked the final day which culminated in
Banks' election after the election rules were changed (as had been
done in a similar standoff five years before) to permit a plurality,
rather than a majority, to make the selection.[13]

324

Republican leaders were jubilant. "Thank God, there is at
last a great United North!" one correspondent wrote to Speaker
Banks. It was a triumph that went beyond the personal to "that
of the principle for which, although in separate organizations, we
have all been contending." And, some Republicans looked at the
contest as a model for coalition building in the future. It had been
a hard struggle, one "involving sacrifices of no ordinary character" on everybody's part. Giddings sighed with relief as "the most
discordant elements were brought to the support of principle, and
the power of the truth in political contests was very fully and
beautifully illustrated." Thurlow Weed, a long-time Whig leader
and editor, wrote on the day after Banks' victory, that "this
triumph is worth all it cost in time, toil and solicitude. For *once*
the North has been faithful. . . . The Republican Party is now
inaugurated. We can now work 'with a will.'"[14]

This assessment might well have seemed true. But would the
bitterness, disarray, and polarization among the potential Republicans readily disappear? There were still powerful divisions
among them. It took the House eleven ballots, for example, to
elect a public printer—and he was the Democrats' choice. Apparently the inclination of the anti-Nebraskas to work together re-

13 New York *Tribune*, various issues, Jan. 1856. See, as an example, Greeley's dispatch
from Washington, dated 27 Jan., in the issue of 30 Jan.; Harrington, "First Northern
Victory."
14 Charles Congdon to Banks, 5 Feb. 1856, Banks Papers; Thurlow Weed to Banks, 3
Feb. 1856, *ibid.*; Giddings, *History of Rebellion*, 389.

mained fragile, despite the unity that had been achieved. The *New York Times* complained of "the strange folly of the opposition in working at cross purposes." Republican leaders continued to express uncertainty even amid the euphoria caused by the Banks victory. Clearly, "much has got to be done to combine the discordant elements [of the anti-Nebraska blocs] and mould them into shape." It was still only a hope that "all who think alike may be enabled to act together." In early 1856, Seward lamented to Weed that "more than half of the majority are Americans engaged in demoralizing the Congress and the country."[15]

It was not certain that the Republicans and their allies in the speakership fight had as yet evolved beyond the stage of being a congeries of blocs and developed lasting common loyalties—the consciousness of being a common party—that ensured permanence. Banks' initial behavior as Speaker suggests how far from secure was the Republican victory. He and other party leaders used their finely honed political instincts when they dealt with the other anti-Democratic members. Their pragmatic behavior toward the latter was occasionally at odds with the demands of an aggressive antislavery pressure group. Committee construction was particularly difficult. In the absence of seniority norms and in the presence of a new party and many new congressmen, it could, Banks realized, become a minefield. He consulted broadly among the blocs, including Ohio's Lewis Campbell, his main rival for Speaker from the anti-Democratic forces.[16]

Fortunately for Banks, many of those consulted responded in the spirit expressed by Congressman William A. Howard of Michigan, who held himself "in readiness to serve in any place on any committee as the Public Interest, the harmony of our friends or the good of the cause may, in your judgment, require." Others weighed in with suggestions designed to improve anti-Democratic unity under Republican leadership. Representative George Dunn of Indiana was recommended for the Kansas In-

325

---

15 *New York Times*, 13 Feb. 1856; "H" to Banks, 23 Feb. 1856, Banks Papers; Thomas J. Marsh to Banks, 19 Mar. 1856, *ibid.*; Seward, *Seward at Washington*, II, 270.

16 "Excuse this bundle of suggestions, which you must reproach yourself for having invited." Colfax to Banks, n.d., 1856, Banks Papers. See also, James Bishop to Banks, 7 Feb. 1856, Lucian Barbour to Banks, 7 Feb. 1856, J. R. Tyson to Banks, 8 Feb. 1856, Banks Papers; New York *Tribune*, 13 Feb. 1856. On Campbell, see William E. Van Horne, "Lewis D. Campbell and the Know-Nothing Party in Ohio," *Ohio History*, LXXVI (1966), 202–221.

vestigating Committee even though he had not supported Banks for Speaker because "we must conciliate and win to us just such men and factions as find their type in Mr. Dunn and his clique in the House." Further, to "secure an advantage" in Massachusetts and "put the Republicans in possession of an element that they must have," it was suggested that Banks introduce a bill to remodel the naturalization laws.[17]

At the same time, careful consideration was given to particularly sensitive—and potentially divisive—problems threatening Republican dominance and party integrity. Giddings, the House's most veteran opponent of the extension of slavery, wanted certain rewards and refused to be placated with lesser gifts from the Speaker. Edward Wade, his Ohio colleague, told Banks that he had "endeavored to show him that his [Giddings] appointment to the *first* place on one of the 'political committees' would tend on the one hand to *alarm* our more *timid* friends and to dissatisfy and discourage the more ardent and strongly anti-slavery of them." Giddings wanted the Territories Committee but would accept the District of Columbia panel, and Wade suggested that it would be better to make him chairman of the latter. "I would rather, however," he concluded, "offend enemies than dissatisfy friends."[18]

Banks could not give everyone what he wanted, and there were violent complaints about the results of his efforts. One member felt that he had been "disgraced" by his assignment and his "noble and generous constituency" humiliated. Others relegated to a "trifling committee" found themselves similarly unhappy. One such appointment was viewed as "a rebuke to the Anti-Nebraska party" and an "insult to the district." Banks acted largely as "the harmony of our friends" required. He recognized the need to find political means to establish and maintain the anti-Democratic coalition, which was largely rooted in opposition to the administration's Kansas policy, while remaining sensitive to other issues and priorities among potential allies.[19]

---

17 William A. Howard, et al. to Banks, 2 Feb. 1856, Banks Papers; Benjamin Stanton to Banks, 1 Dec. 1855, *ibid.*

18 Edward Wade to Banks, 9 Feb. 1856, *ibid.*

19 Rufus King to Banks, 27 June 1856, *ibid.*; Editors of the *Chicago Tribune* to Banks, 20, 23 Feb. 1856, *ibid.*; Stanton to Banks, 3 Mar. 1856, *ibid.*

The final distribution of committee chairmanships and memberships hardly reflected secure Republican hegemony. Self-identified Whigs, Americans, and members of various other blocs in the potential Republican pool all chaired committees (Table 1). Giddings, for example, did not become the chairman of the Territories Committee. Instead, the appointment went to Galusha Grow, a Free Soil Democrat from Pennsylvania who was less threatening, less extreme, and more in need of wooing. Campbell became chairman of the Committee on Ways and Means "and had substantial control of the business of that Congress." Of eight major house committees, Republicans chaired two, Whigs three, Americans one, and Free Soil Democrats one; the last was chaired by Campbell, who might best be called a Whig-Republican (Table 2). All of this careful parceling out of committee assignments to the various groups was necessary, but it had a cost. Banks' "maddening impartiality" as Speaker calmed matters down and helped bring people together but "left still in the air the terms of Republican union." And it did not resolve whether they would be able to continue together in a more permanent fashion than they had effected to that point.[20]

327

Table 1 Party Affiliation of Chairmen:
All Committees, House of
Representatives, 34th Congress

Republican	11
Whig	9
Whig and Republican	1
American	6
Whig and American	2
Native American	1
Soft Democrat and American	1
Free Soil Democrat	1
States Rights Democrat	1
Democrat	4

20 Sherman, *Recollections*, I, 134; Richard Sewell, *Ballots for Freedom: Antislavery Politics in the United States, 1837–1860* (New York, 1976), 276. The committee lists are in *Journal of the House of Representatives*, 34th Cong., 1st Sess., 501–503.

Table 2 Makeup of Key Committees: House of Representatives, 34th Congress

COMMITTEE	CHAIRMAN	COMPOSITION	
Ways and Means	Whig and Republican	2R	2D
		2W	
		3A	
		1W&A	
Commerce	Republican	2R	2D
		2W	
		2A	
		1W&A	
Public Lands	Whig	4R	2D
		2W	
		1A	
Judiciary	Whig	2R	2D
		2W	
		2A	
		1W&A	
Manufactures	American	1R	2D
		4A	
		1W	
		1W&A	
Agriculture	Republican	2R	2D
		2W	
		2A	
		1FSD	
Foreign Affairs	Whig	1R	2D
		2W	
		2A	
Territories	Free Soil Democrat	2R	2D
		3W	
		1A	
		1FSD	

R Republican
W Whig
W&A Whig and American
A American
FSD Free Soil Democrat
D Democrat

The House finally received President Pierce's message—the traditional opening of congressional business—in February. From then until adjournment at the end of August, congressmen faced a crowded agenda, dealing not only with matters related to Kansas and the extension of slavery, but with more traditional concerns as well. The tensions originally seen in the speakership contest continued to erupt among the anti-Democratic blocs throughout the session. Elements of political obtuseness, self-interest, and obsolete commitments to defunct parties still obtained. But ideological and policy differences also splintered the potential Republican blocs, and greatly magnified party-building difficulties. As Congressman Francis S. Edwards, elected as a Whig and American from New York, explained, he had voted for Banks. But, he continued, "I am no Republican—but intend to act and think for myself—there are very many of the principles of that party which I shall carry out—but not all."[21]

329

Several different votes relating to sectional and slavery issues indicated the extent of potential Republican strength. There was an almost immediate series of votes about Kansas, for example, specifically concerning the legitimacy of the election of a territorial delegate there. On these roll-calls, sixty-two of Bank's supporters in the speakership contest voted together, and none voted against the main bloc. The other forty-one did not vote, suggesting either a refusal to cooperate, indifference toward the issue, or individual situations which prevented attendance. "The absenteeism of members of Congress," one observer noted, "continue a grievance of a very serious character."[22]

But too much should not be made of the failure of certain congressmen to vote, even if they constituted a large group. There was a more telling set of votes on Kansas affairs—three roll calls highly symbolic of the elements that created the anti-Nebraska party in the first place. The first of these, Congressman Dunn's resolution that no one should be elected speaker who did not favor restoring the Missouri Compromise line, took place before the election of the Speaker (and was defeated 103–102); the second, a bitterly controversial resolution setting up an investigating committee to look into conditions in Kansas, took place shortly thereafter; and the third, the vote to expel Congressman Preston

21 Republicans and potential Republicans disagreed, for example, over territorial matters relating to the propriety, timing, and conditions of the admission of Kansas and Oregon as states, leading to constant bickering and divisions among the anti-Democratic blocs. When one bill to admit Kansas as a free state went down to narrow defeat, the *Tribune* harshly condemned the "treachery and faithlessness" of some of the congressmen on whom Republican leaders had counted. *Congressional Globe*, 34th Cong., 1st Sess., 1450 ff.; New York *Tribune*, 1 July 1856; Francis S. Edwards to Greeley, 13 June 1856, Greeley Papers.
22 JSP [James S. Pike], "Letter from Washington," New York *Tribune*, 14 May 1856.

Brooks, occurred in July. The votes on all of these remained remarkably stable from beginning to end. The vote to expel Brooks for his assault on Sumner indicates the nature of the reactions of the anti-Nebraska group to the entire subject. Banks' supporters stayed together and added a crucial eight votes from Whigs and Americans that they had not received in the speakership contest.[23]

The voting pattern suggests the classic historiographical picture. The issues were decided over a six-month period, providing the Republican leaders with ample opportunities to rehearse the slavery issue, to denounce the iniquities of the Democrats and the South, and to press hard for unity among the Northern opponents of the Democrats. As one, not unfriendly, observer noted, the Brooks matter aided Republicanism. "Now that the prejudices of the North can be appealed to in aid of a sectional controversy for the presidency, we roll up our eyes in holy horror at the offense." The combination of Bleeding Kansas and Bleeding Sumner helped create a Republican hegemony. Senator William Seward commented that he saw the House of Representatives "steadily, from the first day of the session, becoming firmer and more true and steadfast in the cause of justice, freedom, and humanity."[24]

Further, few people abstained on these roll-calls. Greeley exuberantly noted how much it did "a Republican heart good to see how the uprising of the people for Free Kansas and [John C.] Fremont braces and stiffens the Anti-Nebraska majority in the House. Never before were such majorities given there for the righteous cause as yesterday." These were great triumphs indeed. As Giddings put it, "the election of Speaker[,] the appointment of the [Kansas investigating] Committee and the passage of the bill [to admit Kansas as a free state] are the three greatest political miracles of the age." Kansas had brought the Republicans into being; Kansas united them with other Northern anti-Democrats. The issue was a powerful political solvent. Throughout, Anti-Nebraska caucuses met regularly "with an eye to harmonious action." The Republicans began as a minority, "yet this minority has been steadily strengthened alike by accretion and internal

23 Three of Campbell's supporters voted with them, one against; five of the seven who voted for other candidates also joined the Banks bloc.
24 *Congressional Globe*, 34th Cong., 1st Sess., *Appendix*, 941; *ibid.*, 34th Cong., 2nd Sess., 60; Gienapp, "The Crime against Sumner."

assimilation until it became barely less than a majority of the House." The Northern Know-Nothings had come over on the territorial issue because they realized that "the slavery issue was paramount, and that of Americanism subordinate." As John Sanborn, a correspondent, summed it up to Banks, "these Free Soil Americans begin to see that [the] first real paramount question for this country to settle is the question of Freedom or Slavery, and that true Civil and Religious Liberty firmly established in fact as well as in theory, Peace, Prosperity and the fullest development of all its resources . . . shall be added onto it."[25]

Nevertheless, Kansas was not the only issue on the congressional agenda in 1856. There were other matters debated, other votes taken. Differences over economic policy in American politics were long-standing, and, in 1855 and 1856, they complicated party building. The persistent differences between Whigs and Democrats over general questions of federal power to shape the economy remained vigorously contested. At the same time, issues related to internal improvements and railroad land grants had also divided Democrats from one another since the middle-1840s. Neither division provided much promise for anyone seeking to build Republican unity out of those same groups if these issues remained on the congressional agenda. They did. The issues could not be avoided.[26]

Two of the roll-call votes taken on economic issues, one before and one after the Brooks expulsion vote, suggest some of the potential problems among the Northern anti-Democrats. The first one is of particular interest because Speaker Banks had to cast a vote to break a tie on it. The Michigan Land Office Bill seemed to be a simple housekeeping measure. Representative Henry Bennett, a Whig from New York, suggested that the bill was "one which involves no principle. It is one merely of convenience."[27] Nevertheless, the ensuing short debate predictably brought in questions of presidential authority, general versus local

331

---

25 Joshua R. Giddings to Joseph A. Giddings, 4 July 1856, Giddings Papers; New York *Tribune*, 29 June, 2, 3 Sept. 1856; John A. Sanborn to Banks, 9 Apr. 1856, Banks Papers.
26 New York *Tribune*, 7, 25 Mar. 1856. The range of economic policy matters considered in the 34th House were, as always, loaded with specific policy directives, symbolic differences over government power, and attempts to include government initiatives that went beyond the original purpose of a particular bill.
27 *Congressional Globe*, 34th Cong., 1st Sess., 503.

power, the appropriateness of special interest legislation, and the administration's position on the matter, all of which reinvigorated memories about economic policy differences. When the vote was taken, Banks' supporters and their potential allies were more fragmented than they had been on the Kansas roll calls (Table 3).

Table 3 Distribution of Anti-Democratic Blocs on Michigan Land Bill

	AYE	NAY	NOT VOTING
Banks bloc	9	53	41
Campbell bloc	2	1	1
Others	2	2	3

The split on this vote among the anti-Democrats did not appear to be overwhelming, but several disturbing facts present in the roll call had to be factored into the Republican leaders' calculations. First, the extent of the defection among the Republicans' potential pool was notable. Thirteen of the sixty-nine voting did not stay with the majority. Although that figure was less than 20 percent of the whole, in a closely competitive political environment, both in Congress and outside, it indicated difficulties for Republican efforts to transform a coalition into a permanent second major party. Second, the number of congressmen who did not vote on the issue, forty-five from the potential Republican pool, could also be seen as a sign of difficulties ahead. Although it is impossible to determine why so many failed to vote, it is not unreasonable to suggest that some might have abstained because of cross pressures growing out of their Republican commitments, on the one hand, and their long-standing and continuing disagreements over economic policies, on the other.

One other vote is suggestive on this point. The bill to establish a naval depot in Georgia split the Republicans dramatically (Table 4). There are some indications that the Know-Nothings and Northern Whigs opposed Republicans on this bill, indicative of a conflict between those who supported expansive government expenditure policies generally and those who agreed with them but not when such expenditures benefitted the South. Since no debate was recorded on the bill, it is hard to analyze this issue further except to note that the splits existed. But, no matter the reason, tendencies against unity in this general area were present.

Table 4 Distribution of Anti-Democratic Blocs on Georgia Naval Depot Bill

	AYE	NAY	NOT VOTING
Banks bloc	48	31	24
Campbell bloc	1	0	3
Others	6	1	0

Interestingly, the division among Republicans and their would-be colleagues was more apparent on this vote, even though it occurred after the vote to expel Brooks, than it had been on the earlier economic policy bill.

Such individual votes are not by themselves conclusive, only suggestive, but it is possible to arrive at a more comprehensive view. A Guttman scale of the role calls on the economic policy issues considered in the first session of the 34th Congress extends and clarifies the picture. The scale contains votes on internal improvements, land policy, and railroad land-grant measures which, although affected by procedural and constitutional elements (override of presidential vetoes, delaying or tabling various measures, and so forth), and, occasionally, highly specific amendments, do provide a more complete and precise picture of the nature of voting in the economic realm.[28] Table 5 indicates the distribution of congressional votes on these issues.

Most of the Republicans clustered together, with fifty-nine of the eighty-five potential Republicans, 69.4 percent of the whole, occupying the first three scale types at the pro-activist end of the scale. But the key issue remained the additional support that they needed to give them control and policy direction on the floor of Congress, and this need posed problems. A substantial bloc remained outside. The eighty-eight Banks supporters on the scale occupy twelve different scale positions and are widely scat-

333

28   The roll calls include six votes on different railroad land grants, three votes on rivers and harbors bills, two votes to override the president's veto of the latter, two land bills, and a bill to establish a naval depot in Georgia. The roll calls can be found, in the order in which they appear on the scale, in *House Journal*, 34th Cong., 1st Sess., 1068, 601, 942, 1055, 1015, 969, 957, 1017, 929, 960, 1046, 1470, 1499, 1175. Unfortunately, many congressmen could not be placed on the scale due to their failure to vote frequently enough to establish their position. They include such interesting and important figures as John A. Bingham, George Dunn, Joshua Giddings, and John Sherman.

Table 5 Economics Scale: Representative Types

CONGRESSMEN REPRESENTATIVE OF EACH TYPE	STATE	PARTY	SCALE TYPE	NUMBER IN TYPE	ROLL CALL → RESPONSE → 1	2	3	4	5	6	7	8	9	10	11	12	13	14
					A	N	A	A	A	A	N	A	A	A	A	A	A	A
Sapp[ac]	Ohio	R	0	(44)	+	o	+	+	+	+	+	+	+	+	+	+	+	+
Perry[ac]	Maine	R	1	(16)	–	+	+	–	+	+	o	+	+	+	+	+	+	+
Flagler[ac]	N.Y.	W&A	2	(22)	–	–	–	+	o	o	+	o	+	+	+	–	+	+
Colfax[ac]	Ind.	R	3	(8)	o	+	–	+	o	o	+	o	+	+	+	+	+	+
Todd[ac]	Penn.	W	4	(5)	–	–	o	–	+	+	o	+	–	+	+	–	+	+
Morrill[ac]	Vt.	W	5	(5)	–	+	+	+	–	+	+	+	+	+	+	+	+	+
Albright[ac]	Ohio	R	6	(9)	–	o	–	+	–	–	o	+	+	+	+	+	+	+
Spinner[ac]	N.Y.	FSD	7	(3)	o	+	–	o	–	o	–	–	o	o	+	+	–	+
N. Scott[bc]	Ind.	R	8	(12)	–	–	–	–	o	–	+	–	–	+	+	+	+	+
Galloway[ac]	Ohio	R	9	(7)	–	o	–	o	–	o	+	–	o	+	+	+	+	+
Purycar	N.C.	W	10	(2)	–	+	–	–	o	o	–	–	o	o	o	+	+	+
Dick[ac]	Penn.	W	11	(3)	–	+	o	–	o	o	–	–	o	o	o	+	+	+
Allison[a]	Penn.	W	12	(3)	o	–	o	o	+	o	–	o	–	o	+	o	+	+
English	Ind.	D	13	(7)	–	–	–	–	–	–	o	–	–	o	–	–	o	+
A. Oliver[c]	N.Y.	D&A	14	(37)	–	+	+	–	–	–	–	o	o	o	o	+	–	–

NOTE   The Guttman scalogram is an attitudinal segregating and measuring device which has been widely used by students of legislative behavior. It allows analysts to deal with a great many votes on the same subject and to refine the responses into an attitudinal shading from one extreme to the other rather than rely on a simple yes or no dichotomy. For an explanation of its use, see Silbey, *Shrine of Party*, 149–153.

a   Voted for Banks for Speaker
b   Voted for Campbell for Speaker
c   Voted to expel Brooks
R   Republican
W   Whig
W&A Whig and American
A   American
FSD Free Soil Democrat

tered. The Campbell and Henry M. Fuller voters were similarly scattered on the scale. The same pattern occurs among those additional members who joined with them in voting to expel Brooks (Table 6). They were most united on outrightly partisan votes to override President Pierce's vetoes of internal improvements bills. On specific railroad land grants and measures specifying particular river and harbor improvements, tendencies toward disagreement and fragmentation increased.

Most of the Republicans and their potential allies, however, did take positions distinct from those held by the large mass of the Democrats. And to underline a major point, policy differences within political parties have always existed and are often bitter and divisive. But, in an era of realignment such as this one, when parties are forming, disagreements take on a deeper, and more threatening, existence than they would once a party had been firmly established and its members had grown accustomed to working together and being more tolerant of the differences among them. Factions existing without the traditional partisan

335

Table 6 Economics Scale: Divisions within Potential Republican Blocs, 34th Congress

SCALE TYPE	NUMBER VOTING TO EXPEL BROOKS	PARTY AFFILIATION			
		R	W	A[a]	FSD[b]
0	31	10	8	13	0
1	14	2	11	1	0
2	14	4	6	4	0
3	4	3	1	0	0
4	3	1	1	1	0
5	1	0	1	0	0
6	5	3	2	0	0
7	1	0	0	0	1
8	5	3	2	0	0
9	4	2	2	0	0
10	0	0	0	0	0
11	1	0	1	0	0
12	1	0	1	0	0
13	1	0	0	0	1
14	2	0	0	1	1

a Including those labeled Whig and American, Democrat and American, and so forth.
b Free Soil Democrats

loyalties and commitments are likely to be more independent, intractable, and inflexible, and less likely to compromise for the good of a larger organization. The powerful events that were to tie these people together in a "Grand Old Party" had not as yet occurred among these former enemies and presently distinct blocs. Although the Republicans and their potential allies differed from the Democrats, they were not united, a major problem at that moment for party development and permanent alliance.

336

Congressmen also had to consider an important third set of policy matters that had created the anti-Democratic surge of the mid-1850s: nativism and anti-Catholicism. Amid the constant attention to, and excitement about, the Kansas issue, the Know-Nothings in the House were never strong enough, by themselves, to accomplish a great deal. As Greeley said, they had power only "to obstruct, none to advance business." The one initiative which they pushed is revealing: they were exercised by the "foreign influence" in elections, believing that immigrants illegally voted in areas under the Democrats' control. Many of the Republican congressmen were sympathetic to their efforts; others were not. The House and Senate both passed bills to impose suffrage restrictions on naturalized citizens in the District of Columbia (one place where Congress had authority on such matters). The bill inspired by the Know-Nothings prompted Howell Cobb, the Democratic leader, to ask if there were "no relenting of that stern American sentiment against the naturalized citizen." The early spring of 1856 saw much angry debate, a good deal of procedural maneuvering, and several attempts to set the bill aside. During the debate, Humphrey Marshall, a Know-Nothing, asked for Republican support since he believed that the latter's views "more nearly coincided" with those of Americans upon suffrage questions. As Cobb pointed out, Marshall was suggesting that "his party and the Republican party were nearer together than were the Republican party and the Democratic party."[29]

The debate proved troublesome to the Republicans. Cobb accused them of absenting themselves from the floor at crucial moments in order to avoid taking a stand.[30] When the House

29 New York *Tribune*, 28 Mar. 1856; *Congressional Globe*, 34th Cong., 1st Sess., 1224, 1235, 1236. The vote on the District of Columbia suffrage bill is in *ibid.*, 980–981.
30 *Ibid.*, 763

voted on the issue in a series of largely procedural roll calls, the Republicans split. As one of the substantive votes indicates, most of them voted for it (Table 7). But, in moving toward the Know-Nothings on this vote, the Republicans lost some of their past supporters, including Giddings, a radical antislavery Republican, Grow, a Free Soil Democrat, and Cadwallader C. Washburne, a Wisconsin Republican, as well as his brother Israel, from Maine. Again, there was also a large number of non-voters among the Republicans.

Both the debates and the votes suggest the potential difficulties for party building which were present in the 34th Congress. Despite procedural maneuvering and evasive tactics designed to defuse the issue, the problem never went away. It was too important to many of the anti-Democrats. Republican leaders realized that there were too many "such *Republicans* in the House" who were willing to, or who needed to support aspects of the Know-Nothing program, for the issue to disappear despite the efforts of the party hierarchy.[31] They did, often successfully, work with such friendly Know-Nothing leaders as Campbell to minimize the attention paid to the issue. They knew its potential power and acted accordingly.

337

The existence of such differences over economic policies or nativism is not surprising (as it is not surprising that the Northern anti-Democratic blocs stayed together on issues relating to Kansas). But how much did these policy divisions slow the powerful impulses pushing toward Republican unity? Giddings breathed good will when he suggested that Republicans and Northern Know-Nothings should "agree on the restoration of freedom to Kansas, while each man entertains his own views on all other matters." But the non-Kansas issues did not fall away in the face

Table 7   Vote Distribution on District of Columbia Suffrage Bill

	AYE	NAY	NOT VOTING
Banks bloc	51	10	42
Campbell bloc	2	1	1
Others	5	0	2

31   Greeley to Colfax, 10 July 1856, Greeley Papers.

of the rising concern about territorial matters in the late 1850s. In fact, Republican leaders constantly had to deal with these potentially divisive issues at state and national levels, as a glance at their maneuvering with the Know-Nothings in key Northern states, or the Christmas tree of items added to their national platform in 1860, attests.[32]

In Congress, too, even in the first session after their victory on the speakership, when so much attention was given to Kansas, the other main agenda items, with their potential to delay or prevent complete anti-Nebraska coalition, received significant play on the House floor. In terms of angry exchanges and divisive explosiveness, there may be little to choose among the different issues. But it is obviously not easy to measure emotion or its implications. When time spent and actions taken are measured, Kansas dominated Congress. Nevertheless, the pages of the *Globe* and *Journal* show how much of the chamber's business involved other difficult policy areas. A simple measure of the roll calls taken suggests something of the proportions among these crucial matters. Kansas was voted on about seventy-five times, economics and nativism together about fifty-five.

There was an obvious imbalance, but the data are not precise (for example, some votes on procedural matters had substantive implications, some did not). And the number of votes on "routine" matters, appropriations for example, greatly exceeded those on the policy areas discussed here. Nevertheless, the raw numbers do allow some judgments about the boundaries within which congressmen operated. The opportunities were there in congressional action for missteps to be made on the road to Republican unity.

What remains at issue is the continuing significance of the difficulties posed for the party by the disunity evident in the potential Republican pool on a set of new issues and the evidence of persisting divisions, born in an earlier party system, that were still potent even as Republican leaders worked to harmonize the anti-Democratic blocs. Some Republicans complained about Campbell's stewardship of the Ways and Means Committee. They

338

---

32 *Congressional Globe*, 34th Cong., 1st Sess., *Appendix*, 44. For an example of Republican-Know Nothing maneuvering in one critical state, see Silbey, *The Partisan Imperative: The Dynamics of American Politics Before the Civil War* (New York, 1985), 127–165.

were chided in return that "there might be and there ought to be, harmony between the members of the opposition and their own committees." So far as Republicans were concerned, the familiar litany was repeated: "with all who stand firmly on the anti-Nebraska platform, no matter what their views on other topics, we wish to have the least possible controversy." As Greeley told his managing editor, "let Lew Campbell alone as much as possible [in the pages of the New York *Tribune*]. He is a strange creature but we must make the best of him."[33]

The divisions continued to surface, even among those who normally worked for unity. Dunn of Indiana, a particular thorn in Republican sides (he should have supported them, they believed; he did, occasionally), "evinced in various ways," they claimed, "a spirit of bitter, implacable hostility to the Republican party, its candidates and its ascendancy." Such men responded in kind. "I have no political affiliation with the Republicans in or out of Congress," a New York Know-Nothing congressman told the House, "and cannot indorse [sic] them, either in principle or practice. . . . I can have no fellowship with them, or act otherwise than in opposition to them and their purposes." This kind of bickering, although not unexpected, drove party builders to despair and depressing conclusions. "As to dunn [sic], Scott, Moore[,] Harrison & Co.[,] the best they can do for us is to bolt—openly and finally. We can make more out of their opposition than their support."[34]

One can see in all of the feverish activity the efforts of a party being born, or rather made, in the interplay among its leaders, the existing political situation, and the members of its rank and file. Throughout, the Republicans had to move warily, determining how aggressive to be on questions of slavery and how to handle issues from the old agenda. At the end of the session, the New York *Tribune* summarized the Republican's situation with cold and grim reality. "There is not an earnest Free-Kansas majority in the House." The Republicans' victories were due to their opponents' divisions. The Democrats and Southern Whigs-Know Nothings "might have beaten Banks for Speaker and the Kansas investigation had they been united. . . . We have

339

---

33 New York *Tribune*, 7, 10 May 1856; Benton (ed.), *Greeley on Lincoln*, 129.
34 New York *Tribune*, 27 June 1856; Greeley to Colfax, 20 June 1856, Greeley Papers.

no majority, and never had, in the present House when full; when we have carried any point, it was by the help of a small segment of the Fillmoreites, who realize that to vote against Free Kansas is to forfeit the favor of their constituents and renounce all hopes of a reelection."[35]

It is possible to overemphasize the amount of potential or real division present and its importance—perhaps it represents nothing more than a temporary condition reflecting a political time lag. As Alexander's careful analysis of House voting in the 1840s and 1850s suggests, there was an increase in partisan voting in the 34th Congress compared to the previous few sessions. The nascent Republicans, with all of their problems, did better than their predecessors (the Whigs) had recently done.[36] Still, as interesting a point as that is in macrocosmic terms, the situation at the time neither was, nor seemed, all that positive to the seasoned politicians trying to build a permanent party coalition. To them, the situation remained ominous. It seemed clear that the emergence of a new political party in the frenetic, divisive, atmosphere of the United States in the 1850s, with the strong partisan memories of earlier battles, was neither easy nor foreordained, no matter how powerful antislavery sentiment had become on the political agenda. The Republican leaders knew how hard new party building was in an intense partisan atmosphere. Their understanding was confirmed by their experience during the 34th Congress. As Edwin Morgan, a New York politician lamented, "I knew that there are many Whigs at the North who still hold in good faith to the old principles of the Whig party of the North." Others echoed similar sentiments. And little could be done except to wait on future events. As a result, Republicans remained one faction of several, a protest movement, not yet a party, when the 34th Congress recessed in August 1856. Divisions and hesitations among the anti-Democrats posed important stumbling blocks and would continue to do so for some time to come.[37]

340

35 New York *Tribune*, 18, 25 Aug., 1 Sept. 1856.

36 Thomas P. Alexander, *Sectional Stress and Party Strength: A Study of Roll-Call Voting Patterns in the United States House of Representatives, 1836–1860* (Nashville, 1967), 94.

37 *Congressional Globe*, 34th Cong., 1st Sess., *Appendix*, 1220. Three years later, in another speakership contest, it took forty-four ballots for an anti-Democrat (who was not a Republican) to be elected. Ollinger Crenshaw, "The Speakership Contest of 1859–1860," *Mississippi Valley Historical Review*, XXIX (1942), 323–338.

Party and Section: The Senate and the Kansas-Nebraska Bill

Gerald W. Wolff

THE KANSAS-NEBRASKA ACT of 1854 was one of the most important bills ever passed by an American Congress. The legislative struggle surrounding it and succeeding events profoundly affected, not only the American party system, but also ultimately the very structure of the nation itself. The Whig Party was destroyed, the Democracy was seriously weakened, and intense animosities were created between northerners and southerners as a result of this piece of legislation.

341

The Kansas-Nebraska Bill was not only controversial and far reaching, but was also confusing and enigmatic. Roll-call material as it bears upon this legislative proposal in the Senate helps to unravel some of that mystery. By applying to these roll-calls a variation of a technique developed by sociologist Louis Guttman, it is possible to derive what amounts to rather sophisticated attitude patterns. These patterns, in turn, can be compared quite precisely with certain other factors, in this case, their relationship to party and sectional affiliation.[1] Put in another way, this paper will be mainly concerned with discovering the attitudes of Senators toward the Kansas-Nebraska Bill and the role played by party and sectional affiliation in shaping those attitudes.

The voting pattern or scalogram used in this analysis was derived by a method of trial and error. We first began with the final vote taken on the Kansas-Nebraska Bill and then attempted to scale with it every roll-call whose contents were directly related to the Nebraska struggle. This involved those votes concerned with parliamentary procedure, as well as the various attempts to amend the measure. In the end, the scale consisted of ten roll-calls and provided seven clear-cut scale types or attitudes on this issue. To facilitate discussion and comparison, however, the seven types were collapsed into three main attitude blocs in a way that would not distort the findings. These blocs could have been assigned several different labels, but it was decided that the following would be most useful: anti-Kansas-Nebraska Bill, moderates, and pro-Kansas-Nebraska Bill. The "moderate" category was the most useful and important of the three, and its meaning must be defined precisely. The term "moderate," as used here, has meaning and relevance only

---

[1] Of the many important works dealing with roll-call analysis, perhaps the best starting place for those interested in the subject is Lee F. Anderson, *et. al. Legislative Roll-Call Analysis* (Evanston, 1966).

Originally published in *Civil War History*, 18 (December, 1972). Reprinted by permission of Kent State University Press.

within the context and perimeters of this particular scale, and is relative to the two more extreme classifications. For example, besides those who were very much for or very much against almost every aspect of the Kansas-Nebraska Bill, the scalogram indicates those who were less polarized in their attitudes toward it. These men were not extremists on the Kansas-Nebraska issue as defined by this scale, and hence can be labeled moderates or non-extremists on that issue. The types of moderate vary from scale to scale and within the scales and must be analyzed. From the standpoint of attitudinal analysis of roll-call material, however, the moderate classification provides a more meaningful and sophisticated approach than the dichotomous breakdown provided by roll-calls taken individually. In fact, it would seem that the major utility of the scalogram over individual roll-calls is that by using scales it is possible to obtain more than a simple yea-nay opinion from Congressmen on a given issue by using roll-call material.

342

Sectionalism was the first variable tested against these attitude blocs. All historians dealing with the Kansas-Nebraska question have recognized that it involved, to some degree, North-South sectionalism because of the slavery issue it enveloped. However, in interpreting that sectionalism, most scholars have concentrated largely upon the words and actions of the Senate leaders. The scale data, on the other hand, provide one type of opportunity to gauge systematically the magnitude and intensity of sectionalism, as it involved a large portion of the Senators. The voting patterns clearly revealed a North-South split, but the division was milder than was anticipated. While nearly 60 per cent of the southerners enthusiastically endorsed virtually every aspect of the Nebraska measure covered by the scale, over one-third were less vigorous in their support and voted as moderates. Similarly, although 45.8 per cent of the northern senators strongly opposed it, one-third appeared in the moderate category, and over one-fifth were actually strongly in favor of the bill. A similar pattern emerged when East-West sectionalism was tested (see Table One).

More can be shown about sectionalism, however, in this regard. Of all the northern senators, those from the Northeast manifested the greatest hostility toward the Kansas-Nebraska Bill. Almost three-fourths of them turned up in the anti portion of the scale, and not one appeared in the pro section. The most adamant opponents of slavery extension appeared here. The northwestern senators, on the other hand, reacted quite differently. Only 23.1 per cent of them were strongly antagonistic toward the measure, while 38.4 per cent were moderates, and a like percentage were actually very much in favor of the bill. So despite the demonstrations of public anger in the Northwest over the Kansas-Nebraska Bill, a rather small proportion of that section's senators strongly opposed the measure. There was then a rather severe contrast on this issue between the voting behavior of the northern senators from the East and those from the West.

As for the Southeast and Southwest, an interesting voting pattern emerged. While almost 80 per cent of the senators from the southern inland states gave solid support to the Kansas-Nebraska Bill, three-fourths of their colleagues from the South Atlantic coastal states were only moderates (see Table Three). The favorable response of so many of the southwesterners seems reasonable enough, but the moderate voting posture of such a high percentage of the senators from the Southeast is curious in some ways and merits further scrutiny.

At first glance, one is tempted to account for their position largely in terms of apathy brought on by the realization that the geographical position of their states would preclude their constituents from ever having a decent opportunity to take practical advantage of the repeal of the Missouri Compromise, popular sovereignty, and the economic opportunities that would result from the organization of Kansas and Nebraska. Yet this analysis is inadequate, for it ignores the complexity of the situation and the passion with which southeastern Senators so often defended state rights. It is virtually impossible to probe the motives of moderate Jackson Morton of Florida because he chose to remain silent during the Nebraska debates, and there are no other sources, as far as we know, which indicate why he took the position he did. With respect to the other five southeastern moderates, however, there is enough evidence to suggest an explanation for their voting behavior.

For some of these senators, a primary and dominant element in any interpretation of their moderate stance must involve intensity of feeling rather than indifference. Harboring an extreme position on the rights of slaveholders, they withheld unqualified support for the Kansas-Nebraska Bill. Believing that the bill did not go quite far enough in protecting slavery in the territories, they felt compelled to rationalize the bill's usefulness at great length before supporting it. Robert M. T. Hunter of Virginia and Andrew Butler of South Carolina, two of the most powerful members of the Senate, shared what one historian has called the common property doctrine regarding the authority of the federal government over the territories.

In its pure form, the common property position was that, although the federal government managed the territories, it governed only in the capacity of a guardian, subject to the desires of all the states, who owned the territories in common. As a guardian, the federal government must allow citizens from every state to move to the territories with their property, including slaves, if they wished. It must also ensure that territorial governments protected that property once the migrants arrived and had become residents. Therefore, not only was the Missouri Compromise unconstitutional, but also the principle of popular sovereignty, which would allow territorial legislatures to sanction or to disavow slavery. If the federal government could not exclude slavery in the public domain, then it was not possible, legally or logically, for the national government to grant that power to one of its own creatures,

343

namely a territorial legislature.[2] This was the most extreme position to evolve in the South regarding the rights of slaveowners in the territories. In the process of reaching a final decision on the Nebraska question, Butler and Hunter adhered strictly to certain parts of the common property doctrine, while agreeing to compromise on other aspects of it. Because the position taken by these two senators is so important to a major portion of the thesis of this study, it is necessary to scrutinize their views carefully.

Both Hunter and Butler declared emphatically that the Missouri Compromise was unconstitutional and should be repealed, just as the Nebraska Bill proposed. To Hunter, the compromise impaired the constitutional guarantee of equality of the states.[3] Similarly, Butler declared that the South had never acknowledged any constitutional obligations under the Compromise of 1820. The government in Washington, as the agent of the sovereign states, had no constitutional right, either explicit or implicit, to run an arbitrary line through the common territories of the states in a calculated move to prohibit slavery and disfranchise an entire section. Given the northern majority in Congress, if the slave states continued to acquiesce in the reasoning and process of accommodation associated with the Missouri Compromise, then those states would ultimately fall victim to the most arbitrary, uncontrollable, and unlimited of all powers, namely legislative discretion.[4] The Missouri Compromise, in Butler's opinion, made a mockery of the constitutional concept of equality of the states in the name of majority rule and compromise. "Suppose a gallant crew," he asked,

trusting in each other's honesty and good faith, were to embark in a vessel at sea, under definite articles of equal copartnership, and that one portion should assume, in violation of the fundamental *principles—not terms only—*of equality, to construe the terms of the copartnership so as to give and distribute the fruits of the voyage to one recognized class in preference to another; what would be thought of such a proceeding? . . . Sir, rather than remain on such a ship—talked of as an equal, but spurned as an inferior—would not the weaker party be doing the highest office of duty and honor to quit the ship, and take to the boats, trusting to the winds and

[2] An excellent description of the common-property doctrine is contained in Robert Russel, "The Issues in the Congressional Struggle Over the Kansas-Nebraska Bill, 1854," *Journal of Southern History*, XXIX (May, 1963), 188. Russel also pulls together a great deal of material showing that the Kansas-Nebraska Act fell short of what the congressional advocates of this position wanted, despite a long list of painful concessions made to them by many northern senators. He does not recognize any of them as moderates, however, but states only that the supporters of the common-property doctrine accepted and voted for the bill in the end. See also Arthur Bestor, "State Sovereignty and Slavery: A Reinterpretation of Proslavery Constitutional Doctrine, 1840-1860," Illinois State Historical Society, *Journal*, LIV (Summer, 1961), 117-180.

[3] U. S. *Congressional Globe*, 33 Cong., 1 sess., XXIII, Appendix, 221 and 224. For the general views of Hunter and Butler see *ibid.*, 223, 225, 238-239; *ibid.*, Pt. 1, 423, 689, 690, 1307. Also see *ibid.*, 519, 1064-1065 and *Ibid.*, App. 648-653, 789-801.

[4] *Ibid.*, App., 232, 238.

the waves for their fortunes, and if the ship were to perish, would they not be justified?[5]

Despite their adamant common property stand on the Missouri Compromise question, both senators were willing to accept the doctrine of popular sovereignty as contained in the Nebraska Bill, but within certain strict limits. To Hunter, a territorial legislature should be given "all possible political power as long as it did not impinge upon the equal rights of the states as provided in the Constitution."[6] Butler went to much greater lengths to delineate his position. He refused to concede that "the first comers upon the soil of a Territory can appropriate it, and become sovereigns over it," but rather Congress controlled the territories from their conception until they reached maturity.[7] A territorial legislature, as a child of Congress, could not do what its parent was forbidden to do. If it was unconstitutional for Congress to approve the Missouri Compromise or other unfair territorial restrictions, then it was also unconstitutional for "clandestine squatters" to pass measures of this type.[8] He was willing, in the case of the Nebraska Bill and as a general principle, to trust the people; but he would never assent to "trust the simple despotism of a majority."[9] If the territorial governments of Kansas and Nebraska should act in any way contrary to the common principles of the Constitution both senators agreed that the federal courts should intervene.[10]

Despite all this rhetoric regarding the rights and future of slaveholders in the Kansas and Nebraska territories, both men steadfastly insisted that the Kansas-Nebraska Bill would bring no practical advantage to the South, only psychological satisfaction. "Slavery might go there for a time," declared Hunter, but "it could not survive the formation of a State Constitution."[11] Butler believed that the Nebraska Bill would not provide "anything but an advance to the sentiment of honor."[12] "The South," he concluded, "wants her heart lightened-not her power increased."[13]

Both these gentlemen offered a summary of sorts explaining why they finally decided to accept the Kansas-Nebraska Bill. According to Hunter, the measure was a step toward peace, removing from Congress a primary "cause of strife, disturbance, and collision," namely the slavery extension issue.[14] The Bill had accomplished this, moreover, simply by applying the Constitution "to the question of slavery in common with

345

---

[5] *Ibid.*, 238.
[6] *Ibid.*, 223-224, 226, 289.
[7] *Ibid.*, 239. See also *ibid.*, Pt. 1, 1307.
[8] *Ibid.*, App., 239, 240; See also *ibid.*, Pt. 1, 690, 1307.
[9] *Ibid.*, App., 240.
[10] *Ibid.*, 224, 240; *Ibid.*, Pt. 1, 423, 689, 690.
[11] *Ibid.*, App., 224.
[12] *Ibid.*, 292.
[13] *Ibid.*, 240.
[14] *Ibid.*, 226, 225.

all others . . . ," and all sections could now "live in the peace of conscious security."[15] Hunter seems to have convinced himself that the demise of the Missouri Compromise, even with the subsequent substitution of popular sovereignty, had vindicated the common property doctrine by providing constitutional justice for the slave states, as well as the free states. He may have felt secure in this position because of his narrow interpretation of the prerogatives of territorial legislatures and of the role he envisioned for the federal courts as the arbiters of territorial decisions on the slavery question.

Butler was less enthusiastic about the virtues of the measure; but the alternative was to prolong the life of the Missouri Compromise. "Under one," he declared, "it is certain we can have no rights; under the other we may have some."[16] Even if no slaves ever entered Kansas or Nebraska, this piece of legislation would be worthwhile, because it recognized southern honor. In fact, he concluded, "even if I were perfectly certain that the bill would operate injuriously to the South, with the convictions on my mind that the Missouri Compromise is unconstitutional, I should be bound to vote for the bill."[17]

Like Hunter and Butler, moderate Thomas Pratt of Maryland, although practically speechless during the debates, also favored, or at least leaned toward favoring, the common property doctrine. He was an avid state rights advocate and would barely admit after careful questioning and prodding by several northern senators that under the popular sovereignty principle a territorial legislature could actually exclude slavery.[18]

William Dawson of Georgia also asserted that the territories were the common property of all American citizens and that there should be no obstacle to any of them settling there if they chose. The Missouri Compromise was such an obstacle. That arrangement was unconstitutional, conceived and executed in perfidy by the North, and the South was under no obligation to obey it. The Kansas-Nebraska Bill, by removing it, was performing an act of justice long overdue, and the people of the United States would receive it as such.[19]

Evidently, Dawson believed that under the Nebraska Bill there was a good chance that slavery could be extended to Kansas and Nebraska, and he displayed few if any reservations about the use of squatter sovereignty there. When a territory acquired enough population to become a state, he declared that it should be allowed to "come into the Union with a republican form of government, with or without slavery, as its people may decide."[20] Dawson then accepted popular sovereignty as a

15 *Ibid.*, 226.
16 *Ibid.*, Pt. 1, 689; *ibid.*, App., 233, 239.
17 *Ibid.*, App. 240.
18 *Ibid.*, 937.
19 *Ibid.*, 303-304.
20 *Ibid.*, 304.

solution to the slavery question in Nebraska and Kansas much more willingly than the senators previously discussed. Because he seemed to have few objections to the Kansas-Nebraska Bill, it is difficult to explain his moderate voting posture. Perhaps a discussion of the position of George Badger of North Carolina, the last of these moderates, can shed some light on Dawson's motives.

Badger was the only southeastern moderate who definitely did not espouse the common property doctrine, and he did not believe that the Missouri Compromise or popular sovereignty in the territories were unconstitutional, although he disapproved of both. His moderate voting stance can be best explained, it would seem, by observing the structure of the scalogram. If Badger had reversed his votes on the last two roll-calls in the scale, it would have placed him in the pro category. One of those roll-calls was his own amendment.

347

Toward the end of the Nebraska debates in the Senate, it was suggested that, if the Missouri Compromise were repealed, it would revive the old Spanish laws, which had sanctioned slavery in the Louisiana Territory. Northern senators were aroused immediately. This would not only have given the South a marked advantage with regard to slavery extension, but also would have put many northern senators in the very embarrassing position of having legalized slavery there by voting to repeal the Compromise of 1820. Badger then offered an amendment which removed any such threat by stating that no law dealing with slavery in the Louisiana Purchase prior to the Missouri Compromise would be legal.[21] Later, many southern representatives chastised Badger for making what they believed to be a vital concession to the North. The North Carolinian did not mean his amendment to represent this, any more than did the southern common property advocates who voted with him, including William Dawson. It would appear, however, that Badger was operating under a different set of motives than the proponents of common property. The common-property men, if they truly believed in the tenets of their doctrine, had to vote for Badger's amendment. If all of them agreed that the Missouri Compromise was unconstitutional in terms of their doctrine, and some even had doubts about the constitutionality of squatter sovereignty, certainly a Spanish law, even though favorable to their interests, was also unconstitutional. Badger, on the other hand, introduced his amendment partly to soothe the sensitive feelings of his northern colleagues, but also because, as a lawyer of considerable reputation, he believed that the repeal of the Compromise of 1820 could not possibly activate any earlier provision regarding slavery in the Louisiana Purchase.[22]

Here then are at least a few plausible explanations for the moderate scale positions taken by these senators from the Southeast. However, before leaving this discussion of the relationship of sectionalism to the

21 *Ibid.*, 291, 145-150, 289-296, 836; *ibid.*, Pt. 1, 250.
22 *Ibid.*, Pt. 1, 689-691.

Kansas-Nebraska scale, it might be useful to scan briefly the broader pattern that emerges from the quantitative data (see Table Four). Of the various subsections, the Northeast and Southwest manifested extreme attitudes toward the various facets of the Kansas-Nebraska question embodied in the scale. The Northwest and Southeast, on the other hand, provided some rather subtle variations of opinion. These patterns make it very difficult to explain Senate attitudes toward the Nebraska question primarily in terms of a North-South split, although North-South sectionalism obviously did much to shape the views of senators on this piece of legislation.

If sectionalism was an important factor in the Congressional struggle over the Kansas-Nebraska Bill, so was party allegiance. Although, on the whole, Democratic senators tended to support the measure and the Whigs leaned toward rejecting it, there was no more of a clear cut division between the parties on this issue than between the North and South (see Table Five). Within the Whig Party, however, the slavery extension issue as it burst forth in the Nebraska debates, destroyed that organization along North-South lines. There was absolutely no cooperation between the northern and southern Whigs on this piece of legislation.[23] In the scale, 75 per cent of the southern Whigs appeared as moderates (see Table Six). All of these senators, however, with the exception of one, ultimately voted for the Kansas-Nebraska Bill, despite any reservations they may have harbored.[24] The northern Whigs were even more united on the other side of the Kansas-Nebraska spectrum of opinion. Every one of them appeared in the anti portion of the scale (see Table Six).[25] If there had been a substantial number of southern or northern Whig leaders in the Senate, or better still, a combination of both, who shared a less extreme attitude toward slavery extension, and who were willing to put the well-being of their party first, as had happened so often in the past, the Whigs might have had a much better chance to escape annihilation. But when the Nebraska question surged to the forefront, the Whigs became permanently polarized on the slavery extension issue, and those Whigs, once so famous for their ability to compromise and to harmonize critical issues, dwindled in number and finally disappeared into oblivion, as their party trailed after them.

23 Arthur Cole, *The Whig Party in the South* (Washington, 1913), p. 305.

24 Six men fell in this category; the motives of four of them, Pratt, Morton, Badger, and Dawson, have already been discussed, as far as possible. One of the remaining two, James Jones of Tennessee, was a common property advocate and expressed a point of view very similar to Dawson's. *Cong. Globe*, 33 Cong., 1 sess., XXIII, Pt. 1, 341-343; *ibid.*, App., 1038-1039; *ibid.*, 2 sess., Pt. 3, 1149; Mrs. Archibald Dixon, *A True History of the Missouri Compromise and Its Repeal* (Cincinnati, 1899), p. 443. John Bell of Tennessee was the only southern Whig in this scale who was moderately opposed to the bill. He believed, among other things, that it was simply not worth stirring up the slavery question again. *Cong. Globe*, 33 Cong., 1 sess., XXIII, App., 408-415, 938-948, 437, 755-758.

25 *Ibid.*, 764-765.

With respect to the Democrats, it is clear that the senators from the North reacted quite differently to the Nebraska struggle than those from the South. One-half of the northern Democrats were moderates, while nearly 80 per cent of the southern Democrats appeared in the pro part of the scale (see Table Seven).

The primary appeal of the Nebraska Bill to the southern Democrats was contained in a series of concessions to the rights of slave owners, which their leaders were able to wrest from their northern colleagues. Furnishing the hard core of this leadership were the members of the F Street Mess, a group of southern Senators who lived and dined in the same boarding house in Washington. Each held a powerful position in the Senate. James M. Mason, and Robert M. T. Hunter of Virginia and Andrew Butler of South Carolina headed respectively the foreign relations, finance, and judiciary committees. Missouri's David Atchison, president *pro tempore* of the Senate, was also an important part of this clique.[26] These gentlemen were convinced that President Pierce's patronage program had favored the free soil, "barnburner" faction over their interests, and so developed a plan to improve their position and, at the same time, promote the welfare of their party. According to one leading interpretation, the Mess was determined to save the Democracy from Pierce's blundering by assuming the leadership of the party, and reinterpreting the Baltimore platform of 1852. They would do this by making that interpretation a fundamental test, which the barnburners would be required to accept before the Senate would confirm barnburner appointments. Atchison's personal ambitions and the Kansas-Nebraska Bill were to be key elements in their strategy.[27]

In December, 1853, the bill to organize Nebraska was about to be introduced again without mention of slavery. Atchison had been grappling bitterly with Thomas Hart Benton in the Missouri political arena that past summer. During the battle Atchison had promised to obtain a Nebraska Bill which would not exclude slavery from the area or quit as a candidate for re-election.[28] The members of the Mess concluded that they could use the Nebraska question to aid Atchison against Benton and as a test of party loyalty. The "barnburners," like the President, had accepted the principle of popular sovereignty contained in the Compromise of 1850. The Mess believed that it was only reasonable that these principles should be accepted for all territories, even those, like Nebraska, protected from slavery by the Missouri Compromise. Both the Democracy in general and the barnburner faction in particu-

[26] Roy F. Nichols, "The Kansas-Nebraska Act: A century of Historiography," *Mississippi Valley Historical Review*, XLIII (Sept., 1956), 229-233; William E. Parish, *David Rice Atchison of Missouri: Border Politician* (Columbia, 1961), pp. 115-117; John A. Parker, "The Secret History of the Kansas-Nebraska Bill," *National Quarterly Review*, XLI (July, 1880), 111-112.

[27] Nichols, "Kansas-Nebraska Act," 201-203.

[28] P. Orman Ray, *The Repeal of the Missouri Compromise* (Cleveland, 1909), Ch. IV.

lar must be made to accept this formula.[29] These leaders rejected, once and for all, the exclusion of their states' citizens from the territories because of slavery. Atchison went to Douglas in December and reminded him that he needed at least four southern votes to pass any bill for the organization of Nebraska and that he would never get those votes unless he found some way of allowing slavery to enter the territory.[30]

This interpretation of the role played by the F Street Mess in the Nebraska controversy poses several problems from the standpoint of the motivation of those involved. There is ample evidence to support the contention that Atchison wanted the Missouri Compromise removed and that he believed popular sovereignty would provide an adequate solution to the slavery problem in Nebraska, once the 1820 restriction was eliminated. Yet there is no evidence to show that Atchison wished to promote these ideas for the sake of party unity or as a test of party loyalty. Moreover, he never indicated, either directly or indirectly, that he was aware that the F Street Mess had such a plan in mind.[31] In view of this, it would seem more reasonable to assume that Atchison demanded the removal of the Missouri Compromise, because as a southerner, he thought the measure was unfair, and because he believed it had to be voided to fulfill the promise he had made to his constituents, and so save his career.

But what of the rest of the Mess, namely Hunter, Butler, and Mason? It is true that as state rights, pro-slavery politicians, they were disappointed in the Pierce administration for having doled out patronage to barnburners. It is also true that as major Democratic leaders, they were convinced that they and their friends had been denied the party recognition they deserved. Finally, it is also true that these senators believed that the Missouri Compromise was unconstitutional and that the Nebraska Bill must destroy that measure. At least two of these gentlemen, however, shared another characteristic. They were extremely uneasy about the use of popular sovereignty as a territorial mechanism for resolving the slavery issue. Of the fourteen southern Democrats in the scale, only three fell outside the pro portion (see the Kansas-Nebraska scale). Two of these three were Hunter and Butler, both of whom were members of the Mess, and both of whom, as previously discussed, had serious qualms about popular sovereignty. As for Mason, he did not make clear his views on squatter sovereignty, but he was an advocate of the common property theory, and during the debates, asserted that there were "some provisions in the bill, which as a Southern man, I should be glad to see out of it."[32]

[29] Nichols, "Kansas-Nebraska Act," 202-203.

[30] Ibid., 203-204.

[31] See Ray, Repeal of the Missouri Compromise, 189-193, 257 and Ch. IV; Fred H. Harrington, "A Note on the Ray Explanation of the Origin of the Kansas-Nebraska Act," Mississippi Valley Historical Review, XXV (June, 1938), 79-81.

[32] Cong. Globe, 33 Cong., 1 sess., XXIII, App., 229. See also ibid., Pt. 1, 507.

All this tends to raise some doubts about the validity of the argument that the members of the Mess purposely devised a plan to unite and to save their party by insisting that their fellow Democrats accept the popular sovereignty formula of 1850 and include it in the Nebraska Bill. It seems highly unlikely that these "true heirs of Calhoun" would seize upon that strategy to foster party solidarity.[33] Otherwise, one could reasonably expect their position on popular sovereignty to have been more positive or favorable.[34] Any involvement of the members of the Mess, as a group, in the creation of the Nebraska Bill can most logically be attributed more to sectional and personal motives than to party considerations.

This aside, Douglas realized that Atchison meant what he said, and that he would have to deal with the slavery issue if he wanted the Nebraska Bill passed.[35] Subsequently, before the bill finally became law, Douglas, the F Street Mess, and several other Democratic leaders worked through the Committee on Territories and various caucuses to thrash out a series of compromises and concessions on slavery to meet the demands of a constantly changing political climate. Certain of the decisions made it easier for various northern Democrats to vote for the measure, but because the leadership was largely southern, that section gained the most.[36] One of those compromises involved an altered ver-

351

33 Nichols, "Kansas-Nebraska Act," 201-203.

34 It must be noted that Nichols does not offer any documentation for his assertion that the Mess devised such a plan. Ibid., 203. The reports of Atchison's description of his confrontation with Douglas on this issue make no mention of any discussion of popular sovereignty even though Atchison had long favored it as a solution. The Missouri senator merely told Douglas, that as Chairman of the Committee on Territories, he would have to devise some way to cancel the Missouri Compromise restriction, so that slaveholders could legally enter the Nebraska territory. See Ray, Repeal of the Missouri Compromise, 201-202 and 277-279. It is not beyond the realm of possibility that Hunter, Butler, and Mason had convinced Atchison to forget the popular sovereignty portion of his plan, and to concentrate upon simply gaining the removal of the Missouri Compromise, which all the members of the Mess desired. Moreover, what these men desired to have included in the Nebraska Bill with regard to slavery rights went considerably beyond the doctrine of popular sovereignty as set forth in the Compromise of 1850. See Parker, "Secret History of Kansas-Nebraska Bill," 112; Ray, Repeal of the Missouri Compromise 230-232.

35 Nichols, "Kansas-Nebraska Act," 204.

36 For a generally excellent analysis and description of the slavery provisions of the various versions of the Kansas-Nebraska Bill and the machinations necessary to achieve them, see Russel, "Congressional Struggle Over the Kansas-Nebraska Bill," 187-210 and Nichols, "Kansas-Nebraska Act," 204-208. Also see Cong. Globe, 33 Cong., 1 sess., XXIII, Pt. 1, 221-222, 175; Report on Nebraska Territory, Senate Reports, 33 Cong., 1 sess., No. 15, Jan. 4, 1854; F. L. Burr to Gideon Welles, Jan. 5, 1854, Gideon Welles Papers, Library of Congress; New York Times, Jan. 6, 1854; Detroit Free Press, Jan. 11, 1854, Washington Correspondent, Jan. 6, 1854; Pittsburg Gazette, Feb. 7, 1854, Washington Correspondent, Feb. 3, 1854; ibid., Feb. 9, 1854, Washington Correspondent, Feb. 5, 1854; ibid., Feb. 13, 1954, Washington Correspondent, Feb. 8, 1854; Detroit Free Press, Feb. 8, 1854, Washington Correspondent, Feb. 3, 1854; Robert Toombs to W. W. Burwell, Feb. 3, 1854 in U. B. Phillips (ed.), "The Correspondence of Robert Toombs, Alexander H. Stephens and Howell Cobb," (Washington, 1913), II, 322.

For a description of the various pressures applied to Douglas, see Henry B.

352

sion of the bill, which Douglas presented to the Senate on February 7, and which was approved handily on February 15.[37] An earlier statement that the eighth section of the Missouri Compromise was "superceded by the principles of the legislation of 1850 . . . and is . . . declared inoperative" was replaced by the phrase "which being inconsistent with the principle of nonintervention by Congress with slavery in the States and Territories, as recognized by the legislation of 1850 . . . is declared inoperative and void."[38] The substitution of the words "inoperative and void" for "inoperative" is considered, by at least one historian, as a concession made to southerners.[39] There is reason to believe, however, that it was also a concession made by the southern extremists to their colleagues. The Washington correspondent of the Detroit *Free Press*, for example, wrote on February 5, two days before Douglas made his report, that he was convinced that the caucus had previously reached a decision to repeal the Missouri Compromise outright. "It was originally the intention," he declared,

> to provide for the direct repeal, but the present provision [declaring the Missouri Compromise 'inoperative'] was adopted out of deference to the opinion of Senators who regard the Missouri Compromise as unconstitutional, and who would not therefore vote for its repeal, lest by doing so, they should acknowledge its constitutionality and binding force.[40]

It is plausible, therefore, that the closest thing to actual repeal these doctrinaire southerners would permit was the addition of the word "void."

At any rate, other concessions were made to the slavery interests in general, and they go far in helping to explain the consistently favorable voting pattern manifested by most southern Democrats on the Nebraska issue.[41]

Learned, "Relation of Philip Phillips to the Repeal of the Missouri Compromise in 1854," *Mississippi Valley Historical Review*, VIII (Mar., 1922), 308-311; Archibald Dixon to Henry S. Foote, Sept. 30, 1858 quoted in Henry M. Flint, *Life of Stephen Douglas* (New York, 1860), pp. 172-173; Mrs. Dixon, 445; George M. McConnell, "Recollections of Stephen A. Douglas," Illinois State Historical Society, *Transactions* (1900), 49.

[37] *Cong. Globe*, 33 Cong., 1 sess., XXIII, Pt. 1, 421; Russel, "Congressional Struggle Over the Kansas-Nebraska Bill," 199.

[38] Russel, "Congressional Struggle over the Kansas-Nebraska Bill," 199-200; *Cong. Globe*, 33 Cong., 1 sess., XXIII, Pt. 1, 353.

[39] Russel, "Congressional Struggle over the Kansas-Nebraska Bill," 199.

[40] Detroit *Free Press*, Feb. 10, 1854, Washington Correspondent, Feb. 5, 1854.

[41] There are, of course, other factors which might aid in explaining their attitudes. The fact, for example, that the Pierce administration threw its full weight behind the bill may have been a major reason for their support. Or the bitter accusations and attacks emanating from the North may have raised their ire enough to vote for the measure. It is very difficult, however, to formulate a satisfactory explanation for their decisions because, in most cases, their individual feelings and attitudes toward this piece of legislation are not on record anywhere. For example, during the debates only three of these eleven southern Democrats uttered anything meaningful on the Nebraska question. Benjamin Fitzpatrick (Ala.), John Slidell (La.), and Josiah Evans (S.C.), said absolutely nothing during the Kansas-Nebraska debates. Three others, Robert Johnson (Ark.), Clement Clay (Ala.), and

The northern Democrats were less reticent on the subject, and their words assist greatly in fathoming why half of them voted as moderates. It would appear that these men were torn between two opposing and formidable forces. On the one hand, their own personal attraction and their party's commitment to popular sovereignty enticed them to befriend the Kansas-Nebraska legislation. The administration, although experiencing considerable difficulty controlling its members because of factionalism and the President's patronage policies, was far from impotent. It worked tirelessly through a number of devices to convince Democrats in both branches of Congress to stand by the bill. For example, Caleb Cushing, acting with the President's blessing, went so far as to offer Senator Hannibal Hamlin of Maine control of Democratic patronage in New England in exchange for his assistance in behalf of the measure.[42]

But there was also considerable pressure calculated to defeat it. The northern Democrats were being confronted with the angry protests of a large number of their constituents, who were insisting vehemently and in a variety of ways that they vote the bill down.[43] It may well be that the moderate voting position taken by these Democrats was, in large part, a product of their frustrating attempts to reconcile the conflicting and severe pressures thrust upon them as a result of this Nebraska question.

Senator Lewis Cass of Michigan, for example, was delighted to have squatter sovereignty applied to the Nebraska situation, since he was the originator of the doctrine. His only concern was that the principles of popular sovereignty not be misrepresented in the bill.[44] On the other

353

Stephen Adams (Miss.), made a few remarks and asked a few questions during the debates, but made no speeches. Lastly, William Sebastian (Ark.) and Thomas Rusk (Tex.) made speeches, but these speeches dealt only with a negligible number of aspects involved in the Nebraska struggle. Rusk spoke briefly about a motion to postpone consideration of the bill, and Sebastian made a few short speeches regarding the elimination of certain Indian treaties which would have affected the settlement of the territories. See *Cong. Globe*, 33 Cong., 1 sess., XXIII, App., 411 and *ibid.*, Pt. 1, 353-355. Moreover, there is no other evidence available regarding the opinions of these senators toward the Kansas-Nebraska Act. For these reasons, any attempt to determine the motivations in this situation, regardless of how logical or sensible, must be considered tenuous and incomplete.

[42] Claude Fuess, *The Life of Caleb Cushing* (New York, 1923), II, 192; Charles E. Hamlin, *Hannibal Hamlin* (Cambridge, 1899), pp. 264 and 268-271.

[43] See, for example, *Resolution on the Missouri Compromise by the New York Legislature*, Senate Miscellaneous Documents, 33 Cong., 1 sess., No. 22, Feb. 9, 1854; *Resolution Relative to the Nebraska Bill by the Maine Legislature*, Senate Miscellaneous Documents, 33 Cong., 1 sess., No. 28, Mar. 1, 1854; Edward Pierce, *Memoirs and Letters of Charles Sumner* (Boston, 1877-1893), III, 362-379; Fred Seward, *Seward at Washington* (New York, 1891), pp. 217-218, 222, and 356; Henry Hubbart, *The Older Middle West, 1840-1860* (New York, 1936), pp. 100-101; Grace Clarke, *George W. Julian* (Indianapolis, 1923), p. 150; Charles Hawley, "Whittier of Iowa," *Iowa Journal of History of Politics*, XXXIV (Apr. 1936), 133-141; G. W. Jones to Howell Cobb, Feb. 16, 1854 in R. P. Brooks (ed.), "Howell Cobb Papers," *Georgia Historical Quarterly*, VI (Mar. 1922), 150.

[44] *Cong. Globe*, 33 Cong., 1 sess., XXIII, Pt. 1, 333-344 and 456-458; *ibid.*, App., 270-279.

hand, however, he opposed the destruction of the Missouri Compromise right from the beginning. On January 14, the *Washington Sentinel* suggested that Cass should introduce an amendment to the Nebraska Bill negating the slavery agreement of 1820.[45] He made it clear in short order that he "could not make such an attrocious [sic] proposition, whatever others might do," and that "the measure was frought [sic] with evil."[46] But Cass did not push his opposition beyond this, for he was also a loyal Democrat of long standing.[47] It was reported as early as January 23 that Cass, although "he was not consulted and was decidedly against the renewal of agitation . . . will vote with the pro-slavery side."[48] The Michigan senator sat quietly during the debates until February 20, when he made his views public. He chastised the South for demanding the removal of the Missouri restriction and for its unreasoning attachment to the institution of slavery. Cass had an immense dislike for slavery, but believed that the only possible solution to the question in Nebraska lay in squatter sovereignty.[49] He also revealed the intensity of the public pressure being brought to bear upon him. "It requires but little exertion to swim with the current," he said,

354

while he who opposes it must put forth all his strength and even may become its victim. Popular feeling is a hard power to resist, and the reproach of being a dough face belongs to him who panders to it, and not him who strives to maintain the constitutional rights of all.[50]

In the end, Cass followed his personal convictions and his party's policy, ignoring both the will of a good portion of his constituents and his own antipathy towards the repeal of the Missouri Compromise, and voted for the Nebraska Bill.

Senator Isaac Walker of Wisconsin exhibited the same pattern of frustration, but could not persuade himself to go this far. There were too many slavery clauses in the Nebraska Bill that troubled him. Among them was the abrogation of the Missouri Compromise, which he believed would create widespread agitation throughout the nation and inflict tremendous damage on the Democratic party. He could not lend himself, he said, to a reopening of the slavery question. During the debates, however, he also revealed part of the deeper mental and emotional anguish he was experiencing in reaching these decisions. He grew extremely defensive and went to excessive lengths to answer Senator John Weller's charge that, because of his negative attitude toward the Nebraska Bill, he was being disloyal to his party.[51] At the same time,

[45] *Washington Sentinel*, Jan. 14, 1854.
[46] Quoted in the diary of Gideon Welles, June 29, 1855 in Gideon Welles Papers.
[47] Hamlin, *Hannibal Hamlin*, 268.
[48] Salmon P. Chase to E. S. Hamlin, Jan. 23, 1854 in "The Diary and Correspondence of Salmon P. Chase," 256.
[49] *Cong. Globe*, 33 Cong., 1 sess., XXIII, Pt. 1, 450-451; *ibid.*, App., 270-279.
[50] *Ibid.*, App., 277.
[51] *Ibid.*, 291.

it was clear that Walker also dreaded the probable reaction of his constituents if he failed to placate them on the issue of slavery extension. In 1850, he had voted for only one of the several compromise measures, and by doing so, he asked if any other Senator had "brought upon himself more of abuse, more of censure, more of condemnation, and involved himself in greater danger with his constituents . . ."[52] Here was a man, sensitive to the desires and pressures of his party on the Nebraska question, but unable to comply completely for fear of voter retaliation. When the final roll-call was taken on this controversial measure, he cast a negative vote.

Although no neat and clearly defined sectional or party cleavage developed on the Kansas-Nebraska question, both party and sectional influences played a major role in determining the voting behavior of Senators on this issue. Of the two factors, sectionalism appears to have been most potent. Even the moderate voting stance assumed by most of the southeastern senators on the Nebraska legislation seems ironically to have been the product of an extreme interpretation of the rights of slaveholders. Again a similar pattern emerged among the southern Whigs, most of whom also voted as moderates on the roll-calls in question. In the heat of the Nebraska controversy, the party polarized along North-South lines, and organized Whiggery disappeared forever. As for the Democrats, the high percentage of southern senators who backed the bill enthusiastically was the result, in large part, of the many concessions that were made to the sensibilities of the slavocracy. Within the southern Democratic group, moreover, the powerful F Street Mess promoted the measure, it would seem, more for sectional and personal reasons than a desire to use the bill to strengthen the Democracy. For a substantial number of northern Democratic senators, however, the process of reaching a decision on this legislation involved a painful personal choice between party and sectional loyalty. The frustration entailed in this situation goes far in explaining why half of them voted as moderates. In the end, for most of them, the urgings of the administration that they accept the bill, combined with their own attraction for all or part of the measure, held sway over the demands of their constituents that they reject it. But this partial triumph of party allegiance over sectional considerations was exceptional when Senate voting behavior on the Nebraska question is viewed as a whole. The pattern did not augur well for the future of the Union.

[52] *Ibid.*, 294-296; Also see *ibid.*, 285-286 and 288; *ibid.*, Pt. 1, 344 and 692.

TABLE ONE

The Relationship Between Sectional Membership and Voting Positions on the Kansas-Nebraska Act in the Senate of the Thirty-Third Congress.

	North		South		East		West	
	No.	%	No.	%	No.	%	No.	%
Anti	(11)	45.8	(1)	4.5	(8)	42.1	(4)	14.8
Moderate	(8)	33.3	(8)	36.4	(9)	47.4	(7)	25.9
Pro	(5)	20.8	(13)	59.1	(2)	10.5	(16)	59.3
Total	(24)	99.9	(22)	100.0	(19)	100.0	(27)	100.0

North—Conn., Me., Mass., N. H., R. I., Vt., N. J., N. Y., Pa., Ill., Ia., Ind., Mich., O., Wis., Calif. *South*—Del., Fla., Ga., Md., N. C., S. C., Va., Ala., Ky., Miss., Tenn., Ark., La., Tex., Mo. *East*—Me., Mass., N. H., R. I., Vt., N. J., N. Y., Pa., Del., Fla., Ga., Md., N. C., S. C., Va., Conn. *West*—Ill., Ind., Mich., O., Wis., Ia., Mo., Ala., Ky., Miss., Tenn., Ark., La., Calif., Tex.

TABLE TWO

The Relationship between Northern Sectional Membership and Voting Positions on the Kansas-Nebraska Act in the Senate of the Thirty-Third Congress Controlling for East-West Sectionalism.

	East		West	
	North		North	
	No.	%	No.	%
Anti	(8)	72.7	(3)	23.1
Moderate	(3)	27.3	(5)	38.4
Pro	(0)	0.0	(5)	38.4
Total	(11)	100.0	(13)	99.9

TABLE THREE

The Relationship Between Southern Sectional Membership and Voting Positions on the Kansas-Nebraska Act in the Senate of the Thirty-Third Congress Controlling for East-West Sectionalism.

	East		West	
	South		South	
	No.	%	No.	%
Anti	(0)	0.0	(1)	7.1
Moderate	(6)	75.0	(2)	14.3
Pro	(2)	25.0	(11)	78.6
Total	(8)	100.0	(14)	100.0

TABLE FOUR

The Relationship Between North-South Sectional Membership and Voting Positions on the Kansas-Nebraska Act in the Senate of the Thirty-Third Congress Controlling for East-West Sectionalism.

	East				West			
	North		South		North		South	
	No.	%	No.	%	No.	%	No.	%
Anti	(8)	72.7	(0)	0.0	(3)	23.1	(1)	7.1
Moderate	(3)	27.3	(6)	75.0	(5)	38.4	(2)	14.3
Pro	(0)	0.0	(2)	25.0	(5)	38.4	(11)	78.6
Total	(11)	100.0	(8)	100.0	(13)	99.9	(14)	100.0

TABLE FIVE

357

The Relationship Between Membership in the Major Parties and Voting Positions on the Kansas-Nebraska Act in the Senate of the Thirty-Third Congress.

	Democrats		Whigs	
	No.	%	No.	%
Anti	(4)	13.3	(6)	42.8
Moderate	(10)	33.3	(6)	42.8
Pro	(16)	53.3	(2)	14.3
Total	(30)	99.9	(14)	99.9

TABLE SIX

The Relationship Between Whig Party Membership and Voting Positions on the Kansas-Nebraska Act in the Senate of the Thirty-Third Congress Controlling for North-South Sectionalism.

	North		South	
	Whigs		Whigs	
	No.	%	No.	%
Anti	(6)	100.0	(0)	0.0
Moderate	(0)	0.0	(6)	75.0
Pro	(0)	0.0	(2)	25.0
Total	(6)	100.0	(8)	100.0

TABLE SEVEN

The Relationship Between Democratic Party Membership and Voting Positions on the Kansas-Nebraska Act in the Senate of the Thirty-Third Congress Controlling for North-South Sectionalism.

	North		South	
	Democrats		Democrats	
	No.	%	No.	%
Anti	(3)	18.7	(1)	7.1
Moderate	(8)	50.0	(2)	14.3
Pro	(5)	31.2	(11)	78.5
Total	(16)	99.9	(14)	99.9

Key to Votes on Legislation to
Organize the Nebraska Territory,
Thirty-Third Congress, First
Session, Senate.

Scale
Number   Issue and Vote

1. Chase amendment, to make the Nebraska Territory one instead of two sections. March 2, 1854. Def. 8-34. Vote no is pro.
2. Chase amendment, to provide for the immediate popular election of officers for the Nebraska Territorial Government. March 2, 1854. Def. 10-30. Vote no is pro.
3. Chase amendment, to allow the people of the Territory to prohibit slavery if they wished. March 2, 1854. Def. 10-36. Vote no is pro.
4. Douglas amendment to strike out in section 14 the words "which was superceded by the principles of the legislation of 1850, commonly called the Compromise Measures" and inserting: which being inconsistent with the principle of nonintervention by Congress with slavery in the States and Territories, as recognized by the legislation of 1850, (commonly called the Compromise Measures) is hereby declared inoperative and void; it being the true intent and meaning of this act not to legislate slavery into any Territory or State, nor exclude it therefrom, but to leave the people thereof perfectly free to form and regulate their domestic institutions in their own way, subject only to the Constitution of the United States." February 15, 1854. Carried 35-10. Vote yes is pro.
5. Motion by Seward that the Kansas-Nebraska Bill should be engrossed for a third reading. March 2, 1854. Carried 29-12. Vote yes is pro.
6. Motion by Hunter that the Kansas-Nebraska Bill should be engrossed for a third reading. May 25, 1854. Carried 35-13. Vote yes is pro.
7. Douglas amendment, to strike out in section 14, the words "was superceded by the principles of the legislation of 1850 commonly called the Compromise Measures." February 6, 1854. Def. 13-30. Vote no is pro.
8. Motion by Cass calling for a vote on the question of whether or not the Kansas-Nebraska Bill should pass. March 3, 1854. Carried 37-14. Vote yes is pro.
9. Motion by Wade to postpone consideration of the Kansas-Nebraska Bill from then (Friday, February 3, 1854) until Monday, February 6, 1854. February 3, 1854. Carried 23-17. Vote no is pro.
10. Badger amendment, that nothing in the Kansas-Nebraska Bill will be thought to revive any law before the Missouri Compromise "protecting, establishing, prohibiting, or abolishing slavery." March 2, 1854. Carried 35-6. Vote no is pro.

Anti   = Scale scores 4, 5, 6.
Moderates = Scale scores 2, 3.
Pro   = Scale scores 0, 1.

358

Kansas-Nebraska Bill Scale

Senator	Party	Score	State	Anti. Y Y Y N N N Y N Y Y 1 2 3 4 5 6 7 8 9 10	Pro N N N Y Y Y N Y N N 1 2 3 4 5 6 7 8 9 10
S. Chase	FS	6	O.	XXXXXXXXOO	
W. Fessenden	W	6	Me.	XXXOXOOXOO	
S. Foot	W	6	Vt.	XXXXXXXXXX	
H. Hamlin	D	6	Me.	XXOXXXXXXX	
W. Seward	W	6	N.Y.	XXXXXXXXXX	
T. Smith	W	6	Conn.	XXXXXOXXXX	
C. Sumner	FS	6	Mass.	XXXXXXXXXO	
B. Wade	W	6	O.	XXXXXXXXXX	
P. Allen	D	5	R.I.	OXOXXXXO	OO
H. Dodge	D	5	Wis.	XXXXXXXX	XX
H. Fish	W	5	N.Y.	XXXXXXXX	OO
S. Houston	D	4	Tex.	XXOOXXX	XXX
J. Bell	W	3	Tenn.	OX XXX	XXXX X
L. Cass	D	3	Mich.	X XO	OOOXOX X
C. Stuart	D	3	Mich.	X X XX	XXXXX X
I. Walker	D	3	Wis.	XXXXOX	OOXO
G. Badger	W	2	N.C.	XX	XXXOXXXX
R. Brodhead	D	2	Pa.	XX	XXXXXXXX
A. Butler	D	2	S.C.	XX	XXOXXXXX
W. Dawson Jr.	W	2	Ga.	XX	XXXXXXXX
W. Gwin	D	2	Calif.	XX	XXXXXXOX
R. Hunter	D	2	Va.	OX	XXXXXXXX
G. Jones	D	2	Ia.	OX	XXXXXXXX
J. Jones	W	2	Tenn.	XX	XXXXXXXX
J. Morton	W	2	Fla.	OX	XXXXXXXX
M. Morris Jr.	D	2	N.H.	X XX	X XXXXXX
T. Pratt	W	2	Md.	OX	XXXXXXXX
J. Williams	D	2	N.II.	XX	XXXXXXXX
D. Atchison	D	1	Mo.	X	XXXXXXXXX
J. Benjamin	W	1	La.	X	XXXXXXXXX
C. Clay Jr.	D	1	Ala.	X	XXXOXXXXX
A. Dixon	W	1	Ky.	X	XXXXXOXXX
A. Dodge	D	1	Ia.	X	XXXXXXXXX
S. Douglas	D	1	Ill.	X	XXXXXXXXX
J. Evans	D	1	S.C.	X	XXXXXOXXX
B. Fitzpatrick	D	1	Ala.	X	XXXXXXXXX
J. Mason	D	1	Va.	X	XXXXXXXXX
J. Pettit	D	1	Ind.	X	XXXXXXXXX
W. Sebastian	D	1	Ark.	X	XXXXXXX X
J. Shields	D	1	Ill.	X X	X XOXXXX
J. Slidell	D	1	La.	X	XXXXXXXXX
J. Weller	D	1	Calif.	X	OOXXOXXXX
S. Adams	D	0	Miss.		XOXXXOXXXX
A. Brown	D	0	Miss.		XXXXXXXXXX
R. Johnson	D	0	Ark.		XXXXXOXOX
T. Rusk	D	0	Tex.		XXXOOXOXOX

Thirteen Senators are not included because of absences, vacancies, or ambiguous voting records.

Reproducibility=98.9%

359